UNIVERSITY of PENNSYLVANIA
PRESS

THE AMERICAN HISTORICAL ASSOCIATION

PREPARED AND PUBLISHED UNDER THE DIRECTION OF THE AMERICAN HISTORICAL
ASSOCIATION FROM THE INCOME OF THE ALBERT J. BEVERIDGE MEMORIAL FUND
FOR THEIR ZEAL AND BENEFICENCE IN CREATING THIS FUND THE ASSOCIATION IS
INDEBTED TO MANY CITIZENS OF INDIANA WHO DESIRED TO HONOR IN THIS WAY
THE MEMORY OF A STATESMAN AND A HISTORIAN

Robert Morris

REVOLUTIONARY FINANCIER

WITH AN ANALYSIS OF HIS EARLIER CAREER

by

CLARENCE L. VER STEEG

University of Pennsylvania Press

Philadelphia · 1954

TO DOROTHY

With gratitude for innumerable
hours spent in the preparation
of this book, but most important
with love

The two points which should have been the great objects of governmental attention have been in a manner totally neglected. One is the establishment of the army for the war; and the other the business of finance. These are the two hinges on which the whole dispute turns. It is a point pretty well established in European politicks that the longest purse will prove the longest sword.

General Greene to Lewis Morris, 14 September 1780, in "Letters to General Lewis Morris" in New York Historical Society Collections, VIII, 468.

The Art of war is so well and so equally understood by the great nations of Europe, and they are so equally furnished with Statesmen, Generals, Admirals, and other Officers, capable of conducting it well, that it is now generally considered as a contest of finances; so that the nation which can longest find money to carry on the war, can generally hold out the longest.

John Adams to the President of Congress, 27 March 1781, Paris, in Sparks MSS 52, Houghton Library, Harvard University (copy).

ACKNOWLEDGMENTS

B<small>Y THE TIME A MANUSCRIPT IS BEING PREPARED FOR THE PRINTER, IT IS</small> impossible to know where to begin in acknowledging the aid received in its preparation. My debt to those who preside over the manuscript depositories mentioned in the bibliography of this work bulks large, but without timely financial assistance, I should not have enjoyed the opportunity to exploit this material. I am grateful to Columbia University for two appointments as a Fellow and for their generosity in purchasing microfilm for my use. My appointment as a National Fellow of the Committee on Economic History of the Social Science Research Council in 1948-49 was particularly important, for their support enabled me to spend a full year on research without being hampered by other commitments. Moreover, the Chairman of that Committee, Professor Arthur H. Cole, was generous with his time and consideration far beyond what was required of him in his official capacity. It is also a pleasure to acknowledge the research funds made available to me by Northwestern University.

In its various stages of development, this study has been read by a number of scholars. Professors Carter Goodrich and Joseph Dorfman detected several embarrassing inconsistencies, and Professor Richard B. Morris, after a careful reading, made important suggestions for its improvement. A number of perceptive comments offered by Professor Oscar Handlin were also incorporated into the final revision. To the Albert J. Beveridge Committee of the American Historical Association, under whose auspices this volume appears, I am especially indebted, for their sympathetic, thoughtful, pertinent observations proved to be highly important in the final revision. In the same regard, I must mention the invaluable assistance of my friend and colleague Professor George T. Romani, who sacrificed time from his own work to criticize my volume in the light of his own high standards of historical craftsmanship. Although the timely encouragement and counsel of close friends will always remain a treasured memory, I must reserve my deepest appreciation for Professor John A. Krout, Vice-President of Columbia University. He not only read my manuscript when burdened by far more important tasks, but also advised me in matters quite apart from scholarship.

These scholars have endeavored to improve an imperfect book. For their time, consideration, and kindness I am profoundly grateful; for my failings, I appeal to your charity.

C<small>LARENCE</small> L. V<small>ER</small> S<small>TEEG</small>

ABOUT THE NOTES

The notes will be found on pages 200-254. In the text, referential notes are indicated by superior numbers in roman type; discussion notes by superior numbers in italics. In the note section, at the upper right-hand corner of each recto page and the upper left-hand corner of each verso page, will be found numbers indicating the pages of the text to which the notes on these two pages refer.

CONTENTS

INTRODUCTION ✧✧✧✧✧✧✧✧✧✧✧✧✧✧✧✧✧✧✧✧✧✧✧✧✧✧

IF CERTAIN KEY FIGURES WERE TO BE SINGLED OUT TO REPRESENT VARIOUS spheres of action in the Revolutionary generation, the selections would be relatively simple. For early Revolutionary politics the choice of Samuel Adams would meet general agreement. In military affairs the Commander-in-Chief, of course, would win universal approval, while few would quarrel with the selection of Franklin on the diplomatic front. In economic and political-economic affairs the choice would inevitably rest on Robert Morris.

It does not seem necessary to make any apologies for offering a book on Morris—or, for that matter, a volume that concerns certain aspects of the economic and political developments of the Revolutionary Era—because a half-century has passed since a serious biography has appeared. Much new source material has been made available in the intervening years, and a large number of valuable books on the period have been published. Although this material alters our picture, it does not entirely erase the work of the biographers of Morris. Two of them in particular still merit any student's attention: William Graham Sumner's *The Financier and the Finances of the American Revolution* (1891) and Ellis P. Oberholtzer's *Robert Morris: Patriot and Financier* (1903). Although Sumner's volumes were comparatively thorough for their time, the author's method of organizing his study limited its usefulness. Moreover, Sumner realized, as he indicates in his preface, that the story would have to be rewritten in the future on the basis of new material. Oberholtzer took advantage of the Letter-books and Diary of the Office of Finance, primary sources unavailable to Sumner, but his analysis of Morris was, unfortunately, much less profound. Because of his persuasive presentation, however, Oberholtzer rather than Sumner became the recognized biographer of Robert Morris.

The present volume is not intended as a biography; rather, it is concerned primarily with Robert Morris as Superintendent of Finance in the American Revolution. To understand him in that significant role, however, it has been necessary to describe and analyze his experience, which was highly important, before he accepted the position in the Office of Finance, and to examine the nature of the crisis in 1780-81 which preceded his acceptance of the office. An effort has also been made to indicate the ideas that were reflected in Morris' immediate policies, to demonstrate the formulation of an important long-range program, and to trace the operation of this comprehensive program. The major portion of this volume is devoted to the last of these aims, where an attempt has been made to investigate the interplay of controlling circumstances and policy changes throughout this period by assessing the impact of the Morris program on the political and economic life of the nation, and the undercurrents which, in turn, tended to forward or retard his plans.

It is scarcely novel to state that these activities of Morris did not take place in a vacuum, but it has not been sufficiently emphasized that his career was intimately related to two of the most compelling forces in the western world of the eighteenth century: the rise of modern capitalism and the emergence of modern nationalism. Both movements, of course, had roots that threaded deep down into the late Middle Ages, but perhaps it is not too much to say that commercial capitalism was reaching its climax in the eighteenth century, while certain reflections of national consciousness were so exalted that the flowering of nationalism early in the following century was assured.

Influenced and stimulated by these larger movements, the British colonies in North America were transformed from separate political appendages to a constitutionally established nation, and from a rather backward commercial area to a highly developed one. As Gouverneur Morris, that perceptive and urbane young American, asserted in 1782: "Highly commercial, being as it were the first born children of extended commerce in modern Times, we must be maritime."[1] The validity of this observation on the rise of commercial capitalism is everywhere in evidence—the estimates of trade, the growing importance of the merchant, the problems involved in credit arrangements, and the rise of commercial cities. The history of Philadelphia alone, where the mercantile career of Robert Morris began and where it was nurtured, reflects this significant economic development. With respect to the growth of a national consciousness, the Revolution is persuasive in itself, although the conditions which prepared the way for the formation of the new nation, a topic still too much neglected, reached back at least into the early years of the century.

The career of Robert Morris spanned those formative years, and, as the substance of this book will indicate, it was highly important to these movements. Trained in mercantile affairs and eventually accepted as a partner by a respected Philadelphia firm, Morris, through a combination of good connections and unusual business talent, rose to prominence in the commercial community of Philadelphia by the outbreak of the Revolution. During the course of the conflict he emerged as the foremost merchant in America, equipped with widespread connections and extraordinary experience in mercantile and financial affairs. It was this background of success which prompted the Continental Congress, faced with the gravest financial crisis of the War, to appoint Morris to the position of Superintendent of Finance in the spring of 1781.

In that position, Morris, in addition to his mercantile and financial experience, used to advantage the political and administrative abilities which he had developed by serving in the Continental Congress dur-

---

[1] Gouverneur Morris to Matthew Ridley, 6 Aug. 1782, Ridley Papers, Massachusetts Historical Society.

ing the early years of the Revolution. Although many of the policies that were invoked did, of course, parallel ideas expressed by other leaders in the country, it was Morris who was actually responsible for establishing the first deposit bank, one acting also as the first national bank, in America. It was also Morris who, with unusual imagination, mobilized private credit to bolster the public credit, regularized public finance, introduced contracting as a money system to supply the troops, and recognized the dynamic nature of the public credit and the public debt. Morris, as his ideas matured during his term of office, became increasingly aware of the possible relationships between the public credit of the country and nationalization. Following for the most part the natural inclinations of his own interest as an interstate and international merchant, Morris tended to become so concerned with the prestige of the Union that he willingly staked his entire financial program, for the most part, on the outcome of a measure to fund the debts of the national government; for he was convinced that its adoption was necessary to preserve the Confederation established during the war.

It is surprising that one of the many themes which runs through this volume, the resemblance between the matured Morris program and the Federalist policies as expounded by Hamilton, has not been previously noted with any particularity. Both men, in reality, were working out their programs under the profound political and economic influences of the western world in their time. The story of Robert Morris, therefore, as a prospering merchant who plays a significant public role as Superintendent of Finance in the American Revolution is highly important for a variety of reasons, not the least being the combination he represents, perhaps better than any of his contemporaries, of the rise of modern capitalism and the emergence of modern nationalism in eighteenth-century America.

Robert Morris, as a person, was a controversial figure in the eighteenth century, and he has been the center of dispute ever since that time. In writing about him it has not been my aim to pass a moral judgment on his confusion of business and political activities, but rather to analyze those factors which prompted him to act as he did. Much attention has been given to the question of the dispute about Morris, and my conclusions have been inserted at an appropriate place in this volume. But it has seemed unwise to permit the controversy to overshadow the much more important developments of the period with which Morris was concerned.

CHAPTER – ONE ❖❖❖❖❖❖❖❖❖❖❖❖❖❖❖❖❖❖❖❖❖❖

The Early Career of Robert Morris (1735-78)

A GENIUS FOR SUCCESS IN BUSINESS WAS MANIFESTED BY ROBERT MORRIS early in his career. On the eve of the Revolution, Morris was acknowledged as one of the leading figures in the mercantile community of Philadelphia; by 1778, he had attained a position among the ranking merchants in America. This rise to prominence had been largely achieved by means of a partnership that Morris had been fortunate in making with Thomas Willing, the scion of an important Philadelphia family, almost two decades before the Revolution.

When the separation from Great Britain presented new challenges and opportunities to those engaged in commerce, the mercantile house of Willing and Morris was in a position to use its substantial resources and experience to advantage. By adjusting to the new conditions which controlled trade, and by relentlessly pursuing the business opportunities which were unleashed, the efforts of Morris, who managed the activities of the firm, were crowned with success. That Morris profited in all of his ventures, however, is false. In the West India trade and in privateering, for example, the evidence indicates that Morris was richly rewarded, but his efforts to open an important commerce with the French were so thwarted that financial gains were severely limited. Despite the unequal results of numerous enterprises, Robert Morris, the Philadelphia merchant who surveyed the business scene in 1778 looking for new worlds to conquer, was a man who enjoyed an outstanding reputation in commercial circles founded upon long and varied experience and extensive and important connections.

The second preëminent feature of Robert Morris' early career was the important role he played in the realm of Revolutionary politics and political administration. In his case, and it could be compared with that of many contemporaries, the Revolution seemed to unlock hidden capacities. Morris' participation in the political events of his native state of Pennsylvania was of significance, but he received his most important experience and training in the arena of national politics. The vigorous enthusiasm with which Morris threw himself into his work in Congress and several of its most important committees soon set him apart as one of the leading members of that body, and the scope of his activity quickly made him conscious of most of the primary problems confronting the new nation. His duties, both designated and assumed, also provided him with an unusual opportunity to use and develop his latent talent as an executive, an opportunity which he grasped with obvious relish. The powerful impact of these politically formative years was immeasurable in the light of Morris' reappearance in a much more significant role during the final years of the Revolution as the Superintendent of Finance.

Morris acting in his private capacity as a prominent merchant and Morris acting in his public capacity as a member of Congress and Congressional committees was technically two entities, but the distinction was not always preserved. This dual role was complicated by numerous extraordinary conditions arising out of the Revolution; these conditions affected individuals and government alike. Both were forced to adapt their efforts to such changes as shifting lines of trade and adjustments within the structure of the mercantile community; both attempted to obtain goods under similar conditions. That a coincidence in correspondents and avenues of trade occurred is an expected development, but when the coincidence was cultivated, as happened with Morris in certain instances, the results were so involved and intricate that it is not surprising to find accusations leveled against the Philadelphia merchant challenging his integrity as a public servant. But these charges, important as they were, should not obscure the two preëminent forces in the early career of Morris—his commercial expansion and success, and his political experience and growth—for these are essential in appraising the early period and in understanding and interpreting the later role of Robert Morris as Superintendent of Finance.

The earliest career and experience of Robert Morris was intimately connected with the growth of the mercantile firm of Willing and Morris. Morris had been apprenticed to the important Philadelphia commercial establishment of Charles Willing—later Charles Willing and Son—soon after he arrived in America. To serve as an apprentice in a mercantile house in order to acquire training in business was a common practice in eighteenth-century America; it was somewhat rarer to be accepted eventually as a full-fledged partner, as it happened with Morris, because such positions were often reserved for members of the immediate family. Because of an unusual combination of circumstances—the death of Charles Willing which shifted the entire burden of business upon the shoulders of his son Thomas and the remarkable promise that Morris had demonstrated as an apprentice with the Willing firm—Thomas Willing and Robert Morris entered into a partnership, the conventional form of business organization at the time. On the one hand, the birth of the firm of Willing and Morris on May 1, 1757, recorded an important achievement for Robert Morris after many years of training, diligence, and friendship; and, on the other hand, it marked the commencement of an illustrious career that carried Morris to mercantile heights unparalleled in early American experience.[1]

Robert Morris had come from a comparatively humble background. In 1747, while only a lad of thirteen, Morris had been brought to America from England by his father, who maintained a residence in Oxford, Maryland, while acting as a tobacco agent for a Liverpool firm. The son was soon sent to Philadelphia in order to continue his education—and probably to permit his father a freer personal life. When the elder Morris died of an accidental wound a few years later, Robert Morris faced the world alone except for the support of a small legacy that remained from his father's moderate estate after the fulfillment of bequests in favor of friends, and particularly for a common-law wife who was with child. About this time, it appears that Robert Greenway, a friend of the elder Morris in whose care the son had been placed, obtained an apprenticeship for Robert in the mercantile house of Charles Willing, where his resourcefulness and talent quickly revealed his natural ability in business matters. Morris was soon rewarded with more responsible duties, and eventually served as a supercargo in several voyages to the West Indies, a customary step in the training of a trusted employee. Upon being released from capture by French privateers, which resulted from one of his voyages, Morris, at the age of twenty-three, entered into the mercantile connection with Thomas Willing.[2]

The significance of this connection with Willing, and the close friendship which grew up between the two men, can scarcely be overestimated. Thomas Willing—more affectionately known to his admirers as "Old Square Toes"—was a young man of ability and training who had been reared in the genteel fashion expected of a family occupying an important position in the economic and social life of Philadelphia. Following the practice of the well born in the other colonies, Tom had been placed in the care of his grandfather in England at a tender age in order to secure an "adequate" education. This training had consisted of the usual round of preparatory schools and, in the best colonial tradition, had eventually led to the Inns of Court, the fountainhead of English jurisprudence in the eighteenth century. Upon his return to Philadelphia, Thomas had entered his father's mercantile house and quickly assumed a conspicuous place in the affairs of the colony. The death of Charles Willing, Tom's father, only a few years after the son's return, not only placed the weighty responsibilities of the business upon Tom's shoulders, but also thrust upon him the worries connected with the provision and upbringing of his father's large, young family.

Robert Morris, who was Thomas' junior by three years, remained with the Willing firm even though his term of apprenticeship had expired; and he assisted Thomas in discharging both of these responsibilities, with the result that the connections between the two men transcended a strict business relationship. It was the union of two personal friends. When Morris prepared for his first trip to the West

Indies as supercargo, Thomas Willing cautioned him to be attentive to his health and safety, and wished him a safe return to Philadelphia "where my house shall be your home and myself your friend." The passing years strengthened this personal bond. Only an intimate friend could write as Willing wrote to Morris during the British occupation of Philadelphia nearly twenty-five years later: "I hope still to be happy in the esteem and friendship of the Man in the World I love most, and for whom I have every feeling of affection and regard." [3]

The maiden years of the firm's operations, although seriously complicated by the problems arising out of the Seven Years War, reflected a blend of growing experience and vitality. Despite some of the existing conditions, uncertain markets and embargoes, the lines of trade established by the firm during the war followed a relatively well-defined pattern. Their correspondents clustered around the focal points of Great Britain, Portugal and Spain, and the West Indies. Thomas Willing of London—the Philadelphia Thomas Willing's uncle—presided over the British end; Mayne, Burn, and Mayne were important in Lisbon; and Scott, Pringle, and Company in Madrid; Samuel Bean, Coddrington Carrington, and Andrew Lessly figured prominently at Jamaica, Barbados, and Antigua, respectively. These men handled the ingredients of trade—flour and wheat to Ireland or Britain; lumber and provisions to the West Indies; dry goods from Britain; salt, lemons, and wine from Portugal and Spain; and rum and molasses from the West Indies. Apart from their own trading, Willing and Morris acted as correspondents for firms from other mercantile communities, handling their goods and drawing bills of exchange. In addition, Willing apparently headed an insurance group.

These commercial activities were conducted on a rather limited scale. An enterprise involving 1,000 pounds sterling was relatively rare, while one of 2,000 pounds sterling was almost inconceivable. In addition, an enterprise that called for extensive credit operations was looked upon by the firm with as much suspicion as their tutor, Charles Willing, had shown many years before. Still, the firm demonstrated an important optimism in carrying on their trade. Although they owned only a few vessels—probably three—Willing and Morris refused to be discouraged when one of their ships was captured, and they immediately arranged for a second voyage. Within the firm, Willing rather than Morris was primarily in command, for ships were sometimes chartered three-fourths Willing and one-fourth Morris, and letters and instructions of the firm plainly bore the imprint of the elder partner. But this relationship did not last indefinitely, and, by the eve of the Revolution, an important change had taken place. [4]

Although an unfortunate gap exists in the materials from 1761 to 1775 and only isolated islands of correspondence appear, it is clear that Morris had replaced Willing as the most active partner within the firm of Willing and Morris by 1775 and that he managed most of its affairs. It is also manifest—as the ship holdings alone bear witness —that the firm had enlarged its commercial establishment to such an

extent that it was acknowledged as one of the leading firms in Philadelphia. Moreover, the investments of Willing and Morris transcended
strict mercantile boundaries to branch out into landholding in Pennsylvania and elsewhere. A choice example is their Mississippi plantation—which Morris called *Orange Grove Estate* because he thought
the name would be highly suitable as soon as a fine orange grove could
be planted. Indeed, his plans for an establishment utilizing a hundred
slaves make a fascinating episode in early absentee ownership. On the
eve of the Revolution, Morris himself was living very comfortably,
having acquired a celebrated country home outside of Philadelphia
which was well known as a showplace. It was with considerable pride
that Morris assured a correspondent in 1775: "It is known that besides
our capital in trade we possess valuable landed estates, [and] that we
are totally free from encumbrances." [5]

Despite the obscurity which envelops many phases of this significant
formative period in the development of Robert Morris, the main out-
lines are clearly perceptible. Morris had enjoyed over two decades of
mercantile experience in a firm that had achieved a substantial trading position after twenty years of commercial activity, a considerable
life span for any such concern in that period. And the firm had grown
up in the thriving and comparatively young commercial community
of Philadelphia, which was soon to receive an added distinction as the
seat of the national government. In many respects, circumstances and
fate seemed to combine in preparing Robert Morris for the challenges
and opportunities which the Revolution injected into American political and economic affairs.

While the firm of Willing and Morris was building up its mercantile position, events of international importance were taking place
within the British Empire. The conflict between the mother country
and the American colonies which had been intensified during the
course of the eighteenth century was aggravated after the British triumph in the Seven Years' War. The reasons for this conflict are so
complex that it would serve no purpose to discuss them in this study,
but there can be no question that the events in the years 1764-76
touched every person in the American colonies in one way or another.

Willing and Morris as prominent Philadelphia merchants took an
active part in the colonial opposition to British policy. Both men
staunchly supported the merchant groups in Philadelphia and other
port towns who protested against the revenue measures involved in the
Grenville program and the Townshend acts, the two plans which reflected the dispute between the mother country and the colonies. In
fact, Willing's name headed the list of Philadelphia subscribers to the
Non-Importation Resolutions, and that of Morris appeared among the
earliest signers—as could be expected of anyone who figured prominently in the Philadelphia Committee of Merchants to oppose the
Stamp Tax. [6]

Although the issues involved in the crises subsided somewhat after 1770, the Boston Tea Party revived them with fresh intensity, and Morris, like every colonial, was soon confronted with a difficult and delicate question. Would the grievances of the colonists be best satisfied by remaining within the empire, there to exert unremitting pressure for a change in colonial policy, or was a complete break with the mother country the best solution? Like so many of his contemporaries, the Philadelphia merchant did not find the answer altogether simple. In many respects, Morris reflects the temper of the colonials—people torn between forces moving toward independence and restraining allegiances.

On the one hand, Morris believed in what he called the "equity of the American Claims." These he found securely rooted in reason, justice, and in the "Principles of the British Constitution." Yet he definitely wanted reconciliation if it could be had on such terms that "undisturbed enjoyment of the freedom we claim" would be insured. And what was encompassed in the word "freedom"? "Every line of liberty and atom of property . . .," he declared.[7]

On the other hand stood the restraining forces: the trading connections with English merchants which Morris greatly respected; the close family connections in England of his partner Willing; the apparent reluctance of his good wife Molly to meet the issue of independence; and, of course, the allegiance to the homeland. In late July, after the Declaration of Independence had been passed in the Continental Congress, Morris wrote Joseph Reed: "I am sorry to say there are some amongst us that cannot bear the thought of reconciliation on any terms. To these men all propositions of the kind, sound like high Treason against the States. . . . I cannot help Condemning this disposition as it must be founded in keen resentment or on interested Views. . . . I think with you that if the Commissioners have any propositions to make they ought to be heard."[8]

But what if the sands of reconciliation ran out? Morris had already committed himself definitely in January 1776. "When it [independence] happens," he had written, "I am content to run all hazards." Why then did Morris as a member of the Pennsylvania delegation to the Continental Congress fail to vote for Independence when that all-important issue was raised six months later? Apparently the pull of the restraining forces remained strong, and his hopes for reconciliation still lived. Equally important, Morris thought the hour for separation had not yet arrived; the issue of independence would divide those previously united in opposition to British policy. Thus the cause would be weakened by a declaration at the time rather than strengthened. Morris signed the Declaration of Independence in August 1776, however, when it was presented to Congress in finished form. This action apparently signified that his long-cherished hopes for reconciliation on honorable terms had flickered out; Morris' signature certainly marked his definite commitment to absolute independence, a principle from which he did not waiver in the ensuing struggle.[9]

The movement toward Revolution introduced Morris to political life, and the experience he gained in it proved to be almost indispensable in his later career. It is customary when speaking of this political career to thrust Morris into a slot neatly tabbed "Conservative, unalterable species," and proceed from there. But this is to make him, and one might add much of the Revolutionary Generation, incomprehensible. After all is said and written, the most important, and most obvious, characteristic of the Revolution was its moderation, and the bulk of its leadership can be described in such terms. The present writer has found it difficult to understand Morris' actions in terms of any set pattern such as revolution and counterrevolution, or even in terms of radicals and conservatives. Morris seems most explicable as a political moderate leaning slightly toward "conservatism" whose actions on policy are conditioned for the most part by the existing situation rather than by any fundamental precept.[10]

In Pennsylvania, Morris served in the Assembly from 1775 to 1781, with the exception of one year. In 1775-76 he was a member of the important Council of Safety—being vice-president for a time when Franklin was president—where he vigorously implemented the measures passed for the defense of the colony. Later he took part in various committees on financing, in skirmishes on constitutional matters, and finally in fighting for the repeal of legal tender laws. To a limited extent this state activity helped to shape Morris' legislative experience, but his attendance in the Continental Congress, the chief agency for carrying on the War for Independence, as one of the leading delegates from Pennsylvania during the years 1775-78 proved infinitely more important.[11]

In Congress Morris served on the usual round of Committees—naval armament, trade regulations, consideration of a war office, ways and means, prisoner exchanges, clothing acquisitions for the army, proposed treaties with foreign powers, and the commissary department. Although the multiplicity of appointments was commonplace in itself, the enthusiastic role which Morris played as a committee member was distinctive. Many members of Congress were content to let others carry on the time-consuming and often burdensome committee work, but Morris threw himself into these tasks with such energy that he soon distinguished himself as the driving force in many committees. And it was his work on these committees that soon set him apart as one of the leading figures of Congress.[12]

One of the earliest indications of this trend was the appointment of Morris as the representative of Congress in Philadelphia when that body scurried to Baltimore in the final months of 1776 to escape Howe's advancing Redcoats; in performing his duties, Morris displayed all his boundless energy, his executive capacity, his zeal for detail, and his appetite for important position. At first his only delegated powers were those entrusted to him as a member of certain important committees, such as the Secret Committee on Commerce and the Marine Committee, but, according to his own statement, the barrage of complaints, the "loud, large, and constant" pleas for money, and the other extreme necessities obliged him "to advise in things not committed to me." Still he felt that such an assumption of authority was fully justified. "Circumstanced as our affairs now are," he assured Congress, "I conceive it better to take liberties and assume some powers than to let the general interest suffer." But Morris was uneasy about Congress' reaction, and longed for approval "of these things which I have undertaken for the sake of serving my country." Morris' anxiety was not relieved until a harassed Congress—whose membership sorely missed the comforts of Philadelphia—ratified his past actions and followed his suggestion to set up a committee in Philadelphia to act in its stead. Though George Walton, George Clymer, and Morris were appointed, it meant in reality that Morris took charge.[13]

Morris accepted his role with obvious relish. With a characteristic burst of energy, he plunged headlong into the immediate problems. First on the list was the safety of the Continental vessels at Philadelphia which the British threat had placed in jeopardy. He hurried the completion of the ship *Delaware* and wrote optimistically of his hopes to Congress. "If General Howe will but give me a few days more, and Lord Howe keep away his myrmidons, I shall have the pleasure to despatch the *Randolph, Hornet, Delaware, Security, Fly,* and a large ship laden with tobacco; all which you may deem as saved from the flames." [14]

But the British had different ideas, and they bottled up the American fleet by sending cruisers to guard the bay. Though Morris feared that his "labours appear to be lost . . .," he acted decisively. He dispatched the *Fly* to report on the movement of the British cruisers; he sent an express to Captain Baldwin aboard the *Wasp,* anchored in a Jersey cove, to cruise outside the British men of war and warn incoming vessels of the danger; he stationed the *Hornet* in "Christeen Creek" where he thought it could best defend the stores located there; and he rushed repairs for the *Independence,* newly arrived at the port of Philadelphia. Morris even conceived a plan—which was approved by the Captains, according to the Philadelphian—to break past the blockade, but fortunately its effectiveness was never tested because Washington's surprising victories at Trenton and Princeton relieved the immediate threat.[15]

This primary task claimed only a part of Morris' attention; he was here, there, and everywhere at once. He urged Congress and Washington to make an agreement with the British for the proper care of prisoners "as we are inclined to believe our People suffer by the peculation of the Commissarys that have the care of them," while in contrast British prisoners in American hands "are feasting on the fat of this land"; he urged defense measures on the Pennsylvania Council of Safety; he prepared for the evacuation of Continental stores— though here it was General Washington's prodding that brought action; he sent blankets from the ship *Independence* to Washington, and handled an assortment of war goods recently arrived aboard the

Andrew Doria; he sent $40,000 in hard money to Washington by means of the Commissary Department and the following day dispatched another $50,000 with the assurance that "if further occasional supplies of money are necessary, you may depend on my exertions either in a public or private capacity"; he lamented that Congress had sent a man from Baltimore to set up the Loan Office in Philadelphia with only some $60,000 worth of certificates and urged them to send $300,000 to $500,000 more, "as we shall use our utmost endeavours to get the money into his office, and [I] doubt not but pretty good success will attend his endeavours." Still there was time enough to condemn the wasted feed and the inefficiency of the Continental stables, to applaud Congressional resolutions giving Washington extensive powers, to provide a superintendent for the building of a magazine at Carlisle, to order salt to Lancaster, to urge the promotion of Cadwalader (with Washington's recommendation) to Brigadier General, and even to write lengthy letters to the American Commissioners in Paris.[16]

Morris was not above some subtle self-approbation. "We are now at 31st December, twelve o'clock [midnight], and have just received your Honour's letter of the 27th . . .," he replied to the President of Congress. "No time shall be lost in carrying into execution such things as Congress have ordered." In a letter to Washington he placed his zeal beyond doubt. "I am up very early this morning to dispatch a supply of $50,000 to your Excellency . . . but it will not be got away so early as I could wish, for none concerned in this movement, except myself, are up. I shall rouse them immediately."[17]

Morris' actions, letters, and reports as a member of the "Philadelphia Committee" reflect the pleasure with which he carried on his responsible duties; they also placed him in the Congressional and, to a degree, in the national limelight. As a man of action, Morris could make decisions and execute them; moreover, the sweep of his decisions and the extent of his powers encouraged his executive capacities. As an added reward, Morris received a round of applause from some distinguished leaders. Hancock, the President of Congress, assured him that "without the least appearance of Flattery I can assure you your whole Conduct since our Flight is highly approv'd, and happy I am that you Remain'd, many agreeable Consequences have Resulted from it, and your continu'd Exertions will be productive of great good. . . ." William Hooper was equally enthusiastic. "Congress seems unanimously sensible of the Obligations which they owe you, and you may boast of being the only man whom they all agree to speak and I really believe think well of." Morris, humanly enough, was pleased by such praise. "I am hon'd [honored] *indeed* if Congress think and speak of me in the style you mention and feel myself truly happy and greatly encouraged by their approbation." Indeed, it was a high point in Morris' early political career. He gained such stature that, according to Mary Morris, his wife, the "Presidentship" of Congress was offered him, but he declined.[18]

Of equal significance with the "Committee on Philadelphia" in representing Morris' emergence as a leading figure in the Continental Congress was his work on two of its most important standing committees, the Secret Committee of Commerce and the Committee of Secret Correspondence. On occasion these two Committess have been thoroughly confused, and their functions, especially that of the Secret Committee of Commerce, completely misunderstood.

The Committee of Secret Correspondence was set up on November 29, 1775, "for the sole purpose of corresponding with our friends in Great Britain, Ireland, and other parts of the world. . . ." The primary reason for Morris' appointment to this Committee on January 30, 1776, was to secure conveyances for dispatches. For a time, however, the default of other committee members, together with his own initiative, placed the burden of correspondence squarely upon his shoulders. Morris handled this task until December 1776, when the appointment of new members to the Committee relieved him of much of the responsibility.[19]

In contrast to the declining importance of his position in the Committee of Secret Correspondence, Morris' role in the Secret Committee of Commerce expanded until it claimed the major share of his time and energy. The Secret Committee of Commerce had been formed by the Continental Congress before Independence—September 1775—and Morris was appointed to the Committee in December. Although the official function of the Committee was never clearly defined, its duties were apparently threefold: one, to procure arms, powder, cannon, clothing, and other ingredients to strengthen the sinews of war; two, to pay for them; and three, to distribute them upon arrival. It is important to examine the work of the Secret Committee of Commerce in some detail because it provides an insight into the experience and development of Morris while a member of Congress, and it later figured prominently in the charges against Morris' integrity.[20]

The existing letters—only a fragment of the whole—and the *Journals* of Congress indicate that the Committee was occupied not only with such vital matters as indispensable stores for the Marine department but also with such minutiae as delivering six pounds of powder and 24 pounds of lead to two rifles companies "to try their rifles." Innumerable run-of-the-mill items ranged within the extremes.[21]

The Secret Committee obtained the countless necessary articles and in many cases paid for them by contracting, a procedure authorized by Congress. A person or a firm would make an agreement with the Secret Committee to buy goods and receive as compensation a commission—usually 2½ per cent or 5 per cent—on the amount purchased. Often the Committee advanced funds to initiate the purchasing. Firms or persons employed in contracting were to account for their purchases by producing vouchers. Contracting was employed not only in acquiring goods, but also in purchasing commodities in the states, which in turn were used as Continental exports to pay for the incoming goods. Upwards of a score of individuals and firms made contracts with the Secret Committee totaling, according to Arthur Lee, some $2,000,000.[22]

The Secret Committee's method of obtaining supplies by offering contractors a commission was comparable to that used by the British during the early years of World War I when J. P. Morgan and Company acted as their purchasing agent in America. The British, however, concentrated the purchasing function in a single agent, while the Secret Committee used many agents. Although the Secret Committee, in contrast, offered more alluring commissions, the percentage allowed corresponded with the business practices and risks of the time. As some of the contracting agents quickly discovered, the new Republic was woefully delinquent in its remittances.

A certain amount of confusion surrounded the activities of the Secret Committee of Commerce; among the many factors responsible for this confusion was the overlapping of functions in several committees of Congress. The Correspondence Committee, for example, issued the instructions on purchases to United States envoys—Silas Deane and William Bingham—while the goods arrived under the care of the Secret Committee of Commerce. Even the Marine Committee appeared to figure in purchasing goods for Congress. It is seldom clear what happened to each Committee's order after its request was sent.[23]

This mixture of overlapping Committee functions was thoroughly spiced by a profusion of personal business activities of the envoys engaged by Congress, a confusion in accounts, occasional mixed cargoes of public and private goods, and a long lapse between the placement of orders and eventual fulfillment. Silas Deane is undoubtedly the best-known example of multiple representation, although his was scarcely an isolated case of triple and quadruple duties. He acted as an agent of Willing and Morris; he was concerned with his brothers in setting up a commercial establishment in Virginia; he, together with others—among them Morris—was commissioned by the Secret Committee to buy 40,000 pounds sterling of goods and trinkets for the use of Congress in making Indian treaties. Such commitments, of course, complicated Deane's primary task, which was to obtain enough supplies for the Secret Committee of Commerce to equip 25,000 troops; the result was a confusion of accounts which the necessary shuttling of the records books of the Secret Committee—to avoid capture—did little to remedy. An element of uncertainty was also introduced with the shipment of cargoes that were partly public and partly private goods. Although mixed shipments, that is numerous shippers, constituted a form of marine insurance frequently employed during the Revolution —it diminished the chances of losing one's entire capital by the loss of a single vessel—there was considerable trouble when adequate bills of lading failed to accompany the cargo. This sometimes happened with the goods received by the Secret Committee. All of these foregoing complications were aggravated by a lapse—often a matter of years—between the time an agreement was made and the time the contracted goods arrived. This delay resulted in prolonged and perplexing accounts that overtaxed the eighteenth-century bookkeeping system; the confusion was compounded by the many changes in the membership of the Committee and a fluctuating currency.[24]

Finally, a cloak of secrecy that has often been misunderstood and construed as a deep forbidding conspiracy enveloped the activities of the Secret Committee of Commerce; in reality, such secrecy was specifically authorized by Congress, and it was perfectly accountable at the time. The Secret Committee of Commerce, like the Committee of Secret Correspondence, was activated before Independence, so it is quite understandable that any moves to obtain arms and court alliances during that period were carefully guarded. Equally explicable is the secrecy after the Declaration of Independence, for Congress did not propose to alienate the French by exposing publicly that country's façade of neutrality. Indeed, the intensity of their feeling on this matter is clearly revealed in the sharp rebuke handed Tom Paine for his "imprudence" and "misapplication of public papers" when he disclosed the character of the French support in the public press.[25]

The career of Robert Morris, for a time, was intimately involved in these varied, complex operations of the Secret Committee; as a member and later as chairman, the Philadelphian often acted as the Committee's propelling force. The nature of the position inevitably developed Morris' administrative talent and widened his personal contacts; indeed, no future program of Congress in obtaining supplies or in handling finances would find the Philadelphia merchant without considerable experience. The work of the Committee not only thoroughly acquainted Morris with the entire procurement program of Congress but also enabled him to play a leading part in managing the purchase of goods and ships on a scale unprecedented in American experience. In addition, Morris' work on the Committee probably broadened his personal mercantile foundations and enlarged his business scope. Certainly the firm of Willing and Morris figured prominently in the contracts of the Secret Committee, a situation that led to ugly rumors and serious charges that Morris was using his public position for private ends—accusations which plagued him to the end of his career.[26]

In addition to the "Committee on Philadelphia," the Committee of Secret Correspondence, and the Secret Committee of Commerce, the general political career of Morris in the Continental Congress was significant. Working on the committee responsible for treaty proposals, for instance, widened Morris' perspective and made him more conscious of national and sectional interests, while the concerns of the committee on "ways and means" familiarized him with the problems of providing support for a new government. Moreover, Morris observed Congress in operation—the membership, the problems faced, and the decisions taken—with the result that he possessed a full knowledge of the proceedings of Revolutionary America at first hand. Such "first hand" knowledge is not to be taken lightly, for only members of Congress were in a position to grasp the complete picture of what was taking place. It is true that correspondents of members of Congress received some information, but such knowledge was of necessity incomplete, specialized, or one-sided. The *Journals of Congress* were late in being published, and they scarcely provided more than a skeletal framework of Congressional proceedings. In view of his later role as Superintendent of Finance, it is probably fortunate that Morris was active in Congress from 1775 to 1778, the first years of the Revolution, since the general lines of Congressional policy were established in that period. Thus, it was relatively easy for Morris to pick up the threads later in the War, especially in finance, where no major policy changes were introduced after the early years.

As for a personal estimate of Morris' contribution in Congress, it would be difficult to improve upon the shrewd evaluation made by John Adams much earlier:

I think he has a masterly Understanding, an open Temper and an honest Heart; and if he does not always vote for what you and I should think proper, it is because he thinks that a large Body of People remains, who are not yet of his Mind. He has vast designs in the mercantile way. And no doubt pursues mercantile ends, which are always gain; but he is an excellent Member of our Body.[27]

When Robert Morris found himself caught up in the demands of numerous political activities at the outset of the Revolution, he declared that he expected to do "very little more business as a merchant until this affair is ended." Within two months, however, the Philadelphia merchant was engaged in sizable private ventures, and at no time during the Revolution did he completely abandon such interests.[28]

Two characteristics in the business activities of Morris during the early years of the Revolution (1775-78) stand out clearly. First, most of his mercantile concerns were conducted through the firm of Willing and Morris; and second, the business itself was closely identified with government—that is, Continental Congress and state assemblies.

The latter correlation would be expected—especially at the beginning of the war. When the first Continental Congress met in 1774, the delegates had adopted a measure, familiarly known as the "Continental Association," that was intended to apply economic coercion upon Great Britain by shutting off imports and, in time, exports. The sweeping terms of this policy worked against the best interests of the colonials when the fighting broke out in 1775, because they were deprived of ways and means to obtain war matériel. In order to remedy this situation, Congress by specific authorization permitted certain individuals or committees to obtain the necessary supplies, with the result that Congressional sanction, for a time, was the only legitimate avenue of business.

Willing and Morris were favored very early under this arrangement when they agreed to obtain arms and ammunition for the Secret Committee of Congress in September 1775. This contract provoked some open criticism about exorbitant profits, but such censure did not prevent Congress from allotting the firm additional projects. Indeed, the warehouses of Willing and Morris apparently contained so many goods for Congress that Continental guards were placed there to insure the proper protection of Continental property. When the entire policy of restricted importation was revoked, the business interests of the firm continued to parallel those of government, and they contracted to supply the continent with goods and to purchase commodities that would be sent to Europe as Continental remittances.[29]

Many of these first wartime transactions and all of the later enterprises posed the difficult question of new channels of trade. With the familiar connections in England severed, merchants were forced to explore trade possibilities with other countries in Europe and to find reputable correspondents in those countries. The cautious manner in which both Congress and private individuals experimentally tried to determine the attitude of various countries on American trade and to sound out trustworthy mercantile houses for correspondents plainly demonstrates the delicate nature of the problem.[30]

Willing and Morris solved the problem by creating what could be designated as a mercantile framework. Correspondents were selected in various states to handle incoming goods and to purchase commodities that could be shipped abroad as remittances, agents were sent to France to administer the European end, and a representative was appointed in Martinique to act for the firm at that important pivot post. Benjamin Harrison Jr., Carter Braxton, Hewes and Smith, Jonathan Hudson, and Stephen Stewart were among the correspondents in the states; Thomas Morris, Silas Deane, and John Ross represented the firm in Europe, although French correspondents in many ports were eventually necessary to implement their business; and finally, William Bingham occupied the pivot post. Of course, this was a loosely knit organization. With most of these men, the affairs of Willing and Morris made up only a small part of their total operations. Perhaps it should be stressed that these connections grew up to meet a definite problem in trade rather than to promote ulterior designs.

Why did Willing and Morris employ Silas Deane, one of Congress' Commissioners to France, and William Bingham, its envoy to Martinique, when these men represented primarily the public interests of the United States? First of all, their respective political assignments placed them in convenient locations to perform services required in the new pattern of trade, but equally important was the matter of credit. Willing and Morris had not traded with French merchants, and therefore no funds had been placed in French hands to establish a credit. If the money and credit resting with Willing and Morris' British mercantile correspondents could be transferred to French hands, it would help to alleviate this situation. However, this possibility evaporated when the British government, to use modern terms, immediately froze the assets of American colonial merchants.

An obvious way to create a credit in France would be to send commodities—that is, tobacco, rice, masts, etc. But this procedure had serious drawbacks because most of the goods, particularly tobacco and masts, were exceedingly bulky and required large vessels to carry a paying cargo. Ships of such size moved ponderously and thus became easy prey for alert British cruisers. The smaller, lighter vessels, which through sheer maneuverability and speed could escape the British squadrons, were invaluable for short trips to the West Indies, but such vessels in turn were entirely inadequate to carry commodities to Europe, at least in the quantity necessary to stockpile a fund that would establish a credit there. Moreover, any attempt, however successful, to build up a credit by commodity remittances was destined to foster a delay in trading; such trips took time and immediate credit was the great need.[31]

Willing and Morris circumvented this entire problem neatly and conveniently by using men who were agents of Congress to represent the firm as well, thus utilizing the credit invested in these agents in their official capacity to bolster the credit of their firm in dealing with French exporters. Goods could then be purchased without delay and shipped; payment could wait until remittances appeared. The accent was on speed; immediate delivery of goods would meet magnificent markets.

Only part of this general framework functioned well. Such correspondents as Benjamin Harrison Jr. and Carter Braxton of Virginia, and Stephen Stewart and Jonathan Hudson of Maryland purchased tobacco for Willing and Morris, while Hewes and Smith in North Carolina and John Dorsius in Charleston concentrated on buying indigo and rice. Although it is clear that the rice and indigo were usually sent to the West Indies while the tobacco was shipped directly to France, further details, such as the extent of the buying program, are fragmentary. Morris wrote Bingham in February 1777 that they were buying tobacco for Europe "pretty deeply," but the evidence in the letters written to the purchasing agents at the time indicate that his observation applied to the Secret Committee of Congress, which was attempting to send remittances to France for war matériel, rather than to the operations of Willing and Morris.[32]

What is clear is that there was a decided lag in commodity remittances from this side of the Atlantic, due in large measure to British patrols and to the general scarcity of shipping throughout the states. But part of the explanation for the delay was spelled out in the almost illegible scrawl of Stephen Stewart, a correspondent of the firm. Newcomers, including to a certain extent Willing and Morris, were unfamiliar with the tobacco trade. Stewart wanted to purchase the more expensive tobacco, explaining that it would meet a more favorable market and lose less by storage; Willing and Morris did not accept his advice. Stewart suggested that Holland would be the most profitable market; Willing and Morris designated France. To confirm this lack of experience, Morris himself admitted later that there were no persons in Philadelphia "sufficiently judges of it [tobacco]."[33]

At Martinique, there was William Bingham. This "young gentleman of good education, family, and fortune," to use Morris' appraisal, had served as secretary to the Committee of Secret Correspondence before he was entrusted with the direction of United States affairs in Martinique. On the day Bingham received his orders to proceed to the West Indies, Willing and Morris suggested to the young envoy that some good mercantile houses in that area might wish to ship West India goods to the United States and to receive, in return, colonial produce. In addition to the commission that would result from such sales, there was the possibility that "Linnens or other European Manufactures" could be purchased on credit, to be paid for eventually with commodity remittances shipped by Willing and Morris. Each party, it was agreed, would share equally in such adventures; for "In this way we will keep up a constant intercourse with you." [34]

Although the early correspondence of Bingham, in the judgment of Morris, reflected "a good deal of the fanciful young man," the connection proved to be highly successful. Morris' confidence that the envoy to Martinique possessed "abilities and merit, both in the political and commercial line," was fully justified, for all kinds of goods—sugar, molasses, dry goods, etc.—flowed in from the West Indies while a less constant stream of commodities—rice, indigo, tobacco—flowed out. In prompting Bingham, Morris emphasized that all goods would do well, although woolens would command the greatest profit. But most important, he insisted, was "to keep doing something constantly," for "where cargoes arrive either one way or the other, the profits are now so great it is well worth risquing largely." Indeed, "one arrival will pay for 2 or 3 or 4 losses." [35]

Particularly advantageous was the shuttle trade between Martinique and Morris' correspondents in North Carolina, Hewes and Smith, and in Charleston, John Dorsius—a commerce described by Morris at one time as a "golden voyage." By April 1777, Morris spoke of it as the "usual" trade. There was reason enough for such a happy description; the route was short, the vessels swift, and the profits high. Such success in the West India trade was not, however, a foregone conclusion. When the course of the war had cast a forbidding shadow over the Middle Region, it had been necessary for Willing and Morris to warn Bingham that it might not be advisable to forward any property, public or private; they urged him, moreover, to sound out a trustworthy French merchant who would take over any goods, should the situation require it. In addition, some specific enterprises ended dismally. One Mr. Prejent, for example, a merchant from the West Indies who had been recommended by Bingham, began a voyage for Willing and Morris that promised "a ministerial fortune," but it ended as a tremendous financial drain. Such incidents were exceptions to the general rule, however, and the existing correspondence, although incomplete, with its record of many voyages and rather infrequent losses, suggests that the West India trade proved to be one of the most profitable ventures for Willing and Morris in the first years of the War. [36]

In France, the story differed significantly. Early in the spring of

1777, Morris began to anticipate shipments of goods from France via Martinique, and he carefully instructed William Bingham to rush them forward when they arrived. Hopes were high with glowing prospects to boost them. "If we have but luck on our side," he wrote Bingham, "much money will be made." Some of these goods did arrive, but by no means on the scale expected. Perhaps Goddess Fortuna was so busy protecting the West India excursions that it would have been ungrateful to ask for a further extension of her favors; certainly all was not running smoothly in France.[37]

Confusion has surrounded much of the activities of the French agents of Willing and Morris—Silas Deane, Thomas Morris (Robert Morris' half-brother), and later, John Ross. Deane, able, active, at times extraordinarily perspicacious in analyzing economic trends, had been commissioned as one of Congress' agents in France when his native state of Connecticut failed to reappoint him to its delegation in Philadelphia. Thomas Morris, young, capable, talented, with an appetite for the gay life, had been snatched from the pleasures of traveling in Europe with unlimited funds. Tom was to be under Deane's wing, but with the promise of a "proper appointment" if "he shews himself capable of serving his country" and, of course, the firm of Willing and Morris. Tom's knowledge of European mercantile houses, thought Morris, would prove advantageous; but even more important, he emphasized, they were armed with an inestimable asset—opportune times. ". . . The present oppert'y [opportunity] of improving our Fortunes ought not to be lost," declared Morris, "especially as the very means of doing it will contribute to the Service of our Country at the same time."[38]

To exploit this glowing opportunity, Morris sketched his plan with sure strokes. "I therefore propose that Tom and you should try your and our Credit jointly and propose to some of the most wealthy Houses in France to ship out quantities of suitable Goods to Martinico and Cape François to be reshipped from thence, hither." What goods were suitable? Sheetings, table linen, sailcloth, cambricks, cutlery ware, tin, lead, indeed almost anything. And the extent of the purchase? "The more the better." Morris suggested that the goods come out two-thirds Willing, Morris, and Company and one-third Deane or, if a French or Dutch house wished to join, then make thirds "or in any proportion you like better." To quiet the fears of any shipper, Deane was instructed to point out that no danger existed if the American cause were successful; should matters take a turn for the worse, the goods could always be halted in the West Indies. Here, then, was outlined the plan of action which Morris felt deserved Deane's "utmost Exertion and attention so far as your mind is engaged in making of money, for there never has been so fair an oppert'y [opportunity] of making a large Fortune since I have been conversant in the World. . . ." Though Morris suggested certain additions later, he did not deviate from this recommended "trading plan."[39]

By December 4, 1776, Deane had received Morris' letter of instructions. Although he was soon writing that various proposals had been submitted to send out goods, the available evidence indicates that the Connecticut enterpriser decided that the best proposition was to be "jointly concerned" with a mercantile house in Europe. This firm would ship the goods; Deane, in turn, would draw bills on Willing and Morris to pay for their share. At least that is the type of venture which began to materialize.[40]

A vessel, well armed and equipped, in which Deane and the Philadelphia firm would hold one-fourth interest, was scheduled to sail by January 15 with a cargo of 20,000 pounds sterling in goods. Deane looked to London for insurance "or rather to know at what rate insurance may be had under such and such circumstances *viz.*, French bottoms, French goods, no warlike stores, cleared out for St. Domingo with proper ostensible as well as secret orders." Promising even greater things, Deane wrote: "It is probable I shall send out this winter, and early in the Spring about 200,000 pounds stlg [sterling] in this way." A rosy picture indeed!![41]

But this optimism was scarcely warranted. The vessel and cargo about which Deane had been writing was unquestionably the *Union,* shipped in conjunction with Chaumont, a highly successful and influential French merchant. When Morris learned of the project, he resented and fiercely criticized the entire adventure. Consigning the cargo to Captain Roche, the master of the vessel, and to Bromfield, Chaumont's supercargo, rather than to Willing and Morris, in addition to remitting the entire net proceeds back to France without even consulting Morris, amounted to "a Certain degree of indignity in the terms that I will not submit to again." Morris pointedly declared he wanted no further interest in such commercial matters unless "they were to come on such a footing as is Consistent with that Credit and Character I am entitled to." Though Morris' anger cooled and cordial relations with Deane were eventually reëstablished, the handsome promise of 100,000 or 200,000 pounds sterling schemes ended in a single voyage.[42]

It would be an error to assume, however, that this temporary flareup was alone responsible for the lack of success. Many developments conspired against fulfillment: Deane's preoccupation with the goods of Beaumarchais, the famed French agent, and the general work of the American Commissioners in France; the ill feeling which at times cropped up between major parties involved in the trading plan; and Deane's intense interest in promoting the commercial affairs of his brother, Simeon Deane, and others. The dual role assigned to young Tom Morris as a Congressional agent and as a representative of Willing and Morris, together with his inattention to those duties, also contributed to the failure.[43]

When Benjamin Franklin departed from Philadelphia bearing the appointment of Silas Deane, Arthur Lee, and himself as Commissioners to the court of France, he also carried a letter defining a new role for Thomas Morris. The Secret Committee appointed Thomas

"Superintending Agent over all their European Concerns" with instructions to purchase goods for Congress through the best mercantile establishments in France and other parts of Europe and to receive and sell all consignments from America on public account. In fulfilling this task, the young Philadelphian was instructed to use his utmost discretion and judgment in purchasing the best goods at the cheapest price and to obtain the best market for American commodities. For compensation Thomas was to share in the commissions. In addition to these public duties, Willing and Morris loaded him with "a good deal of Private business."[44]

Here Thomas Morris was offered choice fruit from the Continental vineyard, but bungling, unsteady fingers dropped much of it to the ground; here was a task of responsibility in public affairs which was treated with gross irresponsibility. Though the details of the young man's trials go unrecorded in these months, his movements left a trail of complaints from friend and foe alike. The trail started in Paris and led to England, where he had gone in the early summer of 1776 to settle the affairs of Willing and Morris. After winding through the highways and byways of London, apparently more attentive to private satisfactions than to business affairs, the trail doubled back into France and finally terminated at Nantes, where he assumed his new duties.[45]

Thomas soon entrusted most of the public affairs as well as private matters to the firm of De Pliarne, Penet, and Gruel. The decision to operate through a French firm fell within his instructions, but Penet, Gruel, and Company had acquired a somewhat questionable reputation. Coupled with this injudicious choice was young Tom's overindulgence in wine, women, and song—his specialty was the first—and his general negligence. It is not strange that the private business of Willing and Morris suffered, that public affairs were confused, or that the chorus of complaints—Deane's voice among them—steadily grew. Some time elapsed before the echoes of such misconduct reached Market Street in Philadelphia, but the whispers in January of 1777 had noticeably increased in volume by late June. At this time Morris rallied to the defense of his brother—Tom's reputation should not be blasted "merely because he was fond of pleasure"—and sent him a letter of approval, even though he entertained many misgivings about Tom's behavior. By December, the complaints rose to such a crescendo that they could no longer be ignored. Morris reviewed his actions before Congress, sent his unqualified apologies to Deane and Franklin, and insisted his brother be removed from public office.[46]

In the meantime, Morris had authorized John Ross, a Philadelphia merchant who was trading in France, to take over the functions of Thomas as the representative of Willing and Morris in France. Ross, at this time, was purchasing abroad for himself, for Willing and Morris, and for others. He was jointly concerned in a renewed contract with Willing and Morris and the Secret Committee of February 1776, as well as one with Morris and the Secret Committee of March 1776. In both cases, Ross was actively implementing the agreements. Despite such extensive operations and previous commitments, Ross attempted to follow Morris' directions, and he took charge of Tom's private affairs. However, the change was not effected without much recrimination; indeed, it took Tom's tragic death in February 1778 to stabilize the uncertain state of affairs.[47]

Scanty evidence makes it practically impossible to measure the extent of Tom Morris' shipments on account of Willing and Morris, but the available material indicates that John Ross' efforts averted an entirely disappointing French trade experiment. The account books of Ross show shipments grossing nearly 70,000 pounds sterling up to May 1, 1778. How much of it was shipped in fulfillment of the contract with the Secret Committee and how much for private importation is not clear, although the records of a "preliminary" account book of Ross suggest an approximately equal division. Although this sum was not inconsiderable, it is clear that the returns fell far short of the enthusiastic predictions made when the operations commenced.[48]

During the first years of the war, Morris was also engaged in enterprises outside the immediate framework of France, Martinique, and the United States, but still closely aligned to governmental activity. His concern with five others in an "Indian Contract" with the Secret Committee of the Continental Congress fitted into this category. For a 5 per cent commission, the five venturers agreed to purchase domestic commodities and ship them abroad to pay for goods and trinkets that would be desirable bargaining merchandise in treating with the Indians. Obstacles on both sides of the Atlantic prevented the realization of the agreement, however, and nothing more substantial than source material for lingering disputes was provided. Another agreement was made between Willing and Morris and a Virginia firm— J. H. Norton, C. M. Thurston, and Samuel Beale—to supply the Virginia Committee of Safety with powder and arms, but this adventure also reads like a chapter on lamentations, with delay, capture, and shipwreck alternating as causes of despair. Contracting with the Maryland Council of Safety to supply arms and gunpowder constituted yet another enterprise of Willing and Morris, but delay hampered the fulfillment of the agreement at every turn.[49]

In contrast to these engagements, the interests of the Philadelphia merchant in privateering fared well. Although he avoided this warborn enterprise in the opening stages of the Revolution—he conceived that seizure and possible destruction of property belonging to British merchants was incompatible with his peacetime relationship to these men—Morris gradually changed his position. Early in 1777 he became involved in a clandestine privateering engagement with one Captain Ord and William Bingham; by April, he was ready to announce that his "scruples about privateering are all done away." Why this change of heart? "I have seen such rapine plunder and destruction denounced against and executed on the Americans that I join you in thinking it a duty to oppose and distress so merciless an enemy in every shape we can . . .," Morris confided to Bingham. Furthermore, he was now disposed "to increase the number of my engagements in that way." Of course, Captain Ord's success argued persuasively; Morris had heard from authentic sources that Ord had sent nine sail of transports and two "guinea men" into Martinique and two sail of transports into St. Eustatia. If this were true, Morris was confident "we shall make a fine hand of it." Apparently stimulated by his spectacular success with Ord and Bingham, Morris entered a privateering adventure with two business acquaintances, Oliver Pollock and Captain Le Maire. He also sent one Captain Bell to France for the express purpose of cruising, and it is possible that he participated in other privateering engagements.[50]

All these business engagements were capped by a variety of miscellaneous affairs—purchasing provisions for the army with Jonathan Hudson of Baltimore, buying tobacco with Carter Braxton of Virginia, transporting goods from South Carolina to Virginia and Pennsylvania for sale in conjunction with both men, speculating in currency and clothing with David Stewart, carrying on a tobacco purchase and currency discount business with Benjamin Harrison, and purchasing indigo with Alexander Gillon in South Carolina.[51]

The demands of lucidity call for a topical treatment of Morris' multiple activities, but for proper perspective it should be emphasized that all of them were being carried on at one and the same time. He was, on occasions, figuratively swamped with work. When Morris functioned as Congress' representative in Philadelphia, for example, he was also conducting much of the work of the Committee of Secret Correspondence, the Secret Committee of Commerce, and the Marine Committee, not to mention devoting energy and time to transacting a plethora of private business. And in almost every case the persons employed in public purchasing were also engaged by Morris privately in some adventure or another. Combine this coincidence and the manifold activities of Morris with some unusual accounting procedures, and you find letters such as that of Morris to the Secret Committee of Congress:[52]

I am corresponding with every part of the Continent to promote your exports and expedite remittances and you could only do this was [*sic*] I with you and then not with equal facility . . . Jenifer and Hoe at Alexandria are buying a cargo of tobacco for a ship I ordered to them. Mr. J. H. Norton of Wmsbourgh [Williamsburg] has bought 1000 hhds [hogsheads] or thereabouts and only one ship ordered to him. Mr. Benjamin Harrison Jr. has made the largest purchases but I don't exactly know the quantity. A ship or two is ordered to him. One he has loaded and dispatched and is loading others [.] I expect he will make up his purchase about 3000 hhds. Mr. Braxton is also buying some tobacco part of which is only for the publick. Messers Hewes and Smith in North Carolina expect to make their purchase amount to 2000 hhds, upwards of 1000 they had sometime ago and are chartering vessels there to carry it. They write me pressingly for more money and there is at Baltimore a Mr. Mushraw [?] that came express from them. I request you will send by him eight or ten thousand dollars which may be charged to me in the Committee books and I will charge them [—] for so our accts run. Mr.

Hewes did not think it quite prudent to trust too large a sum by this man or else I would wish 20,000 dollars to be sent to them and the same sum to Benjamin Harrison junr. And if you do this, send some other person that you can depend upon along with this Mushraw for if it is not done now, it soon must, and I think you had best do it at once and write Mr. Harrison to credit me for the money on account of the tobacco purchase. Smith and Hewes at Edenton in N. Carolina must do the same and I shall credit the Committee for the sums sent and charge them for the tobacco bought.

Obviously, the combination of interlocking activities, of difficulties involved in shifting to a war economy, and of intricate, numerous, and unusual financial transactions was pregnant with possibilities for confusion and error. That it eventually produced serious criticism about the manner in which Morris conducted the government's affairs is scarcely unexpected.

The dispute which implicated Robert Morris in 1778 and early 1779 was only one in a contentious season where an historian of the American Revolution can garner a harvest of charges and counter-charges. Tempers flared over the personalities involved in the Dr. Benjamin Rush-Dr. Shippen affair in the Medical Department, over the whisperings of Washington's incompetence, and over the accusation against Silas Deane, who was charged with mismanagement and even fraudulent transactions. Complaints against Morris had been simmering in the Congressional caldron for several months, but it was the heat generated by the last of these disputes which brought the brew to a boil.[53]

In January of 1779, a specific complaint was leveled against Morris: that he had been dishonest in discharging his public duties as a member of the Secret Committee of Commerce because he had received compensation from the public treasury for a loss, by capture, of private goods and shipping. The story behind this indictment ran as follows: Henry Laurens, South Carolina's able delegate to the Continental Congress, charged that a ship called *Farmer*, under the command of Captain Dashiel, had been loaded in Baltimore in January 1777 by the firm of Willing and Morris on their private account. When the ship was captured by the British, the accusation continued, Morris had claimed that the vessels had been loaded on public account by Willing and Morris except for fifty hogsheads of tobacco which constituted the firm's private share of the cargo. Willing and Morris, in pressing their claim, requested and obtained compensation for their purchases from Congress' Secret Committee of Commerce, of which Morris was an important member. Thus Morris had used his government position to such an advantage that Willing and Morris had received Continental funds for personal losses. The fact that Laurens' informant was one Francis Lewis, also a member of the Secret Committee, lent important weight to the charges.

A committee of Congress was appointed immediately to determine the validity of the charges, and the actual story, as it emerged from the records, was much different from that related in the complaint. The Secret Committee of Commerce, which was sending goods to France as remittances for war matériel shipped to the United States, had authorized Willing and Morris, as one of their many purchasing agents, to outfit the vessel *Farmer* and to buy a cargo of tobacco. Although it appeared on the surface as if the firm were preparing the ship for sailing on private account, Willing and Morris were, in reality, implementing the order of the Secret Committee and thus fulfilling an agreement with the government. In order to complete the transaction it was necessary for the Secret Committee to repay Willing and Morris for the money which the firm had expended in assembling the cargo and in outfitting the *Farmer*. The firm, to receive payment, was required to submit vouchers and receipts of their expenditures to authenticate their claims. In this case, the evidence indicates that all of these conditions had been met. Certainly the specific indictment proved false, and Henry Laurens himself produced proof supporting Morris. In summary, the firm of Willing and Morris had not received public funds as compensation for private losses; Morris' version that the vessel *Farmer* was loaded on public account with the exception of the fifty hogsheads of tobacco which had been purchased for and listed in the firm's private account was accurate.[54]

Although never fully expressed at the time, a second allegation much more sweeping and destructive lay in the shadows behind the specific indictment. Stated simply, it was strongly intimated that Morris, as an important member of the Secret Committee of Commerce and later its chairman, applied public funds to his private use. In fact, in later years, when the issue became a political football, it was sometimes asserted that the basis of Morris' wealth lay in the public money that he had used to line his own pockets. Morris, it was maintained, had been corrupt.[55]

To settle this question definitely, five groups of evidence would be indispensable—the books and papers of the Secret Committee of Congress, the Willing and Morris correspondence, the Thomas Morris letters, the complete Bingham letters, and the Deane papers. Of these, the first group was unfortunately burned, and the fourth, although useful, is incomplete. The Willing and Morris correspondence for these years remains highly fragmentary, and the Thomas Morris papers, an indispensable link, cannot be found, which presumes at this writing that they are lost. These papers—Willing and Morris and Thomas Morris—were still intact, however, at the time of Morris' death—over a quarter of a century after the transactions occurred; if Morris wished to destroy them as incriminating, he certainly neglected an ample opportunity. The Deane correspondence is comparatively full, though still incomplete. In view of the relatively fragmentary data it is impossible to settle the issue once and for all.[56]

This fact, however, does not invalidate a few pertinent observations both for and against the well-known Philadelphian. Morris, though

the most important member of the Secret Committee of Congress, did
not execute the business of that group singlehandedly. The contracts
that were made and the actions taken required a quorum of the Committee. When Morris was delegated to act for the Secret Committee—
such as the time he stayed in Philadelphia—he seems to have described
fully what decisions he had made and what actions had been taken.
Indeed, the letter quoted in this volume with relation to the profusion
and confusion of Morris' tasks—section III—supports this conclusion.
By welcoming the appointment of William Lee, brother of Arthur Lee
who later became Morris' most persistent critic, as co-purchaser of
continental supplies abroad with Thomas Morris, the Philadelphia
merchant certainly placed himself in a compromising position if he
was surreptitiously draining off public money for his private use. And
his constant invitation to investigate, when the first flurry of criticism appeared, scarcely sounds like a man shielding a fraud.[57]

The manner in which the criticism against Morris originated is also
noteworthy. With the exception of Francis Lewis' early misinformation and, as it turned out, his forgetfulness about the ship *Farmer*—
for he had been told of the entire transaction at one time—the members of the Secret Committee who worked with Morris did not initiate
the complaints. This is particularly important with respect to Richard
Henry Lee, later a vigorous critic of Morris. All during 1776-77
Richard Henry Lee and Morris were members of the Secret Committee, but there is no hint that Lee was dissatisfied with his colleague's
conduct; much less was he concerned with any charges of fraud.
Richard Henry Lee began to attack Morris only when his brother
Arthur Lee, one of the American commissioners in France, became involved in mutually acrimonious charges against Silas Deane in France
and in bitter denunciations of his colleague Benjamin Franklin. In
short, the drift of complaint was from France to America, with Arthur
Lee largely if not entirely responsible for the first whispers. And yet,
the persons at home were infinitely better informed as to the procedures of Congress and its Committees, and they were familiar with
what actions had been authorized and required. Here is something of
a key, for it was Arthur Lee who appointed himself a committee of
one to investigate the actions of the Secret Committee when he returned from France, and it is the allegations of Arthur Lee, for the
most part, which have been handed down through the years.[58]

What prompted Arthur Lee's actions? Though he nowhere declared
it in so many words, Lee was following pretty closely the advice which
Francis Lightfoot Lee had sent him, "to provide yourself with all the
means necessary, both for attack and defense." To Arthur Lee such
counsel meant to gather evidence on Deane and, of course, on Deane's
friends, Franklin and Morris. Though all of the Continental accounts
were shot through with confusion—as anyone who has examined the
existing Journals and Ledgers can testify—Arthur Lee was content to
direct his attention to the work of those he conceived to be his
enemies.[59]

Arthur Lee's temperament ill suited him for this self-appointed task. Even his fondest admirers found him intemperate in writings and speech, and by nature jealous and hot-headed. Lee was quick to accuse but slow to prove. "You know too," he addressed Sam Adams, "that a person may be well satisfied of the truth of a thing without being able to produce legal proofs necessary to conviction." But accusations directed toward Lee quickly drew his retort: "Where was it you learnt that accusations and proof were the same?" The acrid comments which he inscribed on some of the extracts of material of the Secret Committee of Congress, now lodged in his personal papers, reveal that he was not genuinely interested in understanding what happened or in fulfilling the demands of justice, but rather in an almost pathological desire to vindicate his personal judgment and actions on all things at home and abroad. He was somehow impelled to twist any fact until it came out to his own advantage.[60]

Part of the explanation of Arthur Lee's actions probably lies in the fact that many of the transactions of the Secret Committee which took place in secrecy—a secrecy called for by Congress—appeared sinister in his eyes. He had been in England and France during the period, and he was not familiar with the circumstances surrounding those first months or with the early procedures of Congress. And yet, after almost a decade of investigation upon his return to America, first as a member of Congress and after 1784 as a member of the Board of Treasury, Lee could only allege rather than specify. The books of the Secret Committee apparently balanced. But in the case of Willing and Morris and some others there existed a "defect in the necessary documents to support many credits as well as a difference in opinion betwixt him [an accountant of the treasury] and Mr. Morris' agent. . . ." In other words, vouchers had been submitted on claims, but some of them were thought inadequate by Lee and Samuel Osgood, a comparatively severe critic of Morris. It is wholly conceivable that vouchers submitted immediately after a transaction while it was still fresh in everyone's mind would appear adequate, whereas ten years later, when examined by unfamiliar and unfriendly investigators, these same vouchers might seem unsatisfactory—especially in light of the accounting system.[61]

However, it should be emphasized that the preceding observations, regardless of their validity, do not offer any specific proof of Morris' innocence; certainly the facts do not all add up on the Morris side of the balance sheet. The mercantile correspondents used by the Philadelphia merchant in his role with the Secret Committee were also those used by him in his business capacity with the firm of Willing and Morris. One can find some plausible explanations for the overlap. In any war, a country appeals to established firms in submitting its contracts and carrying on its war business. Usually they receive this business because they are equipped to handle it; the pressure of events seldom permits a calm, judicious distribution. In the perspective of historical development, therefore, the connection between government contracts and a business firm where the latter continued to act in its private capacity while fulfilling its engagements as a public agent—a combination assumed by Morris—does not, during periods of war, stand in isolation. However, this explanation does not eliminate the possibility of corruption. In fact, such a close relationship between government and business would tend to breed many evils.

Morris in his private capacity often used the Secret Committee as a quasi-bank, a practice that was certainly highly exceptional. For example, Carter Braxton, a Virginia merchant, was purchasing tobacco for the Secret Committee and also for Willing and Morris. Morris, as chairman of the Secret Committee, requested the other members of the Committee, who were residing in Maryland at the time, to send Braxton the sum of $40,000 which was to be used to purchase tobacco for the government. (The tobacco was to be sent to Europe as a remittance for supplies being purchased in Europe.) This transaction eventually became involved with Morris as a private person. Some six months later, when the Secret Committee was preparing to report to the Continental Congress, Morris instructed Braxton as follows:[62]

The Secret Committee are preparing their accts and papers to lay before Congress and make a report. In order to do this properly, they must write to all the Agents employed to furnish their accts and as it is probable these must also be laid before Congress, I desire you will open an account with me as Chairman of the Secret Committee and credit thereon the 40,000 sent you from Mr. Hillegas in March last by Mr. David Stewart. This being the only public money I did ever send you credit it on the very day you received it and charge against it the ship Virginia and her outfitts as that ship is to be on public account. Charge the tobacco you have bought on public account, specifying the dates when you made the purchases and as I expect the ship *Virginia* and her cargo and the Brig *Braxton* will exceed the amount of 40,000 dollars you will ballance the public acct by charging that balance to me and I will charge it to the secret committee.

The quasi-bank relationship involved in this letter was not only dangerous, but the very best accounting habits were also indispensable to insure accurate, comprehensible accounts. This prerequisite was seldom present, what with the Secret Committee separated and the committee books temporarily stored out of the reach of any member. There is no graft or corruption intended in the letter quoted or in the type of transaction it mentions, but these practices widened the possibilities for graft. In the case of Braxton, the vouchers submitted for the tobacco and ship purchases would be crucial. If they contained some "padding" or some inaccuracy, it would be impossible to detect it unless an immediate inspection were made. Whether Braxton presented adequate vouchers in this particular instance is now impossible to determine because the books and papers of the Secret Committee, as has been previously stated, were later accidentally burned.

At the time Morris was under fire from his critics, he did not always reply to all the complaints with painstaking accuracy. When Henry Laurens demanded an investigation of the *Farmer* incident, he also brought up the issue of settling the general accounts of the Secret

Committee. In the exchange which followed between Laurens and Morris, neither adhered strictly to the record. Morris asserted that he had made important progress in settling the accounts of the Secret Committee while the books of the Committee were in his possession during the first months of 1778. From all reports, he had actually straightened out little of the confusion—a fact asserted by Laurens and later confirmed by Morris. Nor did Morris ever face the important question which Laurens posed. "You plead in excuse many other avocations," wrote the South Carolina patriot, "but will this considera- tion excuse you before the Public—by no means. Why did you en- gage in so much more business than you were competent to? If private affairs would not admit of a close attention to your Public duties for due execution of which in the particular case before us Congress had altogether depended upon you, you should have relinquished in time and delivered up the Books in good order." [63]

The preceding observations do not, in turn, prove Morris guilty of the charges against him. Indeed, it should not be assumed that Morris because of his dual role embezzled public funds, that he engaged in graft, or that he was a party to corruption. If pressed for an opinion— for an opinion it must ever remain—the present writer is inclined to believe that the charge against Morris of appropriating public funds for private adventures cannot be supported. This opinion is held in part because the present investigation has not been able to prove the charge; and allegation should not be accepted as fact, nor would it be just to condemn without convicting evidence. Indeed, where the mate- rials exist—such as in his relationship with Silas Deane in France— Morris' general assertions check with the facts. If one is to err, it is better to err on the side of innocence.

All this does not mean that Morris stands blameless, that he con- ducted public affairs with the greatest efficiency or at all times scrup- ulously in the public interest; nor does it mean that one must condone the carelessness that unquestionably crept into the accounts. Indeed, for his own reputation, if for no other reason, the future Financier should have taken pains to follow the advice he often sent his subor- dinates in private business: "Short accts are best, they keep things clear, and good Friends will then remain so." It is hardly necessary to add that he would have done well to recall the ancient wisdom embraced in the Biblical injunction on the danger of serving two masters. [64]

CHAPTER —TWO ❖❖❖❖❖❖❖❖❖❖❖❖❖❖❖❖❖❖❖

Robert Morris: Prince of Merchants

THE BEGINNING OF A NEW YEAR, 1778, MARKS SOMETHING OF A BREAK in the career of Robert Morris. This is true not only of his private business but also of his public position.

Morris had been unusually active in the Continental Congress from the fall of 1775 until January of 1778 as a delegate from Pennsylvania, but late in 1777 he requested and received a temporary leave of absence from Congress. From that time forward Morris rarely participated in the work of that body, although he did resume his seat formally in July 1778; after fulfilling certain commonplace tasks, Morris left Congress permanently in November 1778.[1]

The break in the business career of Morris occurred when the successful firm of Willing and Morris expired with the final days of 1777, although the decision was not announced publicly until July 28, 1778. According to Morris it was prompted by a combination of Thomas Morris' misconduct abroad, which had injured the reputation of the firm, and Willing's decision to remain in Philadelphia during the British occupation. Willing, at this time, was rather gentle with young Tom. "He has ruined himself, and I dare say he has hurt us, both in our pockets and reputation in some degree." But Morris, whose patience was apparently exhausted, regarded his brother's downfall with less charity. "He has now sacrificed his own credit and character and disgraced his connections, so that I . . . renounce him forever[.] You will therefore not have anything to say to him on my account."[2]

Willing's residence in Philadelphia during the British occupation, however, did provide a convenient channel for the settlement of old British accounts, and the firm apparently took advantage of it. Rumors that eventually proved false reached Willing of vast claims against their firm, and for a time he was greatly distressed. "You may be assured the report has been spread far and near and with design to stab Us to the Vitals in the Mercantile World. Curse on the Malice of those who have invented it, or those who with bad designs have spread it." Much later he added, "I believe they tho't we were going to the Devil headlong." Willing looked forward to "winding up our English affairs" when Morris could lodge his funds "in Safe hands in some part of Europe, but not in France, I never did like those people."[3]

Following the termination of the old firm, there was a most important development in the individual mercantile affairs of Robert Morris during the period 1778-81; his interests became so extensive that he was elevated to a position where he was acknowledged as the most prominent merchant in America. With Morris' attention devoted almost exclusively to his private business for the first time since the beginning of the Revolution, his interests reached out to envelope nine major business partnerships and a great number of lesser concerns, that is, ventures in which Morris was engaged but where the business organization was less formal than a partnership. Indeed, at this time, the Philadelphia merchant might well have conceived the design of a network of mercantile connections which was completed, as he later remarked, in 1784. The following pages attempt to show the extent of these connections, to indicate the expansion of Morris' business operations and the types of enterprises where he invested money and time, and to provide a background that will be valuable in understanding Morris' use of this experience and these associations when he entered the Office of Superintendent of Finance.[4]

When Morris determined to carry on his business, as he stated it, "in my own name and in my own acct," everything indicates that his strong financial situation warranted such a decision. "[I] still thank God," he declared in January 1778, that "I am as well provided with funds to carry on business as any [every?] occasion I can have will require." Morris underscored this assertion by purchasing 12,000 pounds sterling or upwards in bills of exchange before withdrawing from Philadelphia. He punctuated it by declaring that he found it unnecessary to draw on the money in the hands of Jenifer and Hoe of Virginia and John Dorsius of Charleston—the terminal points of the lucrative short run between Charleston and the West Indies where a handsome sum must have accumulated—because he had no "occasion for the money."[5]

Among the former connections continued by Morris in his new capacity was that with William Bingham at Martinique, whose interests blended a little of the old and new. The privateering ventures in the West Indies in which they were engaged tapered off, and Captain Ord, their chief privateering captain, turned to normal shipping. Ord continued to justify their faith in his ability by making profitable trips to "Hispaniola" and L'Orient, each venturer holding his accustomed share—Morris, one half; Bingham, one third; and Ord, one sixth. A little of the new was included in Bingham's request to purchase $40,000 worth of loan office certificates. In trying to fulfill the request, Morris discovered that in the Philadelphia area, "people will not part with them." Indeed, the demand for certificates was so widespread that his best efforts only yielded a value of $8,000.[6]

Meanwhile, Morris tried to impress Bingham with the necessity of speeding along the goods that were now flowing into Martinique from France in quantity; Bingham, on the other hand, urged Morris to push remittances. This led to a series of exchanges which endangered the whole connection, but Morris smoothed the troubled waters by assuring the young man at Martinique "that my regard and Friendship for you never altered nor abated . . . perhaps we have both said rather too much. Therefore let us stop." [7]

Morris, in these years (1778-81), always intended to do "something worthwhile" in the West Indies, but in reality such ventures never measured up to the old Willing and Morris business. One need not seek far for the reason. With the consummation of the French Alliance in 1778, much of the urgency for a place like Martinique as an entrepôt vanished. The protection such a "neutral" spot provided, of course, ceased with France's active participation in the war; and trade and shipping, previously carried on in quasi-secrecy via the French island, could now take a direct route. It should also be emphasized that the market for West India goods was less favorable, in relative terms, after 1778. When Bingham left Martinique in 1780 and returned to Philadelphia, his move merely accented the fact that his tasks had been completed, in his public as well as his private capacity. [8]

Another connection which continued from the days of Willing and Morris was that with Jonathan Hudson. In contrast to the retrenchment in the Morris-Bingham affairs stood the enlarged operations of Morris-Hudson under a totally new concern named Jonathan Hudson and Company. Initiated with a capital of 20,000 pounds—each man supplying one-half—the partnership was launched into the mercantile waters under full sail. Hudson set the course with occasional advice from Morris, although the "occasional" tended to become constant. [9]

A gap of four months in the correspondence leaves the firm's early course uncharted. By late October, however, Hudson was speculating in salt, an operation disapproved by Morris; by November, Hudson was purchasing large quantities of tobacco, but the execution of the operation did not satisfy the Philadelphian. Skeptical of "such wild expectations about the price of tobacco," Morris warned that such an event was "to be dreaded and not wished for." He also cautioned Hudson against West India goods which he thought "too high to be meddled with." [10]

However, the firm did decide to make additional large-scale purchases, although at times it jeopardized the entire connection. Extensive acquisitions of tobacco, rum in quantity, plantations, and lands fell within the scope of this far-reaching business; but they were not acquired without misgivings. Although general economic conditions were partly responsible, the main difficulty lay in the decisions of Hudson, whose enthusiasm to overextend the interests of the firm threatened to founder the entire enterprise. ". . . By eternally pushing beyond your strength you harrass and distress all your Friends and Connections," lamented Morris. "It is absolutely necessary that you shou'd curb that very keen eager desire of missing nothing." But Hudson was not easily restrained, and when the difficulty recurred, Morris' patience gave way. "In short you reduce me to an absolute necessity of distressing myself to help you at times when I have not a leisure moment to cast about for resources." Moreover, Hudson's job was to run the business and relieve Morris of such worries, "and yet there is not a week passes that you do not press some difficulty or other upon me[.] This ought not to be and no gains you can make is a compensation to me." Morris even threatened to end the concern. Any shock provoked by such exclamations was measurably softened when Morris agreed to advance another 10,000 pounds—a language embodying its own eloquence.[11]

Some of the purchases, particularly tobacco, were being made on "triple account"—the third member of the triumvirate being Peter Whitesides and Company. Morris had entered into this firm with Peter Whitesides in July of 1778 because he wanted someone to take care of his private affairs in the Philadelphia area while he completed his public business. Morris suggested that the two firms could nicely complement each other, advice that was apparently followed. Indeed, their tobacco purchases reached such a volume that Morris warned Hudson: "You must stretch yourself tightly to pay for it. don't depend on me for I am exhausted."[12]

This entire buying program reached its peak in May 1779, when Morris instructed Hudson "to sell off the goods, settle all accounts, pay off all debts, and get ready for such new matters as may occur." At the time, Hudson was in advance to Morris some 60,000 pounds—presumably Pennsylvania currency—but Hudson, in turn, had goods in Whitesides' hands whose sale was to cover part of this advance.[13]

The holdings of Jonathan Hudson and Company were not completely liquidated, and, spurred on by attractive prices in the fall, the firm plunged vigorously into another tobacco-buying scheme. Hudson's eagerness to "miss nothing" seized him once again, and soon his substantial purchases—at least 2,000 hogsheads—had swallowed up Morris' available funds. Indeed, the letters between the principals after 1779 revolve around a theme, Hudson's request for funds and Morris' inability or unwillingness to supply them. In the spring of 1780, Morris complained that "altho I have plenty of effects yet I can't find that anything will command money." Some months later Morris disclosed to Hudson that he would be unable to purchase a new vessel "as it is impossible even with my stores full of goods to keep way with the heavy demand for money occasioned by concerns in shipping. . . . Being pinched myself I must cut close until better times. . . ." Attributing his lack of specie to his advances to the French forces, Morris, to judge from his actions, was not overly pessimistic. Despite signs of austerity, the purchase of an occasional plantation and "another mill" found its way into the correspondence of Hudson and Morris.[14]

The business relationship of Morris and Hudson was subjected to additional storms. Morris criticized Hudson's bookkeeping and his lack of promptness, reminding his partner that punctuality was "the best part of a man's trading capital." When Hudson proposed schemes that apparently would evade certain state restrictions in trade, Morris explained that "even the most Lucrative of Trade" could not balance a "sullied reputation and a Reproaching Mind." Apparently such friction was only momentary, for Jonathan Hudson and Company extended into the later period when Morris became Superintendent of Finance.[15]

Towering above all his other concerns, however, were Morris' dealings with John Holker, a celebrated French enterpriser. The picture of the Morris-Holker relationship, as it appears in the record, is slightly out of focus, for the materials which make up the design and shadings were brought together to substantiate Holker's claim in court. Yet the central pattern can be discerned although the edges are decidedly blurred.[16]

In the fall of 1777, John Holker together with some French friends —among whom were Bustault and St. Seine, Chaumont, and later Grand—concocted a scheme of speculation in American funds; Holker left France shortly thereafter in order to implement the plan. After he arrived in the United States, Holker was awarded the post of Purchasing Agent for the Royal Marine, a position which clothed him with additional prestige and promised him considerable financial return. Morris became involved when Holker, acting in his official capacity with the Royal Marine, approached the Philadelphia merchant and urged him "to undertake the transaction" of his affairs. The Frenchman offered the promise of commissions—to be divided between them —and "great sums of money," which coming to hand "might be occasionally employed in usefull speculations on our joint account. . . ." But Morris was not favorably disposed to the proposition, "tho urged . . . for several days." He pleaded that settlement of his private affairs had long been postponed because of public occupation, and to enter new pursuits before these affairs were completed might incur injury to himself and others. Holker persisted and finally, according to Morris, "drew from me my reluctant consent." From that time (July 1778) until the "spring of 1780" (probably February 17) the Philadelphia merchant acted as Holker's purchasing agent in Pennsylvania and apparently in Maryland and Virginia as well.[17]

Despite some encouragement, Morris did not develop any deep interest in this type of business. The arrival of D'Estaings' fleet in Boston in the fall of 1778 touched off a considerable expenditure in the Royal Marine that eventually amounted to more than 235,000 pounds, presumably Pennsylvania currency, with resulting commissions to Morris of some 7,500 pounds. But he apparently found the problem and worries of procurement burdensome, for he informed Holker the following year: ". . . I will do everything in my power to secure them [supplies] . . . however I wish to decline the moment you can find proper persons to employ in it." To attribute Morris' dissatisfaction solely to the difficulties involved in the position, however, does not seem warranted. Although Morris made no issue of it, he must have realized that his time was ill spent. One successful voyage in shipping to the West Indies—taking three months—would net him almost as much profit as a year and a half of commission business. It was in line with the wishes of Morris, therefore, that in the spring of 1780 new arrangements were made. Under the name of William Turnbull and Company, Holker, Turnbull and Morris became partners, with the intention of carrying forward the official purchasing program. Morris supplied $200,000—amounting to $5,000 in specie—of the firm's capital, and he agreed "to throw in a large share of his business and concerns." How well this new relationship functioned is difficult to determine, but it continued, part of the time under the name of Turnbull, Marmie, and Company, until 1784 when a dispute between Holker and Morris interrupted its affairs.[18]

Holker, acting in his private capacity, also consulted Morris. The French entrepreneur was particularly anxious to enlist the Philadelphia merchant's counsel on speculating in American funds, but Morris apparently misled him. Morris believed, early in 1778, that paper currency was going to appreciate and advised Holker accordingly; Holker's object, then, was to purchase currency at once and to invest in loan office certificates at leisure. Although Morris attempted to assist Holker in this project, he encountered the same difficulties that he had found when he tried to fulfill Bingham's request to purchase loan office certificates. Holders simply were not anxious to sell. In following Morris' advice, Holker evidently suffered losses, because this complaint combined with conflicting theories on depreciation and forms of accounting called for a most prolonged dissertation in his "Observations" on the Holker-Morris dispute.[19]

These connections with Holker were important to the experience of Morris. He gained some valuable business advantages by freely utilizing considerable amounts of money which came under Holker's care—one of the inducements the Frenchman had originally offered him. Morris later testified that "all the monies I received I put into one common chest and as my occasions required it, I took from thence without knowing whose particular money it was." Although he hastened to add, "If at any time this money was used I was always ready and able to replace it," the fund unquestionably served as an important source of credit, and in consequence a stimulus to Morris' personal business expansion. This relationship was also important because it formed a close tie between Morris and French representatives in America; it expanded the boundaries of Morris' business experience; it taught him more thoroughly than ever before how paper currency was subjected to a partly illegitimate function; and it formed a basis for business concerns which were in force at the time Morris entered the Office of Finance.[20]

In addition to William Turnbull and Company, Morris participated in two other concerns with Holker: Benjamin Harrison Jr. and Company, and Stacey Hepburn and Company. Information is scanty on the Harrison connection aside from the firm's general concern in tobacco shipments and in purchasing supplies for the French. Material on the interesting activities of Stacey Hepburn and Company is more complete.[21]

Morris and Holker "concerted together," in the spring of 1779, to establish this firm to buy and ship indigo from South Carolina. At Holker's insistence, Chaumont and another French firm of Sabatier, Fels, and Desprez were included—Holker apparently representing both firms. Morris issued the general instructions—characteristically they were complete down to the final consignee—to Stacey Hepburn, who was designated as the acting partner. Indigo to the amount of 120,000 pounds (Pennsylvania currency) and rice to the amount of 10,000 pounds (Pennsylvania currency) were to be purchased, depending on Hepburn's ability to fulfill the order at $3 per pound (continental currency). In case prices exceeded the limit, alternate plans were outlined. Hepburn was supplied with 10,000 pounds (Pennsylvania currency) and $300,000 in bills and credits with permission to draw on Morris for an additional 20,000 pounds (Pennsylvania currency). Finally, if the indigo purchase could not be executed, Hepburn was given wide discretion to buy goods, hard money, or landed property "most likely to turn out advantageous to this concern."[22]

The plan enjoyed moderate success. After purchasing at least 40,000 pounds of indigo, Hepburn sent part of it to the St. Eustatia market. He also engaged in shipping ventures and land purchases, at times for the concern and then again for Morris personally. In December, Morris proposed that all purchases be liquidated, except "well bought confiscated [?] lands"; the proceeds, he continued, should be invested in loan office certificates that would be sent to Philadelphia where they would be used to purchase bills of exchange. As an alternative Morris suggested buying hard money in Carolina, where it was cheap, and transporting it to Philadelphia, where it was dear. At that city, once again, the money could be invested in bills of exchange. But the reluctance of Congress to sell bills of exchange, the changing outlook on paper money, and the British military moves in the South prompted a radical change of plans. Instead of liquidating in Carolina, wrote Morris, "I wish the whole was invested in good lands or other Solid Secure property." There is no indication which advice Hepburn followed, nor is there sufficient evidence to estimate the amount of profit or loss, but a general account between Hepburn and Morris shows a gross business of slightly over 200,000 pounds (Pennsylvania currency). With the capture of Charleston in May 1780, the entire adventure was concluded.[23]

On another business front was Silas Deane who, in the spring of 1780, was preparing to leave for Europe to fortify his claims against Congress and to execute some private business; in his bag of enterprises Deane carried a new informal agreement with Morris. It appeared that the Morris-Deane friendship was cemented rather than destroyed by the criticism which had surrounded each man; Morris seemed to consider that Deane, Franklin, and himself had been "fellow laborers in the vineyard" whose "works will speak for themselves before that impartial Master who knows all actions and the secret springs that give rise to them." Morris thought it wisest to implement the divine judgment, however, by arming Deane with a letter to Franklin mentioning the injustices against Deane and professing his continuing veneration of Deane and Franklin. Although the plan was rather loosely knit, Deane and Morris proposed to sell "vacant lands" in America to European gentlemen who desired to increase their fortune but were "too ignorant as well as proud and indolent, to engage in commerce. . . ." When Deane arrived in France the outlook for the scheme appeared favorable, but Morris' inability to find the opportunities and time to forward the domestic end checked any immediate fulfillment. When Deane, in 1781, abruptly adopted the British side— a move which caught Morris and others, such as Franklin, unprepared —the project was halted altogether.[24]

Three more firms rounded out Morris' primary business concerns. One was a new Philadelphia house under the name of Samuel Inglis and Company. It included Samuel Inglis, a Virginia merchant who had been crippled financially by the burning of Norfolk; Willing, Morris' "late partner"; and Morris. Inglis as the managing partner conducted a variety of mercantile affairs, handling consignments, and engaging in shipping ventures. Another concern was founded with Isaac Hazlehurst in a joint partnership, based on a capital of 10,000 pounds sterling, to purchase European goods for sale in the states. This engagement was being implemented when Morris became Financier. Finally, a third concern—consisting of Morris, Samuel Beall, and John May and capitalized at 48,000 pounds—was interested in "procuring waste or unappropriated lands in the sd [said] state of Virginia. . . ."[25]

But these associations did not conclude the business affairs of Philadelphia's most important merchant, for a great number of additional ventures were intertwined among these full-fledged connections—that is, adventures in privateers, purchases, or shipping where Morris was engaged for anywhere from 1/8 of an interest upward. With Carter Braxton it consisted of tobacco purchases and shipping; with John Ross, goods shipped from Europe; with Conyngham and Nesbitt, privateers; with Matthias Slough, purchase of commissary needs; with Hewes and Smith, tobacco buying and shipping; and with Thomas Mumford, Thomas Russell and John Bradford, shipping. And this brief summary does not include Morris' numerous and widespread mercantile correspondents.[26]

During 1780, the powerful surge of expansion that had marked the business affairs of Morris tapered off, but by that time his interests had broadened out to include at least nine major partnerships and a host of less important ventures. All the principal connections remained in force in the years immediately following except those with

William Bingham, who returned from Martinique, and Stacey Hepburn, whose project had been interrupted by the British capture of Charleston. Although primarily related to trade, the activities of these concerns branched out into lands, some manufacturing, and occasionally securities.

It is important to note that the connections were concentrated from Pennsylvania southward; in fact, Morris was at a loss to recommend a reliable merchant to Holker when D'Estaing's fleet anchored in Boston harbor in 1778. In succeeding years Morris cultivated the New England community, but his knowledge of the Southern region and its mercantile, business, and political leaders remained superior to his acquaintance with Yankee-land. In turn, Morris was very well known in Pennsylvania and to the regions southward, but in traveling in the opposite direction the glitter of his name faded, particularly beyond the Connecticut Valley.[27]

Morris' experience, as has been stated, led him, for the most part, to shipping, trade, and securities; as a result, he was familiar with the problems touching these areas. He was also acquainted with the difficulties of purchasing supplies for military forces, although his experience in this field was much more limited. All of this activity, however, was important to the Philadelphia merchant when he became Superintendent of Finance.

There is some indication that Morris' prosperity was threatened a bit in the spring of 1781. "Miss Fortune is fickle and coy," he observed. "Therefore if you court her you must not only be bold, adventurous, and attentive to her humours, but persevering in your endeavours to win her. She has played the Devil with me last summer, fall, and winter, but still I hope to put her in better humour this Spring and a few of her smiles may make amends for all the frowns her ill temper cast on me. But to be serious. . . ." As long as Morris could speak of "Miss Fortune" in jest the situation was not too depressing. Indeed, he hoped to retrieve his losses soon.[28]

Despite such momentary fluctuations, the vast connections and activities of Morris reflect his unchallenged position as the leading merchant in America. One would err in assuming that Morris sought out all these connections; he was more often solicited by others. To include Morris in a plan was usually more advantageous for the other partners than for him. But Morris reaped benefits. By pooling his resources with those of others, he expanded his own credit enormously and, in consequence, his volume of business. It also enabled Morris to spread his risks. Indeed, Morris' mercantile activities were so numerous and substantial that it seemed almost inconceivable that only two decades had passed since the Willing mercantile house had entrusted a cargo, for the first time, to their apprentice "for his encouragement." And how important was this mercantile experience to Morris? It was as intimate a part of his life as his physical self, the ideas that raced through his mind, or the family he fondly embraced.[29]

When one witnesses the swift rise of Morris to prominence there is some danger in overlooking the force of his personality and the nature of his ideas. Traits of character and personality are so subjective that there is great danger of claiming too much or too little, but several characteristics stand out clearly. The personality of Morris was warm and cordial rather than cold and austere; he was self-assured rather than timid; temperate rather than intemperate; generous rather than vindictive. Those who read an avenging spirit into Morris' personality are misjudging their man.[30]

Perhaps the princely life, although an arduous one as well, of which Morris was so fond fostered such a temperament. Good company, claret "of a quality rarely to be met with in America," gay parties, and enjoyable conversation was as much a part of the household as Morris' affection for his young family or his concern with everyday business affairs. He described it well when he wrote Benjamin Harrison in the crucial winter of 1776 that he had dined at "The Hills" on Sunday in spite of the recurring crises. "You see I continue my old practice of mixing business and pleasure, and ever found them useful to each other." [31]

When Morris married Mary White in 1769, he was already a successful merchant in his middle thirties, and the Morris home quickly blossomed into one of Philadelphia's social centers. In addition to the town house, they enjoyed the Hills, their luxurious country seat which Jay so happily described as "the little temple you erected to hospitality." There nature's majestic landscape was interrupted by some of man's newly fashioned contributions to a luxurious life—ice houses, hot houses, imported fruit trees, and, of course, the handsome residence itself.[32]

When the British threatened Philadelphia for the second time, Morris purchased a house in Manheim, Pennsylvania, that had been built by Baron Henry Stiegel, whose attempt at large-scale operations in iron and glass work had ended so disastrously. Although the house enjoyed a reputation for magnificence, it could not lure the Morrises from their beloved Hills until imminent danger from the British threat to Philadelphia required it. Mary Morris hoped to continue at the Hills and enjoy "all that's beautiful to the eye and grateful to the taste; for, as if to add to our mortification, are we obliged to leave it; nature never appeared there so lovely, nor promised such a profusion of her gifts." [33]

Wherever the Morris family made its home the social whirl began anew. Sometimes it was a large body of friends who were attracted by a gay ball; sometimes the children played host to their friends, and their admiring mother could bask in the afterglow of her children's accomplishments. At other times Morris sought the quiet companionship of close friends such as Richard Peters, whose wit and humor he found so refreshing that even in recollection it helped "to revive drooping spirits." Or there was Kitty Livingston, who lived up to the approving appraisal of her brother-in-law, John Jay, as "a charming correspondent as well as a charming everything else" when she captivated Philadelphia society during her stay with the Morris family.[34]

In his business and in his personal and social life, Morris distinctly revealed that he was primarily a man of action rather than one of reflection. So it hardly comes as a surprise to discover that he offered no carefully defined scheme of thought. However, on certain questions such as the nature of commerce, the function of money, and the relation of government to private enterprise—questions he had wrestled with in his everyday life—Morris had formed rather definite opinions.[35]

Nowhere did Morris comment more freely on commerce and the role of government in economic affairs than in his forthright letter to William Hooper, dated January 1777, where he discussed a proposal before Congress to form a Chamber of Commerce. In considering what the attitude of Congress should be on certain questions, Morris declared that commerce should not be tortured by restrictions and restraints, but be "free as air to place it in the most advantageous state to mankind." Here lies the ideological root of Morris' protests against embargoes and other regulations of trade during the Revolution. Hinged to this idea was his concept of the function of government in relation to private enterprise. The projected Chamber of Commerce, which in actuality would represent the government in this instance, should certainly not try to foist any commercial system on the traders or promote measures that would favor monopoly. But such an attitude was merely negative; there were positive steps that such a committee should take. "To do any good," wrote Morris, "they must infuse into traders of Am [America] a spirit of enterprise and direct their attention to such objects as will most benefit the publick." In the new Republic, thought Morris, such actions seemed, at the moment, unnecessary; "our traders are remarkable for their spirit in trade and are dayly forming those enterprizes you wish for." Why had such a happy concurrence taken place? "Their own interest and the publick good goes hand in hand and they need no other prompter or tutor." This explained, in the mind of a man like Morris, the compatibility of private and public affairs; actions that would benefit you in turn enhanced the public welfare.[36]

How did Morris translate such ideas into actuality? He wrote to Deane at one time that some people might infer that they were more interested in private gain than public good. But this was not true, Morris asserted, speaking unmistakably by his own guide to conduct: "I shall continue to discharge my duty faithfully to the Public, and pursue my Private Fortune by all such honorable and fair means as the times will admit of." Two presumptions were evident in this credo. First, the aims of the two duties were not considered at cross purposes; second, the definitions of "honorable" and "fair" were assumed. More than that, these definitions, to be made, so it seemed, by the individual involved, would be limited only by the standards and considerations in the mind of the person concerned. Morris, for example, instructed Stacey Hepburn to refrain from any type of operation "that has the least tendency to obstruct the operations of our army or that can be detrimental to the cause of America," a personally imposed restraint to otherwise limitless action. By designating Bingham's duties with the public "more important concerns" than those undertaken for private persons, Morris again made some individual choice by a priority in time and effort; at the same time, he did not find the dual duties of Bingham—as a representative of Congress and of private business concerns—antagonistic to each other.[37]

Although less distinct and forceful than his views on commerce or the relationship of government to the economy, Morris' ideas with regard to the role of money warrant consideration. Most important, he thought, there should be a sufficient quantity of money to supply the needs of commerce—with a very general meaning given to the word "commerce." No unalterable concept on "hard" or "soft" money—that is, for or against paper money *per se*—was revealed by Morris in his correspondence. He considered the bills of credit issued by the colonies as wholly satisfactory, and apparently approved those issued at the outset of the Revolution. In brief, he did not quarrel with the use of paper money; he was concerned only with its careful supervision.[38]

The social concepts of Morris, his ideas on man, the relationship between man and the universe, classes in the social structure, the meaning of liberty and revolution, and the role of property were blurred for the most part. Scarcely any of the standard nomenclature of the Enlightenment—man's state in nature, the laws of nature, nature's God, and social compact—is found in the writings of Morris. He did believe in a God, though the nature or the importance of that God is not distinct. There is no indication that he believed in deism; nor, on the other hand, did he speak of a powerful Calvinistic God of righteous indignation, but rather a God whom one could mention with a certain casualness without fear of eternal damnation. Some scattered material of Morris indicates, though not too clearly, that he conceived of man as a rational creature and one who is primarily virtuous rather than evil. When Morris' actions rather than his thoughts are examined, however, there is usually a presumption of progress, an important eighteenth-century concept, and to a lesser degree, of man's perfectability. What seems strange is that Morris did not comment specifically on classes in society; and practically no mention is ever made of the "meaner sort" in his writings of this time. There was no tirade by Morris against the excesses of the Revolution, although many so-called eighteenth-century radicals like William Livingston felt compelled to deliver them. Indeed, Morris wrote that "Revolutions such as ours cannot be effected without violences," although he hoped that improved measures in carrying forward the war would mean that the people "will grow less turbulent." When he used the term "liberty," his meaning was not clearly defined; it was vaguely related to property, but it transcended such specialized meaning. On property itself, the

Philadelphian was more explicit. "This you may depend [on]," he assured Deane upon becoming Financier, "that I will never give countenance to any measures that tend to deceive and mislead individuals in matters of property, for I hold it as essentially necessary for governments to practice moral honesty, if they wish for success or support, as it is for an individual that wishes to maintain a fair character."[39]

It is not strange that Morris' social thinking should be, at best, fuzzy and amorphous in contrast to his crystal-clear concepts on certain economic matters, for he never seriously addressed himself to such questions. When a specific issue arose, his opinion about it focused on the immediate problems and not on principle. Morris' mental qualms on involving Europe in the British-American dispute furnish a choice example.[40]

It appears clear to me [he wrote] that we may very soon involve all Europe in a War by managing properly the apparent forwardness of the Court of France; its a horrid consideration that our own Safety should call on us to involve other nations in the Calamities of War. Can this be morally right or have Morality and Policy nothing to do with each other? Perhaps it may not be good Policy to investigate the Question at this time.

Perhaps the closest that Morris ever came to stating a personal credo was included in his candid letter to William Hooper. "Happy is that man who has judgment and fortitude to preserve a proper medium of conduct throughout the eternal conflict between passion, prejudice, and principle."[41] Much wisdom was condensed into this short passage —wisdom which emanated from a man endowed with a certain sensitive quality despite the rigors and materialism of the counting house.

★ ★ ★

The picture of Robert Morris in the first months of 1781 does not require any artificial retouching in order to produce a powerful impact. Here was a man with a warm, outgoing personality whose considerable talents were exercised with tremendous energy and perseverance. His mind was practical rather than philosophical, with the result that his ideas on those matters touching his everyday life, such as trade, were much more fixed than, for example, his speculations on man's place in society. In his significant role as a member of the Continental Congress, Morris' actions well illustrate the point because he performed as a "doer" rather than as a "thinker"—with the important exception of ideas respecting politico-economic affairs.

Although Morris had resigned his seat in the Continental Congress in 1778, his experiences in that body did not melt away. How could Morris forget those exciting days in the winter of 1776 when he had acted as Congress' representative in Philadelphia? The nature of the decisions made and the broad sweep of his authority had stimulated Morris' natural inclinations toward executive work and, as an added measure, had set him apart as one of the leading figures in the Continental Congress. His other duties had given him an education in all the problems that arose in supporting the War for Independence.

Moreover, the vigorous part that Morris had played in such key committees as the Secret Committee of Commerce had brought him into the center of a governmental purchasing program so extensive in scope that it shattered any precedents in American experience. In fulfilling these duties as a public figure, Morris the private merchant had become involved, with the almost inevitable result of charges against his integrity. Although the bitterness aroused by the dispute had been diluted by the passing years, the effects still lingered. In 1781, however, these effects were definitely subordinate to the more endurable features of Morris' career as a member of Congress and as an executive and administrator in political affairs. If Congress had held any deep-seated suspicions respecting the honesty and integrity of Robert Morris in 1781, they certainly would not have requested him to take over the finances of the government as Superintendent of Finance.

But the feature of this man, Robert Morris, which stood out most prominently in 1781 was that of the Philadelphia merchant deeply rooted in the counting house and ambitious for material advancement and position. His business genius had been amply documented by substantial achievement. In his early years as a partner of Thomas Willing, Morris had shared in the ownership of no more than three vessels; by the time of the Revolution, he had shared in the ownership of seven to ten vessels; during the Revolution, he actually lost as many as three vessels in a single year without seriously restricting his operations. At first Willing and Morris had been engaged almost exclusively in trade by means of a limited number of correspondents; by 1775 the firm had been concerned with trade and lands, and the number of their correspondents had been greatly augmented; by 1781 Morris, in his individual capacity, had interests in trade, land, mills, privateering, and securities—to list the most important—which were handled by a whole network of mercantile correspondents. In the early years the firm of Willing and Morris had been held in respect by its contemporaries; on the eve of the Revolution, it had been numbered among the leading firms in Philadelphia; after three years of war, Morris enjoyed the reputation of being one of the leading merchants in America; five years after Independence Robert Morris was almost universally acknowledged as the outstanding merchant in America. In 1757 Morris had commenced his mercantile career as a partner of Thomas Willing; by 1778 Morris had made a number of connections outside of the firm of Willing and Morris; by 1781 Morris' vast concerns reached out to include at least nine major partnerships and numerous lesser engagements, not to mention an extensive network of mercantile correspondents.

Although many enterprises never fulfilled the hopes of their author, the life of Robert Morris until 1781 is largely a story of almost incredible success—a person of humble birth whose spectacular advancement crowned him as the Prince of Merchants, the giant figure in the business world of Revolutionary America. There were many weaknesses in the structure erected by Morris, as he eventually discovered, but as yet—in 1781—those weaknesses were not apparent. In the eyes of most if not all observers it appeared as if the path of Robert Morris leading into the future was paved with gold.

It was this demonstration of business success which attracted the attention of the Continental Congress and eventually led to the reappearance of Robert Morris on the political scene; but it was the combined experience of political administration and mercantile success that proved indispensable to Morris after he accepted his new role. The Revolutionary government was tottering on the brink of financial collapse, and, in searching for solutions to the crisis, Congress looked to the giant of the business community in the hope that he could somehow find a remedy. This service in the Confederation government as the Superintendent of Finance proved, by all odds, to be the most important public role in the career of Robert Morris.

CHAPTER —THREE

A Crisis in Revolutionary Finance

THE PROBLEM OF FINANCE HELD THE SPOTLIGHT ON THE REPUBLICAN stage in the winter and spring of 1781. Of course the question of ways and means to support the Revolution had been extremely important from the beginning, but at this time it developed into such proportions that it dwarfed all other considerations in the conduct of the War. A clutter of resolutions, letters, and committee reports of Congress witness the facts; but what testimony is more eloquent than the actions of Tom Paine, whose pen now praised taxation rather than denounced Kings?[1]

It was the Continental Congress which faced the persistent and difficult financial problems throughout the fight for Independence. In retrospect, the most remarkable characteristic of Congressional action on finance was its boldness and its enormous assumption of power. Without any constitutional structure or some like instrument as a basis, Congress issued paper currency and borrowed money on the credit of a central government that had no existence in fact, and carried out these financial functions with amazing success. It is something of a paradox that the final traces of this success faded away just at the time the financial powers of Congress were being secured formally by the final adoption of the Articles of Confederation early in 1781. The measure of this eventual failure was reflected in the near collapse of the credit of the central government.

These developments are so closely connected with the career of Robert Morris that the essentials must be clearly comprehended. It is necessary, first of all, to examine the reasons for the crisis in finance in the winter and spring of 1780-81. Then it is important to evaluate the relationship of the finances to general conditions within the economy in order to determine more precisely the exact nature of the crisis. Finally, it is indispensable to place Morris in this large movement of events.

In order to understand the condition of the finances it is necessary to summarize the measures used by Congress to finance the Revolution from its outbreak until the winter and spring of 1780-81. In this synopsis, the four well-known means employed by that body—issuing bills of credit, domestic loans, foreign loans, and requisitions in money and commodities—must be examined briefly.[2]

Emission of bills of credit, that is, paper money, was the first step taken by Congress to obtain funds to support the war. That they turned to this means was quite natural, for it had been resorted to during the colonial period with comparative success, and it was also the most accessible resource. The first emissions of bills of credit were authorized by Congress a year before the Declaration of Independence. They were intended as notes of anticipation, that is, temporary notes to serve as money until specie resources could be tapped; Congress planned to redeem them with hard money to be brought in by taxes. Their "temporary" character soon became fixed, however, and issue followed issue under the mounting pressures of war until this means of financing the war completely overshadowed all the others.[3]

Domestic loans, the second method used by Congress, consisted of loan office certificates and certificates of indebtedness, the latter issued by such purchasing agents as the quartermaster and commissary departments. Loan office certificates were the government bonds of the Revolutionary generation. Congress had become alarmed by the amount of paper money thrown into circulation, and finally, on October 3, 1776, despite considerable opposition, voted to borrow money

from the citizens of the states. The citizens who loaned their money
to Congress received a certificate, a bond which called for an interest
of 4% and later 6%. Loan offices were established in each state, and a
commissioner was placed in charge of each office. These certificates
were purchased almost exclusively by the wealthier groups, because
they were the only ones who had money to lend; furthermore, the
resolution stated that no certificate should be issued for less than
$300, another condition restricting the number of purchasers. Thus
this type of certificate became the avenue by which the more affluent
citizens supported the war, in contrast to paper money which touched
more directly the rank and file.[4]

The remaining interest-bearing certificates, those issued by various
purchasing agents of the army, made up an important part of domestic loans. In return for goods supplied to the military forces, the proper
agents of the services would issue certificates of indebtedness for the
value of the goods received. Of course this method sometimes led to
malpractices. The owners often received a value in certificates, properly adjusted for depreciation, far in excess of the normal market
price, while agents who had relatively few checks on their conduct
were often tempted to enhance their personal comfort at the expense
of the army and Congress. In addition, this method tended to become
a forced loan at certain times in the war. If the army needed supplies
and did not have the funds on hand to obtain them—a condition that
became increasingly frequent—goods would be seized from the surrounding countryside, and certificates given as compensation.[5]

The use of foreign loans as a means of financing needs little explanation. In the period from 1775 through 1780, such loans came exclusively from France. The first assistance had been given in the form
of secret subsidies—although the secrecy was scarcely more than surface obscurity—through the agency of Beaumarchais, the celebrated
and colorful French playwright and man of affairs. When treaties were
signed with France in 1778, however, aid from the French Court was
given directly and openly rather than through subterranean channels.[6]

The final method employed by Congress to obtain funds to support
the war up to January 1781 was requisitions, the only form of taxation
that was available to it. It is a well-known but still important fact that
the Continental Congress did not possess the power of direct taxation.
As a result, Congress, in casting about rather desperately for additional
sources of support, finally resorted to a requisition upon the states on
November 22, 1777, for $5,000,000. The total sum was apportioned
among the several states in a ratio worked out in Congress as a temporary compromise, but it was understood that, as soon as the value
of the land and buildings in each state could be assessed, a permanent
proportion would be established according to the ability of a state to
pay. When the general situation of the revolutionary government is
considered, these early requisitions produced surprisingly good results.
In 1780, Congress turned to requisitioning commodities or, as it was
called, "in specifics," from the states. Some success was achieved, but

the problems of transporting the commodities, the deterioration of perishable goods, and the difficulty of making a proper assessment of the value of a commodity seriously hampered its operation.[7]

These four methods composed the sources of financial strength for the central government, but the key to an understanding of conditions in the winter of 1780-81 lies in the relative contribution made by each method to the whole up to January 1781. Using round numbers and stating the amounts in specie value, these contributions range as follows: foreign loans—$1,600,000; requisitions—$4,000,000; domestic loans—$20,000,000; and bills of credit—$37,000,000. In terms of percentage, these results are even more startling. Foreign loans provided approximately 3% of the whole, requisitions approximately 6%, domestic loans, 32%, and bills of credit, 59%. But even these percentages are somewhat deceiving because they tend to underemphasize the bills of credit and overstress domestic loans and requisitions. Over 60% of the support drawn from requisitions and probably as high as 35% of that drawn from domestic loans was received in continental "revenue" furnished by the bills of credit was greater than 59%; a realistic appraisal would indicate that they paid for approximately 70% of the whole cost of the war between 1775 and January 1781.[8]

These figures and percentages take on an importance that can scarcely be exaggerated when the financial crisis in the spring of 1781 is analyzed. The core of the matter was unmistakably apparent. The indispensable financial prop of the central government, the bills of credit, was being swept away in a torrent of depreciation, while the second buttress, domestic loans, was crumbling rapidly.

The story of depreciation in the bills of credit is well known, although its precise character for any specific area was obscure until the recent publication of Professor Anne Bezanson's excellent study of *Prices and Inflation during the American Revolution: Pennsylvania.* At first the bills circulated at par or very close to par. Declining slowly and even appreciating at certain intervals, the continental currency began to depreciate so rapidly by the winter of 1779-80 that any quotation of its value was valid for a very limited time. Each surge upward was punctuated by local, state, and even interstate meetings to establish price regulations. The value of these efforts was definitely short term, however, for depreciation was caused by basic factors quite outside the influence of a single group.[9]

In an attempt to halt the decline of public credit which resulted from the depreciation, Congress adopted a measure that has become popularly known as the forty-for-one funding measure of March 18, 1780; but this enactment did not stay the trend. The most important provisions in the resolution included (1) that the old bills of exchange be recalled at forty paper dollars as against one of specie; (2) as quickly as the old bills would come in, new bills were to be issued, valued at one dollar in specie, and thus forty to one in terms of the old bills; (3) the new bills were to be issued on funds provided by the individual states on the basis of a tentative quota; (4) six-tenths of the total of the new bills issued were to be reserved for the use of the states and four-tenths for the use of Congress; and (5) the new bills were to be redeemable in specie within six years and bear interest at 5%. Because this measure failed to stop the depreciation, quotations of the value of continental currency scarcely remained valid for a day; and by Spring 1781, when the paper money became more expensive to print than it retained in value as a medium of exchange, it ceased to exist as a means of paying for the war.[10]

The story of domestic loans through these years is much more obscure, although there is no doubt that this source of financing the war was seriously crippled. Congress did manage to continue the interest payments to the holders of the loan office certificates by drawing bills of exchange on Benjamin Franklin, their emissary at the French Court, which helped to bolster their market price. But the certificates did depreciate, sometimes at such a pace that the rate of loss swallowed up the interest return. As a result, this source of financing the war had dried up for the most part by 1780-81, although the burden of paying the interest as an item in current expenditures continued. Certificates issued by the commissary and quartermaster agents were used in the crucial early months of 1781, but the precise amount is indefinite. Because these certificates were also a form of paper, however, there can be little question that they too were carried along with the pressures of depreciation.[11]

The situation with relation to the bills of credit and domestic loans was bad enough, but it should be emphasized that the prospects for supporting the war by the less important means were also unfavorable. Requisitioning had bogged down in apathy and mismanagement; furthermore, Luzerne, the French foreign minister, had received instructions to offer Congress unlimited affection—but no funds.[12]

Although this discussion has been focused upon the finances of the central government, which are indispensable as a background to the crisis of 1780-81, it should be remembered that this condition was aggravated by similar problems within each state. In order to shoulder its share of the burden of the war, each state was compelled to search for means to support its war effort. All of them turned to the same solutions as those used by Congress, occasionally supplemented by the sale of Tory estates and the introduction of state import duties. It is not pertinent to outline the details of each state program, but it is important to note that acute distress within the states tended to parallel that of the central government. Although it cannot be stated that the financial situation of every state was as desperate as that of the national government by January 1781, most states were wrestling with a severe financial crisis, as Governor Thomas Jefferson of Virginia and Governor William Livingston of New Jersey could well testify.[13] Joseph Reed, President of the Executive Council of Pennsylvania, spoke for many of them when he declared to Washington:[14]

It is difficult for your Excelly [Excellency] to form a competent Judgment of the Difficulties and Embarrassments with which the procuring Supplies is attended. The Confidence of the People in Paper Money is so shaken that the Produce of the Country is furnished to the Commissioners with much Reluctance, and even of this Money we have but a very incompetent Sum when compared with the Amount and Value of the Supplies. Credit may be said to be at an End; the innumerable Certificates granted by the Quarter Master and Commissary Departments and by the Authority of the state having extinguished all Confidence.

With the two major props in financing the Revolution—the bills of credit and domestic loans—either useless or disintegrating, with the prospect for support from the lesser sources unfavorable, and with the condition of the state finances little better than that of the central government, the situation confronting Congress was nothing less than the near collapse of public credit. If this situation had coincided with the end of the struggle, one could cheerfully join with the many who quote Franklin on the virtue of paying for a war by unlimited issues of paper money. But the two did not coincide; the war was still to be won; without victory, there would be no Independence. The government which was established to carry the war to its conclusion had no funds and, what was far worse, no credit at its command.

The army itself, the most articulate source of complaint, was placed in a precarious condition which was symptomatic of the crisis. The Northern army grouped around the British stronghold in New York had encountered the customary trio of troubles—lack of pay, inadequate clothing, and scarcity of supplies. After warning Congress in October 1780 that no supply magazines had been furnished for winter, Pickering, the Quartermaster General, had stated he held little hope that this deficiency could be remedied. General Heath informed Washington that the army at West Point existed on a day-to-day basis; "one long storm or spell of severe weather," he declared, "would drive us on the verge of want." Later Heath was compelled to write that the garrison was "totally destitute of flour" and that the situation "on account of provisions is really alarming." Washington's pen strengthened the pleas of his subordinates, and the picture he sketched was not pretty. ". . . The prospects of the army, especially of that part which is to winter in the Highlands, were never so alarming in respect to the want of Bread as at this time." For this situation James Thatcher, the much quoted Revolutionary diarist, could well attest, when he confided to his Journal: "For three days I have not been able to procure food enough to appease my appetite; we are threatened with starvation." General Wayne, in command of the Pennsylvania Line, pleaded for adequate supplies, particularly clothing. Receiving no satisfaction, the General begged for needles and thread so his troops could repair their garments, for otherwise, he continued, "we shall be naked within the course of two or three weeks." But his troops did not wait for this chilly prospect in the snow-covered New Jersey hills and their revolt climaxed the long season of troubles. In order to salvage the situation,

Washington began to discharge a considerable part of his army; but this action brought only temporary relief.[15]

Although other detachments such as that of Captain Brodhead at Fort Pitt faced similar situations, it was the army in the South which was destitute. When Nathanael Greene, newly appointed to the Southern Army, arrived to assume command he was appalled. "Nothing can be more wretched and distressing than the condition of the troops, starving with cold and hunger, without tents and camp equipage. Those of the Virginia line are, literally, naked; and a great part totally unfit for any kind of duty, and must remain so until clothing can be had from the northward." He feared that it might be impossible to subsist the few remaining troops because of the devastation by British horsemen. Had Greene been able to inspect the correspondence of his predecessor, General Gates, before arrival he would not have been so shocked, for Gates, when writing to the Board of War, had withheld nothing. "The unspeakable distress which the army has suffered, and still likely to suffer from want to provisions," he had written, "requires your instant interposition to save it from utter ruin." [16]

The difficulty, of course, lay simply in the lack of money. The Quartermaster General found himself "distressed beyond measure from the want of money." Indeed, he discovered that his funds were so low that "the expences of one express to Philadelphia would take all the money I have." Such a situation was not unusual for the army; it had been in dire straits most of the war. But this time—and the new twist was of supreme importance—the army was addressing a central government whose public credit was, for the first time in the war, on the brink of collapse.[17]

Even the British command was sufficiently encouraged by the depressing state of the American finances to base a part of their policy upon it. Lord George Germain, the British colonial secretary in charge of the general war effort, instructed General Sir Henry Clinton, one of the chief commanders in America, to dispatch troops to Maryland and Pennsylvania in order to subdue those regions while General Arnold and Lord Cornwallis disposed of Virginia. Why at this time? "For such is beyond all doubt the low condition of the Congress [*sic*] authority and Finances, and so weak the state of Washington's army that little opposition is to be expected in that quarter." [18]

"Credit, either public or private, may always be kept good, where there is sufficient estate to support it." If this statement, written by that careful observer, Peletiah Webster, in an essay published June 8, 1780, be accepted as valid, then the economic condition of the country looms large in assessing the nature of the crisis in the winter and spring of 1781.[19]

Sometimes the severe crisis in the national finances is not distinguished from the general economic situation. To be sure, the two are interdependent, yet each must be considered separately if the nature of the crisis is to be understood and interpreted. It is also essential to make this appraisal in order to establish a firm base from which general economic trends can be traced, for only in this way can the later policies of Morris as Financier be analyzed and their reception, in large part, explained.

Superficially it might appear that the revolutionary effort had exhausted the economic resources of the country, and that this situation in turn caused the financial crisis. But there is little substance to such an interpretation. Indeed, despite the many qualifications that must be made, the most impressive characteristic of the economy in the winter and spring of 1780-81 is its favorable outlook.

Some signs of economic strain were apparent in the winter of 1780-81. The inflationary spiral, caused largely by the depreciation of paper currency, had discriminated against certain elements within the community. Obviously, people who were on fixed wages either in military or civilian life were caught between rising prices and stationary incomes. Even when wages were increased they tended to lag behind the rising prices with the result that many a laborer felt the pinch of inflation in declining real wages. Speculation and profiteering were also encouraged by the inflation, though it should be quickly added that this would have happened regardless of the inflation. Merchants, farmers, or craftsmen could hold their commodity or commodities off the market in anticipation of the expected increase in prices. Such tactics naturally were oppressive to those members of the community who needed them, and they banded together in price-fixing committees and conventions on numerous occasions to protest. The inflationary trend also disrupted normal trade channels, and discrepancies in the rate of inflation between one area of the country and another encouraged speculation in a fluctuating currency as an article of commerce.[20]

On the other hand, one merely elaborates the obvious in pointing out that only a handful of Americans in the Revolutionary generation were on a fixed income. Laborers too composed a minor segment—that is in relation to the whole—of the population. Both groups did everything in their power to avoid personal jeopardy by receiving their income in terms of real wages—either in commodities or in specie. Also, those workers who were relatively skilled—such as bakers—participated in the price increases just as much as the more important business groups in the country. Professor Anne Bezanson has stated it accurately and well in her recent study on prices when she writes that "anyone who made provision for the future became in his own way a speculator." All members of the society had to hedge against the future, and the point where an attempt to preserve financial stability ended and speculation began is obscure, to say the least. Certainly it is easy to string a number of quotations together to prove almost anything during this period of changing conditions. And some historians, though by no means all, have strung them together without reference to time, place, or immediate circumstances. A careful analysis of the basic factors in the economy in the various sections, however, indicates that the country was relatively prosperous in the winter of 1780.[21]

The agricultural element within the New England area, in the winter of 1780-81, fully supports this generalization. The reason for this comparatively happy prospect lay in the type of agriculture carried on before the Revolution. The characteristic Yankee farmer had been and continued to be self-sufficient for the most part, and his key crops of maize, barley, and oats were not exported extensively before the war; the activities of the British cruisers, therefore, did not seriously affect him. The only threat which could imperil his economic existence was actual conquest of his land by the British forces, and the destruction of his crops. But this threat never materialized, for the deepest penetration had been made by the enemy forces in their memorable expedition against Concord in 1775. Those farmers who exported meat products—the only important cash commodity—unquestionably suffered at the outset by the disruption of coastal commerce. Fortunately, however, new markets appeared in the form of Continental troops, state militia, and somewhat later, the French fleet and troops. Droves of cattle on their way to military posts became a familiar sight on the New England countryside, and such towns as Great Barrington mushroomed into important supply centers. Rochambeau's arrival at Newport in 1780 brought this warborn market to a climax, for soon additional fingers of trade reached out into the entire region. Jeremiah Wadsworth, an experienced Connecticut enterpriser, acted as the French purchasing agent and carefully supervised the outflow of French coin and bills and directed the incoming cattle and produce. In view of these circumstances—self-sufficiency and a market for the one significant exportable commodity—it is hardly surprising to learn that complaints from the agrarian community were infrequent or that travelers failed to note any real signs of distress.[22]

The commerce carried on by the New England port towns, however, was much more vulnerable. What had happened to it by 1780-81? Outbreak of hostilities had not only severed the direct trade with Great Britain, but the alert British fleet cast a menacing shadow over the important carrying trade and coastwise commerce. The fishing industry was seriously crippled and shipbuilding was temporarily halted. These developments, plus the occupation of Boston and later Newport, certainly indicate that the commercial life of New England was gravely impaired by the outbreak of hostilities. Still, no one mentions any graveyard of ships from late 1776 to 1780 because the commercial community did not die. It changed its form; it turned to privateering, a war commerce of distinguished and familiar lineage for many New England seamen.[23]

Privateering more than flourished; it took on the character of a bonanza. In Portsmouth, New Hampshire, William Whipple found its attractions so strong that regular vessels of the marine, militia quotas, and farmers needing laborers all suffered from manpower shortages.

The pull of privateering was so overpowering in Rhode Island that restrictions had to be placed upon it and limitations set up on the complement of men that each vessel was permitted to enlist. In Boston, Abigail Adams repeated the sentiment of many observers when she informed her husband, John, that "the rage for privateering is as great here as anywhere." Sensational captures like that of the brigantine *Charlotte,* an extremely rich prize, by the privateer *General Sullivan,* or the arrival in Salem harbor of the privateer *Brutus,* heavily laden with nine rich prizes of specie and jewels, scarcely cooled such ardor.[24]

Each year the number of privateers swelled, reaching flood tide in 1781, with profits apparently reaching a maximum the previous year. Massachusetts, of course, with the towns of Boston, Salem, and Beverly in the forefront, led the assault. In 1780, the crucial year for this analysis, approximately 165 ships carrying some 6,000 men sailed forth as privateers. When compared with the available manpower, this figure is staggering. According to the best estimates available, the number of males over sixteen in ten of the leading port towns in Massachusetts totaled slightly over 9,000. If this figure is discounted for the aged, the disabled, the non-seamen such as storekeepers, and the men under arms—the quota for these towns in 1780 alone exceeded 500—the available manpower can be more accurately assessed at 7,500. A very high percentage of men over sixteen, therefore, were involved in privateering, and this figure reëmphasizes the overwhelming concern of New England port towns with this type of enterprise. The fact that commercial activity did decline in some port towns like Marblehead and Ipswich suggests that the remaining ports attracted men either from the declining ports or the surrounding countryside.[25]

The various towns in New England seemed to flourish. George Williams, a Salem merchant whose aptitude for pessimistic predictions was well established, wrote a friend in 1780 that "this town stands the war at present well, by the exertion in privateering and merchant vessels." As late as 1782, the Frenchman Chastellux traveling from Newburyport to Boston was continually astonished with the prosperity of the towns, and he remarked frequently on the "springing up" of houses, warehouses, and the like. A complaint of John Eliot—"the town of Boston is really poor. If some brighter prospects do not open, it is my opinion we cannot subsist"—often quoted by historians, should not be taken too seriously. This is the only comment Eliot makes on the matter in a year of correspondence where his views on theology and his indispositions compete for attention; moreover, at the time he wrote the letter, his gouty, "game" leg did bother him no end. As late as December 1781, Boston, in sensible instructions written for its delegates to the General Court, mentioned the "astonishing successes that have hitherto attended that kind of enterprize [privateering]."[26]

It would be a mistake to think that privateering crowded out all other trading activity. The mercantile community traded with the Continental powers—France, Spain, and Holland—and with the West Indies. Cargoes of rice, tobacco, flaxseed, lumber, and even codfish—

300,000 livre to Nantes alone—together with remittances in French bills were sent to Europe, and lumber and fish to the West Indies. In return—sometimes direct, often via St. Eustatius or some other entrepôt—came fine and coarse cloths, linens, cutlery, glass, sugar, molasses, West India rum, and even "English goods." These wares and commodities, together with the prize cargoes, favored the region with an abundance of goods and its almost inevitable counterpart, criticism of luxurious tastes. Special items such as gray sable muffets and fashionable silk shoes moved many a patriot to orate on the vices of plenty. Indeed, moaned a staunch New Englander, a "worldly spirit" was abroad in the land.[27]

The available merchant records are much too incomplete to assess precise gains and losses in 1780. However, those that exist reflect a business confidence and absence of complaint in the fall of that year quite striking in contrast to their letters in the fall of 1784, for example, or to the correspondence of Charleston merchants in November 1783. Whether the sum total of all mercantile activity substituted for prewar commerce is equally impossible to determine, but the foregoing analysis certainly demonstrates the surprising vitality of seafaring New England in the winter of 1780-81.[28]

Not all the signs, of course, point to economic prosperity for New England. The farmer was plagued with occasional threats of invasion, some shortage of manpower, and increased taxes, while his seafaring brother faced unexplored channels of trade, possible loss or capture of men and vessels at sea, and increased operating costs. In addition, some fishing ports declined, and shipbuilding lagged—but it collapsed when the peace finally came in 1783. The port of Newport suffered because of its occupation by British forces, and its use as a British base hampered a part of the mercantile community; but Newport showed remarkable recovery by the time the French troops arrived in the summer of 1780. And some of the unfavorable developments throughout the region were certainly compensated by the increase in internal trade, by an improvement in shipbuilding, and by the well-known spurt in domestic manufactures.[29]

Although most New Englanders could not match the stately mansions built during the period by the conspicuously blessed, they could more than agree with the well-known Brattle Street Church minister, Samuel Cooper, when he proclaimed in his election day sermon of October 1780, "The Lord . . . hath not forsaken us nor our God forgotten us." Well might they have gone on to echo the psalmist, "Thou crownest the year with thy goodness; and thy paths drop fatness. . . . The pastures are clothed with flocks; the valleys also are covered over with corn; they shout for joy; they also sing."[30]

Even though the British continued to occupy the port of New York and its surrounding countryside, the economic outlook of the Middle Region was also favorable in the winter of 1780-81. Of course, there are some exceptions to this generalization, but an analysis of the fundamental factors at work supports this conclusion.

The agricultural community of the Middle Region was especially favored in this period. On the whole, crops in 1779 and 1780 had been good, and attractive prices could be had for the commodities produced. Cereal crops, the most important staple, met a ready market because of the demands of the Continental Army and the French troops and fleet. The market provided by the French forces proved most alluring, for payment was usually made in French coin or French bills of exchange. Leading the exploitation of the convenient French market in Rhode Island was New York, especially after its embargo was lifted; but other parts of the region did not lag far behind. Purchases by the continental and state commissaries also formed an essential link in the economic chain of the agrarian community, although continental currency, commissary certificates, quartermaster certificates, and various kinds of state paper issues were somewhat less desirable as compensation for commodities. When the demon of depreciation did rear its head, various allowances were made by the state legislatures and by commissary officers who appraised goods considerably beyond their worth and issued certificates on the basis of the inflated valuations. Then, too, the paper, whether it was in the form of currency or certificates, was freely used in paying taxes, in buying goods, and, above all, in purchasing lands. Many farmers had averted severe loss through depreciation by investing in more durable goods, a practice which in itself had tended to lessen the value of the paper. When paper issues depreciated precipitously in the fall of 1780, the farmers who had commodities to sell demanded specie payments or the equivalent.[31]

Although it is sometimes stated that the agrarian community of the Middle Region suffered from lack of imports in general and, more specifically, imports of agricultural equipment, there is little indication that this factor was important in 1780-81. In fact, there is little evidence of heavy imports of such equipment before the Revolution, for the farmer of the middle colonies was almost as self-sufficient as his New England brother. If the agricultural community was pinched economically because of restricted imports, that condition was greatly improved by 1780 when goods flowed in from New England, Philadelphia, and Baltimore, and quite possibly from the port of New York itself. By 1780, imports at the latter port reached prewar levels. It is scarcely plausible that the Loyalists had suddenly developed such a voracious appetite for goods—even after making allowances for the supply of British troops. Much of it must have dribbled through the lines into Connecticut, New York, and New Jersey.[32]

In summary, the farmer of the Middle Region enjoyed good crops, favorable prices, and channels to invest surplus funds in 1780-81. Still, these encouraging signs would be meaningless if hostilities laid waste their crops and despoiled their lands. Such destruction did occur, but it is easy to exaggerate its impact upon the agricultural prosperity of the region.

On the New York scene—particularly in Ulster, Dutchess, and

Orange counties toward the south and Tryon County on the frontier
—the tendency to over-assess the ill effect of war upon the rural area
is most pronounced. The real test must be made in southern New
York where the British and American forces maintained a consistent
point of contact. In the early years of the war, a swift-moving British
marauding party had pierced the Continental lines to set fire to Kingston, but the main body of troops had not advanced beyond White
Plains. Even this limited penetration had been momentary, and by
1780 the American troops were once again entrenched at Dobbs Ferry,
a scant twelve miles north of Manhattan Island. Thus the British
troops never truly burst through the rugged barriers below Poughkeepsie—or for that matter Fishkill—to spill out on the fertile plains
of Ulster and Dutchess counties. In northern New York, the British
had penetrated to Saratoga in their elaborate campaign of 1777, but
this fort was an outpost, and the big prize, prosperous Albany County,
lay untouched. Her historian has summed it up well. "During the hostile years of revolutionary War," he asserts, "the agricultural interests
of this country were not materially affected." The western areas such as
Tryon county had been harassed by Indian raids, but by 1781 the Indian campaign of General Sullivan did much to spike their guns and
sheathe their scalping knives.[33]

It is also easy to magnify New Jersey's agricultural distress due to
fighting. To be sure, early in the war farm houses had been burned,
crops destroyed, and livestock confiscated, but this should not be interpreted as a general sacking. Indeed, the British command had frequently taken great pains to prevent destruction, for they had entertained high hopes that the entire countryside would become loyalist.
An occasional building burned in a village or the partial looting of
two or three isolated farm homes was described in terms of "wanton"
destruction by writers long after the event. The vast majority of citizens heard of rather than saw either the British or the American
armies. The counties of Sussex, Morris, and Hunterdon in the north
and Burlington, Gloucester, and Cumberland in the south went virtually untouched. In the central and northeast counties, where the
maneuvers were carried out, only a small area and a limited number
of citizens were involved. Indeed, 10 per cent seems a generous estimate for those who felt the brunt of war, even at high tide, and of
this group only a handful incurred permanent damage. Those who
listened to stories about the war rather than being directly involved
might become excited and experience some mental uneasiness, but
such uncertainty did not injure the corn and wheat or reduce the milk
production of their herds.[34]

The invasion of Pennsylvania in 1777, of course, had centered on
Philadelphia, and the receding wave of Redcoats had left some damage
to the countryside in its wake. But much of this destruction had
been repaired by 1780. In fact, invasion by British troops had carried
with it some compensation, for here was a market that paid in gold.
Many observers agreed that such an attractive market was not entirely

neglected even when the British Legions had retreated to their New York headquarters. No one asserted it more quaintly—and bluntly— than John Hunt, who confided to his Diary that "The Eastward market opened again and people fell on to tradeing and strugling after the treasures of ye Earth." [35]

In short, by 1780, favorable conditions had nearly erased whatever ill effect the war might have had upon the agricultural community. Moravians, fortified by the prayers of their friends, traversed the Pennsylvania back country and delighted in the beautiful plantations, houses, fields, and orchards; and their only complaints refer to the roughness of the road, a minor obstacle to such devout churchmen. Even the venerable New Jersey parson, Reverend Nicholas Collin, who had diligently inscribed in his Diary the woes of 1778, now devoted almost exclusive attention to such memorable events as the baptism of Maria Kelley, a visit to the Stringer Glass Works, and the marriage of a middle-aged couple who had long shared bed and board. [36]

To speak of the mercantile community in the Middle Region at this time is to speak of the Philadelphia merchants, because the New Jersey seafarers, although apparently prospering, were comparatively unimportant. Late in 1779, shrewd contemporary observers such as Peletiah Webster found the Philadelphia situation generally good. This is supported by the existing records. The merchants were occupied with the tobacco trade; they "trafficked" in West India goods; they traded with continental Europe and even the Baltic region. According to reports some surreptitious trade in wheat and flour occurred despite the embargo placed on these commodities by the state. Much of the general trade, it is true, had to be carried on by remote control through Maryland, Virginia, or even West India ports, because the British cruisers intermittently threatened Delaware Bay. Yet the Philadelphia business community fairly bustled with energy. [37]

Although the South revealed the greatest variance in economic health, the pleasing appearance of much of the upper South was encouraging. The well-being of the upper South began with the fertility of the soil and the favors of nature. Despite the weevil in 1779 and the abnormally cold spring of 1780, crops had been plentiful. Their abundance prompted John Hanson, a well-known Maryland agrarian, to write: "The account you have given me of my plantation affairs, and the plentiful crops in general, is very pleasing." Moreover, he had heard that "the harvest throughout the country . . . is very great." This agricultural produce found an accessible market. Supported by the King's monies, John Holker, the purchasing agent of the French forces, bought substantial quantities of wheat, corn, and cattle in Maryland and to some extent in Virginia, while the Continental army and the state militia served as markets equally important to this region as to the middle states—and for the same reasons. Tobacco, the most important agricultural staple of the upper South, was also much in demand. Exploited by merchants from almost every state in the Union, the tobacco trade had witnessed an intensified competition early in the war because of the purchases of Congress and various state governments who were employing the commodity as a remittance for loans and goods from abroad. This combination had stimulated prices, and there is no indication that, in relation to other commodities, the price of tobacco declined by 1780.[38]

The fact that the upper South witnessed virtually no fighting up to 1780 is significant. Only French troops invaded Maryland—to the delight of the belles of Baltimore. But late in 1780, storm clouds in the form of British troops under Generals Arnold and Cornwallis appeared on the Virginia horizon to break eventually upon parts of that state. These clouds contained a streak of silver, or more properly gold, lining, however, for not only did the British troops require rations, but the British merchants following in the wake of the troops also made plans to export tobacco.[39]

The stimulus given to the trading communities in the upper South is so well established it requires little more than mere mention. Favored in location with respect to British military operations—that is, during most of the war—and convenient to the sources of tobacco, the merchants in the Maryland and Virginia area enjoyed an advantage which they did their best to exploit. Certainly an abundance of goods was provided by returning vessels and by captured privateers. In fact, privateering when it reached its highest level in 1780 was significant in its own right.[40]

As one proceeds southward from Virginia, economic conditions worsen. Still, North Carolina, with minor exceptions, suffered little from the war up to 1780 because of her self-sufficiency and her relative freedom from disruption by military activities; for one time in that state's history, its uninviting coastline proved to be a blessing rather than a curse. Her sister state to the south was much less fortunate. During the early years of the war the economic prospects of South Carolina promised much, but the new British strategy to choke off the South directly affected the Queen of that region. The scene on that wet and dreary fall day in 1780 on the crest of Kings Mountain marked but one in a series of widespread skirmishes throughout the state— warfare intensified by civil discord. Charleston's capture some six months earlier crippled the economic life of the region; the military penetration inland killed it. Each side complained of the other's destructive pillaging; yet each side continued its depredation on what it conceived "enemy country." Each side commented on the genuine distress of the citizenry; but both partisans were too busy with their problems to offer any aid. There was some compensation for Charleston when the British finally gained possession. Limited quantities of indigo and rice were exported to Britain, and an equally limited supply of British goods and gold trickled into the city.[41]

The exception of South Carolina and the qualifications discussed in relation to each section should not obscure the fact that the economic life of the country showed remarkable vitality. This conclusion is evident despite the fact that the nature of the evidence on economic affairs in the Revolutionary era is prejudiced against it. The generation following the Revolutionary period—and their intellectual heirs, the town and county chroniclers—was zealous to record every complaint, every suffering, every sign of destruction. They were enthralled by the one house destroyed, the one family turned from its home, the one farmyard looted, and neglected the fifty houses untouched, the hundred families undisturbed, and countless farmyards intact. In brief, matters on economic life so commonplace as to go entirely unrecorded emerge in consequence as material to bolster the conclusion of a relatively prosperous economic situation.[42]

The nature of the crisis in 1780-81, therefore, resulted almost exclusively from the collapse of the credit of the central government rather than from general economic exhaustion. To be sure, the continued strain in the finances could have an important deteriorating effect upon the economic life of the country. But the reverse was also true; the economic situation could bolster the depleted credit of the country. The trend either way would be importantly influenced by the measures introduced to meet the situation. Certainly any program, if it were to be realistic, would have to recognize the nature of the crisis.

The career of Robert Morris became intimately connected with the crisis in finance when he was elected to the position of Superintendent of Finance, a newly created executive office, in the spring of 1781. The establishment of this office was but one measure among many which came before Congress. It is not too much to say that the crisis had riveted the attention of Congress to financial problems; they debated plan after plan until the Journals were crowded with suggestions, but relatively few reports of action. Among the positive measures, however, was the revival of a plan to create executive departments where responsibility would rest upon a single person.

Such a plan, which had been advocated early in the Revolution but never adopted, was involved with an important difference of opinion about the function and organization of Congress. Some members of Congress had suggested that executive agencies should be created which would be responsible to Congress but composed of persons who were not members of that body. The advocates of this view were primarily interested in separating the deliberative from the executive duties of Congress. In supporting their case, they argued that this type of organization would result in better administrative efficiency and responsibility, and at the same time the members of Congress, in being freed from excessive detail, would be able to concentrate on policy making. Other members of Congress were interested in the continued combination of executive and legislative powers, and insisted that the committees appointed to carry out the executive functions be composed exclusively of members of Congress. Those who favored this type of organization argued that these executive duties were so important that immediate supervision should remain directly in the hands of Congress; it would be a mistake, they asserted, for Congress to relinquish any part of its prerogatives with respect to the executive function.[43]

During the course of the Revolution the trend was toward the separation of the executive from the legislative functions, and this is reflected in Congress' actions on finance. At the outset, special committees of Congress had been appointed to supervise such executive financial tasks as the inspection of the bills of credit. On February 17, 1776, this tentative arrangement was replaced by a more formal one, calling for a standing Committee of Congress, later named the Board of the Treasury. Although some minor changes were made in this general establishment during the following years, no major revisions took place until July 30, 1779. On that date a new Board was set up, which included three members outside of Congress as well as two members of that body. It was this Board which was presiding over the Treasury as the financial crisis of 1780-81 took shape.[44]

In view of the financial crisis, it is not surprising either to find that the plan to create executive departments with individual responsibility was reactivated and adopted or to discover that the first position filled was the Office of Superintendent of Finance. To veteran observers of Congress, however, this action appeared somewhat incongruous, for that august body had long guarded its functions as jealously as a mother hen shelters her brood of chicks.

Although opposed by some members, a resolution creating the Office of Superintendent of Finance was adopted by Congress on February 7, 1781. Its adoption did not signify a clear-cut triumph for those who agitated for a greater concentration of executive power to meet the exigencies of war. Clauses such as "to examine" the public debt, expenditures, and revenue, "to digest and report plans for improving the finances" reflect the lack of any policy-making power. More positive authority was delegated in settling public accounts and in directing and controlling "all persons employed in procuring supplies for the public service, and in the expenditure of public money." Obtaining accounts, compelling payment of monies due the United States, and reporting to Congress the need for any assistants also came under the duties of the Financier. All this indicates a very limited, if not to say weak, authority. The key phrase in the deputization of powers, however, was "to direct the execution of all plans which shall be adopted by Congress respecting revenue and expenditure." Should the man holding the Office interpret the executive power broadly—as some chief executives did on the establishment of the present form of government—the Office of Finance could develop into a very positive force.[45]

When the Office of Finance was established, almost all eyes turned to the successful and capable Philadelphia merchant as the most likely candidate for the post. Indeed, with a passing nod toward Hamilton— and it was scarcely that—Congress elected Robert Morris "unanimously" as Superintendent of Finance and dispatched a letter to inform him of their action.[46]

Morris did not accept the offer outright. In his reply of March 13—a letter which Gouverneur Morris declared opened "the way to his acceptance"—the Philadelphian, with becoming modesty, explained that he had delayed his reply while inquiring as to his own fitness. He then stressed the personal considerations which made him reluctant to accept the appointment. Tranquillity, ease, and retirement lay at his doorstep because of "twenty years (and upwards) assiduous application to business as a merchant." Moreover, "providence has so far smiled upon my endeavors," and acceptance would certainly mean "a sacrifice of that ease, of much social and domestic enjoyment, and of every material interest." He recounted his devotion to the cause of Independence and asserted that this devotion alone could force him to shoulder the burdens of the Office. After these preliminaries, Morris approached the vital matters; there were some contingencies that Congress must meet and some clarification of powers that must be made before he would accept.[47]

Foremost among the conditions stood Morris' relationship to his commercial connections. Many of them had been formed, said Morris, to relieve him from active mercantile affairs; and now he declared positively that he would not take the appointment unless Congress permitted these connections to continue regardless of his public post. "These establishments I am bound in honor and by contract to support to the extent agreed on. . . . I cannot on any consideration consent to violate engagements or depart from these principles of honor which it is my pride to be governed by." Furthermore, if Congress agreed that his mercantile connections could continue, "an express declaration of their sentiments should appear on the minutes, that no doubt may arise or reflections be cast on this score hereafter."[48]

Why such explicitness? Undoubtedly the charges leveled in 1779 at Morris' dual role earlier in the Revolution, and the bitter criticisms that followed, remained much too fresh in his memory to be easily forgotten. Then too, Morris' statement on his word of honor was unquestionably sincere. Anyone familiar with the mercantile community of the Colonial and Revolutionary periods knows that a merchant's word constituted his bond in business, and a merchant who failed to live up to his commitments in dealing with his correspondents soon discovered that his business was short-lived. In Morris' case the records reveal that his word as a merchant was greatly respected; and he always prided himself upon this acceptance of his mercantile integrity. The theme runs constantly through Morris' correspondence and that of his contemporaries.

The question raised by Morris, that of holding a public position while carrying on private business affairs, was a particularly troublesome problem for merchants. To withdraw from business altogether entailed a special hardship for a merchant, because his trading position depended on the network of correspondents and connections

which he had built up over the years. It amounted to the good will
established by a firm. This network would not only be severed at a
single stroke, but it would be difficult to rebuild. These circumstances
contrasted with those of the landholder, for example, whose lands remained intact regardless of his participation in public affairs. The
landholder might suffer some decrease in income but no diminution
of capital, and no one ever suggested, of course, that a person should
sell his lands upon assuming a public position. A second part of the
problem concerned the investment of surplus capital. If a merchant
who entered public service decided to sell his business, where could
he invest his funds? Land and commerce offered the most likely prospects, with the latter preëminent, for it was the kind of business activity
with which he was familiar. There was a high probability, therefore,
that the merchant might end where he had started—in mercantile
affairs. In short, the personal problem encountered by a merchant who
held a public position while carrying on his private affairs did not
have an entirely simple solution. Certainly it was not unusual during
the Revolution for a person to carry on both activities; and Congress,
despite some opposition, did accept Morris' condition.[49]

Morris included a request for clarification on other points. He
wanted complete control of appointments in his Office; he requested
absolute power to dismiss all persons "that are concerned in the official expenditure of public moneys"; he had misgivings that the Congressional resolution creating the Office "requires the execution of
many things for which adequate powers are not provided." Congress
eventually met most of these demands, but not until the indefatigable
Sam Adams, and others who suspected any delegation of authority,
had spent their last efforts defending the outworks of Congress' executive power.[50]

The power of appointments met little opposition; not so with the
powers to dismiss. Convinced that he was right, Morris asserted that
unless this control was granted, the reforms so sorely needed could
not be effected. What agencies were to come under this control? Certain functions of the Quartermaster General, the Paymaster General,
the Commissary General, expenditures in the Medical Department,
and those who settled accounts. Did that complete the list? Morris
thought that some department probably existed of which he was unfamiliar, but still legitimately within his jurisdiction. Then, too, Congress might create new agencies in the future that should fall into the
"expenditure of money" category. The best solution, he felt, lay in a
blanket resolution outlining those powers. Although Morris thrust
aside the fears of Congressmen that such powers might be construed
to include Washington, he made it clear that the persons employed by
the Commander-in-Chief in the expenditure of public money "ought
to be accountable and subject to dismission." Only the secret service
should be excepted.[51]

After lengthy deliberation, from April to May, Morris was in substance granted authority over all persons engaged in the expenditure

of funds. But the matter of executing "many things" where powers were not expressly provided would have to wait for future interpretation. Morris, in turn, accepted the position of Superintendent of Finance on May 14, but he did not take office officially until July.[52]

Reaction to Morris' acceptance ran the expected gauntlet from praise to protest. Very early Joseph Jones of Virginia had commented that "Our Finances want a Necker . . . Morris is I believe the best qualified of any our Country affords for the arduous undertaking." Mrs. Jay assured Mrs. Morris of the "universal satisfaction" which Morris' acceptance had "diffused among the friends of our country." The French Minister, Luzerne, was pleased. "Everybody wants him to accept, and it is thought that this post could not be in better hands." Although he wrote of his "great expectations" in Morris' appointment, Washington was sensible enough to know that it would be a long hard pull to recover "from the labyrinth into which our finance is plunged."[53]

There were many persons who held honest misgivings about the delegation of power to Morris; many of them recognized, however, that the situation demanded some positive action. Nowhere is this quandary revealed in sharper detail than in the spirited letter of William Churchill Houston, a New Jersey patriot, to Thomas McKean of Delaware:[54]

I will frankly confess to you that my mind labours under a Load of Anxiety respecting the Settlement of the Powers of the Superintendent of Finance, and indeed the whole Business of that Department. It appears to me that there is no Alternative. Those Powers, or similar ones, must be vested in some one Person, in Order to extricate our Affairs from the Confusion in which they are at present involved. The Board of Treasury only make bad, worse. To go on in the present Train is *absolutely impossible. A total Stagnation* must soon take place, and Ruin cannot be far off. Were our Affairs in a State of *Beginning,* Powers so extensive would not be necessary; but perplexed, deranged and clogged with Abuses and Mismanagements as they are at present, it really appears to me that less Powers would be altogether unavailing. . . . As to the Gentleman who is elected Superintendent of Finance, I have no great Acquaintance with him, nor more Predilection for him than any other capable and upright Man. He is acknowledged a Man of Abilities and Character, and I believe if he has Time given him will yet retrieve our Affairs, Almost hopeless as they are in that Line. But it is the Trust I speak of and not men. What he has to do cannot be done without efficient Powers, when a less capable Man must have them.

Those people who shared the views of Sam Adams were more critical but still thoughtful. Only on the outer fringe does one find the comments of a few like John Armstrong who spoke of the "high price" of "Bob" Morris and the childlike qualities of Congress in one breath and the dictatorship of Washington in the next.[55] Franklin's shrewd observations with relation to the new position must have caught Morris' eye.[56]

You are wise in estimating beforehand, as the principal advantage you can expect, the consciousness of having done service to your country; for the busi-

ness you have undertaken is of so complex a nature, and must engross so
much of your time and attention, as necessarily to injure your private interests; and the public is often niggardly even of its thanks, while you are
sure of being censured by malevolent critics and bug writers, who will abuse
you while you are serving them, and wound your character in nameless pamphlets; thereby resembling those little dirty insects that attack us only in the
dark, disturb our repose, molesting and wounding us, while our sweat and
blood are contributing to their subsistence.

All of this should not obscure the fact that Morris himself definitely
felt, as he expressed it to Schuyler, the *"necessity,* the absolute *necessity,* of a change in our moneyed system."[57] Assuming that this responsibility should be shouldered by one person, Morris unquestionably
agreed with those who regarded him as the only man capable of setting
the financial house in order. With an eye toward posterity, he carefully recorded the circumstances surrounding his appointment.

This appointment was unsought, unsolicited, and dangerous to accept, as it
was evidently contrary to my private interest, and if accepted must deprive
me of those enjoyments, social and domestic, which my time of life required
and to which my circumstances entitle me; and a vigorous execution of the
duties must inevitably expose me to the resentment of disappointed and designing men, and to the calumny and detraction of the envious and malicious.
I was, therefore, determined not to engage in so arduous an undertaking. But
the solicitations of my friends, acquaintance, and fellow-citizens, a full conviction of the necessity that some person should commence the work of refor-
mation in our public affairs by an attempt to introduce system and economy,
and the persuasion that a refusal on my part would probably deter others
from attempting this work, so absolutely necessary to the safety of our country;—these considerations, after much reflection and consultation with friends,
induced me to write a letter to the President of Congress. . . .

It would have pained Morris if he could have foreseen how near
this passage came to the rubbish heap of a paper pulp mill in an obscure village in France.[58]

That the newly elected Financier recognized the realities of the
overall financial situation seems evident; what influenced him most
profoundly is less apparent. The arguments and counter-arguments
which enveloped the issue of finance and the general economic measures of Congress during the course of the Revolution, the reports of
Congress on finance, especially those of 1780-81, and the discussions of
Congressmen "out of doors" must have played as prominent a part in
his conversation as the pamphlets on financial topics written by his
friend, Gouverneur Morris, and Peletiah Webster. It is also true that
the Financier was conscious of contemporary British economic thought
as embodied in Adam Smith, and at least somewhat informed on the
Bank of England and other financial institutions.

To evaluate or measure how much influence these reports, writers,
or general concepts had upon the newly elected Financier, however, is
a difficult if not impossible task. It has been pointed out earlier in this
volume that Morris' ideas on such questions as commerce, the rela-

tionship between government and business, and money, were set comparatively early. Those convictions came out of his experience, for the most part, and he adopted ideas congenial to that experience. The evidence indicates that Morris' basic concepts on policy were not greatly swayed by others, but that in considering means and measures to implement those ideas he was indebted to external influences.[59]

The most enlightening specific disclosure of Morris' general attitude at this time is his unpublished draft of a letter dated June 15, 1781, to Necker, the French Director-General of Finance, where he describes some of the ills in the nation's financial policy—according to his own views—though he pays less attention to the cures. After paying proper homage to Necker, Morris embarked upon an explanation of the bills of credit. They had been used, and with impressive success, in the colonies before the Revolution; and it was only natural that this resource should be utilized when the conflict began. All that was fine, continued Morris, for "people by Habit were fully prepared to give their Confidence." But the failure to levy taxes which could absorb the emissions resulted eventually in depreciation, despite the fact that the first few emissions passed at par with gold and silver. Gradually this implicit confidence of the people in the public credit— this "precious jewel"—was undermined when it should have been preserved at all costs. As Morris saw it, the embargoes and the excessive number of officers and civil servants intensified rather than relieved this troublesome problem. The Financier acknowledged the limitations which faced the Congress in the early years, however, and conceded that they had done well despite the handicaps. But this did not alter, in Morris' eyes, the present circumstances. "We are likely to become an unruly ungovernable nation [.] the confidence of the people being destroyed, the credit of the government lost, its vigour is of course gone, and this unhappily at a time when exertion is most wanted." [60]

And what remedies were suggested for the sick finances? An ample quantity of "free and open commerce" and a strong measure of "unrestrained liberty of disposing of private property at the pleasure of the owner" must take precedence over other medicines. Add to this a "few wholesome laws" mixed with economy in expenditure, and the cure would soon "bring the minds of the inhabitants to cool reflection, encourage their industry, and restore the necessary confidence to invigorate the measures of government."

Although, as we have seen, the ideas of Morris on commerce and property were deep rooted, this is only a partial explanation for his pronouncement to Necker. Public credit had collapsed; private credit existed. In order to resurrect public credit, it must be harnessed to existing private credit. Thus, individuals and the action of individuals, Morris felt, should be given the freest license to enhance that private credit. In conjunction with this concept, the Financier recognized that the private resources of the country were surprisingly strong:

When I speak of our imbecility and distress, let it be understood of the government of Congress and of the governments of the several states for as to the People individually they are active [,] numerous [,] and tho not rich yet in very good circumstances, except in those parts laid waste by the ravages of the enemy. . . .

It is possible that he mentioned how little of the country had actually been "laid waste" by the enemy in the early spring of 1781, but this cannot be determined because the remaining pages of his draft are missing. The resources certainly were in evidence; the only require-ment was to bring them "to the true point of exertion" by means of a system.

But the resurrection of public credit and the establishment of a "system" could not be completed overnight, observed the Financier. ". . . Method, economy, and punctual performance of contracts" had to precede it. "Time is necessary to each; and therefore the removal of those evils we labor under can be expected from time only. To hold out a different idea would deceive the people, and consequently injure the public service." Robert Morris, never a person who was subject to inertness, obviously intended to make this lag as brief as possible, for his first measure to promote the resurrection of public credit was hurried to Congress three short days after his acceptance of office. It had been a long time since the Republican audience had witnessed such a flurry of activity.[61]

CHAPTER — FOUR

The Immediate Policies of the Superintendent of Finance

ON HIS RETURN TO PUBLIC OFFICE IN THE CAPACITY OF SUPERINTENDENT of Finance, Robert Morris inherited the crisis which had arisen in the winter of 1780-81, the near collapse of the public credit of the central government. At the outset Morris faced this situation by devising expedients in order to salvage the crumbling financial structure; in time he proposed a long-range program to establish the finances of the government, and in effect the Confederation itself, upon what he considered to be a secure foundation. Being confronted by a condition, however, did not cause Morris to lose sight of his fundamental purpose.

The first major action of the Financier, submitting a proposal for a national bank, is the most reliable evidence of this purpose, but the fact that its implementation in the first months of the new financial administration was subordinated to immediate needs indicates the nature of his early policies and decisions. Although the duties of two additional positions held by Morris, the one as Agent of the Marine and the other as Agent for the State of Pennsylvania, tended to emphasize the immediate, the unsatisfied requirements of the army was the most important element which determined the earliest policies. To provide supplies, to make arrangements for transportation, to find means to meet present obligations—these were the burdensome problems dominating, and at the same time limiting, the actions of Morris. Until the pressure of these needs had diminished, it was difficult if not impossible for Morris to concentrate on a long-range program.

The idea of some kind of bank was figuratively "in the air" at this time. The colonials had been experimenting with such institutions during most of the eighteenth century, and the Revolution permitted a freer expression of those ideas. Under the pressures of the financial problem, Congress itself debated the wisdom of a central bank, and Peletiah Webster and Gouverneur Morris were numbered among the many who advocated such a measure. Alexander Hamilton, the future

Secretary of the Treasury, sent a long letter to Morris which not only discussed the advantages of a bank but also outlined in detail a plan for its establishment. The only specific measure approaching the concept of a national institution, however, was the Bank of Pennsylvania set up in 1780. But its purpose was concerned exclusively with the purchase of supplies for troops rather than with the functions of a commercial or national bank.[1]

Morris' plan to establish a bank was submitted to Congress three days after he had accepted the Office of Superintendent of Finance, thus emphasizing the fact that he had been attracted by the idea for some time and that the need for such a measure, in his judgment, was impelling. The plan called for a subscription of $400,000 in shares of $400 each "to be paid in gold or silver," but provision was made to enlarge the capitalization. Twelve directors were to guide the bank in its operations, and a president would be selected from among the directors. In this choice, one share equalled one vote. A very important section of the proposal asked for the issue of bank notes which would be payable on demand. Further, these notes "shall by law be made receivable in the duties and taxes of every State in the Union, and . . . by the treasury of the United States, as specie." The entire operation of the bank would come under the close scrutiny of the Superintendent of Finance. He was "to examine into the affairs of the bank" at all times, and this meant "access to all the books and papers." Last, but not least, the bank was to be incorporated under the name of Bank of North America. In the letter which accompanied the plan of the bank, the Financier asked for a prohibition of all other banks "at least during the war."[2]

What Morris proposed, therefore, was a private bank under governmental auspices that would in turn serve the government as a national bank. As he observed: "The public will have much connexion with the bank, and at times deposit considerable sums of money in it, and always be availing themselves of its credit." Here, then, was an instrument to revive public credit by enhancing the aggregate private credit as drawn together under the Bank of North America. This did not mean that private interest would be subordinated to public interest. The two would march hand in hand and be so successful that subscribers to the bank would clamor for more shares of stock. As Morris remarked: ". . . It is not doubted but every subscriber will increase his capital in the bank so soon as he finds not only the national advantages it will produce, but sees clearly his private interest advanced beyond his most sanguine expectations."[3]

Morris realized that the capitalization of the bank would not answer completely the purposes of government. "It is . . . evident at the first view," he wrote, "that four hundred thousand dollars are not sufficient for those purposes, nor those of private commerce, because no considerable circulation of paper can be founded on so narrow a basis. . . ." But to provide a bolder design and require a much larger capitalization in order to satisfy all the needs entailed great risks. "To ask more than could be obtained would have a fatal effect," Morris observed. He conceived $400,000 to be attainable. If it proved far short of the possible resources to be tapped, the remedy would be simple and easy —enlarge the subscription.[4]

Acting with unusual speed, Congress passed a resolution approving the plan on May 26, together with subordinate resolutions to implement it. The only opposition seemed to arise when Lowell and Ward of Massachusetts, Smith of Pennsylvania, and Madison of Virginia voted against the provision on incorporation. The final vote, however, was overwhelmingly in favor of Morris' proposals. Indeed, the bank plan did not seem to create much of a stir in Congress. Perhaps the proposal coincided with the thinking of most members of Congress; certainly their letters are void of any significant comments on the Bank of North America at this time.[5]

With the assurance of Congressional support, the Financier's arguments in favor of the bank, in his public as well as private correspondence, took on a bolder and, to some extent, a more definite tone. In an address "To the Public," in which subscriptions were solicited, the Superintendent of Finance defined precisely the role of the bank in governmental operations. First of all, the government was to derive great advantages from the institution, and consequently should lend it wholehearted support. Support of the Confederation by sufficient revenue from the states was the first object, of course, but obtaining the revenues would require time. Meanwhile the government had no credit on which to operate, for the confidence of the people had been lost. "The use, then, of a bank is, to aid the government by their monies and credit, for which they will have every proper reward and security. To gain from individuals that credit, which property, abilities and integrity never fail to command. To supply the loss of that paper money . . . and to give a new spring to commerce. . . ." For the subscribers, the prospects were equally pleasing. "They will receive that advantage from this investment of their capital which has invariably attended the business of banking in every free commercial country."[6]

In corresponding with his friends Jay and Franklin, Morris was even more explicit. "Among those things which, after the experience and example of other ages and nations, I have been induced to adopt, is that of a national bank," he wrote Franklin. "I mean to render this a principal pillar of American credit, so as to obtain the money of individuals for the benefit of the Union, and thereby bind those individuals more strongly to the general cause by ties of private interest." Morris was hopeful that Franklin could interest the French bankers in the plan and perhaps establish a credit for the bank in Europe. The Financier also confided that he intended to increase the $400,000 subscription gradually to "ten times that sum."[7]

The Financier wrote Jay with equal candor. Although he repeated some familiar arguments, he elaborated particularly on the role of bank notes. Depreciation had sharply curtailed the availability of ac-

ceptable currency for commerce and taxation, observed Morris. If taxes
were levied and collected under these circumstances, injury and distress might be inflicted upon the "men in the community." Not only
would the bank notes help to avert this situation, but they would also
supplant all other currency, thus relieving the people "from those
doubts and anxieties which have weakened our efforts, relaxed our industry, and impaired our wealth." It was absolutely necessary to have
some paper, Morris stated, otherwise "our commerce would suffer for
the want of that facility in money transactions which paper alone can
give." Bank notes circulating at par would help to carry out this essential function. Other considerations favorable to the government would
be realized, according to Morris. By combining the credit of numerous
individuals in this institution, the financial resources accessible to the
government would be augmented significantly. And Morris was sufficiently concerned with his "one very strong motive" to repeat it for
the benefit of Jay. The bank, he emphasized, would serve "to unite
the several States more closely together in one general money connexion, and indissolubly to attach many powerful individuals to the
cause of our country by the strong principle of self-love and the immediate sense of private interest." Here, indeed, were delineated all
the arguments which were raised in support of the Hamiltonian bank
scheme a decade later.[8]

News of the bank plan gained wide circulation immediately. Most
of the citizens throughout the states first learned that Morris was
Superintendent of Finance by reading the plan as it was published in
their respective newspapers. As early as June 18, within a month of
adoption, the news was heralded in Boston by publication of the complete plan in the local *Boston Gazette and Country Journal* even
though newspaper space was limited. Rendon, the Spanish observer in
America, also included the plan when reporting to his superiors.[9]

Publicity and a lively interest in the project were highly desirable,
but it was money which would move the wheels of finance; the bank
scheme needed to be implemented. Subscriptions trickled in slowly,
but it took time to establish faith in this new venture. To encourage
the fulfillment of the subscription, every possible impediment was removed. When the Financier thought that the debt which Congress
owed to the subscribers of the Bank of Pennsylvania hindered the
process, he proposed that Congress pay this debt and at the same time
give him jurisdiction over the bills of exchange which they had retained as security. Congress honored Morris' request immediately, as if
enjoying its break with the past when delegated authority had been so
jealously scrutinized.[10]

Morris entertained the prospect of acquiring specie outside of the
United States to inaugurate the bank. He had urged this action on
Franklin and the Paris bankers, but his hopes rested primarily on
Spain via Havana. Spain, thought Morris, had hesitated to carry
some of her West Indian treasure to Europe for fear of the British
squadrons. Now, he reasoned, this specie could be shipped to the

United States and considered as a loan from Spain, especially since that country would incur no hardship because expediency already restricted her use of these funds. A project to bring Spanish money from Havana, therefore, would benefit everyone concerned.

Under secret orders from the Financier, the *Trumbull,* Captain James Nicholson commanding, sailed for Havana in July. She carried a cargo of flour, bills of exchange on Madrid, important letters to Navarro, Governor of Cuba, and Robert Smith, an old acquaintance of Morris who had been newly appointed United States consul at Havana. Morris hoped to receive $400,000 from the Spanish Governor which would double the capital in the Bank of North America and consequently multiply its effectiveness. The bills of exchange would pay for a part of the sum, the cargo of flour would add a mite, but Morris banked on friendship and the future promise of flour to secure the balance. Unfortunately the mission was never completed. The British cruisers—which were exceptionally successful at this time— captured the *Trumbull* and with her the hopes of the Financier to augment the bank's capital in the immediate future. The capture of that vessel, Morris wrote later, was a great loss to the public and a distressing blow to his promising plan. "However, we have learnt to bear losses and endure disappointments and what is still better we have courage always to try again. . . ." Still, the fate of the Havana scheme reflects the fate of the Financier's attempts to effect any long-range policies at the beginning of his administration.[11]

With the exception of the bank, Morris did not propose any general program of finance during the first months he held office. Part of the explanation lies within Morris himself. Although he grasped the essentials with respect to public credit and envisioned the bank as an instrument to resurrect that confidence, the Financier failed to work out a full-scale program to complement and supplement his general objectives. Morris readily recognized this to be the case. After writing a long letter to Jay analyzing the requirements from Spain—a letter written for the eyes of the Spanish Court—Morris asserted in a private note: "I would gladly now give you details of our situation and plans for reforming it; but I have not yet sufficiently obtained the one nor matured the other."[12]

Why the delay? First, it took some months before the Financier began to comprehend completely the problems which confronted him and the possibilities of his new position. A second factor, and an important one, was the conglomeration of duties which were heaped upon him from the outset; they diverted his attention from policy-making to expedients. A third factor centered on the needs of the army; everything was subordinated to the summer campaigns which eventually led to the fateful siege of Yorktown in the fall of 1781. Until these matters were disposed of, long-range policies would have to wait.

★ ★

Two of Morris' most important duties, apart from the position of Superintendent of Finance, were those he performed as Agent of Penn-

sylvania and as Agent of the Marine. Morris had not only been called
on to assist in righting the federal finances, but also those of his native
state, a summons to which he responded with little reluctance. During
the entire Spring he had battled for the repeal of the tender and penal
laws in Pennsylvania. In fact, his stand on these questions was so determined that he did not take the oath of office as Superintendent of
Finance until this objective had been achieved. At that time he had
also urged—and apparently with great effectiveness—more efficient
taxation.[13]

On the 25th of June, after Morris had accepted the post of Financier but before he had actually taken the oath, the assembly of Pennsylvania assigned him extensive powers. He was to procure the specific
supplies required of the state by Congress, and he was to pay into the
national treasury, for the credit of Pennsylvania, paper bills of credit
emitted under the funding resolution of March 18, 1780. In order to
fulfill these tasks, he was authorized to be the sole drawer of warrants, countersigned by the President or Vice-President, on the state
treasurer.[14]

Morris took on this additional task of procuring supplies for Pennsylvania with characteristic energy. Some of the first supplies were
furnished by two of his friends, Philip J. Schuyler and Thomas Lowrey,
but the largest proportion was obtained by means of contracting. Individuals would make engagements with the Financier to supply the
military posts in Pennsylvania at a specified sum per ration. The
money paid to the contractors from the fund furnished by Pennsylvania would be credited to the state as payment toward its share of
the Congressional requisitions for specific supplies. By August 1781,
the system was in operation throughout most of the state.[15]

Meanwhile Morris as Agent for Pennsylvania became sorely pressed
for funds. This situation was due in part to the large number of engagements which had been incurred, but more important was a decision by Congress to draw upon the respective state treasurers for the
four-tenths of the paper emission due them under the Congressional
funding act of March 18, 1780. It was true that Morris had been
ordered to provide for the payment of this sum; the timing of Congress' action, however, was scarcely propitious. The fund on which the
Pennsylvania legislature had authorized Morris to draw was composed
of new bills of credit which had been issued with land as security.
Although the land value exceeded the value of the bills, and despite
the fact that only 130,000 pounds (Pennsylvania currency) of the authorized 500,000 pounds had been issued, these bills had depreciated.
In view of the circumstances, Joseph Reed, President of the Executive
Council of Pennsylvania, saw no alternative except additional issues
of the state paper even though such a decision would make further
depreciation inevitable. Reed "deplored" such depreciation, but he
thought the case was of such magnitude that it was "beyond the reach
of private credit"—in other words, beyond the ability of Morris. Assuming a contrary position, the Financier opposed further issues of

bills of credit under such conditions. As an expedient he proposed a rather intricate system of drawing bills on Franklin with a design of gaining additional time to make the payments—in short, bill kiting. This plan of Morris' was delayed; by late August it had apparently been abandoned.[16]

By that date, August 1781, the financial stringency of the Agent of Pennsylvania had been somewhat relieved. Morris had pledged his personal credit to the amount of some $80,000 for flour and for other payments to the contractors. Moreover, the bills of credit, which had been gradually appreciating, reached the point where two dollars of paper bought one of specie. Morris did not fail to point out, in reporting these engagements to the President of the Executive Council of the state, that if the flour had been paid for at the time of the purchase, the payments would have been made in bills of credit selling at five, six, and even seven for one; now payments would be made at two for one. His operations and the use of his personal credit, Morris correctly asserted, benefited the state by saving it a considerable amount of money. To fulfill these engagements and to take advantage of the savings, Morris urged the effective collection of taxes, a recommendation which met a surprisingly successful response.[17]

In time other expenditures rose to becloud these promising prospects for complete relief. In September, a decision was made to call out the militia because of a possible threat from General Clinton and his British forces at New York. Morris, who was busy attempting to curtail expenditures, opposed such a move unless more definite signs of Clinton's plans were perceptible. Perhaps the militia might live up to Joseph Reed's earlier appraisal: "My people [the militia]," he had written, "behave with a regularity and discipline beyond anything I ever saw in militia. A flock of chickens would go untouched thro the camp." Still, the militia had to be fed and a few of them might require a musket or two. Morris eventually went along with the plan to call out the militia, but he did so with reluctance. Indeed, after Yorktown he used his influence with everyone he knew to dismiss the militia as an unnecessary expense—a move which produced additional friction between Reed and the Financier.[18]

The work of Morris as Agent of Pennsylvania was confined almost entirely to his first year in office, though some of it, such as settling the accounts of Pennsylvania on specific provisions, carried over into 1782. But his actions in his native state, to a limited extent, do foreshadow in miniature a part of the program he later introduced on a national level. Such diversion, however, delayed formulation of a long-range national program.[19]

Acting as Agent of the Marine was another duty which Morris performed outside the Office of Finance. Congress had provided for a Secretary of the Marine at the same time it had created a Superintendent of Finance, but the position had never been filled. General McDougall had been elected to the post; the stipulations which the General had laid down as prerequisites, however, were unacceptable to

Congress. A movement to place this department under Morris' jurisdiction came up in July, but it proved abortive. Formal action was
postponed until September 7, 1781, when Morris was appointed as acting Agent of the Marine.[20]

The delegation of power to the Agent of the Marine was limited. It
did not authorize him to fit out vessels, much less to determine their
orders. These decisions were to remain with Congress, while the Agent
of the Marine was merely to execute their wishes. But Morris always
leaned towards a broad interpretation of authority; he had, in fact,
undertaken some of the duties which would normally fall to a Secretary of the Marine long before he actually received his most recent
appointment. The *Trumbull* had been sent out under his orders, and
he had prepared the *Alliance* and the *Deane* for cruises. He had also
urged Congress to complete the 74-gun ship *America*. Some of these
actions transcended his explicit duties by a generous margin, but Morris circumvented any trouble with Congress by informing that body
that he had taken the liberty to outfit the two vessels while matters
had been "pending." If Congress had any express wishes, he hoped
they would communicate them. "On the other hand if it is intended
that I should employ these ships from time to time as may to me appear most for the public interest, I shall submit whether it might not
be proper that such intention should be explicitly declared." Congress,
in sheer abandon of its customary position on delegated power, again
responded with a resolution which gave him the authority for which
he asked.[21]

With that license, a veritable flood of correspondence issued from
the Agent of the Marine. Though naval affairs stood at a low ebb,
Morris sought to infuse "system" into the department. Most of the
orders centered on preparations to dispatch the *Deane* and the *Alliance* to sea. John Brown, the former Secretary to the Admiralty Board,
Governor John Hancock of Massachusetts, John Bradford, and Tench
Francis were enlisted to dispatch the vessels with haste; cruising orders
were dispatched to Captain John Barry. Morris also prepared to close
the offices which had existed under the previous administration of the
Admiralty Board, and took preliminary measures to settle the accounts
up to the time he assumed office. Some opposition to this move developed within the department, and the deputies of Morris were unable to obtain the books. However, most of these obstacles were eventually disposed of.[22]

Although Morris' work as Agent of Pennsylvania and as Agent of
the Marine continued to demand much of his time, they were merely
offshoots of his major task, fulfilling the needs of the army during the
summer campaigns and especially during the all-important operation
against Cornwallis' forces at Yorktown.[23]

When Morris accepted the job of Superintendent of Finance, he had
not intended to participate in the task of supplying the army. Indeed,

he specifically informed Congress in his letter of acceptance that it should expect very little from him in the ensuing campaigns. But the demands of the army became so critical that Congress was soon urging Morris to take some action.[24]

The distress in the army, which had never been fully relieved since the winter of 1780, continued to persist everywhere. Many commissary agents echoed the experience of David Duncan, a purchasing agent for troops at Fort Pitt, when he complained that creditors had become so insistent that he did not dare "to pet [sic] my head out of doors." It was Washington's plea, however, which brought Morris into the struggle for supplies. "If there is not a very great and sudden change of measures," the Commander-in-Chief had insisted, "it will be next to impossible to keep the army together." At the same time that Washington wrote Congress, he dispatched General Heath to the New England states with a disturbing message. Unless salted provisions and beef cattle were provided, "the Garrison of Fort Schuyler must inevitably, that of West Point may probably *fall,* and the whole Army be disbanded." [25]

But the strongest argument that spurred Morris to act was a resolution of Congress which gave Washington the express power to impress supplies. The Financier, after conferring with a Committee of Congress on Washington's earnest appeals and "reflecting on the nature of the motion made in Congress," immediately dispatched letters to his friends Philip J. Schuyler and Thomas Lowrey, asking them to purchase 1,000 barrels of flour at once for the use of the army. To grease the wheels of action, Morris pledged his personal credit in hard money. As he explained to the Commander-in-Chief: "I found myself immediately impressed with the strongest desire to afford you relief and also to avoid such measures as are proposed in the said motion. . . ." [26]

These efforts were successful, but they merely marked the beginning. Throughout the summer and fall the Financier's primary concern was directed toward the army. In order to fulfill his commitments, Morris marshaled those men with whom he was familiar. John Holker, his partner in several private enterprises; Matthew Ridley, his personal friend and business acquaintance; William Turnbull, his partner in private business affairs; Jonathan Hudson and Stephen Stewart, both associated with Morris—all figured prominently in implementing the measures of the Financier to support the army in the important campaigns of 1781.

Why did Morris choose these men? First, he knew them intimately and apparently respected their ability to carry out his wishes. Second, the location of these associates coincided with movement of troops and supplies in the Yorktown campaign. Third, when Morris pledged his credit to these men, he was in reality pledging his personal share of their private business and thus extending the effectiveness of his private credit. Fourth, the Financier unquestionably believed that the combination represented by these men—that is, personal business partners as well as agents of the government—could be counted an asset rather than a liability. After all, did not private enterprise and public welfare to all intents and purposes work together for good?

In August and September, as the pitch of the campaign heightened, Morris was inundated in work. The Financier met with a Committee of Congress and the Board of War to determine the requirements of the campaign. At the conference, it was decided that Morris and Richard Peters of the Board of War should confer with Washington on "proposed numbers and arrangements of the army for the next campaign." Upon arrival at the General's headquarters, they preached the doctrine of economy in the military establishment. But their advice did not meet a ready reception at this juncture, for the higher command was already involved in extensive plans for the Yorktown campaign. In fact, the cry was for increased rather than curtailed expenditures; Washington requested aid to obtain supplies and vessels for troops at the Head of Elk, a strategic center in the proposed Virginia expedition.[27]

The Financier adjusted his plans to those of the army. After his return from camp, Morris immediately began to make preparations for the oncoming troops. He wrote to his friend Matthew Ridley at Baltimore and instructed him to purchase 3,000 barrels of flour. Characteristically, the instructions were complete to the smallest detail. He also ordered Ridley to hire "as many bay craft as you can" to transport the flour, other supplies, and troops. A few days later he elaborated on the matter of transportation when he directed Ridley, Donaldson Yeates, the Quartermaster of Maryland and Delaware, and William Smith of Maryland, to act jointly in executing his orders. The Financier wanted the boats assembled at the Head of Elk on the fifth of September ready to transport some 6,000 to 7,000 troops. Speed, economy, and credit formed a triumvirate of key words in the operation.[28]

Meanwhile Ridley's flour purchases were going relatively well, although some farmers and millers seemed reluctant to sell because of an anticipated increase in prices. To Morris, the hopes of this group seemed absurd. "What can put it into the heads of either farmers or millers that prices are to rise? . . . if your ports were open, all the shipping that belongs or resorts to America could not carry it [the wheat] off if employed solely in that business. . . ." Besides, he added, the scarcity of hard money precluded a rise in prices.[29]

The governors of Maryland and Delaware were urged to fulfill their requisitions and were told to deliver all supplies to the Commissary General. Morris warned the Agent of Maryland that "the calls for flour and fresh beef will be immediate and constant . . ." and he hoped he would be able to answer the "pressing demands which will speedily be made upon you." It was essential that these states act swiftly, for they were not only "particularly concerned" in this campaign, but the *argumentum ad horrendum,* a "military collection," would confront them unless their "timely efforts . . . spared the necessity." Morris found these arguments equally useful in soliciting the aid of his business associates.[30]

While the Americans were hurriedly obtaining supplies, so were the French, with the result that their combined purchases tended to raise the price of commodities and lower the rate of exchange on French bills. It was almost commonplace for French bills to sell at one-third discount. This tendency worked a hardship on the nation because one-third of the value of its available funds in France was lost as a result of the discount. Morris tried to remedy this situation by setting a minimum rate on bills. Before going to Washington's headquarters, he made an agreement with the French minister to peg the rate at a price which would not exceed a 20 per cent discount; however, the understanding never worked out effectively in practice. When at camp, the Financier also attempted to reach an agreement with Rochambeau on a single group of commissaries or agents for both armies in order to help stabilize the purchasing situation; but the French were satisfied with their own system, and the suggestion was never implemented. Thus the twin problems of competing purchasing groups and of a declining rate on bills of exchange continued to plague Morris during the campaign.[31]

When Washington, Rochambeau, and their respective staffs were gaily welcomed to Philadelphia on their way to the siege of Yorktown, the tempo of activity was stepped up. At Morris' invitation, the two chiefs stayed with him in Philadelphia, and the series of busy conferences which followed were interrupted by a minimum of social affairs. In fact, the first week found the Financier so engrossed "in assisting the intentions and movements of the Commander-in-Chief" and "in hearing the applications of every department" that he was unable to keep up his Official Diary. The letters sent and the conferences attended fully amplify such testimony. If Morris harbored any doubts about the fruits of this joint effort, a reassuring letter from General Anthony Wayne must have encouraged him. Unless something "uncommon" happened, the General from Pennsylvania wrote hopefully, Cornwallis was doomed.[32]

Morris maintained a constant barrage of correspondence with individuals and with the various governors, all with an intent to draw forth their best efforts. The governors of New Hampshire and New York were censured by the Financier because they failed to supply the cattle drivers with money to care for the herds in the long drive to the South. Measures to hurry along Washington's meat supply—which was traveling under its own power—were urged upon the governor of New Jersey. Timothy Pickering, the Quartermaster General, continued to send Morris a small but steady stream of letters requesting decisions on purchases and, of course, money. That part of the army which was grouped around New York under the command of General Heath also demanded attention; the amount of rations issued exceeded expectations, while the contrary was true of incoming supplies. In this instance, Morris called on his friend William Duer, a well-known New York business man, to supply the needs of Heath's troops, but more than one obstacle intervened before the transaction was finally com-

pleted. The promptness of the Financier's response to most requests—
something unusual for an army regardless of time or place—and his
willingness to act planted an important seed of confidence in many of
the department heads of the army for the first time in several years.[33]

In addition to the major demands, literally dozens of minor matters
claimed the Financier's every moment. An unceasing cry for money
from every department head, every soldier, every officer, and every
creditor of the government fell upon him. Applicants for money would
waken him at six o'clock in the morning, and the calls seldom let up
during the remainder of the day. "It seems as if every person connected in Public Service entertained an opinion that I am full of
money," Morris inscribed in his Diary, "for they are constantly apply-
ing even down to the common express riders and give me infinite interruption so that it is hardly possible to attend to business of more
consequence." Indeed, the pressure of events, the stimulation of a
great crisis, the multiple duties and the broad scope of authority
brought back memories of the days when Morris represented Congress
in Philadelphia in 1776. Only this time Robert Morris dominated the
stage.[34]

Some of the actions of the Financier exceeded his delegated authority, at least as far as the original deputization of power was concerned.
But Congress had expressly ratified his earliest actions, though they
had been taken extralegally if strictly construed. They had granted
him the power over the Marine, of course, and they knew of his post
as Agent of Pennsylvania. The scope of his powers had also been enlarged by frequent resolutions. A considerable extension of powers
had, therefore, taken place by a combination of need, assumption, and
Congressional ratification both explicit and implicit. If this same attitude should prevail in the introduction of a far-reaching, long-range
economic program, it would constitute an important precedent of
authority.

Where did the Financier obtain the funds to meet all these engagements? Except for some money furnished by Pennsylvania for specific
supplies, the states contributed no cash. It was the French who supported the Financier. Despite the sincere threats in January and February that further aid was out of the question, the French purse strings
seemed unusually lax after the crucial year got under way. They eventually responded with a gift of 6,000,000 livres, and loan of 4,000,000
more—a total of approximately $2,000,000. In addition they promised
to furnish the credit for a loan from Holland of an equal amount.
Most of this money, however, was used in France by Franklin to
answer the bills which had been drawn by Congress before Morris
came into office, and an important sum had also paid for war materials, purchased by John Laurens in Holland.[35]

Only a fraction of the money made available by France, therefore,
was at the disposal of the Financier. Luzerne, the French Minister to
the United States, had offered to place 200,000 livres at Morris' disposal even before Morris had accepted the Office of Superintendent of

Finance, an indication that the two men were on friendly terms. Later, the Financier was advised that he could draw an additional million—although he understood the authorization as two million. He concluded by drawing on Le Couteulx, whom he had instructed Franklin to employ as American bankers, for approximately 1,200,00 livres, and on Grand, Franklin's preference as a banker, for an additional 400,000 livres. Thus, the Financier received some $300,000 from the French bills placed at his disposal which paid for approximately 50 per cent of the expenditures. The remaining 50 per cent was eventually supplied by a combination of the funds from Pennsylvania, the sale of goods captured at Yorktown, and the use of some of the $450,000 in specie which arrived from France as part of the loan from that country. Indeed, the strategic appearance of the specie from the French court put the Financier in the choice position of not only balancing his budget but also providing a handsome $300,000 surplus. This balance figured importantly in the long-range program introduced later.[36]

With the happy conclusion of the Yorktown campaign, the Financier could direct his attention to other important problems, for, from his point of view, it had been only an episode in the financial fortunes of the newly established nation. His major concern was the formulation of a long-term program. This matter weighed upon the Financier's mind during the summer and early fall; still it remained to be seen whether his ideas could be translated into definite form. More than that, if a program were developed, it would have to be molded with an eye toward domestic rather than foreign support; Luzerne in his communications with Congress had made that point clear. ". . . The King has done on this occasion what he can do no more," he had asserted. "An exertion like the present cannot be repeated." All this emphasized the fact that the most significant period of the Financier's administration was about to begin.[37]

CHAPTER — FIVE ❖❖❖❖❖❖❖❖❖❖❖❖❖❖❖❖❖❖❖❖❖❖❖

The Morris Program: A Financial Plan
for the New Nation

THE GOOD NEWS FROM YORKTOWN DID RELIEVE THE FINANCIER OF SOME
of the most insistent demands, but he continued to be harrassed by
minor detail. His Diary amply recorded the stream of applications for
money, the numerous conferences with Congress and the army, the
vast number of inquiries with respect to adjusting accounts, and the
minute as well as major problems of supplying the army. He was
called upon to decide not only what cattle were to be sold but also
whether the tallow on the slaughtered animals was to be weighed
separately; he attempted to find a mare which a fine "old gentleman"
had loaned to the service; and he was asked to ease the army's shortage
of paper, a condition which had become so distressing, in the eyes of
several high-ranking officers, that Hughes, the Deputy Quartermaster,
wrote: "There is no keeping the ground any longer without a supply. . . . The General is exceedingly importunate. He says it will not
be practicable to govern the army any longer without paper. . . ."[1]

Persons with varied interests, observing the Financier at work in
these months, might note separate incidents. Some would be shocked
by Morris' pronounced favoritism, even though authorized by Congress, in supporting the payment of large sums to William Bingham
and John Ross, his friends and past partners, for old debts from a depleted Treasury, while others in similar circumstances were turned
away. Some might be fascinated by the attempt of Samuel Bean of
New York City to open a correspondence with Morris that might "hit
on" a solution "for the mutual advantage" of England and America;
still others would be equally intrigued by the Financier's gentle but
firm reply. "It is neither in your power nor mine," he wrote, "to render
them mutual service untill certain points are settled and this is not
the proper channell for discussing those points." The correspondence,
in consequence, should be ended, but "with this assurance, that when-
ever this nation shall be at peace with yours you will find me ready,
not only to correspond but also to render you any service in my
power." Several interested spectators might share the sadness of Robert

and Molly Morris when their two eldest sons, but little lads, left America to be educated in France. Still others might fret with Molly that her husband's health would be overtaxed by "his herculean labors." [2]

Underneath all of this detail, however, a most significant program was taking shape—the formulation of a long-range financial policy with important political, economic, and social ramifications. It was a painful, plodding, almost imperceptible process, and sometimes the outer fringes of the plan were fuzzy even in the eyes of Morris. But the policy was deliberate. Morris begins speaking of "general arrangements" early in the fall of 1781, and by the following spring a full-fledged program is in operation. There is no single document which includes the overall program, and no blare of trumpets to announce its completion. Yet administrative reorganization to encourage the more effective operation of the Treasury Department, policies to augment the collection of revenue, and basic changes in the methods used in the expenditure of monies in order to introduce a measure of economy were all included within its far reaching orbit. These three goals revolved around the unchanging basic objective of the Financier, the revival of public credit by the use of private credit. [3]

In this chapter, there will be an examination of those parts of the program presented by Morris that involve administrative reform, that concern specific means introduced to revive the public credit—the Bank of North America, the notes issued under the signature of the Financier, and a national mint—and finally, that touch upon the beginnings of a plan to fund the debts of the Confederation. In the chapter following there will be an examination of those parts of the program more directly concerned with the revenue and expenditures.

One of the earliest forecasts of a comprehensive program was the reorganization of the Treasury Department. In fact, a smooth-functioning administrative system to shift the burden of minor detail from the shoulders of the Financier to those of able subordinates was a necessary preliminary to any effort at policy-making. "The variety of business I am obliged to do in detail," lamented Morris, "so engrosses my time that I cannot pay attention to those general arrangements which are the proper objects of my appointment." [4]

Under the old Board of Treasury, the group which had presided over the executive functions of the Treasury before the creation of the Superintendent of Finance, the department had included an Auditor General, a Treasurer, two Chambers of Accounts consisting of three Commissioners in each "Chamber," and six Auditors of the army. There was considerable overlapping in the jurisdiction of each of these branches within the department, and the division of responsibility was not clearly defined. This situation resulted in considerable animosity among various officers which, combined with a hostility between the Treasury Board, the head of the department, and the respective branches, created an atmosphere of distrust and indecision.[5]

Morris' request for a secretary who would be in charge of the clerks touched off the administrative reform. When a committee of Congress consulted him about the request, Morris presented a more drastic reorganization plan which the committee "apparently approved." At least, the resolution reported by the committee, and immediately approved by Congress, embodied a plan "nearly conformable" to the one Morris had originally submitted. This ordinance, although abolishing the entire structure of the Treasury Department and replacing it with the plan that the Financier had suggested, changed the Office of Finance only slightly by the addition of a Secretary to supervise the clerks. Outside the Office, however, a Comptroller, a Treasurer, a Register, and Auditors were established. The Comptroller was authorized to "inspect and superintend the settlement of public accounts, and all subordinate officers concerned therein." Procedures were also carefully defined to audit, hear appeals, and finally register the accounts. The Treasurer was directed to keep strict account of all revenues and expenditures and have them checked quarterly; the Register was to "keep all public accounts." Moreover, "every warrant on the Treasurer [and these warrants could be drawn only by the Superintendent of Finance or Congress] or others shall be entered and countersigned by the Register before it shall be paid." Except for the clerks, all appointments remained in the hands of Congress. That body soon selected James Milligan to be Comptroller; Michael Hillegas, Treasurer; Joseph Nourse, Register; and William Geddes and John D. Mercier, Auditors.[6]

In many respects, the new organization did not alter radically the previous establishment either in form or personnel, but rather improved it. The duties of the officers were defined more precisely, procedure between the various branches of the department were simplified, and the uncertain element of divided responsibility was practically eliminated by appointing single officers to administer functions previously exercised by a group of men. Further improvement resulted from the Financier's systematic management of the department. Subordinate officers were consulted at regular intervals for their opinions about problems pertinent to their branches of the department, or, as the case might warrant, they were called in and instructed to carry out previous policy decisions more effectively. Although most of the men elected to the new positions within the department had held important offices under the Board of Treasury, the absence of bitterness and complaint within the department, which had characterized the preceding years, testified to the effectiveness of the reorganization. It is also evident that the Financier was relieved of many burdensome minor details, thus permitting him to devote most of his energies to policy-making.

Meanwhile, two positions of importance had emerged in the Office of Finance which Congress, and probably Morris, had not anticipated. When Morris became Superintendent of Finance, he was determined to begin his term with a clean slate and avoid any entanglement of accounts or funds with the old Board of Treasury. To make certain that monies placed at his disposal by the order of Congress did not become involved with those belonging to the Board of Treasury, the Financier brought John Swanwick, one of the clerks in his counting house, into the Office of Finance. Swanwick was to act as a "cashier," according to the Financier, "to receive the monies for Bills sold and to pay the same to my order." Later, Swanwick would settle his accounts "with the Treasury Board or other proper public office when such settlements are or ought to be made." What started as a fluid, temporary arrangement solidified into a permanent position, and, for the remaining years of Morris' incumbency, Swanwick was known as the "Treasurer to the Superintendent of Finance." This office had not been provided for by Congress; it was an extralegal creation of the Financier.[7]

John Swanwick apparently was a man who had cultivated his native talents—his knowledge of French and German had been particularly useful in Morris' mercantile establishment—but the fact that his father, Richard Swanwick, was a Tory made the son's patriotism suspect in the eyes of certain critics. The elder Swanwick had resided in America only a short time when the tension between the colonies and the mother country began to develop. Because he owned a farm, valuable furniture and cutlery, and slaves, there is reason to believe that he was a person of means. But Richard Swanwick also committed the unpardonable error of accepting an office under the King—which the son described as "of the most odious Nature"—and when the Revolution actually broke out, he took the side of the Crown and was exiled to New York. His son John, John's mother, and a sister remained in Philadelphia where, according to a petition of neighbors, they remained loyal to the Revolutionary cause. These circumstances, however, put John Swanwick under suspicion, and on occasion the criticism became vocal. Henry Laurens, for example, suspected the younger Swanwick of carrying on a correspondence with his father in New York that transmitted information to the enemy, but an investigation indicated that these misgivings were without foundation. Yet criticism, however baseless, was not entirely stilled, and those who wished to find fault with the Financier might censure either the nature of the position he had created or the reliability of the person who filled it.[8]

The second and more important position created in the Office of Finance was that of an assistant to Morris. Soon after taking the oath of office, the Financier asked Congress for an aide who could assist him in his extended correspondence and in drafting reports. Congress responded favorably to this request, and an assistant was provided at a salary of $1850. Meanwhile the Financier had made a verbal agreement with Gouverneur Morris that, should the post be authorized, it would be his. Indeed, according to the Financier, "he [Gouverneur] has most cheerfully afforded me every advice and assistance which his genius and abilities enabled from my first appointment to this time."[9]

Gouverneur Morris was a precocious, talented person of distinguished lineage whose family had played an important role in New York and New Jersey politics during most of the eighteenth century. In fact, the close relationship of some members of the Morris family with the interests of the Crown prompted many of Gouverneur's close relatives, among them his mother, to remain Loyalist when events forced a choice upon him. Gouverneur himself, a young man in his early twenties, was not always certain whether Independence offered the wisest course, for he did not look with favor upon a general upheaval or excessive "licentiousness," to borrow the Revolutionary phrase; but he cast his lot with the opponents of the King and, in consequence, played a substantial role in the New York legislature and later in the Continental Congress. In both positions Gouverneur displayed a general conservatism and strong inclination toward centralization which was presented skillfully in speech and in writing. Some of his letters, full of quotable and pithy phrases to delight the historian, must be approached with a measure of skepticism, for the New Yorker had a pronounced weakness for the unusual expression—often Biblical—and for the luscious sentence. There are times when he seemed to be as interested in producing an effect as in offering a precise exposition of his views.

Although he was not yet thirty years old when he took up his office as assistant to the Financier, Gouverneur was no neophyte in finance. Very early in the Revolution he had suggested possible modes of financing the war, and in Congress he had served on the Ways and Means Committee, where he had been instrumental in writing a "Plan of the Finances." Gouverneur's ideas on finance, like his views on politics, were somewhat to the right of the Financier's. Gouverneur, in contrast to the Financier, was not a man of wide personal experience in finance and business, and consequently he drew heavily upon his reading and observations.[10]

The relationship between Robert Morris and Gouverneur Morris ripened into a close friendship during the course of the Revolution. When Gouverneur first attended the Continental Congress as a delegate, Morris, in writing to a friend, observed that the New Yorker possessed "first rate abilities." "I think he will be immensely usefull," he continued, "if he pursues his objects steadily (for I have been told his only blemish is being a little too whimsical)." By the time Robert Morris assumed the Office of Finance the two men were firm friends. "Gouverneur is with me and a most useful and able adjunct he is," the Financier wrote to Jay. Some years later Kitty Livingston, who knew the Morrises well, remarked, "His [Gouverneur's] eloquence joined with Mr. R. Morris's judgement would ensure success in every cause." Only time could determine whether such optimism was warranted. Meanwhile Gouverneur's wit, vivacity, and charm lightened many a moment for the Financier, while his sharp intellect and able pen helped to support the burdens of the office.[11]

In the other executive departments, reorganization was being matured by Congress through the appointment of Robert R. Livingston and General Benjamin Lincoln to the respective positions of Secretary for Foreign Affairs and Secretary at War. In the process, old political wounds were reopened, tempers flared, and recriminations were heard. Arthur Lee had been a leading candidate for the position of Secretary for Foreign Affairs, and, according to the Lee partisans, Morris in combination with others, notably the French Minister, had defeated Lee. It is clear that Luzerne exerted pressure to block Lee and, though there is no real concrete evidence, it takes no imagination to know that Morris would oppose Lee. Yet to take the additional step and say that Morris held such enormous prestige and power that he could thwart the will of Congress in the appointment is a tenuous assertion. One suspects that even some of Lee's friends did not relish the prospect of the Virginian, with his lack of tact, in an important position which demanded this quality as a prerequisite. Certainly the evidence indicates that the election of Benjamin Lincoln as head of the War Department was not dictated or determined in any way by the Financier.[12]

Although there is little evidence that Morris determined the appointment of other department heads, there is no question that the Superintendent of Finance overshadowed the other executive departments. Even though his specified powers hardly exceeded those outlined for the other departments, the Financier, in contrast to the others, assumed a positive policy-making role; as a result, the actions of the other departments, for the most part, merely paralleled those of the Financier. In conjunction with this role, Morris initiated an important administrative policy by calling a conference of the leaders "for the purpose of communicating to each other whatever may be necessary and for consulting and concerting measures to promote the service and public good." The Secretary at War, the Secretary for Foreign Affairs, the Commander-in-Chief, the Secretary of Congress, and the Financier's Assistant were included in the group, and they agreed to meet each Monday evening. This group resembled a semiofficial cabinet which convened to grapple with the countless problems involved in policy and to correlate the efforts of the several parts of the government. Because the problems of finance touched all phases of government, these meetings were of particular significance to the Financier.[13]

To provide a sound administrative unit, which the preceding measures of reorganization were designed to accomplish, was essential to the most effective execution of policy in financial affairs. The changes within the department itself permitted it to function more efficiently and smoothly; the creation of a Treasurer within the Office of Finance separated the old measures from the new; the appointment of an Assistant relieved the Financier from a part of the arduous duties which he was called upon to perform; and the meetings of the semiofficial cabinet made it possible for various parts of government to coöperate in measures which touched them all. The emphasis could now be

placed decisively upon long-range policies rather than upon expedients.

★ ★

With administration reorganization clearing the decks for action,
the efforts of the Financier could be concentrated on his primary objective, a comprehensive program to revive the public credit. Although
the Bank of North America, introduced by Morris immediately after
assuming office, took precedence, it was now closely supplemented by
new measures designed to achieve that goal. Issuing notes to replace
the defunct continental currency and proposing the establishment of a
United States mint were important, but the outstanding measure in
the Financier's program on public credit was his plan to fund the
debts of the Confederation. This measure, in his eyes, would place the
credit of the new nation on a secure and permanent footing.

The plan to establish the Bank of North America had not yet been
fulfilled because stock subscriptions had lagged. Throughout the summer Morris had urged everyone, and particularly his mercantile
friends, to participate in the grand experiment. John Langdon, Jeremiah Wadsworth, William Duer, and John Holker were among those
who responded, but the subscription list read very much like a roll call
of the prominent members of the Philadelphia business community.
This is not surprising. Morris' extensive connections in the South were
useless, for that section—Virginia through Georgia—staggered under
the impact of the war's developments in 1781. In the lower South, conditions were such that it is quite understandable to find Governor
Rutledge of South Carolina reporting: "Not a single subscriber could
be found, nor a shilling of money raised." The solicitations of Morris
produced limited results in New York and New England, for he was
neither as well known, nor did he command as much influence, in
those sections. The list of stockholders was also determined by several
additional factors, the proximity of the Philadelphia community to
the seat of government, and the interest and awareness which its merchant groups had shown in a bank. But all these efforts to attract subscribers had yielded only $70,000 of the desired $400,000 when the
welcome news reached Philadelphia that 2,500,000 livres ($450,000)
under the care of John Laurens, the son of Henry Laurens, had arrived at Boston as part of a loan from France. Indeed, this cheerful
information prompted John Nixon and George Clymer, who were in
charge of receiving funds for the bank's capital, to let it be known that
subscriptions would close on October 1, and that an election of directors would take place on November 1.[14]

Meanwhile Morris prepared an expedition to transport the French
specie from Boston to Philadelphia. He decided on an overland rather
than a sea route because he felt it would be safer, despite the rough,
rugged country and the threat of banditti and guerrilla bands and of
possible British regulars. Tench Francis, a brother-in-law of Morris'
good friend and partner Thomas Willing, was placed in charge of the

expedition. This responsibility, thought the Financier, would afford Francis "an opportunity to shew his firm attachment to the cause of America," an attachment which many persons had looked upon rather skeptically. To expedite matters, Morris not only drew up the instructions in characteristically complete detail—the manner in which the carts were to be built and even the preferred age and number of oxen to draw the carts—but he also wrote letters to key persons along the route to enlist their help in protecting the money. Fortunately Francis carried off his crucial mission without any mishap, and early in November his oxen caravan deposited its precious cargo with the Treasurer at Philadelphia, Michael Hillegas.[15]

In order to complete the establishment of the Bank of North America so it could begin operations, the bulk of the French money was immediately used by the Financier to enable the government to subscribe the remaining shares. In this way the Financier was employing public money to establish a financial institution which, though incorporated by the government and under its general inspection, was largely a private institution. What prompted him to use precious public funds in this way? In the Financier's mind, the Bank represented a beneficial combination of private enterprise and public welfare, vital as one of *the* great engines to revive the public credit. The money would serve most advantageously, therefore, by helping to establish it; for the use of the credit facilities and other functions of the National Bank would multiply the effectiveness of the funds tremendously. Little of this full explanation is specifically expressed in Morris' correspondence, but it is implicit in his actions and is assumed in his earlier circulars on the Bank.

In the meantime the Bank was being formally organized, largely at Morris' direction. On the first of November 1781, under his instructions, the subscribers met to elect twelve directors, most of whom Morris knew well, and at least five with whom he had been associated in business. The following day the directors selected as President the long-time friend and business partner of Morris, Thomas Willing. At this meeting, a committee—Samuel Osgood, Thomas Fitzsimons, Timothy Matlack, and James Wilson—was appointed to formulate a "charter of incorporation" and to "digest and report a plan for conducting the business of the Bank." By the end of November the directors had rented the "commodious store" of Tench Francis, who later became cashier, "for holding the bank," and they had arranged for the engraving of bank notes. After long weeks and frequent consultations with Morris, a charter was finally written which met the approval of the directors and, on the twenty-second of December, the directors agreed to present it to Congress.[16]

But the ordinance of incorporation encountered considerable opposition in Congress, almost exclusively on the theory that the Articles of Confederation did not include such a power. Assuredly, there was a substantial basis for such an argument. The Articles not only failed to mention such power explicitly, but no section or phrase could be construed to contain that power implicitly. For constitutional support the advocates of the Bank could rely only on a broad and rather flimsy theory that the United States as a sovereign nation founded upon sovereign states possessed the power to incorporate.

The directors, on the other hand, reasoned that "the promise of a preceding Congress was binding on a subsequent one," and declared that delay would hamper a recovery of the Continental finances. They also pointed out as a complementary argument that the Pennsylvania legislature, which many members believed could provide the Bank with a legal existence to enable it to function in all the states, was not in session and would not convene until late spring. In brief, objections of theoretical unconstitutionality were countered by exploiting the facts of a real situation.[17]

Morris had already urged individual members of Congress to pass the ordinance, but now he threw his full weight into the balance. According to Madison, the Financier not only "reinforced" these considerations but warned that he relied heavily on "this institution as a great auxiliary to his department, and in particular expected aid from it in a payment he is exerting himself to make to the army." Such "reinforcement" was unquestionably important when a final solution was hammered out in a long conference between the directors, a committee of Congress, and the Superintendent of Finance. The result was something of a compromise, with Congress making the most concessions, and, on the last day of 1781, Congress passed an ordinance of incorporation and breathed legal life into the Bank of North America.[18]

The ordinance provided that the corporation could purchase, receive, hold, or sell lands, goods, etc., to the amount of $10,000,000 (Spanish milled dollars); it could sue or be sued, defend or be defended in "courts of record, or any place whatsoever"; it validated the existing organization of president and directors; it provided for considerable latitude in regulations and by-laws provided the Bank did not try to exercise any power "repugnant to the laws or constitution" of any state; and it "ordained" that "this ordinance shall be construed, and taken most favorably and beneficially for the said corporation." No provision mentions bank notes, nor was there any specific period of incorporation. Apparently the first was presumed, for the virtues of these notes had been widely heralded; the second apparently would be contingent upon the continuing approbation of Congress.[19]

Successful passage of the measure, according to the Virginia delegates, depended upon some members of Congress who felt obligated by the action taken in May and upon other members who consented only "from absolute necessity." Madison thought the vote—which unfortunately is not recorded—as one of acquiescence rather than affirmation. There is every indication that surface approval concealed many personal reservations, but it should be stressed that most of these reservations centered around the power of Congress to "ordain" a bank, not on the question of a bank *per se.* When Congress, in a concluding gesture for the old year, recommended that the various state legislatures pass laws to fulfill the ordinance of incorporation, Madison considered the action a "tacit admission of a defect of power" which he hoped would stand as "an antidote against the poisonous tendency of precedents of usurpation."[20]

On the 7th of January the Bank of North America opened its doors, and the following day the Financier broadcast the news by circular letters which fairly glowed with optimism. "I am confident," he wrote the respective governors, "that with proper management it will answer the most sanguine expectations of those who befriend the institution." According to Morris, the Bank would be advantageous to everyone.

It will facilitate the management of the finances of the United States. The several States may, when their respective necessities require and the abilities of the bank will permit, derive occasional advantages and accommodations from it. It will afford to the individuals of all States a medium for their intercourse with each other and for the payment of taxes more convenient than the precious metals and equally safe. It will have a tendency to increase both the internal and external commerce of North America, and undoubtedly will be infinitely useful to all the traders of every State in the Union. . . .[21]

Although the prospects as described by the Financier promised much, the Bank was not sent out to do battle without reinforcement; rather it was supplemented and supported with several important measures. The second means employed by the Financier in an attempt to revive the public credit was the utilization of his personal credit. There can be no question that Morris conceived that his mercantile standing was valuable in carrying out public operations. "My personal credit which thank Heaven I have preserved throughout all the tempests of the War, has been substituted for that which the country had lost," he wrote in a personal letter to Benjamin Harrison, Governor of Virginia. "I am now striving to transfer that credit to the public."[22]

The primary device used by Morris to carry out this policy was a paper issue which became known as "Morris notes." These notes, "numbered, lettered, signed, and directed" by Morris, were drawn on John Swanwick, the cashier of the Office of Finance, for twenty, fifty, or eighty dollars, and made payable "to the Bearer" at sight. A second type of paper issue, warrants drawn on Swanwick by Morris and payable at specified dates rather than at sight, was also used. Despite the differences in the nature of the paper issues, the warrants were often called "Morris notes." It is difficult, as a result, to distinguish between them in the correspondence of the period. That the Morris notes were circulating as early as November 1781 is clear, although the more extensive use of both types of paper issue was apparent somewhat later, when Morris urged their acceptance in the collection of taxes. Indeed, it is possible, although Morris nowhere indicates as much, that the earliest stages might well have been experimental.[23]

The Financier expected that the Morris notes, and possibly the warrants, would provide an essential medium of exchange and facilitate the collection of taxes. The notes issued by the Bank of North America, the Financier had warned previously, would not be sufficient to meet the need for a circulating medium, now that the continental paper had become worthless. The collection of taxes would aggravate this condition by drawing money, already scarce, out of circulation, and the result would work a great hardship on the people. Thus an additional acceptable paper medium would be invaluable. In relation to revenue, the Morris notes would also serve an important purpose by filling in the gap between the laying of taxes and their collection. The notes would establish a credit, circulate as cash, and provide, by purchase, the necessary supplies for current needs; and they would be eliminated gradually as the revenue flowed in from the collection of taxes. The Morris notes, then, in anticipating taxes and in providing an additional circulating medium, would help replace the defunct continental currency.[24]

To add to this circulating medium and to help revive the public credit, Morris advocated a third instrument, the establishment of a national mint. Preliminary steps had been taken very early by summoning Benjamin Dudley of Boston to assay foreign coins and to make plans for the operation and location of a mint. In January 1782, after considerable thought and labor by the Financier and his Assistant, Gouverneur Morris, a proposal was submitted to Congress for consideration.[25]

The essence of the message from the Office of Finance was an argument for an "American coin." To rely on foreign coins as a measure of value would expose the country not only to the tricks of individuals, it was suggested, but also to the influence of a foreign sovereign; indeed, the message strongly intimated that mischief was abroad in the form of "Birmingham artists" who were circulating coins of inferior value. In addition, the well-known differences in money between the various states created a situation which made a knowledge of the various coins "a kind of science." Still a need existed for "small money" in the "common occasions of trade"—a need, it was pointed out with an eye to groups who might support the plan, "more felt by our soldiery than any other persons." If to these reasons is added the "loose state in which our currency has been for some years past," the present moment indeed seemed propitious for setting up a uniform coinage. And how did the mint fit into the Financier's program?

Neither will anything have a greater tendency to restore public credit; for although it is possible that the new money will at first be received with diffidence by some, yet when it has been fairly assayed it will gain full confidence from all, and the advantage of holding the only money which can pay debts or discharge taxes will soon give it the preference over all, and indeed banish all other from circulation.[26]

Judging from the letters of the various delegates, the proposal of a mint apparently awakened little interest in Congress. A Committee of the States did meet with the Financier and Gouverneur Morris in a long session, however, and they voted unanimously in support of the proposal. When the committee report was submitted to Congress it was approved, and the Superintendent of Finance was asked to implement the resolution. Although its adoption completed the list of specific measures advocated by the Financier to resurrect the national credit, there were other proposals on his agenda involving the past obligations of the Union which, in his mind, would secure the credit permanently.[27]

The bank, with its credit facilities and note issues, the Morris notes, and the mint were important ingredients in the Financier's program for restoring public credit, but the most significant element was missing. This was embodied in a single phrase: Funding the debts of the Confederation. "As I consider national credit to be an object of the greatest magnitude and importance," expounded Morris to Luzerne, the French Minister, "so I think it necessary to bend every possible effort to the establishment and support of it. Provision for our debts," he continued, "is . . . the first object and therefore must take place of every other demand."[28]

The Financier, it should be emphasized, initially introduced his program on funding the debts of the new nation because in his mind it offered the best promise of success in the restoration of the public credit of the Confederation. Like the other measures advocated by the Financier, funding was designed to harness existing private credit to the public credit by inducing men with money to lend it to the government in exchange for securities for which the credit of government was pledged. Of course any plan to fund the debts of the nation would arouse various interests, some between states and others between groups interstate in character. In the following years such interests were aroused, but they can be understood only by tracing an important maturation in the ideas of the Financier in correlation with significant developments in political affairs after 1781. It is inaccurate to assume that a full-blown Morris program on funding existed in 1781, or to state that the Financier clearly comprehended all the implications of the program. It is also a mistake to assume that the differences arising in 1782-83 over the question of funding, which will be set out later in this volume, were clearly discernible at the outset. These developments occurred over the course of several years, and strict respect must be paid to chronology if they are to be properly evaluated.[29]

Between 1781 and 1783 the general plans of the Financier on funding matured into a significant program which paralleled that advocated by the Federalists a decade later. At the outset, many of Morris' ideas with respect to funding were muddled, but in time they became distinct; initially, his arguments in support of these ideas were obscure and sometimes confusing, but they became clarified; his purpose began on a note of public credit, but in time it became inextricably involved with important political questions.

Although the Financier had prepared a detailed message in July 1781 on funding the debts of the Confederation, he did not submit it to Congress until November for fear they would be too busy to give it thorough consideration. The great bulk of this first message was concerned with a general settlement of accounts as an indispensable preliminary to any satisfactory plan for funding the debts of the Confederation.

The state of the nation's accounts was little short of chaotic. In Congress, numerous people had served on countless committees and boards that were concerned with expenditures. In the army, various purchasing officers had kept only haphazard records, and those maintained by the separate states were little better. On the surface, of course, the matter of accounts appeared simple. If a commissary officer was allotted money to purchase supplies, for example, he would be held "accountable." But had he actually received the money which had been allotted to him? What was the rate of depreciation of the currency at the time? Was the rate different in his locality than in some other parts of the country? Did he pay too much for the goods which he did purchase? Of course, several years had elapsed, the money had been spent, the supplies had been consumed or lost, and sometimes the officer himself had died. The state of such records was indescribable. In an examination of any accounts between the Confederation and the states, the same surface simplicity disguised a mass of perplexing detail. Supposedly, the states were to be debited for the amount of the requisitions—that is, taxes—which the central government had requested, and credited with the goods and services which they had furnished. But who was to evaluate these goods and services? What allowances must be made for the rate of depreciation? What must be done to fill the absence of figures, the result of shoddy bookkeeping? It hardly needs to be emphasized that no one had more than an uncertain notion as to the relative status of the various accounts; and it requires no imagination to realize why the Financier considered the settlement of these accounts as the indispensable prerequisite to a funding program.[30]

Morris was convinced that an immediate and final settlement of accounts between the states and the Confederation must take precedence. Each state, according to him, was plagued with twin suspicions: one, that it was doing more than its share for the united effort toward Independence, and two, that its present efforts would "drop into forgetfulness." If this continued, Morris asserted, a general lethargy would pervade the states, for they would reason that everything not furnished would be so much saved. Such indifference entailed a host of ills—a failure to summon resources, increased expenses because of the dubious credit standing of the government, and eventually the use of force as a substitute for credit to supply the needs of war. In addition, an endless stream of disputes, more than equal to those already present, would arise in the future between states and the Confederation;

not only would nothing be accomplished, but these disputes would sow the seeds of disunion.[31]

In consequence, the Financier laid down a basic proposition which he called the "Cornerstone of the whole fabrick": the whole expense of war from its commencement until the present should be determined and a definite quota established for each state. But one important exception was made to the "whole expense"—the public debt of the United States.

Rather than offering positive suggestions for determining the respective state quotas, the Financier shifted this delicate and difficult problem upon the shoulders of Congress with a few well-chosen comments on what not to do. He realized that any given quotas would meet with objections—"I know it is not possible to do strict justice"—but, he declared, they must be set nevertheless. Recognizing that it would be impossible, because of the war, to place an immediate evaluation on the lands within the respective states as a basis for assigning the quotas—a method which was called for by the Eighth Article of the newly adopted Articles of Confederation—Morris suggested that the Eighth Article be interpreted to apply to expenditures *after* the Confederation went into effect rather than to past expenses. As for the past Congressional resolutions which referred to this Article as a manner of settlement, Morris stated: "The Confederation itself must receive a liberal and equitable construction; much more so those resolutions which refer to it."[32]

The determination of the whole expense of the war, the other element making up the "cornerstone" in settling accounts, received the Financier's thoughtful attention. By using a table of depreciation previously authorized by Congress, Morris calculated that the assessment upon the states in terms of requisitions amounted to $5,000,000, a sum which he hoped would be apportioned among the respective states according to a quota decided upon by Congress. To determine what goods and services provided by the separate states would be embraced within the "whole expense of the war" and thus considered as a debt of the Confederation was an exceedingly troublesome problem in itself, but it was complicated further because goods and services accepted in this category would be credited to the account of the state which provided them. Morris toyed briefly with the idea that no state charges should be allowed, for, he reasoned, they had paid most of such "charges" in state bills of credit. If the states had not issued this money the same services would have been performed with continental paper, and the expenditures would have been swept away by "the general torrent of depreciation." Quickly discarding this explosive doctrine, the Financier proceeded to outline in detail a mode of settlement for three distinct time periods of the Revolution based upon key Congressional resolutions on requisitions and financing dated November 22, 1777 and March 18, 1780.

In the period up to November 22, 1777, the date of the first money requisition of Congress, all articles furnished by each state, including militia expenses "expressly authorized" by Congress, would be considered as part of the general expenses of the Confederation. This proposal amounted to a limited assumption of state debts by the central government. In terms of each specific state, the articles furnished would be credited to its account with the Confederation; the quota of the whole expense of the Confederation which was assigned to the state would be charged against its account, and a temporary balance would be struck for this first period. The second period, from November 22, 1777, to March 18, 1780, the date of Congress' forty-for-one funding act, would be considered separately, and an account would be made up in which each state would be charged with its quota of the money requisitions, and credited with its advances to the Confederation. The final account would cover the period from March 18, 1780, to the date when Congress first requested specific supplies. The Financier proposed, in addition, that the Congressional funding act be satisfactorily completed by continuing to accept forty dollars of the old continental currency for one of the new, but the new, he stressed, should not be issued "on any pretence." By following this procedure, the state would receive a double credit—one for bringing in the forty dollars of old continental currency and one for the dollar of new currency which was not to be issued. His proposals, asserted the Financier, would permit a final settlement of accounts, allow the proper balances to be placed on interest, and permit measures to be taken which would provide the income to fund these debts.[33]

In this settlement of obligations between the Union and the states, as expounded by the Financier, together with the funding of the balances, several significant observations emerge. First, general rulings were suggested as guides to a final settlement, but little attention was given to spelling out solutions to the almost insurmountable problems which would be encountered in actually settling the accounts. Second, the Financier proposed a limited assumption of state expenses. Third, the message emphasized the state-Confederation relationship, which suggests that the question of funding the "public debts"—that is, obligations, such as foreign loans, entailed by the central government—was assumed. Finally, and most important, the plan presumed that, regardless of the kind of expenses incurred by the separate states which would be considered as part of the "whole expense," the entire total would eventually be apportioned to the various parts—that is, the states—for payment. It was also taken for granted in Morris' report that the Confederation would be the creditor of the states, and thus the states as debtors would be repelled financially from the Union rather than attracted to it. More than that, the individuals within the states who were creditors for goods or services rendered either to the states or to the Union during the war would be compelled finally to look to the states for relief. To reverse this creditor-debtor relationship between the Confederation and the states proved to be a detail of infinite importance.

But why should the "public debts"—that is, foreign loans, loan office certificates, and certificates given for various goods and services—be distinguished from the other debts in a settlement of accounts? The Financier made his position clear some months before. "I have also heard it suggested," he wrote in July 1781, "that the public debts ought to be divided among the several States, and each be called to provide for its proportion." Such a measure, he added, "would be sufficient to destroy the credit of any country." Why such a dogmatic assertion? "The creditors trust the Union, and there can be no right to alter the pledge which they have accepted for any other, even for a better one, without their free consent." Indeed, "there is in it a principle of disunion implied which must be ruinous." Now he reinforced these views with the declaration that the "public debts" were long-term obligations; they "may subsist until the relative wealth of the states has entirely changed. Those who are now most rich may then be poor, and those who are poor may become rich." Furthermore, the creditors enjoyed the "general promise of government," a government of a union of states and not the states individually.[34]

The "public debts," according to the Financier, should be funded by using the income of uniform taxes throughout the United States that could not be diverted to any other purpose and would be payable only in specie. He suggested that a land tax, a poll tax, and an excise be added to the 5 per cent duty on imports, prize goods, and prizes, a measure adopted by Congress before Morris came into office. But interestingly enough, especially in view of the later development of his ideas, the Financier fails to elaborate either on the questions involving these taxes or on the public debts—that is, with one exception.

The exception concerned the commissary and quartermaster certificates which had been used to pay for articles and services received by the public. These certificates should not be consolidated with the rest of the public debt, observed the Financier, because it would be forcing a loan from the people who had received the certificates, "many of whom are unable to make it." To treat such certificates in the same manner as the loan office certificates would be harsh and probably unjust. Although it might be possible to accept some quartermaster and commissary certificates from various states on account of past requisitions in specific supplies, he added, it would be impracticable to receive them as fulfillment of current requisitions, for they would not produce any revenue.

Relying upon these observations, Morris suggested a separate plan to fund the commissary and quartermaster certificates. These certificates would not be received in taxes, and more important, they would not be transferable. It would be best, thought Morris, to have them adjusted by a commissioner appointed by Congress, so that each certificate would genuinely reflect the value of the original article or service. (The Continental officers had been inclined to issue more certificates than the article or service was worth in an attempt to compensate the farmer or artisan for possible depreciation.) If the amount of this settlement were small, a note would be given which would be due in a year. If the settlement were large, it should be divided into five parts, and notes given in exchange whose due dates would be spaced over five years. Bearing six per cent interest, these notes would be made payable to the bearer and thus transferable; they would also be receivable in taxes upon reaching the due date. These general proposals, asserted the Financier, would give a credit to the government and give relief and perhaps an advantage to the individual, while at the same time the measure would constitute only a limited anticipation of the revenue. What Morris might have added was that this plan would sharply curtail all speculation in this type of indebtedness, because the original certificates would not be negotiable, and the original holder would receive his full compensation if the plan were successful. In this proposal, then, there was no attempt to benefit any restricted, wealthy, speculative group at the expense of the "poor debtors." [35]

Although some members had inspected and apparently approved the proposals of the Financier before he submitted them, Congress' reaction was disappointing. A committee, after conferring with the Financier, was willing to recommend that certificates be refused in payment of quotas. No action, however, was taken to fund those certificates; no action was taken to provide additional sources of revenue to fund the "public debt." Even the suggestions for settling the accounts between the Confederation and the states failed to move Congress to act immediately. [36]

In November and December 1781, upon being presented with a new opportunity, the Financier elaborated on his suggestions to determine quotas and to expedite the settlement of accounts. He suggested that each state send one representative to Philadelphia to meet in May of the following year. There, by "Major Voice," the delegates would settle "finally" the apportionment for all the expenses incurred thus far in the war, again "excepting such part thereof as now is, or may hereafter become, a funded debt of the United States." He also proposed that a Commissioner to settle the accounts of each state be nominated by the Superintendent of Finance and approved by the respective state legislatures. Although the Financier fails to emphasize it, his report strongly suggested that some states might be creditors rather than debtors of the United States. [37]

The legislative machinery moved slowly; only after frequent consultations and debates was a basic ordinance agreed upon on January 9, 1782. On the procedures to begin the settlement of accounts, Congress followed the suggestions of Morris closely; on the matter of adjusting quotas, Congress differed. According to the resolution, an individual commissioner for each state, to be nominated by the Superintendent of Finance and approved by the respective legislature, was authorized to settle all accounts of the Confederation within the state, even "certificates given for supplies by public officers to individuals, and other claims against the United States by individuals for supplies furnished the army. . . ." Although the form of the accounts would be under the direction of the Comptroller, all principal rulings would be made by Congress; and the indebtedness for or against a state would be placed on interest at 6 per cent. Congress also tried to follow Morris' suggestions for getting good men by paying an attractive salary of $1,500. With respect to adjusting quotas, Congress, rather than calling for a convention of representatives, asked the states "to empower" that body to determine the quotas "without being wholly confined to the rule laid down in the eighth Article of the Confederation."[38]

A supplementary resolution setting up additional commissioners, and based on supporting recommendations submitted by Morris in the interim, was passed on February 27, 1782. Commissioners to settle the accounts of the major departments—Quartermaster, Commissary, Hospital, Clothier, and Marine—were to be appointed by the Financier with the approval of Congress. In the process, the Financier expressed himself rather strongly on his powers of appointment. "This is an occasion so important, that I can not sacrifice my duty to false notions of delicacy," he asserted. Persons "fit for such an intricate and difficult business can not easily be found, still less can they be known to the several members of Congress." Furthermore, "debates which sometimes take place when appointments are made deter the most proper persons from putting themselves in the way of nomination." That appointments should be made by one "who can be made accountable for an improper choice," seemed to Morris the essence of wisdom.[39]

Passage of these resolutions marked a beginning in setting at least a part of the funding house in order, and Morris greeted it with enthusiasm. "At present I shall confine myself to congratulating your excellency," he observed in a circular letter to the various state governors, "which I do with the most unfeigned pleasure, on the prospect which begins to open of adjusting these intricate and almost obsolete transactions, of relieving the various public creditors, and consequently of rescuing and restoring the public credit." What he added was of equal interest. ". . . I consider these things essential to the consolidation of our Federal Union, to the promotion of general harmony and generous confidence throughout the United States, and to the establishment of our glorious independence on the solid basis of justice." When Morris actually transmitted the resolutions to the governors, he promised a happy ending if all went well.

Let us settle the accounts of the past expenditures, adjust the shares which each State has to pay, but let the settlement be final, or we do nothing. And if on the requisition of men and money for this and for future years the quotas be finally fixed, and the compliances be made publicly known, we shall banish that distrust which, I am sorry to say, now exists between the States, and in place thereof excite the noble ardor which animated our conduct in the commencement of the contest. The strife will then be which shall be foremost in contributing their share to the support of that war on the success of which depends the political existence of all.[40]

State jealousies had been primarily responsible for the delay in adopting measures necessary as prerequisites to any funding program.

Each state delegation feared that a uniform method of settling accounts would discriminate against their particular state, and that any
quota would force undue burdens upon it. In supporting the best interests of their states, some delegations sought the protection of the
eighth clause of the Articles of Confederation, which called for quotas
based on the value of the lands within the state. Other state delegations, however, whose interests would be hurt by an application of
this principle, were attracted to other methods. Regardless of the
methods supported, state delegations tended to reflect state interests
and state jealousies. At this time there is no real evidence to indicate
any concerted pressure from economic groups of a national character
clamoring for funding according to Morris' plan; rather, the measures
taken were a compromise between states. The Virginia delegates perhaps voiced the opinion of the majority when they reported to Benjamin Harrison, the Governor of Virginia, that the measure which was
adopted "will perhaps be found as free from exception as any that
could be devised." [41]

The combination of measures proposed by the Financier formed a
strong working force to restore the public credit. The Bank of North
America had been established, and its function as a national bank as
well as a deposit bank could soon be exploited; the Morris notes, if
they retained their value, would act as an important source of credit;
the mint, if established, could provide uniform and acceptable coinage
throughout the country; and the first steps had been taken in the direction of funding the debts of the Confederation, a measure for which
the Financier held high hopes as a permanent foundation for erecting
a new structure of public credit. The effectiveness of many parts of
this program on public credit depended eventually upon revenue; and
in this respect, the Financier was hopeful. "The present moment not
only offers the best opportunity of obtaining these revenues," he wrote,
"but requires that they be obtained." And what was more intimately
related to revenue than expenditures? [42]

CHAPTER — SIX

The Morris Program: Revenue and Expenditures

It was to be expected that within the Morris program revenue would hold a place of prominence. Because of the limitations imposed by the Articles of Confederation, the existing constitutional framework, the Financier's actions tended to be confined. His efforts, for the most part, were directed toward the coördination of actions taken previously by Congress rather than toward the formulation of new proposals. In performing this task, he tried to animate the collection of revenue at home and to quicken the efforts of the Republic's friends abroad. But he did something more. In implementing the measures of Congress, the Financier initiated new methods in the collection of taxes which he hoped would not only produce more revenue but also overcome, by administrative techniques, what he conceived to be omissions in the basic Articles of Government.

Closely allied to revenue, of course, was economy in expenditures. This laudable objective is usually greeted with enthusiasm by men of varying shades of political opinion, but there is always less agreement on how it is to be achieved. Although his program embraced frugality in carrying on the operations of government, the Financier did not wish to achieve economy by depressing prices. That the prices of certain commodities were comparatively high he recognized, but a general policy of deflation might conflict with, if not endanger, his entire program on revenue. Indeed, the Financier asserted that he was "desirous the country should obtain prices to sweeten labor and enable them to pay taxes freely." [1]

As an alternative, Morris instituted measures designed to reduce excessive expenditures by eliminating inefficiencies and duplication. Although the complaint of waste was general, it was most often leveled against the military, whose needs quite naturally required the greatest outlay of funds. Prompted by these considerations, the Financier introduced, or more accurately, extended his use of, a system of contracts. This method of supplying the services, he hoped, would satisfy their needs at less cost without impairing their effectiveness as fighting units. The expenses of other governmental operations were to be lowered by careful planning and inspection. Whatever proposal was made, however, it was always intimately linked with the question of revenue.

Revenue was needed for two distinct purposes: one, to supply funds for current expenditures; and two, to provide for the public debt. Although a combination of foreign and domestic sources was required for both purposes, the second would depend almost exclusively on domestic support. And it was precisely in this area that the Financier's actions were most circumscribed. Regardless of these limitations, Morris vigorously employed those weapons at his command to obtain additional revenue at home and abroad.

The impost, which had been proposed by Congress in February 1781, led the assault on the states for revenue to fund the public debt. This measure provided, with a few exceptions, for a 5 per cent *ad valorem* duty "upon all goods, wares, and merchandises of foreign growth and manufactures." The "monies" produced by this duty were to "be appropriated to the discharge of the principal and interest of the debts already contracted, or which may be contracted, on the faith of the United States, for supporting the present war." [2]

The Financier brought his heaviest verbal batteries to bear very early in an attempt to clear away opposition to the impost. The most powerful weapons, fear of disunion and possible defeat because of the lack of credit, were employed again and again. Would the enemy be correct, he asked, when they professed "that we are unworthy of confidence, that our union is a rope of sand, that the people are weary of Congress, and the respective States are determined to reject its authority?" Public credit could not be restored until the public faith was revived, and the best assurance that the United States would honor its pledges would be action on the impost. "No words will induce men to risk their property upon the security of a nominal union." As for disunion, the Governors must judge for themselves whether a union in which any part refuses to be bound by the debts of the whole is or is not nominal. But the close support work for the specific measure was also effective. Could commerce bear a 5 per cent duty? Without question, answered the Financier. Why should the revenue from this duty go directly to the central government rather than be credited to the state in which the tax was levied? The latter course would work a hardship on the non-commercial states and be unjust, for "the tax will fall equally on all, and therefore ought, in justice, to be carried to the general account." These arguments led Morris to one conclusion, "that those who wish to re-establish the credit and confirm the union of these States will comply with this requisition."

But there was a parting shot which hinted at a future development. Morris was worried about the jealousies of the respective states which prompted them to place hampering restrictions on measures of Congress. Congress was composed of representatives "freely chosen," he observed, and thus responsible to their constituents. "Nothing, therefore, ought to prevent the free and generous communication of all necessary powers to Congress; and I am confident that such a communication will more effectually dishearten the enemy, encourage our friends, and promote the general and unanimous efforts of the whole community, than any other circumstance which could possibly happen." Of course, continued the Financier, he knew the "Whigs of America" were more firmly united on the cause of Independence than ever before, but "there has been too little attention paid to give to that union of sentiment a proper political form and consistency."[3]

In reply to the many public creditors who daily requested payment, the Financier shifted their attention and criticism to the states as the source of their difficulties. If permanent revenues were provided to discharge the interest, he wrote to General Glover in a typical letter, "it will afford immediate relief to the creditors." Morris' decision in October 1781, to stop the accepted practice of issuing new loan office certificates in lieu of interest payments on previous issues, accented his words. Issuing certificates on such a basis, he explained, was among those "timid little artifices" which were fraudulent because this device would continue to depress the value of the certificates and "stamp our national character with indelible marks of infamy. . . ." Payment of interest could be provided only by solid revenue, he asserted. "To the public creditors, therefore, I say that until the States provide revenues for liquidating the principal and interest of the public debt they cannot be paid; and to the States I say that they are bound by every principle held sacred among men to make that provision."[4]

The results, as far as the Financier was concerned, were encouraging. He announced with satisfaction that his action with respect to paying interest on the loan office certificates "produced much clamor among the public creditors. This I expected, and I still expect that it will occasion much more." And on the specific measure of the impost, Morris assured Franklin, "there is a well grounded expectation that the clamors of our creditors will induce the several legislatures to comply. . . ." By January 1782, only three states had failed to accede to the wishes of Congress on the impost, and it was expected that they would fall into line momentarily. The Financier entertained high hopes that an important part of the revenue program could soon begin in earnest.[5]

The second need for revenue, to obtain funds in order to meet current expenditures, held a prominent place in the Morris program. Under the Articles of Confederation, Congress could request the states to provide the national treasury with a certain amount of money, but the specific taxes levied to obtain the revenue and the collection of those taxes remained in the hands of the respective state legislatures. In conformity with the authority of the Articles, Congress issued a call to the states in November 1781 for $8,000,000 in specie to carry on the war in 1782. The resolution embodying this requisition contained two additional points of importance. First, they urged that

taxes for the United States should be levied separately from those of
the state; second, the revenue collected should be paid to the commissioners of the loan offices in the respective states or to "such other
person as shall be appointed by the Superintendent of Finance." They
also recommended that such appointees be given full power to recover
money from the collectors and that the funds received should be subject "only to the orders of Congress, or the Superintendent of
Finance."[6]

In carrying out this ordinance of Congress, Morris chose to appoint
a receiver of taxes in each state, thus bridging the gap between the
Confederation and the states in the collection of revenue, and supplying by means of procedural techniques what he conceived to be an
omission in the political structure. Appointing receivers rather than
using the commissioners of the loan offices also tended to make a
clean break with the past practices in the collection of revenue. The
duties of the receivers, who in reality represented the interests of the
Confederation within the states, were defined by Morris with care:
urge the fulfillment of quotas, receive bank notes or specie—Morris
notes were added a bit later—in payment of taxes, transmit weekly
accounts to the Superintendent of Finance, and publish a statement
of the accounts in the local newspapers—including the names of the
persons from whom taxes were received. The purpose of this final instruction, according to the Financier, was to inform "every citizen"
of the sum of taxes collected and actually transmitted to the Confederation "for support of the War" and "at the order of the Superintendent of Finance." Indeed, it was entirely "proper and necessary
that in a free country the people should be as fully informed of the
administration of their affairs as the nature of things will admit."[7]

In reality, this final instruction was designed to meet certain problems that had plagued Congress for some time. States were accustomed
to lumping all taxes; then they would dole out to the Confederation
what revenue they deemed could be spared. Even when collected explicitly for Continental purposes, revenue was often appropriated by
the state to its own use. This practice was complicated by local considerations. Collectors in the various localities were often elected by
their own counties; in consequence, they were really responsible to
their own communities. Any inclination to collect taxes, then, was
seriously hampered at the very source. In short, between the time the
quotas had been determined by Congress and the time the funds were
to be received, after traveling the gauntlet of local, county, and state
collection, there were slips aplenty.[8]

To help the receiver fulfill his duties, the Financier suggested certain aids. The receiver, he indicated, should be given authority to in-
sist, apparently by court action if necessary, that the local collectors
fill their quota of taxes. It is easy to see why such a suggestion would
meet resistance from the states—which, of course, it did. Failing this,
the weapon of social pressure would be employed as much as possible.
Publication of revenues and of a list of persons who paid would place

decided social pressure, first of all, on the state assemblies, who would be answerable to the local communities; second, on those collectors who were delinquent or corrupt in their duties; and third, on the members of the local communities who had failed to pay.[9]

Morris throughout stressed the enormous possibilities of the latter technique. "Your publications of receipts from the collector would stimulate curiosity," Morris later observed to William C. Houston, who had been appointed receiver in New Jersey. "Besides that when persons of influence in the counties have paid, it would be well to hint to them an enquiry why others have not paid." On the other hand, people of influence who had not paid might rapidly make amends for fear of losing their influence. Publication would also keep those collectors in line who, on occasion, would receive money for taxes and somehow forget to include their acquisition on the list of the taxes received. Indeed, the Financier's faith in public pressure was perhaps extravagant.

Public opinion is always useful reinforcement to the operation of laws. It goes farther. Thus in the case before us altho in the first moment men will not consent to very severe laws for enforcing a collection or if such laws were passed would very reluctantly consent to the execution of them. Yet when a part of the community have paid punctually they feel a degree of resentment excited against the negligent and unwilling. Those half tories who want to be considered as Whigs will not suffer the public to know that they do not pay taxes and in a very little time they feel that very payment interesting them to make others pay. Thus the cords of government get wound up by degrees to their proper tone. And what is of infinite importance morals and laws march with an equal pace towards the same object of public utility.[10]

Morris intended the receivers to fill a larger role than mere Continental tax collectors. He wanted them to urge the passage of the impost, to "remonstrate against" any possible paper-money issue in their respective states, to oppose—with "prudence"—any inclination of either public assemblies or individuals "to prefer local to general interest," and to stamp out any hint of fraud or negligence. Moreover, they were to send him not only their comments on money affairs, but also "all the newspapers" of their states and all "political pamphlets or publications." They should observe the political trends in the various assemblies, the course of commerce, the rates on bills of exchange, and the general economic outlook. In a phrase, they would act as the "eyes and ears" of the Financier.[11]

Those chosen by Morris to act as receivers in the various states represent a blend of political attitudes. Although little information is available for some of the receivers, several important figures were selected, such as James Lovell, a very well-known member of Congress, a close correspondent and apparently firm friend of Samuel Adams. He was also the member of Congress who had taken great pride in his subtly written letter recalling Silas Deane from France in 1778. William Whipple, whom Arthur Lee, a severe critic of Morris, called "that most excellent Patriot," was also included among the appointees. On the other hand, there was Alexander Hamilton in New York, whose views on banking and money so closely paralleled those of the Financier, and in Pennsylvania, John Swanwick, Morris' "Treasurer in the Office of Finance." But Swanwick had been a second choice, for Morris had first urged David Rittenhouse to accept, a man who has often been called one of the foremost "radicals" in Pennsylvania. In brief, the representation was remarkably well balanced politically. If Morris planned to stage a "conservative" *coup,* he had enlisted a strange army.

The compensation for the receivers varied according to the size of the state and the amount of revenue which was expected. James Lovell in Massachusetts received $\frac{1}{8}$ per cent, for example, while George Olney in Rhode Island got $\frac{1}{4}$ per cent. The only receiver whose compensation exceeded $\frac{1}{4}$ per cent was George Abbot Hall in South Carolina, who was to be paid $\frac{1}{2}$ per cent for his services.[12]

When methods of procedure in the collection of revenue were being determined, the lower South, because of its distressing economic situation, received special attention from the Financier. In consultation with George Abbot Hall, whom the South Carolina delegates had recommended for receiver of taxes in their state—a policy of Congressional courtesy often followed by Morris—the Financier devised a plan which he thought would meet their needs and at the same time enable them to comply with the requisitions of Congress. A receiver of taxes would be appointed in each state, who, in addition to his regular duties, would be authorized—by the Financier—to issue notes. These notes would function, for the most part, as paper money. Warrants drawn by General Greene to compensate those who sold supplies to the army in the South would be payable in these notes; they would also be acceptable in payment for taxes. The notes would tend, therefore, to be drawn into the state treasury, where they would be credited to the state in fulfillment of its quota of Congressional requisitions. In introducing this plan, the Financier insisted on one definite prerequisite. Each legislature must first pass a tax law to raise its quota of requisitions as called for by Congress and make the notes receivable as specie in the Continental taxes.[13]

The object of this proposal, which is quite apparent, was to provide a paper medium which would diffuse the burden of taxation. If goods to subsist the army were either impressed or paid for by using certificates, the incidence of taxation would rest on those who resided in the immediate area, and especially those within the area who happened to possess the goods needed by the army. The burden, therefore, would be localized. The plan of the Financier would avoid this, because, as he pointed out, if taxes were levied properly all would be compelled to contribute—nonslaveholders, slaveholders, small plantation owners, and persons with large personal property but little that could be used by the military service. And, at the same time, the state would be fulfilling its quota of the requisitions, because the Financier would accept the notes in payment.[14]

When this proposal was presented to the delegates of the states concerned, the initial response was favorable, but only fleetingly so. Although all the states involved except Georgia approved at first, and orders were issued to print the notes, the important South Carolina delegation voiced some reservations about the prerequisite of passing the tax law. They offered a counterproposal, according to Morris, which included a delay in passing a tax law, a legal tender measure, and price regulations on articles wanted by the army. Morris fairly exploded in reply. As Superintendent of Finance, he stated, it was his duty to urge compliance with the requisitions of Congress, and his orders were explicit "to prevent the issue of a single note until such bills shall have been enacted and effectual provision made for the collection." As for the possibility of a legal tender law or the regulation of prices, Morris declared:

My opinion of all such laws is decidedly fixed. I know both from reason and experience that they injure the credit of the paper they appear designed to support. . . . I entreat that on no representation, nor for any cause whatever, any law be passed making the notes a tender, valuing the price of goods, or anything of that sort. I ask for no embargo, no regulations. On the contrary, I wish and pray that the whole detestable tribe of restrictions may be done away, and the people be put in possession of that freedom for which they are contending.

Because of these differences, the plan did not go into effect; it remained to be seen whether the Financier could persuade the southern states to change their views.[15]

In addition to strengthening methods of procedure in tax collection, Morris employed every device and argument at his command to spur the states to fulfill their current requisitions. In each case, the argument was turned to fit the particular state that was being addressed at the moment. New Hampshire, for example, was excoriated for neglecting to do its part when it had experienced relatively no fighting; on the other hand, Virginia, which had found itself the very seat of battle, was told that this trial was only a blessing in disguise. The heavy military expenditures in that region would be "so diffused as to possess its inhabitants of specie"; it was, therefore, a very favorable moment to obtain revenue in hard money.[16]

When addressing the states jointly, Morris argued that the possibility of further aid from abroad was slim. Much misinformation had been circulated concerning past assistance, he observed, so the full story must be told in order "that the meanest individual may be in due time informed of those affairs in which as a free citizen he is interested." To expect further help from either Holland or Spain seemed little more than a futile wish, while the generous assistance from France, which in itself was far short of current needs, could not be repeated. No one could possibly miss the concluding point of his exposition, to draw "solid revenue" from the resources at home. Indeed, the Financier was so intent upon persuading the respective governors that he deliberately included an erroneous account of the French aid.

This gesture, he wrote Franklin, would help "to lower the expectations of the several States" for foreign assistance.[17]

To paint such a dismal picture of expectations from abroad could
be a dangerous business. A circular letter amounted to a public letter,
and the representatives of the French Court could use its contents to
bolster their refusals to give additional aid. Fully aware of this possibility, the Financier hastened to send Luzerne, the French Minister, a
copy of the communication with the comment that it was "an additional proof of my desire to draw from among ourselves the necessary
resources, and thereby to become truly independent." The letter was
designed as a weapon to stir the states to action, but ". . . the sincerity
with which I have always spoken to you, and which I mean to preserve . . . will not permit me to conceal my sentiments on what is to
be expected."[18]

Where the Financier had sketched the resources and abilities of the
states in colorful design and bright shadings, he now exchanged his
paints and brushes to sketch in dark, somber, depressing colors to suit
the skeptical appraisal of the French. The public debts had to be
funded, he commented, and revenue for this purpose had to take
precedence over current expenditures in order to revive the public
credit. Even then, it was not easy to collect taxes, for that power resided in the sovereign states. Moreover, the people were not "accustomed" to such levies, and the legislatures were not skillful in their
application. It was also a mistaken assumption that taxable wealth
was available. Although it was true that western lands were valuable,
Morris admitted, they could not produce revenue at this time. And
many people, injured economically by the war, could not shoulder
extra burdens. In fact, added the Financier, "the use of many articles
not strictly necessary are become so even by that use, and therefore
the mode of living being habitually more expensive than in other
countries, requires greater wealth. A good prince would not suddenly
render the lot of his subjects worse. How, then, are we to expect that
the people themselves will do so?" But Morris was wise enough to
conclude with a much more realistic and effective argument. France
had more at stake than the fate of America, he reminded Luzerne.
Victory would not only restrict "British encroachment and rapacity,"
but it would enhance French commerce. By advancing funds to the
United States, "the subjects of France will for ages derive benefits
from a commercial connection with this country" as well as find "a
warm friend and a faithful ally. . . ." The French, who had long recognized the importance of America to the European balance of power,
needed few reminders on the strength of this argument.[19]

Only in writing to Franklin was the Financier completely candid.
Indeed, in a letter which Congress had urged the Financier to send
along with Lafayette, Morris included a compendium of his actions
on revenue since he had entered the Office of Finance. Although he
emphasized the adverse conditions which still existed—for after all he
had to provide Franklin with material for the French Court—the

Financier professed that the people possessed "the ability and ought to have the inclination." However, if experience was any teacher, they would fail to exert themselves. What was really wrong? ". . . I must repeat again and again that our general system has not grown into that form and vigor which can communicate the impulses of a sovereign mind to the remotest members of subjected power." But Americans should not be criticized. "The exertions of our country have really been very great, and as soon as more consistency shall have been put in the administration, they will again be great." Then the Financier uttered what many of his contemporaries would have considered as one of the great truths of the Revolution. "This is the period of weakness," he asserted, "between the convulsive labors of enthusiasm and the sound and regular operations of order and government."[20]

The Financier urged Franklin to press once again for additional aid from France. He asked for funds to pay the interest on loan office certificates, which he said had been pledged by France very early in the war; he outlined how the money made available by the Court had been expended, and concluded that the pledge of 10,000,000 livres as security for the Dutch was still at his disposal; he included copies of letters which he had exchanged with Luzerne, letters in which some "warmth had crept in." All of this Morris placed in Franklin's care, for he acknowledged that "a paper argument in Philadelphia can have but very little influence at Versailles." If the Court refused any assistance whatsoever, advised Morris, Franklin should subtly threaten that the United States might sever its French connection if Britain should concede its Independence as an inducement. "This would on our part be wrong, and therefore it ought not to be done; but, sir, when this great object shall be presented on the one side and the weight of new and great taxes be felt on the other, with all their ancient prejudices and predilections in aid, will not there be some men who for the shades of ease will quit the paths of virtue?" If Morris had had an opportunity to glance at Franklin's correspondence of long standing, he would have discovered that this threat was an old device to the shrewd sage from Pennsylvania.[21]

Morris' program with respect to revenue did not mark any abrupt departure from previous practices because the measures he proposed and the actions he took had to conform to the existing constitutional instrument, the Articles of Confederation. But his program reflected a greater clarity in objectives than had customarily been the case, and it was more carefully planned in relation to all the other functions of the central government. To achieve results the Financier was somewhat more precise and thorough by tailoring his arguments to fit the audience being addressed and by establishing Continental receivers of taxes in each state with specific duties to perform and clear-cut, simple procedures to follow. But this program on revenue was only one of "two pillars," as Morris stated it, whereby the structure of finance was supported. The second pillar concerned the final segment of the Morris program, economy in current expenditures.[22]

Current expenditures divided themselves very neatly into two categories, civil and military. In the former, which comprised but a small part of the total outlay, Morris was content to institute savings by reducing the number of employees and carefully supervising the minute administrative details. In military affairs, where most of the nation's money was being spent, the Financier initiated a complete change in procurement methods by introducing a new system of contracting, to take effect on January 1, 1782.[23]

The existing manner of supplying the army—that is, by requesting specific provisions—had not functioned satisfactorily. Requisitions lagged; when supplies were provided, much of it spoiled or was pillaged before it could be sent to the necessary posts; transportation costs became excessive; and the army suffered because supplies often failed to arrive. Born out of dire necessity, the system of specific supplies proved valuable, for it enabled the army to remain in the field; still, it was wasteful, and the costs were exorbitant. When circularizing the states, the Commander-in-Chief summed it up quite accurately:

I think I may venture to say, that a great proportion of the specific Articles have been wasted after the people have furnished them, and that the transportation alone, of what have reached the Army, has, in numberless instances, cost more than the value of the Articles themselves.[24]

In contrast to this, Morris expected the contracting system "to prevent the repetition of those evils which have so often arisen from the want of supplies and to husband our resources." The plan itself was simple. Individuals would contract with the government to provide rations for troops at a specific sum per ration. It was assumed, of course, that individuals would be attracted to make such an agreement by the profits which a contract might yield. In theory, several advantages would also accrue to the government and the army. The troops would no longer suffer from "want of supplies" because it would be to the advantage of the contractor—being paid per ration—to make certain that sufficient rations were on hand, while the danger of an oversupply of commodities—such as occurred when commissaries received five per cent commissions on everything they purchased—would be avoided because any spoilage or waste would shrink rather than enhance the profits of the contractor. Because fulfillment of supply requirements would rest with the individual making the agreement, a number of expensive military establishments and practices could be abolished. For example, the costs of transporting the specific supplies of one state to feed the army five hundred miles distant, the cost of the commissariat with all its directing and issuing agents, and the loss by spoilage of specific supplies would all be eliminated.[25]

But where did economy enter in? The profits made by the contractors could be so excessive that the government would pay more rather than less to supply the troops. This possibility, thought the Financier, would be eliminated by the use of sealed competitive bidding. Thus, each prospective contractor would be thinking in terms of minimum rather than maximum profits. Perfectly suited to the Financier's larger concept of the harmony of private interest and public good, the contracting system received extravagant praise from its author. ". . . Contracts with private men, men of substance and talents equal to the undertaking as [are] the cheapest, most certain, and consequently the best mode of obtaining those articles which are necessary for the subsistence, covering, clothing, and moving of an army." [26]

The Financier realized that the system rested on two assumptions: first, that a contractor would not try to squeeze out extra profits by supplying rations of inferior quality; and second, that revenue would provide the necessary specie to fulfill contractual obligations promptly. In answering the first with confidence, Morris wrote General Heath: "I expect that the rations will be good. If they are not the Contractors will suffer the loss of it when condemned so that they are bound in interest to take care that the beef put up be of good quality." "Besides that," he concluded, "bad beef loses more in the weight by being salted than good does." This was a pleasant prospect, indeed, but what if the contractors and the army disagreed on what constituted "inferior" quality? Who was to condemn the supplies? If a quarrel broke out and the contractors temporarily refused to provide the rations, how would the army fare in the interim? These possibilities were pregnant with future misunderstandings and disputes. On the second assumption, Morris hoped that his program on revenue would prove to be the most effective answer. What would happen, however, if it failed and no specie was available to meet the obligations involved in the contracts? Obviously the two assumptions with respect to the contracting system were so basic that they would continue to reappear. [27]

Morris had planned to introduce contracting as quickly as possible after taking office. Though Congress readily acquiesced by delegating him the necessary power, the program as he visualized it did not mature until late fall of 1781. Contracting, as we have seen, had undergone something of a trial run when Morris substituted it for procurement of specific supplies in Pennsylvania, but full-fledged preparations began after Yorktown. [28]

The general procedure followed in all contracts was the same. First, announcements in the various newspapers would specify a certain day when sealed bids would be accepted for a military post or series of military posts. On that day, the lowest bid, if it complied in full with the specifications laid down by the Financier, would be accepted. Finally, a contract was drawn up by the Secretary of War and submitted to the Financier for approval.

A typical contract was made with Jonathan Lawrence and Melancton Smith. They were to "furnish and deliver at the different posts to the Northward of Poughkeepsie such rations or parts of rations as might be required by the Secretary at War." Specified in the contract were the ingredients of the tantalizing ration: one pound of beef (or ¾ pound pork), one pound of bread, and one gill of rum or whiskey. Lawrence and Smith were also to provide one quart of salt and two quarts of vinegar for every 100 rations and eight pounds of soap and three pounds of candles for every 700 rations. In this particular agreement a ration would be provided at 10/90ths of a dollar, to be paid by the Financier in specie. A breakdown in the price for separate parts of the ration was included in case an additional quantity of any item were required. The agreement called for a small advance from the Financier; future payments were to be made monthly on the basis of vouchers produced by the contractors.[29]

Morris was anxious to enlist his friends in the enterprise. "Perhaps, if you are not fully employed otherwise," Morris had written Philip John Schuyler, the celebrated New Yorker, soon after taking office, "you might start some worthy man under your patronage that might render essential service to the public, with proper advantage to himself and connexions in this line." William Duer of New York was also encouraged. "I am glad to hear that you intend to bid for the contract at West Point and hope your proposals may be the lowest as it will always give me great pleasure to find men of integrity and honor engaging in the public service."[30]

But both men were destined to be "much underbidden." Tench Francis and Matthias Slough received the contract for certain posts in New Jersey; Henry Dering at Lancaster; Commodore Hazlewood and Peter Summers at Philadelphia. The two big contracts—for West Point and for the posts above Poughkeepsie—were granted to Comfort Sands and Company and Jonathan Lawrence and Company, respectively. Of these contractors, Morris knew Francis, Slough, and Hazlewood well, but the others were outside his acquaintance. Morris was confident of the latter group, however, and described them as men of "integrity" who possessed the means and experience to carry out the contracts.[31]

Because of the controlling factor of general economic distress, the South was again given special consideration. Contracting for the present could not be employed in that region, he informed General Greene, the commander of the Southern department. "The dubious State of the Southern Country, the want of men who have sufficient capital and sufficient knowledge of their resources even if I should offer, and above all my serious doubts whether any exertions would be made if once I stepped in to their relief [—] these are reasons which oblige me to leave you for the present as you are." If the Southern States adopted his revenue scheme, thought Morris, then it might be possible to introduce the system. The decision to withhold contracting, however logical and sensible, aroused some bitter criticism. Although the Financier had earlier assured Greene that he had "neither forgotten nor neglected your department" in clothing, arms, and hospital stores, it is probable that the Head of the Southern Department—not to mention his biographers—thought Morris' "fullest applause to an officer who finds in his own genius an ample resource for the want of men, money, cloaths, arms, and supplies" the more accurate appraisal.[32]

Supplying the army by contract was the major economy measure, but others were introduced. The hospital department, which Morris thought particularly inefficient and corrupt, was completely reorganized at his request in the interests of "great oeconomical advantages to the public and very useful alterations to the sick and wounded." The position of the Clothier General within the orbit of the Superintendent of Finance was consolidated. Morris renewed his request to reduce the military forces, particularly officers, for he thought it could be carried out without impairing the strength of the service. The virtues of frugality were also preached to what remained of the Continental Navy, but the Financier occasionally reflected a partiality toward that service, and no distinct program was put into operation except for settling old accounts.[33]

The measures to introduce economy into the operations of the Confederation rounded out the comprehensive program of the Financier. The program touched almost every phase of the war and every branch of government. It included administrative reorganization of the Treasury Department, important steps toward the greater production of revenue for the Confederation, and measures for the more effective employment of the revenue. But the driving force of the program was directed toward an important long-range objective, the restoration of the public credit of the Confederation. The specific instruments to achieve this end formed the inner core of the Financier's program, of course, but all the policies were designed to attain that goal.

It is obvious that these policies and measures were not entirely the creations of the Financier. Gouverneur Morris, James Wilson, Peletiah Webster, and Alexander Hamilton, to mention a few, wrote on the advisability of a bank, and Morris himself maintained that he had been in the process of organizing a deposit bank just before the Revolution. Measures on public credit, such as funding, were discussed by many others; and certainly few members of Congress would have considered Continental debts anything less than sacred. The revenue program, as we have seen, was merely an assimilation and strengthening of Congressional measures, while the introduction of contracting may have been derived either from Morris' experience on the Secret Committee of Congress or from reading about the experience of the Europeans. On the other hand, the Morris notes were a creation of the Financier, and most of the policies, although not necessarily originating with the Financier, bore the imprint of his thinking and experience. Certainly the concept of building public credit out of existing private credit was more clearly articulated in the Financier's program than elsewhere.

To trace origins is of minor consequence in comparison to the most significant fact, that the Financier had woven into one comprehensive program the various strands of thinking which had hitherto been widely separated. And what is more, the responsibility resided in one office and, to a large extent, in one man. Many policies had been advanced in theory; here was a program which was to go into operation. The effect of theoretical decisions on paper could in no wise compare with the important impact on the progress of the war, on the economy, and on the government, that would be felt by most of the Financier's actual decisions.

Morris' program on public credit, together with its supporting arguments contained virtually all the essential ingredients of the Hamiltonian program as enunciated during the Federalist decade, with the exception of Hamilton's Report on Manufactures. Although some parts of the Financier's program lacked the boldness and clarity of the Hamiltonian expositions, each was geared to its time. A proposal of a $10,000,000 capitalization for a bank, as Hamilton suggested in his letter to Morris in the spring of 1781, was simply unworkable, and the institution would have been crushed before it had begun. The development of the Morris program in the coming months, particularly on funding, was of such a nature that it soon foreshadowed the Hamiltonian program of the Federalist period in chapter and verse.

If, as Morris conceived it, public credit was at stake, a terrible urgency existed. "The time is hastening on," warned the Financier as the year drew rapidly to a close, "when it must be determined, perhaps forever, whether the United States of North America shall, or shall not, possess the inestimable jewel of public credit." Morris had observed earlier that only this confidence and vigor "can perfect our independence." What might be required eventually to attain this goal? Perhaps increased power for the Congress, a circumstance that was "evident now to many, and will probably become soon very apparent to all." Yet that was still afar off. "All these things are in the womb of time, which can alone disclose the events we plague ourselves with guessing at." [34]

Morris could have added that the fate of the Confederation, in large measure, might well depend upon the fortunes of his program.

CHAPTER—SEVEN

The Program in Operation:
The Instruments of Public Credit (1782)

DURING HIS ADMINISTRATION, THE FINANCIER NEVER DEPARTED FROM the position that the essential core of his program was the restoration of the public credit. On occasion, this objective seemed almost to supersede the support of the war itself. "You will be sensible," he wrote in March 1782, "that my views must first be directed to the support of the War, next to a revival of Public Credit and Confidence by a punctual discharge of the public debts or of the interest annually until the principal can be paid." Certainly those means in the program of Morris whereby he hoped to achieve this end—such financial instruments as the Bank of North America and the Morris notes, and such a plan as that on funding the debts of the Confederation—must be examined in their actual operation during the year 1782, if any evaluation is to be made of their significance and effect. But it is pertinent, first of all, to inquire into the prevailing conditions within which these instruments of the program would operate.[1]

The state of the nation with respect to political trends, economic developments, and foreign affairs was uncertain in the late spring of 1782. Although a decided shift in political attitudes was remote, there were some changes which forewarned that Morris' program might encounter opposition. The general economic situation, for several reasons, had deteriorated since Morris took office as Superintendent of Finance, and the trend either toward prosperity or depression would depend upon such developments as the opening of new markets and the revival of the old. The attitude of foreign powers and their inclination to aid the United States was equally unpredictable. Weighed down by financial demands at home and uncertain about the future course of the war, friendly powers would act as expediency directed. Each of these general developments, to be sure, was important to Morris' comprehensive program.

The general make-up of Congress had changed only slightly during the latter half of 1781, when the relationship between Congress and the Financier had been comparatively harmonious. If this membership remained intact, the immediate future promised a coöperative approach to the financial problems. Looking beyond Congress to the sovereign states, a first glance reveals nothing which might immediately alter these circumstances. Most of the states were interested in solving the financial problems, and Morris' efforts up to this time had received a distinctly audible round of applause. A few events, however, warned of impending change. David Howell of Rhode Island began to emerge in the politics of that state as a champion of anti-centralization, and more than that, an active antagonist of the impost, a step in the funding program. And Arthur Lee, who hated Morris and all his works, began to play a more important role for his native Virginia by his election as a delegate to Congress.[2]

Individual comments on the Financier's efforts were overwhelmingly favorable. Most of the criticism which did exist was heard only in faint whispers, not in loud angry tones; most of the critics of Morris were awaiting a misstep rather than finding fault with the constructive program. No one reflects this more clearly than Joseph Reed, sometime opponent to the Financier. Morris was credited by Reed with an influence over Congress far beyond what powers he possessed. Indeed, Reed did a gross injustice to Congress by sarcastically contending that Morris had so absolved them of deliberation and responsibility that "they are now very much at leisure to read despatches, return thanks, pay and receive compliments, etc." As for Morris, the principal in this matter, "those who know him will also acknowledge that he is too much a man of the world to overlook certain private interests which his command of the paper, and occasional speculations in that currency, will enable him to promote." But not so fast! As humiliating as this power of Morris might be, Reed added, "it has been exercised with much advantage for the immediate relief of our distresses, and . . . the public have received a real benefit from Mr. Morris's exertions." Those who approved the actions of the Financier echoed William Livingston, the "radical" Governor of New Jersey. "But by the blessing of God, and the instrumentality of General Washington and Robert Morris I hope we shall drive the devils to old England before next June."[3]

The opponents and proponents of the actions of Morris—and the former were little more than a handful at this time—do not seem to make up a definite pattern. As far as the evidence indicates, no determined opposition had yet arisen which represented any specific economic, social, or political interest. If one were to develop, it would depend on the effect rather than the formation of the Morris program.

Although the prospect was comparatively promising for the reception of the Morris program politically, a decline in economic prosperity could seriously impair its operation. Was the economy sufficiently prosperous to support the Morris program? Had conditions prevailing in 1780 been improved or worsened since the Financier assumed office? The trend, though not uniform either in sections of the coun-

try or in economic groups within a section, was generally more discouraging early in 1782 than it had been in 1780-81.

The economic chaos which had flooded South Carolina had now
overflowed beyond her borders to engulf North Carolina and Georgia
and to reach into Virginia. The prolonged fighting in Virginia stimulated a market for wheat, flour, and provisions, but it hampered the
export of her important commercial product, tobacco. The gap in the
mercantile correspondence of such men as William Reynolds of Williamsburg from early 1781 to late October bears its own eloquence.
"You have no conception, my friend, the losses and uneasiness I have
suffered for this nine months . . .," Reynolds wrote to a friend when
he resumed business in October. "The British . . . destroy'd the tobacco warehouses and a large quantity of tobacco in this state."[4]

In Maryland, and moving on north into Pennsylvania, New Jersey,
and New York, the situation was somewhat more heartening. Crops
were so abundant that Morris was prompted to exclaim: ". . . Every
part of the country from one end of the continent to the other is so
full of wheat that an army of 10 times the number of ours could not
possibly consume a tenth of the surplus. . . ." Although Morris' ex-
uberance may have misled him, John Hunt, the New Jersey diarist
who could be very sparing in describing such matters, confirmed Morris' appraisal of a bountiful harvest. "We have now had a very plenty-
ful season for grass and corn of every kind." Wheat he found to be
"plentyer here than it had been for many years." Not only were crops
good but prices held up, although there seemed to be a brief decline
in terms of the earlier years. Moreover, there had been relatively little
fighting in this region, and consequently there was no extensive
destruction.[5]

In the Philadelphia and Baltimore mercantile communities there
was a significant downward trend in trade and business. Those who
had engaged in privateering had been less successful, and many whose
attention would normally have been directed toward regular trade
channels diverted their efforts to the immediate threat of Lord Cornwallis in Virginia. Until the welcome arrival of the French fleet under
De Grasse in the autumn of 1781, much of the commerce of the ports
in the Middle Region had been consistently hampered by the unusual
success of the British cruisers. But De Grasse had returned to the West
Indies with his fleet in March 1782; the immediate trade prospects
and prosperity of Philadelphia and Baltimore would depend upon the
lasting effectiveness of his offensive at Yorktown. If the defeat had not
crippled the British fleet, it could resume its deadly assignment of
blockading the coast, seriously restricting all economic activity—as it
eventually did.

Although there was no pronounced change in the economic situation of New England, some weak spots, foreshadowing future trends,
had appeared in trade and agriculture. For the latter, the absence of
the French army and the French navy eliminated an important market
for which there was no immediate substitute in prospect. This devel-

opment helps to explain in part the decline in the price of meat products when that of wheat, flour, and other staples was apparently maintained in most of the other regions. If intercolonial trade could be expanded or West Indian commerce resumed without too much risk, New England could expect a rapid surge upward in its agricultural prosperity; these developments, however, would depend on the strategy of the British fleet. The question of an uncertain market for farm products was complicated by the fact that the heavy tax burden in some states—Massachusetts in particular—was being shifted to the agrarian community. The commercial centers were also faced with a period of transition because their important Revolutionary enterprise —privateering—sharply declined. To most good seamen this would be considered an asset, for they realized that privateering was a risky, temporary activity, and that their real strength lay in normal ventures carried on in regular channels of trade. If the decline in privateering could be balanced by an increase in intercolonial or European commerce, all would yet be well; on the other hand, if the transition to normal commerce did not materialize, then conditions would be aggravated.[6]

In general, then, the economic condition of the states was less favorable than it had been in the winter of 1780-81. It was not an irretrievable condition, for the downward trend could be decidedly influenced for better or worse by the course of events at home and abroad. The fortunes of the Morris program, in turn, would depend in large part upon the degree of prosperity within the country, because any financial program, in the long term, must be predicated upon the nation's economic resources.

To fulfill certain parts of the Financier's program, there was the possibility of aid from abroad, a source that Morris did not intend to neglect. In late November 1781, he had estimated that some 9,313,000 livres ($2,000,000) were at his disposition in Europe—in short, the whole of the expected Dutch loan. Although fresh dispatches from Europe did not confirm this appraisal, the Financier certainly expected a substantial sum to help finance the war in the coming year, or, if terms were made, the transition to peace.[7]

These anticipations were scarcely warranted, for circumstances abroad were, on the whole, less encouraging than at home. The persistent efforts of John Jay, the nation's envoy to Spain, had yielded very little in actual funds, and no promises for future aid. His running commentary of disappointment is summed up in a bitter letter to Gouverneur Morris. "This government [Spain] has little money, less Wisdom, no Credit, nor any right to it." Whatever the real reason, inability or refusal, nothing could be expected from Spain's treasures. Still there was France, but the outlook for assistance from that quarter did not appear bright. Luzerne, the French Minister, had been told by his superiors that no further bills should be drawn by Morris, and none should be authorized "even for a small sum." And Franklin's letters were especially disheartening, although they began to take on a more optimistic note upon the arrival of Lafayette, who had been thoroughly briefed by Morris on the "state of the finances and assistance from the Court of Versailles."[8]

The only shaft of sunlight piercing the gloom was a new loan from the prudent Dutch that finally became available in the early months of 1782. The first flush of enthusiasm which had caught up John Adams, United States Minister to the Netherlands, upon his arrival, had soon given way to less optimistic appraisals. "There is not so much money here as the world imagines," he reported—perhaps as a defense in case he failed to obtain a loan—and "those who have what there is have now no confidence in any nation or individual." In the course of the maneuvers, Adams had become increasingly pessimistic and Franklin increasingly impatient. "Some writer, I forget who," the latter wrote, forgetting his customary caution, "says that Holland is no longer *a nation* but *a great shop;* and I begin to think it has no other principles or sentiments but those of a shopkeeper." But Franklin recovered his usual shrewdness in time to forward a hasty follow-up letter in which he confessed he might have expressed himself "too hardly." "I was a little out of humor when I wrote. . . . It will be well not to let my letter be seen." Caution finally triumphed—or perhaps it might be more accurate to say that France now permitted it to triumph—and the States General agreed to loan 10,000,000 livres to the United States on behalf of France, with the French guarantee as security for the loan.[9]

Meanwhile, in Philadelphia, the Financier and Congress had tumbled over each other in their eagerness to take advantage of any loan made by the Dutch, but their expectations were destined to disappointment. Morris had arranged for the disposition of the loan before he had received any confirmation of a successful conclusion to the negotiations, despite the warnings of Franklin that "sundry great sums" were needed to pay past Congressional drafts and to replace the cargo of the vessel, *Marquis de la Fayette,* which had been loaded with war supplies and lost. Indeed, the whole story of the employment of the Dutch loan was summed up simply by Franklin a few months later. "Unfortunately . . . most of it [has] been eaten up by advances here." Although some funds remained at the disposition of the Financier, the amount fell far short of his expectations.[10]

With the political scene shifting slightly in opposition to some of the policies of the Financier, with the nation's economy, the basis for any financial program, in delicate balance, with aid from abroad dwindling and the prospects for future assistance discouraging, it was safe to assert that the program of the Superintendent of Finance faced an uncertain future. In the light of this situation, the relative success of a substantial part of the Morris program on reviving the public credit was the more remarkable.

Of the two exceedingly important measures on which the Financier based much of his hope in reviving the public credit, the Bank of

North America and the Morris notes, the former was probably the more successful. The Bank, as has been noted earlier in this volume, had been finally established in the last days of 1781. In the course of the Bank's operations during 1782 there were certain periods when it was compelled to curtail operations for fear of overextending its resources, but it was, on the whole, highly successful from the point of view of the Financier.

At the outset, the most important role of the Bank was the part it played in the national financial plan rather than in its assistance to private traders. One of the Bank's significant functions was the discounting of personal notes for the government. When the Financier sold bills of exchange on France, the only method available to tap the resources abroad, he was usually compelled to take personal notes in payment, for few purchasers had the necessary cash at hand. The Financier, who was also in need of immediate funds to meet current expenditures, would then discount these notes at the Bank. This function, important as it was, was subordinate to the credit which the Bank supplied for exploitation by the Confederation. On the day its doors were opened, the Financier borrowed $100,000 for a period of six months at an interest of 6 per cent per annum, and within a month he successfully applied for a second loan, an equal amount on the same terms. In this brief period, then, the Financier had borrowed some $194,000 out of the $250,000 which the government had provided as capital. This was possible because the money used to purchase stock subscriptions to establish the bank was specie; the money borrowed was received in the form of bank notes. The credit created by this financial institution as reflected in its notes enabled the Financier to borrow $400,000, minus discounts—that is, the full amount of its capitalization—within six months after the Bank began operations.[11]

Of course, to maintain this credit and to exploit its possibilities, it was essential that the bank notes circulate at par. At the beginning there was little evidence of discounting in the Philadelphia area itself, but in New England, in the lower South, and to a lesser degree in New York and Virginia, the notes were seldom accepted at full face value. Indeed, the rate of discount seemed to vary in proportion to the distance from Philadelphia. But the history of the Bank during its first year is a story of growing credit, as reflected by wider circulation of its notes and its increased business. When the stockholders met in November 1782, less than a year after the grand opening, Thomas Willing, the Bank's president, cheerfully reported upon "the progress the Bank had made in regard to the number of its customers, and the extensive circulation of its notes," and he commented briefly on its "present flourishing situation and flattering prospects."[12]

The entire year had not promised such a pleasant ending, however, and the Bank had been confronted by a multitude of problems in the course of its operation, many of which had not been resolved by the time the directors met. During the year the question whether the

Bank should invest in public securities was raised. It was decided that the Financier's advice in this instance was sound: "Those securities would be ultimately good," he had assured the directors, "but they would soon absorb their whole capital and therefore too dangerous to the Institution." States had come to borrow money, pledging the income from certain taxes or other securities as collateral. When the case of Pennsylvania arose in April, the Bank decided to loan some 30,000 pounds on this basis, but by the time Maryland applied three months later with a similar scheme, the Bank found itself so short of resources that the directors were forced to disappoint that state. To apply limits to private traders in the discounting of notes had been brought up and decided on the basis of expediency. During a certain period, for example, the officers had stopped all discounting, with respect to the government as well as private traders, because the Bank had overextended itself. In fact, government loans and discounting were chiefly responsible for this condition; beginning in September, as a consequence, delegations from the Bank became frequent visitors in the Financier's office to urge partial repayment of the government loans.[13]

In summary, therefore, the Bank helped the Financier expedite his everyday financial transactions; it provided an acceptable currency to substitute in part for the worthless Continental; it attracted private funds and credit which augmented its role in "mobilizing the existing private credit"; and most important, it consolidated and multiplied the available credit which the Financier could and did exploit for the advantage of the government. There can be no question that the Bank of North America, the first financial instrument instituted by the Superintendent of Finance to aid in the restoration of the public credit, served significantly in facilitating the comprehensive program.

Although somewhat less successful than the Bank, the Morris notes, the second device instituted by the Financier, were equally important in bolstering faith in the public credit by the use of private credit. The Morris notes, as has been previously discussed, were intended first as a medium of exchange to act as a partial substitute for the collapsed Continental currency, and second as notes which would be used as "anticipations" of tax collection in specie. In fulfilling these functions, the notes encountered some difficulties. If their operation during 1782 is compared with the depreciation of the Continental currency, the results were spectacular; if their operation is compared with the hopes of the Financier, the benefits were largely, though not entirely, realized.

The most persistent problem that plagued the Morris notes as a medium of exchange was their initial tendency to depreciate in certain areas of the country. In Philadelphia and the surrounding region, the Morris notes, along with Bank notes, were accepted as cash "with the traders." But as one examines the region "to the Eastward" the situation changes. In New York, for example, a reluctance to accept such notes at par was reported almost immediately. "The little currency there is in your state of Bank notes and Mr. Morris's notes embarrasses me," the Quartermaster General wrote to his deputy in New York. "I depended on their perfect credit and easy exchange for cash, thro the taxes." In the Massachusetts area, the tendency was even more pronounced; James Lovell, the Receiver of Taxes in that state, reported discounts of 10 to 15 per cent. Because the lower South was still functioning under a system of specific supplies, Morris notes were not extensively utilized; but in the upper South, where their use was comparatively widespread, they apparently circulated at par. It appears, therefore, that the rate of discount, with the exception of the South, varied initially in proportion to the distance of the region from Philadelphia.[14]

The Financier was not alarmed by this early depreciation of his notes. He observed that the public faith in any type of paper medium had been thoroughly shattered and that it would take time to restore it. But, he reassured Lovell in Boston where the condition was most pronounced, when those persons who had sold their notes at a discount saw them exchanged at par, the credit of the notes would soon be established.[15]

During the course of the year 1782, the credit of the Morris notes improved greatly in New York, but only slightly in Massachusetts. The notes were accepted as cash throughout much of New York, although the danger of discounting continued because of the actions of the army contractors.

It appears to me [wrote the Inspector of the Army, General Cornell, from New York] that the contractors have crowded your notes too hard. They have lodged them in the hands of the collectors in every part of the country where money is collecting for taxes and disgusts [disquiets?] those who have taken them for supplies, and has I apprehend hurt their credit, and if the practice is pursued I think it will tend to depreciate them.

At the same time Hamilton, who had accepted the job of Receiver in New York at Morris' insistence, wrote the Financier that "bank notes pass pretty currently as cash, with a manifest preference to your notes." In Massachusetts decided discounting continued, despite the fact that a firmer credit had been established for a brief period, and regardless of Morris' decision, in late August, not only to stop issuing the notes but also to destroy them "as they are brought in." In October, Daniel Parker of Watertown, Massachusetts, who had earlier requested notes from army contractors, now wrote: "The notes on Swanwick are in the hands of every person and the rumor is spread among the mercantile people that he has not cash to take them up. . . ." Lovell, the Connecticut Receiver, could not escape the insistent pressure, and his appeals became so urgent that the Financier, in December, finally authorized him to employ whatever funds were on hand to buy up "any of my paper" in an effort to preserve the public credit.[16]

There are several possible explanations why the rate of discount in Morris notes tended to vary in proportion to the distance from Philadelphia, with the exception of the South. The complaint that $20, the smallest note, was unsuitable for such areas as agrarian New York because it was too large for general circulation was possibly valid, but this argument would not hold for the Boston area. The deliberate attempt of a few extreme critics of Morris—most significantly Arthur Lee, the former Commissioner to France—who, according to James Madison planned to discredit Morris by attacking his notes, may have been partly responsible; the influence of these critics, however, did not parallel the rate of discount. The practices of some tax collectors assuredly influenced the discounting of notes, for they could exchange the specie they collected in taxes for Morris notes which they sometimes obtained at a discount. The collectors, in turn, would present the notes at the Treasury and receive credit for them at their face value, thus netting a handsome profit. Perhaps the most satisfactory explanation, however, lies in the influence and previous business connections of Morris. These connections, as has been previously described, were heavily weighted from Philadelphia southward, and in those areas his reputation as a merchant stood without precedent. Morris was known "to the Eastward," of course, but his business relationships were limited, and his fame and word as a merchant was based much more on hearsay than on actual contact. In brief, the notes of the Superintendent of Finance seemed to vary with the credit of Morris as a merchant.[17]

The chief obstacle hampering the second function of the Morris notes, that is, their use as anticipations on taxes, was the lack of specie payment in the collection of revenue. As the Financier remarked, the notes "constantly returned upon me for payment instead of being absorbed by the taxes." This meant, first, that the notes would be in circulation much longer than the Financier had originally expected, and second, that some other source of specie would have to be tapped in order to meet those obligations which called for specie payment.[18]

Only three alternatives could salvage such a situation: one, of course, involved a spurt in tax collection in specie; two, further aid from abroad to provide the new source of specie; or three, the increased use and acceptance of the Morris notes as a circulating medium with a gradual elimination of the Morris warrants.

Although it is almost impossible to determine precisely how many Morris notes were in circulation by the end of 1782, their function in the Morris program was vital. A combination of Morris notes, which were payable to the bearer at sight, and Morris' warrants on Swanwick, that is, bills drawn payable to bearer or to a specific person with a particular due date, amounted to some $400,000. The benefit of this credit equaled that made available by the Bank of North America; and together these two financial instruments supplied a credit to the nation in excess of three-quarter million dollars. To present this figure more realistically in terms of the time, the total expenditures in 1782 amounted to $2,300,000, which indicates that the credit supplied by the Bank and Morris notes was 35 to 40 per cent of the whole. The problem of preserving the important credit of the Morris notes depended, of course, upon the promptness with which the Financier could continue to honor the warrants as they became due, while meeting daily the constant presentation of Morris notes.[19]

Funding the debts of the Confederation had been advocated by the Superintendent of Finance as one of the key policies within his program on public credit. In outlining this phase of his program, he had concentrated on the obligations between the Confederation and the respective states, for the most part, and had proposed that a general settlement of accounts be made as a prerequisite to any funding program. Although the Financier had noted the importance of funding the loan office certificates and had suggested a means by which Congress could fund those continental certificates which had been given as compensation for goods and services, Congress had not taken action upon his proposal.

In operation, Morris' program on funding during 1782 made some progress in settling accounts, but the most important development was the maturation in the ideas and policies of the Financier, particularly in relation to the "public debt"—that is, foreign loans and domestic loans (loan office certificates and continental certificates such as those issued by the Commissary and Quartermaster, given for goods and services). With respect to the settlement of accounts, Morris made most of the necessary appointments to implement the policies adopted, and worked hard to fulfill this enormous task with speed, accuracy, and efficiency. The further refinement of the Financier's ideas in relation to funding the public debt was prompted partly by a growing pressure outside of Congress by groups of public creditors who demanded some kind of action, but it was also the result of a clearer comprehension of the implications of this policy and its place within the entire program. Embodying his ideas in a remarkable message to Congress, Morris presented the same arguments, logic, and design later employed by Alexander Hamilton in his celebrated First Report on Public Credit.

The Financier made every effort to carry out the enormous task of settling the accounts. By December he had appointed commissioners to settle the accounts in nine of the states and in every major department except the Marine, although all the appointees had not yet been confirmed. In making these selections, the Financier made certain that the appointee was neither a resident of the state whose accounts he was to settle nor a member or former member of a department whose accounts must be examined. It was not easy to find persons who were, according to Morris, "men of character and abilities equal to the undertaking and willing to engage in it," because the pay was not particularly good, the problems were endless, and the traveling involved in the job was rigorous.[20]

Instructing these commissioners with becoming brevity, Morris advocated care and accuracy. "Artful men have frequently taken advantage of the public and . . . in many instances public officers have taken advantage of the weak and unprotected," warned the Financier. The commissioners should remember that it was their duty to do justice, and this meant "to discover, bring to light, pursue and punish fraud and peculations of every kind where ever you may meet them." The Financier offered advice to detect it—and Arthur Lee could certainly find grim humor in these suggestions. If the statements made by any governmental officer during the period indicated that he had had funds at hand for a considerable length of time, declared Morris, then the commissioners should investigate more thoroughly. This task, the Financier realized, would be "laborious and painful," but the public interest demanded it.[21]

The real problems, however, started when the commissioners actually began to investigate the mass of unsettled accounts. What vouchers could be accepted as satisfactory? If public officers were given funds, and they, in turn, distributed those funds to others, who was responsible? What about claims based on material that had been lost through the hazards of war? If a state refused to permit an examination of its accounts with the Confederation, could any positive action be taken? These constituted only a few of a legion of queries which began to flood in from the various commissioners. Most of them echoed Jonathan Burrell, one of their number, when he complained that "the issuing part in particular is involved in impenetrable intricacy and irregularity."[22]

In addition to fulfilling the measures already adopted, the Financier took steps to bring the accounts of the loan officers within the general policy of settlement. After some debate and even more delay, Congress authorized the commissioners for the various states to settle the accounts of the loan officer within each of their respective states. Thus, Congress placed another duty upon those public servants who were already overburdened.[23]

Action was also taken on settling the intricate, confused, and extensive accounts in Europe, but only after some six months of Congressional hesitation. In May, the Financier urged that Franklin be authorized to settle the accounts with the French Court and that a commissioner be appointed to settle accounts between the United States and "their public servants" who had served abroad. ". . . There appears to have been but little received for the great sums which have been expended, and therefore it is highly necessary that the public accounts of these States with their servants in Europe be also settled," asserted Morris. "Their magnitude, as well as other circumstances, makes me extremely solicitous to have them adjusted." At first Congress responded with a resolution incorporating the Financier's recommendations, but two months later, without forewarning, that body suddenly recommitted its action. Some personal antagonisms may have been responsible for this move, because Arthur Lee, who played an important part in the reconsideration, had some scores to settle with Franklin, Deane, and others. The hesitation transcended individuals, however, for many members of Congress were reluctant to delegate such extensive powers to one person—that is, settling "finally" the tremendous expenditures and claims abroad. The major difference between the Congressional committee and the Financier was: Should the accounts abroad be obtained and then sent to America where they would be finally settled, or should the commissioner abroad complete the entire settlement? The committee held to the former view, while Morris favored the latter.

Morris' arguments that the commissioner abroad could interview the people, pursue the necessary examinations, command additional evidence, and if necessary bring suit, were apparently persuasive, for his view was finally accepted. Indeed, the final resolution authorizing the commissioner to settle the accounts of those who handled money in Europe contains the precise wording which the Financier had recommended in an earlier letter to the committee.[24]

Thomas Barclay, a man of considerable mercantile experience in Europe and an American consul in France, was immediately elected to the new position. A few weeks later Morris outlined in some detail the general instructions which Barclay should follow: Caution when employing accountants, to insure their competence; care in auditing accounts; zeal in rooting out excessive commissions or fees; scrupulousness in determining the amount of goods lost in captured vessels. To reinforce the insistence of Congress, the Financier again stressed the need for bringing Beaumarchais' accounts under the "strictest scrutiny." ". . . Whatever may have been the character of the persons concerned, either for ability or integrity, the business which has passed through their hands has not been well done." Moreover, Barclay might well find "other large accounts which merit a like attention." There was scarcely a hint of the enormous obstacles which anyone settling such accounts must surmount. In fact, there was hardly a breath of realism in Morris' entire letter. It sounded fine, as did the settlement of domestic accounts, when it was on paper, but in actual operation it was quite another story.[25]

With the settling of accounts being forwarded in one category of debts, the Financier's attention was drawn increasingly toward the "public debt"—foreign and domestic loans. The Financier continued to urge the adoption of the impost, "the first step," in his correspondence and conversation with individuals and in his public letters to the states. For those states adopting the impost, the Financier bestowed lavish praise. He assured Pennsylvania that its action on the impost would always stand as a "flattering monument of zeal for the glorious cause we are engaged in, of regard for the sacred principles of moral justice and of adherence to the exalted dictates of national obligation." If all the states had followed the lead of Pennsylvania, their joint action "would have dried up the tears of many fatherless children and removed from a thousand worthy bosoms the heavy load of affliction." Some of this extravagant prose—not to mention extravagant claims—reflects a bit of Gouverneur Morris' touch.[26]

In February the Financier submitted to Congress suggestions for additional sources of revenue, to provide a uniform tax plan throughout the states to fund the public debt. Although he had mentioned additional taxes previously, Morris now offered more definite advice. He called for a land tax of $1 for every 100 acres of land, a poll tax of $1 on all freemen and all male slaves between 16 and 60, and an excise of one-eighth of a dollar per gallon on all distilled spirituous liquors. Soldiers in the Federal army and persons incapacitated were excepted from the poll tax; otherwise the plan allowed for no reservations. In general, Morris' supporting arguments at this time were mild. The variety of taxes which composed the tax package would equalize the burden, he asserted, while the taxes themselves were comparatively moderate.[27]

These proposals met with unfriendly hands in Congress. A committee composed of Arthur Lee, Samuel Osgood, and Abraham Clark reported unfavorably on the suggestions, and for several months this move choked off any further action to forward the funding of the public debt. Only when Morris once again urged, in a report to Congress, that all interest payments on loan office certificates be stopped did the entire question suddenly become very much alive.[28]

The issue of providing additional revenue to fund the public debt was by no means confined to Congress at this stage; "out of doors" perceptible pressure began to build up. More than that, the men involved enjoyed the express blessing of the Financier. Such men as Colonel Walter Stewart called to see Morris and warned him that unless some action was taken to provide for the interest the public creditors would become "clamorous." When, in the course of the conversation, Stewart suggested a meeting of public creditors, the Financier approved. Morris made it clear, however, that a delegation of "sensible, cool men" should obtain the true information about the cause for their ills, that the states and not Congress were delinquent. At the same time, Morris assured Stewart that he was "very desirous to serve and support" the public creditors "in their claim to justice."[29]

The pressure continued to build up, with the encouragement of the Financier. Within a few days Congress received some letters and memorials, as did the assembly of Pennsylvania, and they were referred to the Financier. He then called in Ewing, Pettit, Rush, and McClenaghan, "the committee appointed by the public creditors to solicit the payment of interest on the public debts," and told them that "the matter rests in this office." He advised them "to make one common cause with the whole of the public creditors of every kind," and "to unite their interest so that they might be able to have influence on all the legislatures in the several states." He would lend them his full support; but they should avoid "the language of threats

which has already been complained of in their proceedings." According to Morris, the committee replied that, if such expressions had
crept into their efforts, it resulted from the ridicule of those who
thought their "pursuit" in vain. Nor were they softened on other
matters. When Morris mentioned that interest payments could not be
made that year, even if his plans should be adopted, they "took up
this point very warmly." [30]

This memorial and these actions served a purpose which exceeded
their immediate importance, because they afforded the Financier a
springboard for the most important single state paper on public credit
ever written prior to Hamilton's First Report on Public Credit. Indeed, its sweep, boldness, and scope might well have provided Washington's Secretary of the Treasury with a model. The document itself,
dated July 29, 1782, set off a chain of reactions which catapulted the
question of public credit into a major political crisis in the spring
of 1783.

In the Financier's Report on Public Credit, he emphasized the need
and the virtue of borrowing. "Taxation to a certain point is not only
proper but useful," he asserted, "but when taxes go so far as to en-
trench on the subsistence of the people they have become burdensome
and oppressive." Such tax burdens were a far greater threat to succeeding generations than was a debt, Morris stated. Borrowing was
beneficial rather than a burdensome, he asserted, as he sketched the
activities of an imaginary husbandman who made imaginary profits
on borrowed funds.

Assuming that borrowing was beneficial, then the relative merits
of foreign or domestic loans must be examined, he continued. Domestic loans entailed some disadvantages because money would have to
be diverted from channels toward which it would normally flow. The
government would have to bid higher than private individuals for
the available funds, a process which might endanger the means of the
individual to extend his industry, particularly when the capital available was limited. But, asserted the Financier, there was an exception
"where the creditor spares from his consumption to lend to the Government, which operates a national economy," and this, in his eyes,
described the situation at hand. Indeed, the advantages of domestic
loans more than counterbalanced the disadvantages. First, ". . . they
[domestic loans] give stability to Government by combining together
the interests of the moneyed men for its support," a prospect particularly useful in the United States where a domestic debt "would greatly
contribute to that union which seems not to have been sufficiently attended to or provided for in forming the national compact." Second,
such a loan would secure a great relief in taxation for the "lower
orders of the community" where the tax burden rested heavily, and
consequently they could extend their "commerce or tillage." Third,
said Morris, such a loan would cut down, to an extent, an excess of
money, which would in turn curtail speculation.

Foreign loans, according to the Financier, provided the same benefits that one individual received when borrowing from another, and he stressed former practices of such credits in the colonies. The only real objection to foreign loans, the idea that paying interest on such borrowings drained the country of specie, was swept away with the argument that the improvements made possible by a loan would be responsible for an increase in wealth far in excess of the interest rate. Foreign loans, however, could not be procured without credit, declared Morris, so it obviously followed that credit must be acquired "at home before it can be extended abroad."

Thus, in order to enjoy those blessings of obtaining loans, public faith and confidence must be revived; and this could only be achieved by funding the public debt—foreign loans and domestic loans. "Justice" must be done.

It is, therefore, with the greatest propriety your petitioners, already mentioned, have stated in their memorial that both policy and justice require a solid provision for funding the public debts. It is with pleasure, sir, that I see this numerous, meritorious, and oppressed body of men, who are creditors of the public, beginning to exert themselves for the obtaining of justice. I hope they may succeed, not only because I wish well to so righteous a pursuit, but because their success will be the great ground work of a credit that will carry us safely through the present just, important, and necessary war, which will combine us closely together on the conclusion of a peace; which will always give to the supreme representative of America a means of acting for the general defence on sudden emergencies, and which will, of consequence, procure the third of these great objects for which we contend, *peace, liberty, and safety.*

Machinery to "liquidate" all accounts had been set up, Morris continued, "and if the States shall make the necessary grants of revenue, what remains will be a simple executive operation." These grants should be made because of the moral obligation if for no other reason, he asserted.

To satisfy those who grumbled over the expense of funding the public debt, Morris stressed the considerable advantages which the community would derive from the operation. First, many persons who were now public creditors were deprived of "the full exercise of their skill and industry" because some of their funds were tied up in such certificates. Thus the benefit which the community would derive from their more extensive economic activity could not materialize. ". . . If these debts, which are in a manner dead, were brought back to existence moneyed men would purchase them up, though perhaps at a considerable discount, and thereby restore to the public many useful members who are now entirely lost, and extend the operations of many more to considerable advantage." Although this would not produce any extra revenue, property would flow into the hands of those who could make it most productive, and in time the sources of revenue would be augmented. Second, foreigners would tend to invest their money in the funded debt and thus help to supply the lack of credit which the mercantile community needed abroad. Third, private credit would be enhanced by the confidence enjoyed by the public credit, securely based on a comprehensive funding program. Hoarding would cease and credit relations would be facilitated. All three of these "advantages," commented the Financier, would increase the available revenue.

Morris calculated the public debt at $25,000,000—$12,000,000 as the value of the loan office certificates and their back interest, $8,000,000 in various certificates given for goods and services, and $5,000,000 in foreign loans. This sum, in addition to loans still necessary for current expenditures in the coming year, would bring the total to $30,000,000. It meant that nearly $2,000,000 was required annually to meet the interest payments of these obligations.

Four general considerations, the Financier continued, had to be borne in mind in meeting this interest. First, funds should be provided before attempting to obtain further loans; second, it would be destructive to borrow abroad to pay domestic debts; third, revenues to pay this interest must be ample and assured; and fourth, the revenues should come from sources which tended to increase in income.

What sources of revenue did the Financier have in mind which would fill these specifications? The impost, of course, which Morris thought "may be considered as being already granted." (Rhode Island still held out, but Morris was convinced after a conversation with Cornell and Howell of Rhode Island that it would soon fall into line.) But the impost was not enough—as he had earlier indicated—and he repeated his plan for a land tax, a poll tax, and an excise on liquor. Each kind of tax would yield, according to Morris' calculations, $500,000, thus totaling the necessary $2,000,000 to make interest payments.

This time the Financier included an extended discussion on the advantages and necessity of each tax. The land tax of $1 for 100 acres might "startle" the "free husbandman" who is "the natural guardian of his country's freedom," but he would find the tax a "trifling object" in comparison to the extensive landholder. Moreover, the large landholders should feel the weight of the tax, continued the Financier, for "they monopolize it [land] without cultivation," and they "impede the settlement and culture of the country." A distinction in the tax rate based on the value of the land would be impracticable because of the delay, expense, and uncertainty in making the appraisals. Besides, land so worthless that the owner will not pay one penny an acre for its defense "ought to belong to the society by whom the expense of defending it is defrayed." The poll tax and the excise tax were not treated as extensively—possibly because the audience addressed by the Financier did not need to be persuaded on the usefulness of these sources. The conventional arguments were presented in each case. The poll tax would be insignificant to the rich, of small consequence to the "middling ranks," and not harsh for the poor "because such of them as are unable to labor will fall within the exception proposed." As for the excise, "the tax will be a means of compelling vice to support the cause of virtue. . . ."

After commenting on the administrative reforms in the collection of these taxes, the Financier explained the method of funding he favored.

It would be as follows: any one of the revenues being estimated, a loan should be opened on the credit of it, by subscription to a certain amount, and public debts of a particular description or species be received in payment of the subscriptions. This funded debt should be transferable under particular forms calculated for the prevention of fraudulent, and facilitating of honest negotiations. In like manner on each of these revenues should subscriptions be opened, proceeding by degrees so as to prevent any sudden revolutions in money matters, such revolutions being always more or less injurious.

The excess of revenue from any one of these taxes—"and care should be taken that there would be a surplus"—should be placed in a sinking fund, to reduce the total obligation.

Recognizing that the method proposed "would enable speculators to perform their operations," the Financier did not conceive that the consequences would be as disastrous as some persons imagined. He listed several reasons why the fear of speculation did not intrude into his funding plan: it was beneath the "dignity of government to intermeddle in such considerations"; speculators always did the least "mischief" where they were left most at liberty; and legislation could not halt their operations. Going beyond these negative considerations, he asserted that speculation was precisely the thing that should not be prevented. "He who wants money to commence, pursue, or extend his business, is more benefited by selling stock of any kind, even at a considerable discount, than he could by the rise of it at a future period." Every man could judge his own situation better than the government could for him, declared Morris. What the Financier presumed—and mistakenly so—was that all the citizens would be equally informed on the proceedings and ramifications of any action by the government on funding.

But should the public debts be funded at their face value, especially in view of the activities of the speculators? Most assuredly, replied the Financier. Many men, "and some of them honest men," let their "zeal against speculation" interfere with sound policy and "even of moral justice." Such men objected that the speculators should be paid no more than their purchase money because they have taken advantage of a "distressed creditor and shown a diffidence in the public faith." What they have done, said Morris, going back to his old argument, is afford the creditor of the government some relief when the creditor wanted it. As for confidence in the public faith, he thought the purchaser showed as much faith as the seller. Even if the "diffidence" existed, Morris asserted that it was far wiser "to remove than to justify it." Funding at face value would tend "to create, establish, and secure the public credit" while the other mode would tend "to sap, overturn, and destroy it." "The debt is a species of property," continued the Financier, "and whether disposed of for the whole nominal value or the half, for something or for nothing, is totally immaterial."

One final subject remained to be discussed, the important question of western lands. Why not use this resource to pay the public creditors? The benefits here are vastly overrated, said Morris, and he outlined succinctly the reasons why western lands would prove inadequate as revenue to fund the public debt.

If these lands were now in the hands of Congress, and they were willing to mortgage them to their present creditors, unless this were accompanied with a due provision for the interest it would bring no relief. If these lands were to be sold for the public debts they would go off for almost nothing. Those who want money could not afford to buy land. Their certificates would be bought up for a trifle. Very few moneyed men would become possessed of them, because very little money would be invested in so remote a speculation. The small number of purchasers would easily and readily combine; of consequence they would acquire the lands for almost nothing, and effectually defeat the intentions of Government, leaving it still under the necessity of making further provision, after having needlessly squandered an immense property.

Later, when public credit had been firmly established and the lands would command their proper value, he observed, this resource could be used as security in borrowing abroad at low interest rates.[31]

This significant document of July 1782, combined with the message sent to Congress in November 1781, constitute the Superintendent of Finance's Reports on Public Credit; these Reports reflect a penetration, a boldness in design, and a breadth in scope perhaps not equaled among the Financier's contemporaries. Although the first message provided for limited assumption of state debts by the central government and contained suggestions for a settlement of accounts as a prerequisite to funding, it was primarily concerned with the state-Confederation relationship on debts; the second report was devoted almost exclusively to the public debt—foreign loans and the various certificates of indebtedness. The latter embodied all the significant arguments and the general outline which was included in Hamilton's First Report on Public Credit of 1790, but Hamilton's Report wove the two threads of state-Confederation debts and public debts into a single strand. It remained to be seen whether the Financier would eventually combine them into one.

Apparently Gouverneur Morris helped to draft much of the second message, but all the evidence indicates that the finished document contained the sentiments and the imprint of the Superintendent of Finance. In writing to Appleton of Massachusetts some three months earlier, the Financier had made his position explicit:

I beg you will remind him [Governor Hancock] that his generosity, humanity, and justice are all concerned in promoting the establishment of permanent revenues sufficient to discharge the interest of our public debt. Nay, more; the political existence of America depends on the accomplishment of this plan. We cannot be called a nation nor do we deserve to be ranked amongst the nations of the earth until we do justice to those who have served and trusted us. A public debt, supported by public revenue, will prove the strongest cement to keep our Confederacy together. Sound policy would also dictate that we should do justice to those who have trusted us, in order that we may have pretensions to credit in the future. We might, then, tax the present race of citizens six pounds, instead of a hundred, and leave posterity to pay the principal of a debt contracted in consequence of our distresses and necessities, but from which they will derive ease and emolument. I could say a great deal more on this subject and probably shall to the world at large, if the just measures of Congress continue to meet with such ill-judged opposition.[32]

When Morris' Report on the Public Credit reached Congress, the entire question of funding the public debt was reviewed, but the ideas and policies involved in his message did not take on their fullest meaning until a political crisis arose in the early months of 1783. The Grand Committee, which was composed of one member from each state to consider "the most effectual means of supporting the credit of the United States," recommended the adoption of Morris' proposals on new sources of revenue to fund the debt, with one exception. That exception was embraced in a prefatory resolution suggesting that western lands would serve as an important fund to repay the debts of the United States, a point of view which the Financier had deplored. Although the report of the Committee commanded the support of a majority of its members, its recommendations on taxation were all defeated on the floor of Congress. Each tax provoked some differences, but the land tax aroused the sharpest conflict. States such as North Carolina which possessed vast reaches of barren territory felt that such a tax would discriminate against them, while states like Rhode Island were interested in shifting the tax from trade to land. Indeed, Morris' entire program on funding tended to become intricately interwoven with the whole difficult and disputatious problem of western lands. The only positive actions of Congress on funding were, first, an additional requisition upon the states for $1,200,000 to pay the interest to the public creditors and, second, the adoption of Morris' recommendation to stop drawing bills to pay for the interest on loan office certificates. Designed to satisfy the Morris program on funding—and the public creditors—temporarily, these measures were considered by the Financier to be feeble gestures. In writing to the Governor of Rhode Island, the hold-out on the impost, about the new requisition, Morris wrote simply: "It is . . . a futile measure."[33]

The expectation that Rhode Island would follow the lead of her sister states and soon adopt the impost was also destined to be disappointed. David Howell, leader of the opposition to a Confederation duty in Rhode Island, had been deliberately shielding his true sentiments on the measure since his arrival in Philadelphia as a delegate. When asked to appear before a Congressional committee which was investigating why the passage of the impost was delayed, Howell made his view known without equivocation. Morris, who was also present, asked for his objections in writing, a request Howell was quick to fulfill.[34]

To the readers of the *Providence Gazette,* the objections which Howell committed to paper would have had a familiar ring: the matter of collection, the fear of high prices, smuggling, etc. But these reservations were subordinated to one primary fear, that Rhode Island as a commercial state would shoulder a greater burden of the finances of the Confederation than she deemed her share, with the result that her strength would be sapped for the benefit of other members of the Confederation. Morris attempted to answer these objections in a letter to the governor of the state, but his efforts were scarcely more effective than saying, "It is not true."[35]

When the Rhode Island legislature failed to act on the impost in its September session, Congress resolved to apply pressure by demanding a "definitive" answer from that state. The Rhode Island legislature responded on November 1, 1782, by voting unanimously against the impost. Congress, in turn, without a single dissenting vote except the delegates of Rhode Island, resolved to send a committee composed of Mifflin, Nash, and Osgood to that state in order to "make a full and just representation of the public affairs of the United States," to urge the adoption of the impost and to answer objections. The news from Rhode Island had prompted this action in part, but the suspicion that information on foreign affairs had been misrepresented to appear more optimistic than it was in fact—and the suspicion rested on Howell, a Rhode Island delegate—supplied its share of incentive. Even Tom Paine, who had commenced writing for Morris, offered to go to Rhode Island to answer the objections of the legislature. The committee's delay in setting off hindered the projected expedition, but the news that Virginia, without any forewarning, had rescinded her consent to the impost, halted it.[36]

Why had Rhode Island taken its stand against the impost? The spokesman for that state's position does not indicate that it arbitrarily opposed payment of public creditors; indeed, such an opinion was seldom, if ever, heard in or out of Congress. "They [the public creditors] ought however to be paid," said Howell, "and we make no doubt they will be paid, to the extent of their just demands and that in a Continental way, and no other." What, then, was the "Continental way?" For the present, the requisitions of Congress. As for the future —the western lands! "And as some States pertinaciously persisted in claiming exclusive rights to sd [said] lands," Howell had told the Congressional Committee, "it was not to be expected that our State would part with all the benefits of its maritime Situation untill some assurance would be obtained of a Participation in common with other States in the back lands, which ought to be considered as a continental acquisition and to be appropriated accordingly." Or, as he stated later in the same report, "They [the "back lands"] would, undoubtedly be a means in our hands of reviving public credit; they are of vast extent and value, beyond what is generally known or conjectured." Here is a good part of the explanation of Rhode Island's view of the impost.[37]

But there were other considerations equal in importance; among them the singular nature of Rhode Island's trade ranked high. Most of the goods imported were not consumed within the state; rather, they were made into finished products and reëxported abroad or to other states. In meeting the general market outside the country, the merchants of Rhode Island, it was thought, would be at a disadvantage in having to add to their selling price the cost of the impost levies. Indeed, it was entirely possible that, in competing with traders outside the country, the merchants would have to absorb the cost of this levy, thus narrowing their margin of profit. With respect to selling to individuals in other states within the Confederation, there was the assertion that, if any import duties be levied, the revenue should be at the disposal of the state. Rhode Island, it was presumed, would greatly benefit because it would be taxing its neighbors—an assumption not borne out in the years following.[38]

In contrast to the other parts of his program on the restoration of the public credit, Morris' program on funding was making, at best, limited progress. Many important preliminary steps had been taken in settling the accounts, but the key proposal to fund the "public debts" without delay, although supported by a powerful message from the Financier, failed to receive a favorable response in Congress during 1782. Moreover, the measure which Morris conceived to be the first step in supporting the funding program—the impost—had been blocked by the unanimous vote of the Rhode Island legislature. For the time being, certainly, a good part of Morris' program on funding as a measure to revive the public credit was thwarted; it would be a great mistake, however, to assume that it had been killed.

CHAPTER — EIGHT

The Program in Operation:
A Story of Growing Tension (1782)

THE LONG-RANGE PROGRAM OF MORRIS ON PUBLIC CREDIT INCLUDED OTHER ingredients besides specific financial devices, and its fate rested in large measure upon these closely interrelated components, his plans with respect to revenue and expenditures. Morris hoped, of course, to increase the revenue while curtailing expenditures; this would enable him to meet promptly the current obligations of the Confederation and thus help to restore confidence in the public credit.

Although the Financier enjoyed a measure of success in both aspects of this program, his expectations were not realized. Not only was the collection of domestic revenue disappointing, but the decline of trading activity seriously hampered Morris in utilizing those sources that became available abroad. Because of these developments in revenue, the contracting system, the most important measure in Morris' program of economy, was endangered; in fact, only extraordinary action prevented its abandonment.

In the revenue program, it should be recalled, the Financier had to operate within the limits of the Articles of Confederation. He had established receivers of taxes in the various states in an effort to narrow, by administrative techniques, the separation between the Confederation and the states in the collection of revenue, and he exploited the only "coercive" weapon available to him—persuasion. Using these devices, the Financier enjoyed a measure of success; in relative terms the contributions of the states, despite a drastic downward trend in economic prosperity, constituted a greater percentage of the total revenue in 1782 than in any of the early years of the war from 1775 to January 1781. Still, it was far short of expectations, and the Financier filled the gap between income and outlay with loans from the Bank of North America, with credit furnished by the Morris notes, and with foreign loans.

In wielding his weapon of persuasion, the Financier wrote two letters in February, one to Congress and the other to the states, which were particularly incisive if not outright aggressive. Congress was warned, once again, that ". . . to expect that foreigners will trust a government which has no credit with its own citizens would be madness." Although financial support at home was the only answer when "even the slightest anticipations of revenue are made on the personal credit of the minister," exclaimed Morris, not a single state had laid taxes to fulfill the requisitions for the current expenditures of the year. The states came in for a verbal lashing in which Morris deplored the delicacy which prevented some members of Congress from censuring the hesitant. "I know that delicacy, and I disclaim it," asserted the Financier. "Nor will I be deterred from waking those who slumber on the brink of ruin." He concluded with a strong plea for Congressional support. "But my voice, sir, is feeble, and I must therefore pray to be assisted by the voice of the United States in Congress. Supported by them, I may, perhaps, do something; but without that support I must be a useless encumbrance."[1]

The Financier's circular letter to the states repeated those arguments used with Congress, but they were couched in softer phrases. He emphasized the benefits which had resulted from the actions already taken in finance and appealed rather eloquently for their support—to keep "little trivial disputes of a private, partial, or local nature" from interfering with the great objects, the defense of the country.

Let us, for heaven's sake, while engaged in a cause the most honorable, the most virtuous, and which must endear the present generation to future ages, let us preserve a conduct noble, dignified, and worthy of that glorious cause; in pursuit of the greatest, the dearest object which man can possess, in the fair road to peace, liberty, and safety, let us not fall out by the way. But, united to and supporting each other, let our efforts be equal to our claims, and let us show that we have the perseverance to obtain what we had the spirit to demand. Let us at once become independent, really and truly independent, independent of our enemies, of our friends, of all but the Omnipotent.[2]

These communications were not conceived on the spur of the moment. The Financier had talked at great length with Washington about some of the problems involved, and when the letter was written, the Commander-in-Chief and the Secretary for Foreign Affairs, Robert Livingston, were called in to examine it and make such alterations as they thought necessary. Morris, according to his own account, told Washington and Livingston that he considered the letters to be extremely important, that they were written "in the spirit of freedom and in terms that may possibly give offense," but he thought that it was necessary to "rouse into spirited action" the groups which were being addressed. He considered the letters as "ministerial" papers, and he wanted the unqualified support of Washington and Livingston when he presented them—"to all which they agreed."[3]

When Morris' confidential letter to Franklin written almost a month later is read, it is difficult to see what prompted the general letters, for

Morris gave Franklin a candid survey of revenue expectations from
the states which showed that an early or ready response was not anticipated.

> . . . All therefore which remains is to shew the Deficiencies which there will
> be in the Grants of the several States. The Quotas assigned to New-Jersey &
> Delaware amount to one million seven hundred eighteen thoud. five hundred
> fifty eight dollars. I expect that these three States will pass Laws for collect-
> ing the sums assigned to them, but from the amount must be deducted first
> the Expence of Collection, which is not, as I can learn, provided for. And
> secondly the Deficiencies from the exposed and frontier Parts which cannot
> pay at all. Even after making the Deductions which will reduce it to less
> than a million & an half, you may depend that a very considerable part will
> not have been paid before the beginning of next year, and very little of it
> will be paid before midsummer. The Quotas of Connect, R. Island & Mass.
> amount to two millions two hundred seventyone thousand four hundred
> seventy six Dollars, and I have no Doubt that they will exert themselves to
> grant what they conceive themselves able to bear, but I should be extremely
> happy to be convinced that I would receive from those States one million of
> Dollars by the first Day of September, and one more by the first of March.
> As to the States of New York & New Hamp. You know, Sir better than I do
> the internal contests which now distract them. These & other Circumstances
> induce me to despair of a Revenue from those States. Mary. & Virg. are
> deluged with Paper Money and have adopted the vicious mode of collecting
> Taxes in Kind; after the late Distresses on their commerce, and the Ravages
> made by the Enemy, they will take time to breathe. Depend therefore that
> we shall receive nothing from them before next autumn, and very little then.
> As to the more southern States their Situation is such, that we cannot hope
> more from them, than meerly to feed the Troops—which are engaged in
> their Defence, and indeed I do not expect that; for you will remember that
> large Demands of Cattle have lately been made by General Greene on the
> State of Virginia. Thus, Sir, you will perceive that, from Causes you are per-
> fectly acquainted with, Prudence will forbid us to rely on more than four
> out of the eight Million Dollars called for. . . ."[4]

This letter indicates that the Financier did not expect any revenue
until summer. And yet the urgent "ministerial" letters were sent out
in February. Perhaps the Financier was preparing the ground for a
future harvest of revenue. Perhaps he intended to maintain pressure
on the states and Congress. Certainly it is apparent that he felt the
states should be prodded early to fulfill their requisitions.

In May, when the pressure on the Financer to fulfill contracting
obligations began to make itself felt, his voice reached a shriller pitch.
After reiterating that expenditures were increasing while adequate
revenue failed to materialize, Morris announced that "little local objects have postponed those measures which are essential to our existence, so that the most fatal consequences are now suspended but by a
thread." And what were these dire consequences? ". . . I shall endeavor
to fulfill engagements which I have already made . . . but I will make
no new engagements, so that the public service must necessarily stand
still." The army, of course, would be forced "to subsist itself, or disband itself." And who would be at fault? The states, answered Morris.

"They have been deaf to the calls of Congress, to the clamors of the public creditors, to the just demands of a suffering army, and even to the reproaches of the enemy. . . ." Morris conceded that "this language may appear extraordinary," yet he thought the prospects justified it.[5]

But the letter never reached its intended audience because Congress, when asked to approve it, decided that the letter presented too revealing a picture of the state of affairs for public consumption. They responded more readily to Morris' suggestion that delegates be sent to the respective state legislatures where the affairs of the Confederation could be unveiled behind locked doors. Morris' reaction, in contrast, was to practice what he had preached. He informed the Secretary of War, General Benjamin Lincoln, that he could not enter into any new engagements in preparing for a campaign without violating his other obligations. "Of the two evils, therefore, the least must be chosen which is that the operations of the campaign must stand still."[6]

Congress and the states were not the only recipients of Morris' attention; individual arguments in opposition, such as a scarcity of money hindering the collection of taxes, or, as John Wendell of New Hampshire phrased it, trying to make bricks without straw, drew a rebuttal from the Financier. The Bank notes and the Morris notes would supply the necessary circulating medium in those areas where it was needed, said Morris, and if a state failed to command either cash or these notes, it indicated that the goods produced in that particular state had been priced out of the market. If such a state would sell its produce or manufactures on reasonable terms, he continued, it would attract expenditure of money, and thus funds would be available for revenue—a statement, it should be added, that neglected other important economic factors. This idea of a free market governed by price as dictated by supply and demand fitted appropriately into the Financier's economic thinking; in fact, it was about this time that he wrote: "I had been long since convinced that nothing could save us but opening all the American ports to unrestrained commerce, all the markets of America to the free sale and purchase of every article of its production and import; and by taking away all restraints on money, leave every individual to judge and act for himself."[7]

In support of the messages stood the practical weapon, the receivers of taxes who had been appointed in each state. Each receiver had been making periodic reports which were compiled into general statements by the Office of Finance. Many of these officials also attempted to supplement the messages of Morris by personal conversations with important citizens within their respective jurisdiction and by providing information for the Office of Finance. But the measure of their effectiveness in combination with the pleas of Morris was disappointingly reflected in the actual revenue returns.[8]

The contribution of the lower South can only be calculated in specific supplies, for those states, as we have noted before, had not adopted Morris' plan calling for an issue of notes receivable in taxes. All who were concerned with the acceptance of specific supplies complained that the valuation of the commodities was excessive, with the result that the sum charged off by the state as revenue paid to the Confederation was also inflated. South Carolina shouldered the burden of specific supplies in the area and, according to its figures, fulfilled its entire quota of requisitions. Regardless of the relative costs, the use of specifics certainly spared Morris from additional burdens.[9]

The response of the remaining states did not measure up to expectations. According to the Treasurer, some $422,000 was received in taxes from the Continental receivers in 1782. If this figure is placed alongside the $8,000,000 requested or the $4,000,000 Morris anticipated, it appears insignificant; if the $422,000 is compared with the total expenditures of 1782—approximately $2,300,000—the figure assumes greater importance. Estimating very roughly, for there is some duplication, the revenue brought in from the states equaled the credit supplied by the Morris notes; or, to put it more precisely, the states—with the important exception of the lower South—furnished about 18 per cent of the total national expenditures.[10]

But the total figure does not tell a complete or intelligible story. New Hampshire and New York, as Morris had anticipated, contributed the least, while Pennsylvania and Massachusetts furnished the most—again excepting the lower South. In terms of percentage, Connecticut, Rhode Island, and New Jersey did well. The flow of revenue chronologically was even more important. Early in May and June it amounted to little more than a trickle, with some $13,000 being recorded in the first month and $17,000 in the second. Beginning in July, the trickle swelled into a small but hopeful stream with a recording in September of some $65,000, but then the stream gradually diminished until December, when a sudden spurt brought in almost $100,000. The Financier had clearly foreseen that revenue would be delayed in collection; yet he had vastly overestimated the total amount which would flow into the treasury in the later months.[11]

It is obvious that the money collected from the states was not sufficient to carry on the current expenses of the war. Although any estimation of the total funds provided to meet the national expenditures must be very rough, the income supplied by the revenue in addition to the considerable credit supplied by the Bank notes and Morris notes did not exceed one and one-half million dollars. Nearly one million dollars was still needed in income to balance the expenditures; in good revolutionary fashion, the nation appealed for foreign loans, and once again her voice was heard.

In Passy, Franklin, overwhelmed with the seemingly unceasing flow of old bills of exchange that had been drawn on him by Congress before Morris assumed office, wrote that he was "quite sick" of his Gibeonite office, "that of drawing water for the whole congregation of Israel." With the help of Lafayette, who had arrived from America armed with information to support Franklin's request, Franklin, prodded by letters from the Financier and the Secretary of Foreign Affairs, redoubled his efforts. The result of this combination was an assurance from the French Court that 6,000,000 livres, to be made available in quarterly installments, would be loaned to the United States for 1782.[12]

When the Financier, hard pressed to fill the difference between income and expenditures, learned of the loan, he presumed it was at his disposition. He assumed that one-third of the money was available to draw on immediately because four months of the year had passed, while the remainder could be drawn upon at 500,000 livres ($100,000) each month. The total sum of approximately $1,000,000 would neatly balance the financial budget.[13]

But Morris' presumptions were unwarranted, as he quickly learned from Franklin, who conceived the new loan as nothing less than an act of Providence to meet the old Congressional bills of exchange. Soon the Financier received a report from his friend at the French Court stating that "every sou we can command during the year 1782 is already anticipated." Despite this disappointing information, which was a clear-cut statement of the matter, the Financier acted according to his original intentions rather than in the light of the undisputed fact. His difficult financial situation persuaded him to continue drawing bills of exchange at the rate of $100,000 each month in the hope that somehow funds would be available to meet those obligations when they were presented for acceptance many months later. Under the exigencies of the moment, therefore, Morris was forced to deal in futures.[14]

During the year, hopes of assistance from Holland also brightened. In January, John Adams described his situation on loans as "very delicate," and later he reported that his major effort to line up some underwriters for a sizable loan failed miserably when subscriptions were opened unexpectedly for a loan to the East India Company. But this chilling news from Adams was perhaps destined to make the information which arrived some two months later the more cheering. He announced that he had opened a loan for 5,000,000 guilders (approximately $2,000,000) at 5 per cent interest with a combination of private firms—Wilhelm and Jan Willink, Nicholas and Jacob Van Staphorst, and De la Lande and Fynje. Adams cautioned everyone, however, that he did not expect more than a million and one half guilders to be subscribed by Christmas. In short, don't anticipate! But the loan filled more rapidly than Adams expected, and by the middle of September—just about the time the Financier first learned of it— some 1,500,000 guilders ($600,000) in cash had already been subscribed.[15]

It was a blessing indeed to be able to draw on European funds, for they provided the indispensable balance to meet current needs; but, in drawing bills of exchange during the year to take advantage of these loans, the Financier was confronted with an unusual impediment. He faced a financial crisis because he could not find persons who would purchase the bills of exchange; individuals could not buy them because a paralysis was gradually creeping over commerial operations.

The finances, therefore, became inextricably interwoven with the course of trade.

The British offensive in 1782 was directed against the vulnerable American commerce rather than against Washington's army, and the results were disastrous not only for the mercantile community but also for a part of the Financier's program. The precipitous decline in trading, on the one hand, upset the normal channels by which the bills of exchange were sold; on the other hand, it introduced the beginning of a period of more restricted economic activity.

All the regions were injured to some degree by the intensified blockade. The merchants of the upper South were quick to experience its effectiveness, but the Philadelphia community was only a scant step behind. By early May, Maryland merchants such as Woolsey and Salmon had lost three ships, and they found the coast "much infested" with enemy vessels; Mark Pringle, a Baltimore merchant of prominence, complained that unless convoys could be obtained, "God only knows what will become of our trade." Faithfully reflecting the anxiety and distress of the Philadelphia merchants, the letters of William Constable spoke eloquently on the hazards of commerce. "The present interruption indeed almost annihilation of our trade," he lamented to his French correspondents, "has wounded most of us so deeply as for awhile almost to extinguish the spirit of adventure." Although the siege against the ports of New England did not endure as long as that against other regions, conditions were severe enough to prompt an important Boston firm to write: "The risk upon our coast is now greater than it has been before during the war. Scarce a vessel gets of [off] safe." [16]

These desperate circumstances in shipping were responsible for a sudden revival of interest in a navy to protect commerce. In April a group of Philadelphia merchants under the leadership of William Bingham, the former American consul in Martinique, presented a memorial to Congress on naval protection. This movement enjoyed the approval of Morris, and in time he responded with a rather elaborate plan to implement the idea. Obviously, the American navy did not possess the necessary strength, asserted the Financier, so French assistance was indispensable. He proposed a force of two ships of the line and ten frigates. The two ships of the line and two of the frigates would cruise outside the capes and northward; the remaining eight frigates would be divided into squadrons of four and would convoy the trade from major port to major port, making a complete circuit in approximately five months. Everyone would benefit, according to the Financier, because American producers would receive better prices and, in return, the goods they purchased would be cheaper; the French would be blessed with American commodities at lower prices and favored with an increase in the consumption of their manufactures.

All of these advantages, of course, could be counted in addition to the rewards of friendship.[17]

Reacting swiftly and favorably to Morris' proposal, Congress ordered him to urge the adoption of his projected operation upon the commanders of the French and Spanish fleets. Morris immediately dispatched the *General Washington,* a vessel owned by Pennsylvania and placed under the command of Captain Joshua Barney, to the West Indies with instructions to deliver letters to the appropriate authorities and return with a cargo of specie. The letters stressed the effectiveness of the British blockade, and the consequences. "Coasts are so narrowly watched that it is only by a kind of miracle that any vessel can get in or go out," the Financier wrote to De Grasse, the French naval commander. "I am within bounds when I say that nineteen out of twenty have been taken." To entice the support of the Spanish governor, Morris dangled an especially attractive argument—cheaper provisions and flour from the United States if the convoy system were established. He concluded with the warning: "It is no exaggeration Sir to say that the obstructions to this commerce however distressing to us will be still more distressing to you." Captain Barney's voyage established a record for speed, but not for results. French or Spanish naval protection was out of the question because the English had regained naval superiority in the West Indies, while merchants would not commit more than $60,000 in specie aboard the swift-sailing *General Washington* for fear of its capture.[18]

Although traders shifted their attention to the West Indies in an effort to avoid the sharpest intrusions of the British cruisers, a complicating factor entered into the commercial picture—the possibilities of peace; for the merchants the question of the moment was not the usual "What is the price?" but rather "What about the peace?" There were few merchants who did not repeat the instructions of Salmon, the Baltimore merchant, in some form or other. "I do not care to touch any goods from France," he wrote in August 1782, "until that matter [the peace] is ascertained." Although he rescinded his order later, he warned that if peace prospects improved, shipments must stop, for "the first cost wd [would] hardly be obtained." Mark Pringle, of the same city, found that each new rumor of peace made it increasingly difficult to dispose of his goods, despite a drastic markdown of the prices. Apparently the effect of the rumors was less pronounced in the Boston area; the available letterbooks do not reflect the same overwhelming concern as those of the merchants in the Middle Region, although an uncertainty crept into most of the mercantile calculations and the thoughts of many venturers turned to postwar plans. In fact, the glowing prospects which many enterprisers envisioned as part of the postwar scene so stimulated their imaginations that planning extraordinary projects became as infectious as a disease. John Holker, the Agent of the French Marine, wrote fervently about so many schemes that his partner in France, Matthew Ridley, warned him against subscribing to ventures "too wild" in scope. "Softly! Softly!"

he cautioned. "Not that I want the will my friend, but I fear wanting the means." And the "means" were crucial, for the effectiveness of the British cruisers and the uncertainty of the peace was so constrictive that all trade relationships had been practically strangled.[19]

Although this factor of a declining commerce had an important long-range impact on the economy and on the Financier's program, its immediate effect was to jeopardize the sale of bills of exchange, Morris' most important single source of revenue. As if to aggravate matters, the danger from Admiral Digby's British cruisers heightened just as the Financier's need for revenue from the sale of bills became paramount. Merchants who found their trade with France practically severed required, of course, few bills on that country. Indeed, Haym Salomon, a Philadelphia broker who handled a considerable number of bills, together with Henry Hill, told Morris in early May 1782, that the current losses "so dispirited" possible purchasers that no bills could be sold "at any price." A few days later Morris informed Grand, the French banker who handled most of the United States operations abroad: "Our enemies . . . have now changed the mode of attack, and strike at our commerce and our resources. . . . The commerce of this country has sustained a severer blow than has been hitherto felt, and the effects of it materially influence my operations. The merchants, deprived of their property, can not command money, and of consequence can not buy bills. I am therefore unable to command by drafts the money in your hands."[20]

To relieve this situation, the Financier turned to several expedients over a period of six or seven months—with varying success. Like the merchants, the Financier was attracted by the possibility of using Havana as a means to escape the worst impact of the British operations. He drew up a rather complicated plan calling for Captain John Barry to sail to Havana where he would fetch a cargo of specie to be obtained by drawing bills on European banks. At the same time, Morris requested Grand to dispatch three vessels to America, each loaded with $120,000 in specie; because of the condition of trade, this maneuver would use the European funds more advantageously than by drawing bills of exchange. Both of these operations failed to materialize, but makeshifts in the sale of bills of exchange at Boston and at Philadelphia enabled the Financier to hobble along for a few months. Each new hint of peace, however, jarred these feeble supports, and in late August the Philadelphia market for bills collapsed. As Morris reported it, Haym Salomon informed him that no bills could be sold, "nor can he [Salomon] raise any money for me."[21]

This collapse provoked a new frenzy of activity. Sales of bills through Lovell at Boston were stepped up and a new expedition to Havana was organized with John Brown, a friend of Morris', in charge. Brown was to sell the ship's cargo and, more important, $200,000 worth of bills on I. L. and C. Le Couteulx and Company at Cadiz and return with the specie. Morris also ordered Captain John Barry to proceed to Havana to assist in transporting the money back to the United States. This operation turned into a dramatic incident filled with frustrating delay and high adventure, but for the Financier it marked only a partial success. Brown found the merchants at Havana so skeptical of the credit of the Confederation that he could only dispose of half the bills intended for sale. Perhaps to flatter Morris, Brown affirmed: "Had I been authorized to draw for your private account I should have found no difficulty in making sale of any sum. . . . But that confidence which would have been readily placed on your private transactions could not be obtained for those done in a public capacity. . . ." The sum received in the sale of bills finally reached Philadelphia safely in the spring of 1783 after some exciting moments with enemy cruisers, but it arrived much too late to fulfill its original function. By that time the peace had been made, and new problems connected with commerce had arisen which were of even greater magnitude.[22]

★ ★ ★

The operation of the Bank and the Morris notes, and the conditions influencing the flow of revenue were quite naturally reflected in meeting the current obligations of the government. Within current expenditures, the Financier had recognized the obvious fact that servicing the military forces was paramount by introducing a system of contracting as part of his program. This system, as he conceived it, was intended to supply the army more efficiently and more economically.

Although many qualifications must be made, the contracting system as initiated by Morris was relatively successful. In general, the smaller contracts seemed to work out satisfactorily, for there was little complaint either from the military, the contractors, or the Financier, but the operation of the largest contracts was less encouraging. A substantial number of recriminations between the military and the contractors mirrored the difficulties involved in settling, without disputes, such smaller details of provisioning as the place where the rations were to be dispensed. These troubles, which fluctuated in intensity throughout most of the year, were seriously aggravated by a new and important development, the Financier's inability to meet his obligations because of the conditions interrupting the flow of revenue. In time, part of these obstacles were resolved. Early in 1783 the Commander-in-Chief could announce that the army, in contrast to the previous winters during the course of the war, was serviced better than ever before.

Although the contracting system seemed to operate with success in the smaller military posts, the fulfillment of some of the larger contracts, such as that held by Matthias Slough and Tench Francis, contractors for certain posts in New Jersey, was quite a different story. Complaints against the firm began to drift in very early, and Morris warned them that they might become "the object of public resentment" unless they mended their ways. But the difficulties persisted and, in March, General Washington called the Financier's attention to the lack of adequate provisions for the brigade which came under the New Jersey contract. The basic cause of the trouble was simple enough. Slough and Francis, like so many of their fellow contractors, engaged in subcontracting, and the organization and rapport between the contractors and subcontractors was so inadequate that misunderstanding piled up on misunderstanding until the whole business relationship tottered and finally fell. Even the Financier conceded that the New Jersey contract "has been badly executed," chiefly, he surmised, because of the "inability of those to whom the management is committed." Of course Morris recognized that the contractors were disgruntled because their bid for the New Jersey posts was lower than those which had won contracts for other regions. "I believe Messers Francis and Slough wish to be clear of this contract and the subs [subcontractors] as far as I can learn are rather sick of it . . .," Morris declared. What the contractors hoped for was a premium "to induce them to give it up," but such expectations were groundless.[23]

The working out of the contracting system can be best followed and evaluated, however, in the most important contracts—first, West Point, which eventually evolved into a combination of West Point and the Moving Army, that is, those combat troops which were not assigned to a specific garrison; and second, the posts "Northward of Poughkeepsie." An appraisal of these two contracts, touching the great majority of troops in the Northern Department, raises several pertinent questions. How did the system reflect the major developments within other parts of the Financier's program? Did the system of contracts supply troops more satisfactorily and economically than previous methods?"[24]

The West Point contract rested in the hands of Comfort Sands and Company, with "and Company" representing his two brothers. We know relatively little about Comfort Sands in spite of his long and rather illustrious career (1748-1834). He was a member of a large family and served as a clerk for various minor businessmen from the time he finished his schooling at the age of twelve until he reached twenty-one. Then Sands opened his own establishment in New York City which to all appearances flourished until the outbreak of the Revolution. During the war he engaged in a variety of enterprises— one was his contract with the Financier—and after the war he settled in New York, formed a partnership with his brother Joshua, and from all accounts prospered. Indeed, Comfort Sands would have had to do well in order to live in moderate circumstances and still support his eighteen children.[25]

General Heath, who was in command at West Point, had not been pleased with the provisioning of his troops during the final months of 1781, but Morris had answered Heath's forebodings by assurances that the problems of supply would subside when the contract became effective. At first this prediction appeared to be warranted. Some of the necessary details such as children's and officer's rations were suitably arranged, and a contract was consummated to supply the hospital. To both the contractors and Heath, the Financier sent reassuring messages. "The opposition therefore which you may meet with from persons interested to oppose a system of public oeconomy need give you no concern," he wrote to Comfort Sands, "for while you do your duty it will be my duty to support you." To Heath he extolled the great advantage to the public in terms of more "effectual and punctual supply of the army" and the economy of the operation.[26]

But the honeymoon did not last, and by March a flurry of bitter criticism and accusation was exchanged between the contractors and the military authorities. A brother of Comfort Sands was confined briefly at West Point, an incident which caused a minor explosion. "If this is the manner that we are to be treated by an insignificant Officer of yours," Sands wrote to Heath, "it is time we knew what we have to depend on." Unless the General assured him that the persons and property of the contractors would be protected, Sands continued, he might withhold supplies. ". . . I am determined at all events not to be trifled with nor suffer any indignity from any officer in the army." Although Comfort's brother was released, this incident initiated a series of recriminations. Heath complained that the beef was inferior, that there was a shortage of vinegar, and that some troops had to travel too far to pick up the rations, while Sands was disgruntled with the difficulties he encountered in settling some of their first accounts when the contractors gave out some "irregular issues" on the orders of the General. The two parties even quarreled as to whether the kidney was or was not to be taken out of the beef—a trivium which eventually had to be decided by the Financier.[27]

Meanwhile, the Financier had taken steps to smooth the troubled waters—but mostly on the theory that to satisfy the army eventually it was necessary first to satisfy the contractors. He not only issued a warrant for $13,000 to take care of the immediate demands of the contractors—apparently without a complete adjustment of accounts—but he also urged them to bid for a Moving Army contract that was soon to be released. When the bids were opened, Morris announced that Daniel Parker—of whom we shall hear more—had submitted the lowest bid. On further investigation, however, it was discovered that Parker had intended his bid to be 8½ pence in "lawful money" rather than in Pennsylvania currency as interpreted by the Financier, and this difference raised his bid so much higher that it was eliminated. The next lowest bidder was William Duer, a New York entrepreneur, but his Philadelphia agent could not—or would not—post security for the contract. As a result of this mixup, discussions were opened between Walter Livingston, Comfort Sands, Secretary at War, Benjamin Lincoln, and the Financier; and a draft of a contract was drawn up with Comfort Sands and Company, the "and Company" now including Walter Livingston, Tench Francis, Oliver Phelps, Timothy Edwards, and Thomas Lowrey. At this point Morris consulted Congress explaining the proceedings in detail and enclosing copies of the various bids. They bestowed their official sanction. The Financier then completed the contract, although it was not accomplished, according to Morris, without "some little altercation in which I could not help getting a little warm now and then." The haste with which the contractors left Philadelphia—a haste which all hoped was prompted by doing good rather than evil—left the final contracts ill drawn and apparently, in certain parts, incorrectly drawn. Despite these inadequacies, the contract met the general approval of the Commander-in-Chief: "You may be assured that I am fully persuaded of the Importance and Utility of the present mode of feeding the Army and that I shall take every Occasion to impress the same Ideas upon the Minds of the Officers."[28]

The contract itself included some new provisions, although most of it fitted into the previous pattern. The most important change concerned an attempt to avoid the disputes that had cropped up under the West Point contract. Instead of three arbitrators resolving a disputed point involved in the contracts, which was the accepted practice, it was decided that an inspector should be appointed who would stay with the army during the entire campaign. If, in the judgment of the inspector, any of the supplies provided were of inferior quality, he was at liberty either to purchase supplies for the troops on his own authority at the expense of the contractors, or to demand replacements from the contractors.[29]

The close relationship between groups interested in the West Point and Moving Army contracts, with the Sands brothers acting as the connecting link, was consolidated further when Walter Livingston assigned one-fourth of his share in the "Moving Army" contract to William Duer, who in turn assigned one-half—that is, one-half of his one-fourth—to John Holker, Morris' friend and partner, a few weeks later. This was important, because Duer had already obtained a contract in February to supply the posts "Northward of Poughkeepsie," replacing the two relatively well-known businessmen, Jonathan Lawrence and Melancton Smith, who had successfully managed their contract by introducing a rather extensive system of subcontracting. In this "Northern" contract, Holker was also an interested participant with Duer.[30]

With the appearance of William Duer and Company among the contractors, three developments in the operations of contracting for 1782 were highlighted: one, Morris, although not privately engaged in any way with William Duer at this time, became more closely linked in general interest with the contractors, for Duer was the partner of John Holker, and Holker was concerned with Morris in several business capacities; second, the alignment of Duer with the other contractors marked the consummation of an important unity of interest in the most prominent contracts—West Point, the Moving Army, and the military posts "Northward of Poughkeepsie"—a unity which was eventually formalized in the first two contracts by the organization of a new firm, called Sands, Livingston, and Company, to supervise both agreements; third, Duer's entry into the ranks of the contractors accidentally coincided with the beginning of a whole series of crises involving the ability of the government to meet its obligations with respect to the contracts—crises which affected all the contractors because they were so intimately connected.[31]

These last two developments represented a dangerous departure from the contracting system as Morris originally visualized it. If a dispute arose concerning one of the contracts, or if one contractor failed, it would probably affect all three major agreements. In addition, the tendency toward consolidation among the contractors meant that the check on profits by vigorous competition was seriously impaired.

Although William Duer figured prominently in the political life of New York and in the Continental Congress during the Revolutionary years, it is not these roles for which he is remembered; since the publication of *Essays on Earlier American Corporations* by Joseph S. Davis, Duer has been almost universally acclaimed as one of the important enterprisers in the Revolutionary period. In contrast to Morris, Matthew Ridley, George Meade, and a host of other enterprisers, Duer did not concentrate on trade; he dabbled in a great variety of businesses. His engagements with John Holker plainly emphasize this diversity—a mast contract, a distillery business, an army contract, and speculation in New York pay certificates, to mention the more important. A man fertile in ideas but weak in their execution, often demanding of others in financial commitments yet lax in his own business conduct, engaged in a great diversity of financial undertakings yet completely successful in none, familiar in the council chamber but more at home in the counting house—this was William Duer.[32]

It appears that Morris first became acquainted with Duer when the two men were attending the Continental Congress, and their correspondence of the period 1779-80 is sprinkled with assurances of mutual confidence and concern. Duer was a guest in the Morris home more than once, and the Philadelphia merchant wrote Kitty Livingston to tell "Lady Kitty," Duer's charming and handsome wife, that they would "take care of him [Duer] for her sake." Later, when Duer conceived a plan to supply the French forces, he made overtures to Morris to enter into the scheme, but these projects never materialized. The two men continued on good terms, however, and when Morris accepted the office of Superintendent of Finance, he solicited the assistance and support of the New Yorker, who responded by providing some provisions for General Heath's forces during 1781. But these amiable relationships did not prevent the Financier from delivering a sharp admonition to Duer, in a private letter dated February 7, 1782, the same day that the latter was officially notified that his bid for the posts "Northward of Poughkeepsie" had been accepted. Morris warned the New Yorker about the necessity for complete and punctual compliance with his contract:

. . . it had been hinted to me that some person whom I have employed to make purchases in your state has not *preserved* that punctuality which is necessary to retrieve and support the public credit. I hope this does not apply to any part of your conduct and let me urge in the most pressing manner that as a contractor you never suffer any consideration whatever to enduce you to deviate in the least degree from that exact punctuality which ought to take place in all dealings and which never fails to procure the greatest advantages to those who practice it invariably.

This reproof referred to Duer's operations in supplying Heath with flour the previous year, but Morris softened a part of its sting by assuring the New Yorker that he would be happy to assist him in any possible way "consistent with that duty which I owe to the public and to myself." [33]

Throughout the summer, Morris was badgered by troubles involving disagreements between the contractors and the army with respect to the precise execution of the contract. Some of the complaints about the conduct of the contractors so rankled the Commander-in-Chief that he fairly seethed in writing to Sands: "Why Sir are the Troops without provisions?" he demanded. "Why are the deposits which have so often, and so long ago been required by General Heath, and pressed by myself, neglected? Why do you so pertinaciously adhere to all those parts of the Contracts as are promotive of your own Interest and convenience . . . and at the same time disregard the most essential claims of the public; thereby hazarding the dissolution of the Army and risking the loss of the most important Post in America?" At the same time, Washington dispatched a letter to the Financier, expressing more forcefully than at any other time in Morris' administration his dissatisfaction with the general supply situation. He strongly criticized the tactics of the contractors; he described the trouble that had arisen over the issue of officer's rations; he denounced the lack of supply magazines and the manner of distributing some of the rations. Indeed, declared Washington, the entire army was complaining bitterly. ". . . We may spin the thread of Oeconomy 'till it breaks," he asserted. "Minds soured by distresses are easily rankled. . . ." [34]

General Heath, whose immediate command was vitally concerned in the primary contracts, continued to exchange complaints with the contractors as well as to furnish Washington with verbal ammunition. "The fresh beef which was drawn this morning . . . was almost spoiled before it reached this post," Heath wrote to Comfort Sands in June. "Judge you, my dear Sir, of the situation of this provision when it arrives at the detached posts, when it stinks on its first arrival here." And the General expressed concern over the limited quantity of whiskey. "The hot weather renders it more necessary at this time than at some other seasons. The soldier at all times expects it." Heath, meanwhile, was busily rallying his officers to present evidence against the contractors showing direct violations of the agreement, for he hoped to strengthen the government's case when it was brought before the board of arbitration. In answering these charges, Sands, the major figure among the contractors, seemed to soften his approach, for his reply soothed rather than irritated. "We trust . . . you will make every reasonable allowance as it is as disagreeable to us to hear any complaints as it is to you. And depend Sir, that if Mr. Morris can fulfill his part of the contract nothing on ours shall be wanting." Indeed, the contractors had occasion to register some complaints of their own. It was with difficulty that they could supply "the lines" which were constantly shifting. They hesitated to set up a supply store near the forward area for fear of losses. If the public would agree to compensate such a loss, the contractors asserted, the forward area would be more effectively supplied. And the contractors were not pleased when some Continental guards broke into one of their stores and had a merry time with "the wine and other articles." [35]

Morris tried to pacify both the army and the contractors. He was instrumental in insisting that General Benjamin Lincoln, the Secretary at War, visit the camp and try to resolve the disputes, a move that enjoyed limited success. The Financier also renewed his efforts to fill the post of Inspector of the Army, which had been designed to arbitrate any question of issues, but his efforts to obtain General Cornell, a highly respected officer, failed. The real solution, as the Financier saw it, lay in a better understanding between the officers and the contractors, a hope that was never completely realized. [36]

Although this series of difficulties grouped around the execution of the contracts was of significance, most of the basic differences at stake could be resolved by improved rapport between the contractors and the army, and by final arbitration proceedings; but a second set of more important problems, which began and ended with money, sprang up in the relationship between the Financier and the contractors. The intermittent complaint reflecting this new difficulty was limited at first, but by September the problem threatened to wreck the entire contracting system; in short, the crisis in the operation of the Financier's program on economy during 1782 paralleled the crisis which arose in the working out of the Financier's program in revenue.

One of the first indications of impending trouble appeared in June 1782, when some of the partners in the Moving Army and West Point contracts began to wonder whether the Financier could meet his obligations. William Duer, holder of the Northern contract, was also filled with the "greatest anxiety" about the money due him. "You must if it is necessary tell *a certain great man* that I must fail if there is a delay in granting the warrant," the New Yorker informed his partner, John Holker. Even though Duer's accounts had not been fully settled by the auditors, the Financier relieved his distress for a time by advancing funds. When writing the contractors at West Point and the Moving Army, the Financier complained that they had failed to keep their word. "I early informed you that I should in May and June find difficulties which you must assist in obviating. I made you very considerable advances and now when I call upon you agreeably to your own promises not to press me I find that you are all alive to suspicions." Morris concluded this reprimand by abruptly instructing the contractors to get their accounts settled so that they could be paid at once. [37]

There was a brief lull when this financial uncertainty seemed to resolve itself, but before a month had passed, new and more numerous
signs appeared. Walter Livingston, one of the contractors, made known
his apprehensions, but the Financier assured him all was well, and
soon forwarded another $20,000 in Morris notes as partial compensa-
tion for rations issued during the previous months. Still, the uneasiness
would not be downed. Calling Morris' attention to an exchange of
letters between Heath and the contractors in which the latter complained of "a deficiency in complying with the contract on the part of
the public," the Commander-in-Chief stated that such representations
differed greatly from "the idea of the state of facts, which I had conceived from my conversation with you." He wanted to know exactly
what the true picture was, so appropriate action could be taken.[38]

Morris' reply was mildly reassuring. In the contract for West Point
the Financier claimed he had been in advance much of the time rather
than a month behind in payments, as the contractors asserted, particularly if the provisions received by them from the remaining specific
supplies were included. Because of necessary delays such as auditing
the accounts before making a final payment, "the Contractors could
not have expected anything else than to have been two months in advance . . .," Morris observed. But the thing which he did not explain
away was the fact that he still had not made any payments to the contractors for the month of July—and he was writing in August—although he was preparing to do so; and he did not explain that he
was committed by contract to pay in specie rather than in notes; moreover, he did not refer to the $20,000 which would be due the con-
tractors during the month of August for clothing. If the contractors
suspected that Morris could not fulfill the full amount of these obligations—probably over $150,000—it could bring on a disaster.[39]

For a few weeks the Financier's prospects brightened. Indeed, on
August 20 Morris thought he had solved the problem, at least so he
assured Washington when he said some $50,000 in Morris notes had
been sent to the contractors. But Morris himself did not actually possess the confidence expressed in his letter to the Commander-in-Chief.
A note to the Quartermaster General had been more accurate. "I find
the most extreme difficulty in performing my own engagements and
live in hourly apprehension of the most fatal consequences."[40]

September ushered in the real crisis when everything seemed to con-
spire to confirm the Financier's worst fears. All the sources of revenue
dried up at once. Bills of exchange were unsalable, relatively little
revenue was obtained from the states, and the Bank was pressing Morris for partial repayment on loans that had been made. It is a story
of ceaseless demands for payment with wholly inadequate funds to
meet those obligations. On August 29 Morris wrote a highly confidential letter to Washington, a letter that Morris wanted the General to
forward to the several states should the situation deteriorate so decisively that the action would be warranted. In this short message, the
Financier informed Washington that there was little hope of meeting

the obligations of the contracts unless a sizable increase in revenue was supplied by the states. "The object of this letter, sir, is to request that you will consider how your army is to be subsisted or kept together if I am obliged to dissolve the contracts. I pray that Heaven may direct your mind to some mode by which we may be yet saved." The Financier did not forward this letter until September 9 when the constant barrage of troubles forced his hand. For the first time in his administration, and really for the first time in his career, Morris was compelled to write ". . . at present I really know not which way to turn myself." [41]

Before this forbidding message was received by the Commander-in-Chief, two developments took place which brought the crisis in contracting to a head. William Duer had written Morris that he would have to forego his contract unless freed from financial difficulties, and the firm of Sands, Livingston, and Company sent a long, comprehensive, confidential letter to the Financier setting an absolute deadline for the payments due them by the government. Indeed, their letter was of such importance that it could not be known except to the Commander-in-Chief and the Financier, said the contractors, "without wounding your [Morris'] credit and weakening still further our own operations which are founded principally on *that basis*." [42]

Sands, Livingston, and Company in their inclusive letter of grievances placed the full blame for the current crisis at the doorstep of the Office of Finance. The company could not replenish their flour supply without money; their failure to build up magazines earlier when supplies of flour were available was due to lack of punctuality on the part of the Financier; the persons who held subcontracts with the firm to provide the beef ration would not continue after the fifteenth (the letter was written on the eleventh of September) unless they received payment in specie—again the Financier. To cap this build-up of circumstances, stated the contractors, they could not expect any payment whatsoever in specie for the August issue of rations. They were "extremely alarmed at this declaration," particularly when the money and notes supplied by Morris were wholly inadequate. Of the $50,000 in Morris notes and warrants sent by the Financier, $20,000 could not be collected until January and February of 1783. These warrants might well work out on a long-term basis, said the contractors, but they would by no means answer the immediate obligations for which the contractors were committed. The $12,000 that Morris had directed Washington to send the firm earlier had failed to materialize; moreover, they were not sanguine about the Morris notes. If the contractors alone received the notes, they could hope for relief from the various receivers of taxes; but many other creditors of the government had also received this kind of payment, the letter asserted. The contractors assured Morris that they had confidence in him and wished his administration success. "When we made this contract we can with truth assure you that we placed more dependence on your personal than your official character." They were also "anxious to sec-

ond the views of your Administration" which they still considered the
best hope of the country, but "seconding" in this case involved serious
consequences with regard to the finances of the firm. So the action
proposed was inevitable. ". . . We [Sands, Livingston, and Company]
are constrained to declare explicitly that we can no longer be answerable for the supply of the troops in terms agreed upon in the contract." Would the company consider any alternatives? Only if two assurances were given by the Financier: one, that the contractors would
be fully indemnified; and two, that upon producing their monthly
accounts the contractors would receive one-half their due in specie
and three times that amount in notes. A deadline of October 1 was
set for a satisfactory answer.[43]

Morris' brief reply was carried in a letter, dated September 20, to
Ezekial Cornell, who had finally consented to accept an appointment
as Inspector of the Army; he could make no such assurances, the
Financier informed the contractors, nor did he wish to. In fact, Cornell
was instructed by Morris to take up the burden of supplying the troops
and thus prepare for the breakdown in the existing agreements. His
letter a few days later was utterly frank and sketched the crux of the
situation.

My engagements are very numerous and weighty and although I have determined to incur no new expence not even the slightest, yet those already
incurred are sufficient to ruin the credit I had taken so much pains to establish unless I can procure some respite. I am reduced therefore to this
point that unless means can be devised to feed the army at a long credit, I
must desire the Contractors to desist and desire the General to subsist his
troops by military collection. I need say no more to impress you with the
necessity of making the best agreement with Colonel Wadsworth which you
can. You will confer with the General on the subject and take his advice.
You will of course keep the purport of this letter secret until I shall find
it proper to make it public.[44]

It is scarcely surprising that General Cornell found his duties arduous when he arrived at camp. "I have experienced more uneasy
hours in transacting this business than in any I ever undertook before," he lamented. Part of his uneasiness stemmed from the attitude
of the contractors, who not only blamed the public as the sole cause
of the breakdown in contracting, but who had also received hints of
the Financier's conversation with Jeremiah Wadsworth, a highly important and successful Connecticut entrepreneur, about the possibility
of the latter's taking over the contracting. In view of the mood of the
contractors, the Inspector "thought that prudence dictated to treat
them gently." But this did not furnish supplies for the troops, and
General Cornell, in consultation with Washington, decided that no
alternative was practicable except to make the best possible terms with
Wadsworth. "At the same time," he confessed, "we were sensible it
must be on his own [terms], as he knew our situation." In the agreement which ensued, Wadsworth and his partner "Carter" were to receive the handsome price of 13/90 per ration, fully one-third higher

than had been paid to the previous contractors; in exchange the firm gave the Confederation three months' credit. As Morris later asserted when he laid the whole situation before Congress, "If it be asked whether this be a good bargain I answer at once that it is not. But I believe it to be the best which could be made."[45]

In the same lengthy letter to Congress, the Financier was artful enough to point up the virtues of quitting the contract with the Sands, Livingston, and Company. It was better to have "vacated" the contract because of the "default or misconduct" which existed rather than because of a complete breakdown in the payment to the contractors, for this would soften the blow against the public credit. "I saw too," continued the Financier, "that any new contract must be more expensive and yet not to have made any would have increased the mischief." These pernicious consequences with relation to the public credit were multiplied, for it was the season to advertise for contracts for the coming year. Moreover, declared the Financier, "I reflected that the loss of our credit (slender as it is) might have some influence on the negotiations for peace. . . . I was reduced to a choice of difficulties."[46]

The failure of the contractors did not rest exclusively with the "non-performance" of the Financier as they had asserted. Although the records of Comfort Sands and Company, and Sands, Livingston, and Company are meager, there is every indication that they entered their contracts with a minimum amount of capital, and consequently cut their resources very thin. In addition, parties to the contract were experiencing some internal quarrels, but the evidence is obscure on the extent of these disputes. It is even possible that the contractors wanted to find some excuse to abrogate the contract because they found it unprofitable. But these factors were subordinate to the dominant reason for the failure of the contractors—the inability of the Financier to command resources.[47]

Meanwhile, the Southern Department of the army command maintained itself, for the most part, by obtaining specific provisions from the neighboring states. Although the high prices at which these supplies were charged against the Confederation—for the benefit of the state—was commented upon by everyone concerned, the troops were sustained, though not always well. Serious anxiety is evident in most of the correspondence early in 1782. In April, General Mordecai Gist wrote to a Maryland friend: "Want of pay and clothing distress the minds of the soldiery and prompt them to desertion, sedition, and mutiny. Instances of all these have happened within these ten days." General Greene, commander of the Southern Department, confirmed such testimony. "For upwards of two months more than one third of our men were entirely naked with nothing but a breech cloth about them . . . our beef was perfect carrion; and even bad as it was, we were often without any." Although the complaints did not dissipate entirely, conditions improved by the end of summer, and the commander spoke more confidently in early fall. What had been partly responsible for easing their situation was the toleration of a clandestine trade that began to spring up with the British in Charleston.[48]

To assist the Southern Department, although in a somewhat limited way, the Financier had dispatched Edward Carrington, Deputy Quartermaster General, with Bank notes and Morris notes to expedite the purchase of goods unobtainable by an assessment in specifics; and he had also worked hard to send clothing. With the exception of a few posts in Virginia, the contracting system was not introduced in the South. The economic situation in that area, in the eyes of the Financier, was such that there was little hope for a successful trial. In addition, the problem of meeting existing obligations had become so acute by July and August that further commitments seemed to him unwarranted. Not until 1783 was the system established universally to provide for the troops, and even then the Financier's previous predictions about the inability of the region to sustain it were validated by actual experience.[49]

It is obvious that the Financier's program with respect to contracting had failed in part; but it did result in reduced expenditures while providing supplies for the troops as well as, or better than, in previous years. On an overall scale it is impossible to compare the expenditures of 1781 with those of 1782 in order to measure any reduction, because the change from specific supplies to specie makes the figures incompatible. If the expenditures of 1782 are compared with those of 1779, the last year in which money was used exclusively in providing provisions, those of 1782 amount to approximately one-third of the earlier year; if compared with 1778, the difference is even greater. The Financier, it is true, did not need to finance a major campaign, but there does not appear to be an appreciable decline in the number of troops in 1782. Contracting did eliminate a small army of issuing commissaries and numerous posts used to issue supplies and to receive specifics. In general, the military commanders seemed to favor the contracting system. Even though Washington viewed Sands with suspicion—"The *low dirty* tricks which were practiced in the time of Comfort Sands . . ."—he advocated the continuance of the contract system. In computing any evaluation, it should also be remembered that most of the lesser contracts ran smoothly, that William Duer and Company, despite its grievances, fulfilled its contracts, and that the efforts to clothe the army met marked success, despite the criticism which was voiced early in the year. Furthermore, in February 1783, the Commander-in-Chief recorded the most important result when he wrote that he enjoyed "the satisfaction of seeing the Troops better coverd, better clothed, and better fed, than they have ever been in any former Winter Quarters." In summary, therefore, the evidence strongly demonstrates that, despite many reservations, the Financier's program to reduce expenditures while maintaining equal or better services and efficiency was relatively successful.[50]

Observing the working out of the Financier's policies on expenditures completes an examination of his long-range program to restore the public credit in its first year of operation; and it is pertinent, therefore, to analyze briefly the composite picture which emerges. The credit facilities and other functions of the Bank of North America had provided an essential support for the Financier in carrying on the duties of his office, while the Morris notes, with some qualification, had served with equal importance in bolstering the public credit. The continued success of the latter, however, lay only in finding sufficient revenue to meet the current obligations of the national government. Funding the debts of the Confederation, the primary objective of the Financier in his program to revive the public credit, had been thwarted, despite Morris' remarkable Report on Public Credit of July; but this measure, being a recent crystallization of the Financier's ideas, could scarcely be expected to pass without lengthy deliberation. The test on funding, as shall be pointed out in the following chapter, was to come when a political crisis arose later.

There had been, then, a substantial revival of confidence in the credit of the Confederation, but it could not, on any account, be considered a complete restoration. Indeed, much of the evidence leads to the conclusion that one of the significant weaknesses was the inability of public credit to divorce itself from the support of private credit. The loan from France, based on war and diplomatic policy rather than upon faith in the credit of the new nation, and the Bank loans and the Morris notes, part of the former and most of the latter based on private credit, combined to supply the difference between the income from requisitions and outlay to support the war.

The failure to achieve the full restoration of the public credit appears, upon initial investigation, to rest upon insufficient revenue either to meet current expenses or to pay the interest on past obligations. Within limits this is true. Although requisitions contributed a proportionately larger share of the total expenditures than in former years, despite a significant downward trend in general economic activity, the collection of taxes certainly did not measure up to the Financier's calculations. But basic to revenue is its foundation—the available economic resources of the country. And, in this respect, the serious deterioration of economic conditions during the course of the year, due primarily to the impact of a declining commerce, was fundamental.

The decrease of commercial activity during 1782 caused a corresponding diminution in general economic activity; this touched the very roots of the Financier's program. Part of the explanation for the dwindling markets lay in the generally adopted policy of constriction. The important French purchasing program had been sharply curtailed; the states, because of their expectations of peace, tended to limit their outlays; indeed, the Superintendent of Finance himself was dedicated to restricted expenditures. Such a general program of constriction in the war-born markets meant that the pressure to find replacements was the more intense. A country that could not find a market for its tobacco, wheat, flour, lumber, fish, and the like would soon be threatened with a severe depression, and this is precisely what tended to happen. The policies of constriction aggravated a most critical development, the trade paralysis resulting from the operations of the British cruisers, and later, the uncertainty over the prospects of peace. The full impact of this situation, it should be reiterated, affected not only the mercantile community, but also most agrarian regions.

By undermining the available economic resources of the country, the foundation upon which the Morris program had been erected, the sharp downward trend in economic activity injured that program at its base. The states, although somewhat reluctant to contribute revenue even under favorable circumstances, would tend to provide a larger proportion in prosperous times because the burden would be less oppressive. If one wishes to consider the depreciation of Continental currency in terms of taxation, the country was in a position to furnish, by taxes, over 70 per cent of the expenses of the war between 1775 and January 1781 largely because of its relatively prosperous economic situation. In contrast, during a period of depression the states would be much less able, if not completely unable, to support any central government, particularly one burdened with comparatively heavy war expenditures.

The economic outlook, depressing as it was, could be changed rapidly by an increase in domestic expenditures or by the opening up of new markets which would stimulate trade. Although Morris' funding plan might plausibly have stimulated economic activity, the first possibility seemed rather remote, for neither the money nor public credit existed to implement such a policy. The fate of the second possibility, opening up new peacetime markets, rested in the hands of Admiral Digby, who commanded the British fleet, or, if a peace were concluded, in the hands of the commissioners at Paris, who needed to make the necessary trade agreements if the new nation were to operate within the mercantile spheres of the various European colonial empires. Much of the success of the Morris program, therefore, depended upon the course of trade; furthermore, any event or policy which would affect commerce takes on a new significance. It is perhaps not an exaggeration to assert that the fate of the Confederation as a form of government rested upon the course of trade.

Although the Financier recognized some of the implications of a breakdown in commerce, he did not grasp the full import of this development with respect to his program. "The effects of this interruption to commerce are truly alarming," he had written De Grasse when asking the French naval commander for protection of American commerce. ". . . The scene of private distress which is opened upon individuals presses with the greater weight as the collection of taxes creates a general demand for money while those who have articles of produce on hand cannot possibly vend them. Few persons even here are acquainted with the extent of this calamity which is now only in its commencement but which if not speedily checked may produce the most fatal consequences." But Morris' later correspondence reveals that he failed to grasp fully the ramifications. When some of the receivers of taxes, like William Whipple, wrote that the states were willing to contribute but did not possess the means, Morris dismissed the argument. When he explained the lack of resources to William Duer, he failed to comprehend that the trade paralysis and the "negligence of the states" marched together rather than as separate developments.

The confidence you reposed in my resources was well founded and had I been able to employ the means submitted to my disposal neither you nor others would have reason to complain. These means were however locked up by a total stoppage of mercantile business on the appearances of peace exhibited by Sir Guy Carleton shortly after his arrival. Appearances which are not yet entirely dissipated and which operate with powerful influence against my department in many different ways. Against an event so unfavorable and against the negligence of the States so unaccountable it was not in human prudence to provide.

In short, the Financier was far too enthusiastic at this time about the country's ability to shoulder the burden of taxes. His original analysis of the condition of the country was based on the relatively promising circumstances of 1780-81, and he formulated his policies accordingly. Despite the significant changes taking place in the economic prospects since that time, the Financier failed to make any adjustment in his policies to tailor them to fit the new conditions.[51]

In casting about for a solution to his financial troubles, Morris became increasingly attracted to a possible remedy which he had mentioned only casually before, strengthening the Articles of Confederation. During the year, 1782, his ideas on that question became more definite, more concrete. In April, Morris had written to General Greene:

The inefficiency of that instrument [the Confederation] is daily felt, and the want of obligatory and coercive clauses on the States will probably be productive of the most fatal consequences. At present they content themselves with the assertion that each has done most, and that the people are not able to pay taxes. Languor and inexertion are the offspring of this doctrine . . . there are in every legislature characters too full of local attachments and views to permit sufficient attention to the general interest.

When Varnum of Rhode Island lamented about some of the defects of the Confederation a few months later, Morris replied: "We are not to expect perfect institutions from human wisdom and must therefore console ourselves with the determination to reform errors as soon as experience points out the necessity for and the means of amendment. A whole people seldom continue long in error." The question, of course, was how much "reform" and how long "in error." At times

Morris grew discouraged. "A firm, wise, manly system of federal government, [and it seems that he had the Confederation in mind] is what I once wished, what I now hope, what I dare not expect, but what I will not despair of." By fall, Morris' thinking had taken a more drastic turn. "Every day's experience convinces me that until some capital alterations take place in our whole system we shall neither be a great, happy, nor an united people," he observed to Lovell. But it would not happen overnight. ". . . The prejudices which are opposed to such alterations are so strong that we must as yet only wish for better prospects." [52]

This trend in Morris' thinking is of major consequence, but it should be stressed that the solution which began to attract him, though important, was not basic in forwarding his program. First of all, the Financier had conceived his program on the premise that it would operate within the existing political framework. In fact, the Financier was attempting to provide a financial and economic program for the Confederation as Hamilton later provided one for the new government under the Constitution. And second, although an alteration in the political structure might noticeably strengthen the possibility of the complete success of his program, Morris realized that that no such change was visible in the immediate future. It is even questionable, in view of the prevailing economic conditions, whether an alteration in the political structure would have improved the chances for the success of the Morris program on the restoration of the public credit. No governmental structure, however realistic, could circumvent the fundamental question of sources of support which, in turn, depended in large measure upon the course of trade.

Meanwhile, a series of events was sweeping the country which could not and did not wait for any upturn in commerce or any alteration in political structure. The public creditors in many states had continued to organize; the intent, of course, was to apply pressure on the states and on Congress so that these political bodies would take action on the public debts. "I am happy to find that the public creditors are organizing themselves," Morris wrote Hamilton with approval. "Their numbers and influence joined to the justness of their cause must prevail if they persevere." Moreover, these forces were being joined by another class of public creditors—the army. It was not a question of food, shelter, and clothing—but pay. In August 1782, General Heath, commanding at West Point, had confided in a letter to General Lincoln, Secretary at War: "I will yet have confidence that a generous country will remember and reward her faithful servants." But the "faithful servants" were becoming restless. The Commander-in-Chief's now famous letter of October to the Secretary at War describing the situation merits repetition:

. . . Under present circumstances when I see such a Number of Men goaded by a thousand stings of reflexion on the past, and of anticipation on the future, about to be turned into the World, soured by penury and what they call the ingratitude of the Public, involved in debts, without one farthing of Money to carry them home, after having spent the flower of their days [and many of them their patrimonies] in establishing the freedom and Independence of their Country, and suffered everything human nature is capable of enduring on this side of death; I repeat it, these irritable circumstances, without one thing to soothe their feelings, or frighten the gloomy prospects, I cannot avoid apprehending that a train of Evils will follow, of a very serious and distressing Nature . . . you may rely upon it, the patience and long sufference of this Army are almost exhausted, and that there never was so great a spirit of Discontent as at this instant. . . .

Indeed, Washington later informed a fellow Virginian that he planned "to stick very close" to the troops and try to be "a careful physician to prevent if possible the disorders getting to an incurable height." [53]

The consolidation of discontent was destined to gather strength. In November, the Secretary of War was informed by Knox that the officers who had been disappointed by the Massachusetts legislature were preparing to address Congress; and less than a month later, in a private letter, he painted a forbidding picture. "The expectations of the army, from the drummer to the highest officer, are so keen for some pay that I shudder at the idea of their not having it. The utmost period of sufferance on that head has arrived. To attempt to lengthen it will undubitably occasion convulsions." Taking advantage of the breakdown in the contracting agreement, the Financier himself circularized the states in October. "Certain arguments" should be avoided if at all possible, he had written, but now the time had approached when every person in authority must ask himself some soul-searching questions.

How long is a nation who will do nothing for itself to rely on the aid of others? In a war waged by one country to obtain revenue from another, what is to be expected in case of conquest? How long will one part of a community bear the burdens of the whole? How long will an army undergo want in the midst of plenty? How long will they endure misery without complaining, injustice without reproach, and wrongs without redress? These are questions which can not be solved by arithmetical calculations.

Yet the only positive action taken by the Financier on the back pay due the service was to order the settlement of accounts through 1781. Thus they were to be placed on interest "in like manner with other public debts of the United States." [54]

This solution was wholly inadequate in the light of the needs of the troops. In September, General Lincoln had observed: "I think it does not require a very penetrating eye to discover, that a heavy cloud is gathering over the United States, nor a prophetic spirit to foretell, that unless the greatest precautions are taken, and those speedily, it will burst and sweep away our feeble confederation, and endanger, if not overturn, the union of these states." Had that time now arrived? With revenue in substantial arrears and commerce on which it depended paralyzed, with public creditors uneasy and an army restless for the lack of pay, and with the loans abroad overdrawn at least 3,000,000 livres, the situation which greeted the New Year was scarcely encouraging. In April 1782, the Financier had written to his Assistant, Gouverneur, in an outburst of enthusiasm: "You may very truly tell your antagonists [the British] that from one end of this continent to the other I can obtain whatever is wanted for the Public Service by a *scrip* of the pen." By January 1783, this optimistic boast had a rather hollow ring.[55]

CHAPTER—NINE ❖❖❖❖❖❖❖❖❖❖❖❖❖❖❖❖❖❖❖❖

The Second Phase of the Morris Program: A Climax in Public Credit

PERHAPS THE PROSPECTS FOR THE SUCCESS OF THE MORRIS PROGRAM, with its aim of completing the restoration of public credit, were more promising than surface events would indicate. It was entirely possible that certain probabilities could be transformed into realities which would encourage hopes of fulfillment. Now that the Financier had sketched a bold, clear-cut plan of funding, for example, pressure from the several classes of public creditors might gain such strength as to command general support, and thus complement, from Morris' point of view, the success of the Morris notes and the Bank of North America. Of greater import, a peace settlement appeared imminent with its postwar dream of new markets and extended commerce. Thus the immobility which gripped a large proportion of the country's trade would be replaced by a flurry of commercial activity, resulting in such a rising prosperity that an atmosphere would be created infinitely more conducive to the full adoption and support of the Morris program. It was possible that the year 1783 could be the decisive year for the program; indeed, some contemporaries were inclined to consider it as the crucial year for the future of the Confederation, to see if the constitutional instrument devised in a period of war would be sufficiently flexible and realistic to survive the problems of a nation at peace.

But a specific condition confronted the Financier as well as a list of probabilities, and an emerging political crisis, in which the Morris program became inextricably involved, did not permit some of the long-range factors to operate. The catalyst in this movement of events was the soldiers. Troubled by its lack of current pay, and especially its uncertainty over the status of its back pay, the army took steps through some of its leaders to make known its grievances. The entrance of this new group of public creditors reopened the entire question of funding the debts and, at the same time, presented the Financier with an opportunity to urge the adoption of his plan, the key measure in his program to restore the public credit. Although other measures involved in the Morris program such as the Bank of North America, the Morris notes, and contracting, operated with increasing effectiveness during the course of the year, his primary objective of funding the public debt was defeated, and in time this outcome decidedly influenced the fate of the Financier's entire program.

Even though the contracting system had sustained a shock when several of the contracts had been "vacated" in the fall of 1782, it was not only continued in the Northern Department during 1783 but also expanded to include the Southern Department. There are several possible explanations for this decision on the part of the Financier. Despite the difficulties which plagued contracting during 1782, the operation of the system did provide an important basis of experience, and the results, with respect to economy and efficiency, were sufficiently encouraging to warrant an extension. Moreover, the success of other parts of the program, particularly the Bank of North America and the Morris notes, had given the Financier greater confidence in his ability to meet the obligations of contracting. Then, too, expectations of an early withdrawal from Charleston by the British as well as growing rumors of a peace settlement had revived hopes that the South would soon find a measure of relief from its discouraging economic situation and be able to support the contracting system. Finally, a budget system was introduced into the national finances at this time by the Financier; and in line with this measure, it was quite natural that orderliness, regularity, and uniformity should also be extended to contracting.

When the Financier prepared to make new agreements, he selected able subordinates to supervise the advertising, to open the bids, and to make the preliminary arrangements for contracts in the various areas. James Lovell, the Continental Receiver of Taxes in Massachusetts, was placed in charge of the Eastern area; George Webb, Receiver of Taxes in Virginia, was assigned to the upper South; General Greene was asked to take that responsibility for the Southern Department; and the Financier himself made the arrangements for the Middle Region.

The response to the advertisements for contracts in the Middle Region clearly reflected the precarious nature of the credit of the Confederation. When the bids for supplying the troops in 1783 were opened in November 1782, Morris was not faced with a parade of contractors such as he had seen when the system was initiated. Only three bids were submitted for supplying the posts in Pennsylvania; a lone bid, that of Wadsworth and Carter, was sent in for the states of New York and New Jersey, and it was pegged at the excessive price of 14 pence (Pennsylvania currency) per ration. After deliberation, John Hazlewood and Company was given the contract for the posts in Pennsylvania at the rather moderate rate of 9½ pence per ration, but Wadsworth's bid for New York and New Jersey was not accepted. According to his own account, the Financier informed the Connecticut entrepreneur that his bid "appears so unreasonable that I think it my duty to try if I cannot do better. . . ." If he did find a more reasonable proposal, Morris assured Wadsworth, the latter would still have an opportunity to match it.[1]

Morris, in seeking for a more moderate offer, approached his friend William Duer. Duer, according to Morris' account, had not made a bid on the contract because he was afraid that he would be unable to fulfill it under the extension of credit demanded in the contract advertisement. At the request of Morris, Duer now presented a proposal, asserting that he needed $150,000 at his command in order to fulfill the contract—$50,000 of this, he specified, would be supplied by himself and his "friends," but the remainder must be obtained from the public, one-half on the 15th of January and the balance a month later. If these advances could be granted, Duer stated, he would supply the troops in New York and New Jersey for 11½ ninetieths dollars per ration. After much discussion and some calculating, the Financier and Duer finally agreed on 11 ninetieths per ration, a figure which was 25 per cent below that of Wadsworth and 10 per cent above those of the previous year. Wadsworth did not elect to duplicate this offer, so the agreement with Duer and his "friends" was formally accepted. The final understanding between Duer and the Financier went beyond the cold terms of the contract. Instead of paying the $100,000 as stipulated, the Financier agreed to pay the contractors an immediate thirty-day bill of exchange on France of $100,000 with the provision that it was to be sold in Boston. Such a handsome advance one month before the contract was to go into effect could not help but propel Duer and "friends" to a whirlwind start.[2]

And who were included among Duer's "friends"? To one of them,

Daniel Parker of Watertown, Massachusetts, albeit an entrepreneur of many parts, Duer scribbled an enthusiastic note. "I didn't bid for the contract nor have I time to tell you the extraordinary [?] manner by which it became mine." What did he expect of Parker? "All I ask of you is the ten thousand dollars you have enjoyed, and for this and your financial service one third of the contract is yours." One more enterpriser of long standing, none other than John Holker, former consul of France and purchasing agent for French forces in America, entered into the picture. Holker's relationship with Morris, as has been pointed out, was not only that of a friend but also that of a business partner. The participation of this Frenchman was essential to the combination of Duer and Parker, for he supplied the remaining capital, according to his own statement, of some $40,000. This combination of Parker, Duer, and Holker was neatly tied up in the firm of Daniel Parker and Company.[3]

The contract itself was drawn up after careful deliberation. During November 1782, the Secretary at War, the Financier, and Duer engaged in long sessions in an attempt to work out satisfactory modes of issuing. They wanted to avoid the disputes which had emerged under the contracts of 1782. In a letter transmitting a copy of the new contract to the Commander-in-Chief, it is obvious that Morris hoped most of the points of conflict had been eliminated.

I hope and believe that these gentlemen will act in such a manner as to attract your Excellency's esteem and instead of endeavoring to screen themselves by the letter adhere to the true spirit of their Contract. I have however drawn the agreement in such form as will I hope obviate most if not all of the inconveniences which you were formerly subjected to.

If the contract lived up to its advanced notice, it would augur well for part of the Northern Army.[4]

In the areas of the Eastern States and the Upper South, familiar names reappeared. Daniel Parker and Company entered a successful bid of 12½ ninetieths dollars for the New England area. Within the company, Parker filled the role of active partner for this contract, as Duer was doing for the one covering New York and New Jersey, while John Holker once again supplied the major proportion of the firm's capital and a generous amount of advice. In the upper South, the firm of Rawlings and Nichols obtained the contract for the military posts in Delaware and Maryland, but it was decided that no agreement should be made for the posts in Virginia. The limited number of troops was given as one reason, and the unsatisfactory prerequisites inserted in the bids submitted was stated as a second. When Arthur Lee applied pressure to introduce contracting in Virginia, however, the Financier, apparently to avoid trouble and criticism, made arrangements to supply the troops at Winchester.[5]

In setting up the contracting system in the South, certain obstacles quickly appeared. Morris had suggested for some time that it would be a major task to find someone who could undertake such a contract, and events proved that his judgment was sound. Although the contracts were advertised for almost five months, no bids were submitted to General Greene. Finally, under pressure from the South Carolina legislature, the General, through his Deputy Quartermaster, Edward Carrington, agreed on a supply contract with John Banks, a Charleston merchant who had previously enjoyed remarkable success in providing clothing for the Southern army. The final contract price per ration was 17½ ninetieths dollars, which was exceedingly high—almost double the Pennsylvania contract—but Banks, as Carrington stated it, "knew too well to be reduced lower, while he stood alone for the business." Indeed, when the Financier learned of the extraordinary expense, he lamented, "I am very sorry to find that the contract for subsisting your army is so high." Yet there was no alternative, as General Greene, Colonel Carrington, and Morris realized. ". . . We must . . .," observed the Financier in writing to Greene, "bear the expence as well as we can for the present."[6]

These contracts indicate that the system was not functioning as Morris originally envisioned it. The pressure of competitive bidding was almost entirely replaced by a bilateral agreement between the government and a firm where the latter maneuvered to receive the best possible terms; the government, in turn, made as many concessions as necessary to obtain an agreement without abandoning the basic aim of the system, to supply the troops more economically and efficiently than by some other method. In order to determine whether this fundamental objective of the system was fulfilled during 1783, it is necessary to follow the operations of the major contractors, John Banks and Daniel Parker and Company.

At the outset, John Banks seemed to be as successful in feeding the troops as he had previously been in clothing them, but he soon became enmeshed in financial difficulties. His situation became so precarious that General Greene himself had to step in to assure Banks's creditors that he would support the contractor in fulfilling his obligations. The General's action with respect to Banks's difficulties was so misconstrued that he was accused in certain quarters of having engaged in private trading at this time. Fortunately, the contracting arrangement was of relatively short duration. Hastening to eliminate every expense, the Financier initiated plans in April 1783 to move the Southern army to the Middle Region where it could be supplied more easily. The sanction of the British command at New York and a contract with Daniel Parker and Company enabled the operation to commence; by late summer, the evacuation was completed.[7]

In New England, New York, and New Jersey, Daniel Parker and Company began its operations at a furious pace. Even before the final contract had been completed, Parker wrote from Brookfield, Massachusetts, that he had taken steps to execute their agreement. A week later he paused long enough to dash off a letter from Boston to say that he was "much pleas'd" with the contract and with the idea of bills of exchange. To hasten the implementation of the contract,

Parker planned to call a meeting in Springfield to make arrangements for the beef, but his operations, which were of such a delicate nature that he could not leave for more than a few days, demanded his presence at Boston. This sensitive business involved the careful manipulation of the price of bills of exchange. Bills on France had been selling at a discount of 20 per cent because of the presence of a part of the French fleet. "It is my intention to reduce them to 33⅓ per cent, and to convince the Major of the fleet that his Bills must go thro' my hands," asserted Parker. The advance to the firm by the Financier had strengthened Parker's bargaining position. "I have now such sums at my command as to furnish him [the Major of the fleet] with 100,000 dollars cash. . . ." With this lever, the New Englander hoped to obtain control of the French bills at the low discount and then "raise them to 10 per cent which will be the case within 15 days. . . ." And how important was this scheme to the plans of the firm? ". . . The negotiation of Bills is our first object."[8]

It would normally be assumed that contractors, whose operations began with speculation, would have a dire effect upon the system, but the early record indicates quite the opposite. Although the initial entrepreneurial strategy was an appropriate index to the later debacle of the firm itself, the smoothness of their operation in supplying the troops was gratifying to everyone concerned. The company gave out subcontracts to individuals and smaller firms to provide the separate commodities which made up the ration. Some suppliers were to furnish beef, others flour, others candles and tallow, and still others casks. Agreements on the rates of officers' rations, and apparently satisfactory ones, were made with the officers of the line, and this eliminated a persistent cause of complaint from the army's most articulate group. Stores providing supplies for the troops as well as operating for the "mutual advantage of the company" were set up by an agreement with Melancton Smith. In short, so untroubled was the scene that Parker informed Holker: "We are making very advantageous arrangements with the army—and we can assure you that the disposition of the *whole* army is infinitely more favorable to the present contractors, than we had reason to expect *so soon* after the commencement of the contract. . . ." Of course, the prospects for the partners were also promising, he continued. "We have no doubt but the contract will afford us all the advantages we had reason to expect."[9]

No major complaints or disputes developed during the succeeding months. Some misunderstanding arose about the issues of rations to the women, but that was quickly resolved; and a passing complaint about the quality of goods was remedied by Parker himself, an action viewed by Washington and the Financier with relief and pleasure. Indeed, when Washington introduced Parker to the Financier, the normally reticent General became profuse in his praise. "I feel myself happy in having an opportunity . . . of introducing to your personal acquaintance Mr. Parker . . . whose character as a Gentleman of amiable manners and dispositions, and as a Man of great integrity

and capacity in business will have preceded him, and almost super-
sedes the necessity of my repeating that the business of the present
Contract has been performed extremely to the satisfaction of the
Army. . . ." What a contrast to the preceding years of the war and to
Washington's harsh judgment of the previous contractors! The great-
coats and fine cloth brought to the Commander-in-Chief by Parker
might have influenced the judgment of the great man, but his opinion
was founded upon much more positive testimony, the general paucity
of complaints about the provisioning of the troops.[10]

Although the contracting operations were going well insofar as the
relationship between the army, the company, and the Financier were
concerned, the firm of Daniel Parker and Company itself experienced
moments of uneasiness; but its troubles did not truly appear until the
company became insolvent the following year. Duer, who was being
sorely pressed by some of his subcontractors in New York, consistently
urged Parker to send him money, and at one time he confided to
Holker: "My situation is delicate to an extreme." Aid from Parker's
quarter came hesitatingly, however, and the New Englander's apparent reluctance to explain the precise state of the bills of exchange
aroused the suspicion of Duer and Holker that all was not as it should
be. A variety of additional enterprises of the company and numerous
individual commitments complicated the situation. The firm held the
contract for the evacuation of General Greene's troops from the South;
they used company funds to purchase a vessel for transporting masts
from Connecticut. Armed with letters from Benjamin Lincoln, Washington, and Morris, the firm obtained an agreement with the British
Commissary—after the peace—to supply flour to British troops in
New York and Canada. This is not to mention the distillery and mast
business of Duer and Holker, Parker's connections with Guild and
Company of Boston, and Holker's criss-cross of interests with Morris,
Ridley and Pringle, and others. Without careful accounting, such di-
verse activities could easily plant the seeds for a host of disputes—as
it eventually did.[11]

Under such circumstances, it is somewhat surprising to find contracting operations carried out so smoothly. Probably the most important explanation lies in the prompt and continual supply of money
from the Financier. In the most important contract, that of New York
and New Jersey, the treasury accounts indicate that the Financier was
in advance to the contractors throughout most of the year. This meant
that the contractors could operate on a minimum amount of personal
credit, for they could purchase the supplies with funds which had already been placed in their hands rather than first purchasing the
supplies, making the issues, and then presenting the vouchers at the
Treasury to receive their compensation. Other factors were involved.
The existing materials clearly reveal that Duer and Parker, through
their previous experience, had learned to handle such provisioning.
It is equally obvious that there was a better understanding between
the firm, the army, and the Financier with respect to the terms of the

contractual agreement, and this reduced the chances of dispute. In addition, the stability of the various posts—that is, a minimum of troop movement—contributed to the ease and effectiveness of supplying the troops. Finally, the contract probably allowed a greater profit incentive than had some of the earlier contracts.[12]

Had the contracts for 1783 fulfilled the aims of the Financier's program? That the troops were better supplied on the whole was everywhere evident; the question of economy is a relative matter. The total amount of money expended for "subsistence" was shaved about 15 per cent from 1782, but, of course, the issues to the army dropped rapidly in the early fall after the army began to disband. Therefore, the increase in the price per ration combined with this figure indicates that contracting was more expensive in 1783 than in 1782, although the added cost might have been more than compensated by the satisfaction expressed by the army. When compared with the years before contracting was introduced, the sum expended for contracting, in a very general fashion, seems to point to a substantial saving, although it is difficult to contrast a year of war with a year of peace. A combination of army satisfaction, efficiency of operation, and comparative savings, on the whole, adds up to a successful fulfillment of Morris' program on contracting during 1783.[13]

There was more to be considered, however, than the basic needs of troops, and particularly at the beginning of 1783 when the ominous rumblings on the question of back pay and current pay reached the sacred Congressional halls at Front Street. Several years earlier, the Financier had established priorities within military expenditures; he had listed food first, clothing second, military stores and equipment third, attending the sick fourth, and "whatever can be spared and oeconomized from these services will be properly applied as pay." But whatever is applied, he wrote General Greene, should be in "solid coin." The proper approach to getting payment, then, was to "urge the grant of so much as will support and equip the army and still leave a sufficiency for their pay" instead of pleading with the states for a small separate grant to pay the troops. Morris' "constant object," as he labeled it, logically followed: "To increase the means of payment by retrenching every other expenditure." The hazardous fortunes of the revenue program, however, had failed to make this possible, and under the stated list of priorities, little hope for relief could normally be expected from the Financier.[14]

Events sometimes move too rapidly for neat and coherent systems, and January of 1783 was definitely one of those times. To Congress, the restlessness of the troops was revealed most decisively in the form of a deputation of officers led by General McDougall who presented a memorial to that body seeking action on back pay. "Our situation compels us to search for the cause of our extreme poverty," the memorial read. ". . . We have borne all that men can bear—our property is expended—our private resources are at an end, and our friends are wearied out and disgusted with our incessant applications." What they needed and wanted was money, immediate pay plus a settlement of back claims and half-pay. Here was a disagreeable situation to sour the joys of impending peace.[15]

For the Office of Finance, the question transcended the matter of back pay for the army pure and simple. It involved the army as public creditors which placed them in the same category as the other members of the community to whom the Confederation was indebted. The Financier, and those close to him, seized upon these circumstances as an opportunity to unite general sentiment behind the proposal to fund the debts of the Confederation and to apply pressure on Congress and the states for its adoption. The question of pay, therefore, became interwoven with the measure which Morris regarded as the most important pillar of his program to restore the public credit and which now began to loom large, in his mind, as a measure to preserve the Union.

Morris' important Report on Public Credit of July 1782 had lain dormant for many months, but in the spring of 1783 his proposal became the center of a political crisis which involved the various states, Congress, the army, and the Office of Finance. An enlargement of the respective state requisitions had been the only action prompted by his message originally, and the Financer had found this response sadly disappointing. But when a class of public creditors, who held muskets, marched on to the national stage in the early months of 1783, the entire question of funding the debts of the Confederation was reactivated with the Financier's proposals often standing in the center of the debate. It was these circumstances which prompted the Office of Finance to alter its strategy, to launch a concerted effort to obtain the adoption of the Financier's plan of funding.

There can be little question that in the fall of 1782 the incumbents of the Office of Finance looked on the approaching peace with some skepticism. What the Financier considered as an indispensable support for the preservation of the Union and for a successful peacetime nation, the restoration of public credit and especially funding as an instrument to that end, had not yet been completed. What better way to forge bands of steel than in the furnace of war? In a private letter to his friend Matthew Ridley, a Maryland merchant who had accompanied the Financier's sons to Europe, Gouverneur Morris stated his position without hesitation. "I am well convinced of two things," he wrote. "One that a peace will not easily be made and another that it is not much for the interest of America that it should be made at present." The country had grown rapidly, he continued, and its resources paralleled and overleaped its growth. "Our Position, our Numbers, our Resources, and our probable Increase are all important. . . . Highly commercial, being as it were the first born children of extended Commerce in modern Times, we must be maritime." The pleasing prospects he outlined did not stop at the edge of political affairs. "Freedom was secured by the several Constitutions; Freedom in the extreme." What was missing in this idyllic picture? Nothing— nothing, that is, except "Vigor, Organization and Promptitude to render this a considerable Empire." And how were these blessings to be secured?

These can only be acquired by a Continuance of the War, which will convince People of the necessity of obedience to common counsel for general purposes. War is indeed a rude, rough Nurse to infant States, and the Consequence of being committed to her care is that they either die Young or grow up Vigorous. We have at least lived thro the Cradle, and are familiarized to her Looks of Horror. The Power of Congress is like a young Tree which when first planted is much endangered but when the Roots once begin to shoot it acquires Strength "[Send?]" in the visitation of the Winds which take the ruffian Billow by the Top." A Tree so visited se[l]dom overgrows. Such a Tree becomes if not large at least solid and tho not showy is surely strong. Metaphors are not Reasons neither are assertations Proofs unless indeed they be taken as the Evidences of opinion. The Confederation has not given to Congress sufficient authority. This becomes daily sensible and that Sense will remedy the Evil. But if the War cease the conviction of our Weakness will also cease until shown by another War, and then perhaps it may be too late.[16]

These comments of Gouverneur Morris represented, in part, the sentiments of the Financier. Some two months later, in a draft of a letter to Washington from the Office of Finance, the following passage appeared:

You observe, in your letter, that a peace is necessary; but if I were to hazard an opinion on the subject, it would be, that war is more likely than peace to produce funds for the Public Debts, Increase of the authority to Congress, and [give] vigor to the administration as well of the Union as of its component parts. These things all appear necessary to our future Prosperity Safety and Happiness.[17]

If there should be any doubt that the Financier entertained ideas which coincided with this letter from the Office of Finance to Washington, all such uncertainties must be dispelled by Morris' personal letter to Matthew Ridley.

Peace seemed for a while to be forceing herself suddenly upon us, and although the prospect is not now so strong and clear as it was yet it seems to me impossible that the war can continue much longer. . . . for my part I wish most sincerely and ardently for Peace that I may get rid of a most Troublesome Office and spend the remainder of my days with more ease and in less hurry than those which are past. But was I to confine myself to the language of a Patriot, I should [this word inserted by Morris] speak in another manner and tell you that a continuance of the War is necessary untill our Confederation is more strongly knit, untill a sense of [this phrase inserted by Morris] the obligations to support it shall be more generally diffused amongst all Ranks of American Citizens, untill we shall acquire the Habit of paying Taxes (the means we possess already) and untill the several governments have derived from experience and action that vigour and self confidence which is necessary to insure the safety and promote the happiness of the People. The expence of the War as now conducted is not very heavy to this country and the payment of our Public Debt will hardly be felt by those that come after us, as this country has abundant resources as yet untouched. In this view of things Peace may not [this word inserted by Morris] be really so desireable as at first view one would think, and perhaps you may be surprized when I tell you that in this City the prospect of Peace has given more general discontent than anything that has happened in a long time, particularly amongst the mercantile part of the community. I have been much surprized at it, but so is the Fact. However, again I repeat my wishes for a speedy and Honorable Peace. It is idle for Great Britain to think of wheedling us into a separate or disgracefull peace—No man in this country seriously thinks of such a thing[.] Even the disaffected are convinced of the impracticability of it—For my own part I will sooner sacrifice all my prospects of ease and enjoyment throughout the whole course of my life than consent to close the contest by any act derogatory to the Integrity Honor and Glory of a young and rising nation.[18]

What does all this mean? Neither the Financier nor his Assistant was filled with dire prophecies for the future of the country; on the contrary, they were highly optimistic. But in viewing the situation, they were convinced that certain fundamental needs had to be satisfied, notably the possible strengthening of the Confederation and more specifically the funding of the public debt. This last measure would be an appropriate ending to a "glorious revolution," and to achieve it, the continuance of the war seemed desirable. As the Financier's letter indicates, this did not mean war at any price; in fact, Morris almost seems to have changed his position by January 1783, when he observed to General Gates: "I am heartily tired of Financiering [.] God send peace and soon." [19]

By early January 1783, peace rumors were multiplying; and, to lend support to such rumors, word was received that the commission of Oswald, the British emissary, had been revised to treat with the Commissioners of the United States of America. If the program on funding required the pressures of war in order to be adopted, therefore, the chances of ultimate success would be seriously diminished with the arrival of peace. Upon this premise, the restlessness in the army with the concluding days of the old year together with the first climax of this uneasiness, the delegation from the army presenting its celebrated memorial to Congress, assumes a special importance. It is not surprising to find Gouverneur confiding to Ridley that "all things says St Paul work together for Good to those who fear the Lord." The question, of course, was: Who is on the Lord's side? This precocious young man did not let such an important question slip by him unanswered. ". . . Those," he thought, "who act justly." If his interpretation of the Scriptures were correct, he declared, "our Legislatures will not derive much good from the fermentation," but such a development was not to be feared. "I shall not be sorry to see Some Thing which may draw forth general attention to our affairs and then perhaps order may be drawn forth from Confusion."[20]

Although there is no specific letter or comment available to determine whether the Financier was of the same mind as his Assistant, the actions of the Superintendent suggest that, for the most part, he would agree with Gouverneur's statement. As the happenings of the next few months unfolded, it became increasingly clear that the Financier had cast his lot with those who considered the new developments conducive to an all-out effort to obtain the adoption of his plan on funding, and the evidence strongly indicates that the movement for uniting the support of the public creditors—civil and military—emanated, so far as it can be traced, from the Office of Finance. Whether the Financier or Gouverneur was chiefly responsible is impossible to determine. The Financier was responsible for the policies of his Office, and he was too seasoned a man of affairs to commit himself to programs which he would consider irresponsible or which he could not support. Before this important series of events had run their course, however, the pen of Gouverneur Morris had carried that young man far in advance of his superior in the Office of Finance.

In re-creating those attitudes and actions of the Financier which prompted him to commit much of his program to the successful adoption of his most cherished measure, funding the debts of the Confederation on the basis of permanent revenue, the starting point must be Morris' own evaluation of the relative importance of his personal credit to the public credit. In September of 1782, Morris had written to Washington: "I . . . shall endeavor . . . to pay the engagements I have already made without which my credit (which has alone supported us hitherto) must be ruined." Later, when a committee of Congress came to ask him about making some kind of payment to the army, he asserted that the only chance of success lay in a very large issue of notes that would be based upon his personal credit. There was, of course, some exaggeration—though by no means a great exaggeration—in such claims, but that is of minor consequence. The real significance of these comments lay in the claim itself. In Morris' view, his personal credit was essential to the nation in carrying on its finances.[21]

Superimpose Morris' idea of his indispensable personal credit upon the quickening pace of events. On the sixth of January the memorial from the army respecting pay was laid before Congress. On the seventh the Grand Committee met with the Financier on the question of pay, and he, according to Madison, informed them "explicitly" that the finances did not permit any payments at present or "any assurances with respect to future pay until certain funds should be previously established." Again, the matter of funding. During this conference, "much loose conversation passed on the critical state of things, the defect of a permanent revenue, and the consequences to be apprehended from a disappointment of the mission from the army"—an interesting combination of topics. On the ninth, Morris asked Congress that a committee meet with him so he could disclose some highly confidential information. This committee was told about the over-

drawn account abroad of some 3,000,000 livres, and a request was
made for Congress' approval in drawing additional bills despite the
overdrafts. In granting this request, Congress ordered the strictest
secrecy, so that further impairment of the public credit could be prevented. On the thirteenth, the Grand Committee and Morris met
with the delegation from the army, and General McDougall, the
spokesman for the delegation, remarked "with peculiar emphasis" on
the "defects in the federal Govt and the unwillingness of the States to
cement and invigorate it." A few days later, McDougall conversed at
some length on this subject with Morris in the Office of Finance.
Called in by the Financier on the seventeeth, the delegation from the
army was told that one month's pay would be given to the soldiers
and noncommissioned officers at the rate of "about half a dollar a
week," and an effort would be made to give the officers a month's pay
with notes at sixty days sight or, if they would wait until the soldiers
received their compensation, in cash. Their major grievances, however, on back pay and half pay would have to wait until a general
settlement was decided upon. On the same day, a committee of Congress which had consulted with Morris about seeking additional foreign loans reported itself in agreement with the Financier "that the
applications already on foot were as great as could be made prudently,
until proper funds [in other words, a program of funding] should be
established." This report was another item which focused attention
on the domestic scene; and, interestingly enough, it was ordered to lie
on the table to be considered along with the matter of the memorial
of the army, for they both centered around the matter of "proper
funds." [22]

With these flames licking the Congressional cauldron, causing the
brew of funding based on permanent revenue to bubble merrily, the
Financier threw an explosive into the fire. On the apparent premise
that his personal credit was indispensable, the Financier, without any
previous warning whatsoever, submitted a letter of resignation to
Congress on the twenty-fourth of January. The finances were confronted with a critical situation; to meet it, in Morris' eyes, depended
in large measure on his private credit. His resignation would act as
an energizer that would practically compel the adoption of his funding program!

Although the timing of the resignation reflects the strategy of additional pressure, the heart of the matter is contained in the letter
itself. The danger of the war had passed, asserted the Financier, and
his purpose to see the finances through the crisis of war had now been
fulfilled. But the matter of funding the public debts on the basis of
solid revenues, "the last essential work of our glorious Revolution,"
remained unfinished. "The accomplishment of this necessary work is
among the objects nearest my heart, and to effect it I would sacrifice
time, property, and domestic bliss." Because little hope was held that
any action would be taken, "I must, therefore, quit a situation which
becomes utterly insupportable." Morris declared that he would vacate

the Office of Finance on the last day of May—with one alternative. "If effectual measures are not taken by that period to make permanent provision for the public debts of every kind, Congress will be pleased to appoint some other man to be the superintendent of their finances. . . . I will never be the minister of injustice." The implication was clear. If the funding measure were adopted, Morris would stay on at this crucial juncture to carry on the finances; if not, Congress—and the nation—would lose what he considered to be the essential support of his personal credit.[23]

The Financier's letter of resignation jarred Congress. "This letter made a deep and solemn impression on Congress," recorded the ever faithful James Madison. "It was considered as the effect of despondence in Mr. Morris of seeing justice done to the public Credrs [Creditors], or the public finances placed on an honorable establisht; as a source of fresh hopes to the enemy when known; as ruinous both to domestic and foreign credit; and as producing a vacancy which no one knew how to fill, and which no fit man wd venture to accept." And it produced the kind of action Morris had intended. On the day following Morris' letter of resignation, Congress inaugurated a full-scale effort to consider the means of "obtaining from the several states substantial funds, for funding the whole debt of the United States."[24]

The effect of Morris' resignation beyond the immediate confines of Congress was blunted by its decision to keep his letter a secret, a decision which probably robbed Morris' action of the full impact he had anticipated. Yet, for those who sympathized with the Morris program of funding and who knew of his resignation, it was a signal for what appears to be a concentrated campaign to enlist support outside of Congress, particularly with the army. It may have been a coincidence, but it is interesting to see Hamilton calling on the Financier "respecting the Report of the Committee on the Army Business" the day after Morris' letter was read in Congress. This interest heightens when Hamilton's correspondence reveals a decided change in tenor after this date. "I view the present juncture as a very interesting one," Hamilton wrote his former chief, George Washington. "I need not observe how far the temper and situation of the army may make it so." But the greatest difficulty was to "keep a *complaining* and *suffering* army within the bounds of moderation," and in this role, Hamilton implied, Washington could perform an important service. "The great *desideratum* at present," Hamilton continued, "is the establishment of general funds, which alone can do justice to the creditors of the United States (of whom the army forms the most meritorious class), restore public credit, and supply the future wants of Government. This is the object of all men of sense; in this the influence of the army, properly directed, may cooperate."[25]

Perhaps these suggestions originated with Hamilton, perhaps they sprang out of his concern over Morris' letter of resignation, perhaps they emerged from the interview with the Financier, or perhaps they came from Gouverneur Morris, for it was at this time that the Assistant to the Financier began to issue his famous letters to key figures in the army. To General Greene, with whom he had long corresponded, Gouverneur wrote:

I am most perfectly convinced, that, with the due exception of miracles, there is no probability the States will ever make such grants, unless the army be united and determined in the pursuit of it; and unless they be firmly supported, and as firmly support the other public creditors.

A few days before, Gouverneur had placed a note, addressed to General Knox, in the hands of Colonel Brooks, who was returning to the army to report on the progress of the army memorial on pay. He warned that the army must look to Congress for relief rather than to the various states. "It is therefore not my persuasion but my conviction that the only wise mode is for the army to connect themselves with the public creditors of every kind both foreign and domestic and unremittingly to urge the grant of general permanent funds adequate to the whole interest. . . . The army may now influence the legislatures and if you will permit me a metaphor from your own profession after you have carried the post the public creditors will garrison it for you." [26]

Although it cannot be firmly established that Hamilton and Gouverneur Morris faithfully reflected the Financier's views, the central theme of combining the influence of the army with that of the other public creditors certainly struck a responsive note. As the Financier wrote to Greene some months later: "My resignation was not made until I was confident of peace, it was then induced by a desire to serve the army and other public creditors." What interested the Financier was the army as a powerful weight of opinion to stand with the other public creditors, not the army as a weapon of internal rebellion. [27]

That the Financier expected the general pressure of circumstances to produce results is evident, and he was determined to bring every persuasive element to bear. When the Financier laid down general propositions for the guidance of Tom Paine, who was now employed to write for Continental measures, he was explicit.

Congress have in contemplation the subject of funds for all the public debts and mean to take it up upon an extensive scale. It is uncertain what particular revenues they will adopt in addition to the impost but I expect that they will consider the subject in a very liberal point of view so that it may be well to impress the general utility and necessity of the provision and shew that from the very nature of it Congress must have the collection and appropriation." [28]

Action it did produce. The battle of funding was waged in Congress for two long months, and only through the efforts of that indefatigable note taker, James Madison, can the record of that campaign be traced—and then in blurred outline. Whether imposts should be state or federally imposed, whether the valuation of lands was possible or even desirable, whether the suffering of one state exceeded that of another, were essential questions that each delegation answered, for the most part, on the basis of the various economic, social, and political interests within its state. But it should be stressed that these were variances in tactics, and nothing more. The general melée should not obscure the obvious, that all members of Congress were interested in satisfying the public creditors, and that most of them favored immediate action. The question revolved around the methods of reaching that objective—not the objective itself. Such men as Arthur Lee of Virginia and Jonathan Arnold of Rhode Island—and who could name more determined foes of Morris' plan to fund the public debt—proceeded on the assumption that "satisfaction of the creditors of the public" was essential. [29]

Although the lines were not clearly drawn, in many respects, on the issue of funding the debts of the Confederation, there can be no doubt that the entire question was complicated by important political overtones. Many members in and out of Congress, who could be called "nationalists," were anxious to use the issue of funding as a means to strengthen the union of the states, while others, who could be called "antinationalists," were equally eager to see that the union was weakened, if anything, rather than strengthened. In perspective, it is apparent that the extremists on both sides overstated their case. The ultranationalists, on the one hand, maintained that unless permanent funds were supplied to take care of public obligations of the Confederation, the union would be dissolved, and this would jeopardize the liberty of the people because they would be at the mercy of internal and external conflicts. Their opposites within the antinationalist group, on the other hand, maintained that a new tyranny was being erected which would endanger liberty because it enhanced the power of the central government to such an extent that it would crush the people. Of course there were countless shades of opinion ranging between the extremes, and the members of Congress reflected this variation.

The stand of most members of Congress with respect to the degree of "nationalism" which they advocated was usually dictated by the political and economic interests of their section, but sometimes it was based on personal conviction or prejudice. An entire state such as New Jersey and regions like the Valley of Virginia, for example, tended to hold to "nationalist" views because their location made them dependent upon their neighboring states, while Rhode Island tended to be antinationalistic because of the nature of its trade and because of the fear of losing power within the Confederation on account of its size. Landholders prominent in large land companies were sometimes nationalists—although their attitude depended upon the circumstances; and some groups of interests who were out of power in their own state tended to become nationalist regardless of their political or economic views. This was also true with regard to certain frontier folk who had not received sufficient protection from their respective states or who were dependent upon a Mississippi River trade outlet for their exportable commodities. A state such as Virginia,

whose citizens, because they were mostly landholders, did not possess
many loan office certificates, took quite a different view on some
phases of the question of funding than did Pennsylvania, for example,
many of whose citizens, because they were engaged in commercial activities, did possess loan office certificates. Such forces, too many to
enumerate and analyze in detail, were at play in the issue of "nationalism" and involved in the specific measure of funding the debts of the
Confederation.[30]

Within these forces, there can be no question that Robert Morris was
a "nationalist" at this time in the sense that he favored a central government that could carry out the powers which he thought necessary
for the preservation of the Union, and that he, with a new clarity,
visualized his plan of funding as a measure towards that end. That he
was a "nationalist" was obviously rooted in the interests he represented; no merchant, particularly one of Morris' vast intercolonial and
international connections, could be expected to hold to any other
view. "Liberty" to Morris as a merchant meant liberty to carry on his
mercantile affairs without meeting separate obstructions from each
state, just as liberty to a large landholder in Virginia or South Carolina meant liberty to own and run his property without any interruption that might endanger this activity.

Insofar as these nationalistic inclinations touched upon the Articles
of Confederation, Morris had time and again urged the strengthening
of that constitutional instrument, but largely in terms of centralization by means of effective administration rather than in terms of an
alteration in the political structure. As has been previously emphasized, Morris as Superintendent of Finance introduced his program
on the basic premise that it would operate within the Confederation.
His overpowering objective, the restoration of the public credit, for
example, would significantly increase the prestige of the Confederation which Morris conceived to be essential to the preservation of the
Union. The funding measure, as Morris saw it, would be the final
step in the "glorious revolution" because it would complete the restoration of that public credit. This would improve the national and
international position of the Union in carrying on foreign affairs, for
example, or in providing the necessary protection on the sea and land
frontiers. Whether the majority of people did or did not favor this
objective is almost impossible to determine, although the widespread
adoption of the impost as a means to that end would indicate that the
goal enjoyed considerable support and that many people of varying
political beliefs and interests were convinced that their future welfare
and prosperity depended upon the whole as well as upon the parts.

In the actual contest in Congress over fashioning a funding measure, the Financier played a subtle role. It is interesting to note, in this
respect, that James Wilson, who entered Congress just in time to participate in the deliberations, placed the emphasis of the Financier's
letter of resignation precisely where Morris intended it. Do not try to
do anything about retaining the Financier, Wilson asserted, but take

action on funding. Wilson hammered on the theme that Congress must first commit itself to the general principle of funding before entering into details, and in his "hints and remarks"—the phrase is Madison's—Wilson's ideas paralleled those expounded in the Financier's Report on Public Credit. Although Hamilton demonstrated many times that his general perspective corresponded with that of the Financier, Wilson unquestionably best mirrored Morris' point of view on this particular issue.[31]

During the debates on funding, the Financier was frequently consulted by Congress, and on one important preliminary report written by Madison a principle was raised which so far had been obscure in the previous reports from the Office of Finance—the assumption of the state debts by the Confederation. "That conformably to the liberal principles on which these recommendations are founded," read the resolution, "and with a view to a more amicable and complete adjustment of all accounts between the United States and individual states, all reasonable expences which shall have been incurred by the states without the sanction of Congress, in their defence against, or attacks upon British or savage enemies . . . shall be considered as part of the common charges incident to the present war, and be allowed as such." The Financier not only moved swiftly to support the resolution of assumption without equivocation, but his views advanced beyond those stated in the original report. Where Madison had intended that the "assumed debts" would be parceled out to the several states on a quota arrangement for payment, the Financier took the position that they should be included within the orbit of the other public debts and be funded on the basis of a permanent revenue which would be solely at the disposal of the Union. In short, the creditors within the states, and the states as creditors themselves, would become a part of a national obligation; the new creditors, in conformity with the idea of the Financier, would look to the Union for relief; they would be wedded by financial ties to the Union; they would be attracted to the Union and cemented to it financially rather than repelled. By this use of the assumption of state debts, the Financier had placed in position the final stone which completed the financial arch of public credit that he had worked so tirelessly to erect. The completed structure now resembled that of Hamilton's a decade later not only in general design but also in precise detail.[32]

Meanwhile, the restlessness in the army became more pronounced and, be it added, more articulate. In fact, the circulars—now known as the Newburgh Addresses—which passed from hand to hand, were models for inspiriting a weary soldiery to take matters into their own hands. In Philadelphia, rumors had been whispered around the Congressional tables that the army would refuse to disband until its grievances were acted upon, even though peace should come, and finally, word arrived that a meeting of army officers which held forbidding prospects had been scheduled. "Congress ought not to lose a moment in bringing the affairs of the army to a decision," Knox scribbled in a hasty note to the Secretary at War. "Push the matter instantly my dear Sir with all your might and main." These events, according to Madison, "gave peculiar awe and solemnity to the present moment, and oppressed the minds of Congs [Congress] with an anxiety and distress which had been scarcely felt in any period of the revolution." Fortunately for all, the impending crisis had already been averted by the magnificent performance of the Commander-in-Chief in calling together the officers and reading his strong message disapproving any type of violent recourse. This piece of news, of course, received a warm welcome from Congress.[33]

The suspicion arose, repeated by no less a figure than Washington, that the Financier had been partly responsible for the new burst of activity that produced the Newburgh addresses. Furthermore, some of the officers thought that they were to be used as mere puppets to establish Continental funds; to be, if necessary, sacrificed to the grand object. Although the Commander-in-Chief first voiced this suspicion to Hamilton, he apparently took the matter directly to the Financier later. Morris' reaction was full of bitterness. "By some designing men my resignation of office . . . was misconstrued. It was represented as a factious desire to raise civil commotions. It was said that the army were to be employed as the instruments to promote flagitious interested views." Let the actions speak for themselves, said Morris. "The factious designing man, who was to have lighted up the flames of mutiny and sedition, has undertaken a most arduous and perilous business [paying the troops] to save this country from those convulsions, which her negligence had hazarded." It is evident that the grounds for the general suspicion about the Financier were based upon the letters of Gouverneur Morris and Hamilton urging the support of the army for the general program of funding, but there is no indication that the Financier was involved in any way with the Newburgh Address or its implications. Robert Morris was interested in properly directed vocal pressure from the army, not mutiny; but such nice distinctions could not always be explained to men with arms in their possession.[34]

Meanwhile, Congress worked hard to find an acceptable solution to the problem of funding the debts of the Confederation, but despite the pressure from the Office of Finance, the measure finally adopted was far removed from the plans and ideas of the Financier as embodied in his Reports on the Public Credit. The Congressional measure recommended the adoption by the states of an impost for a period of twenty-five years, with collectors appointed by the states but removable by the Congress. A requisition amounting to $1,500,000 was also recommended with quotas assigned to the separate states that could be adjusted at a future time under the rules prescribed by the Articles of Confederation. The amount collected from each state on this requisition would be credited to the account of that state. If the revenues from any state should be in arrears, "the immediate deficiency shall be made up by such State with as little delay as possible, and a future deficiency guarded against by an enlargement of the revenues established." A plan was included to hasten the complete cession of western lands, and an amendment of the Articles of Confederation was recommended to the states for adoption which would change the basis for determining quotas from the evaluation of land in each state to the number of persons in each state.[35]

This measure did not win the support of the Financier. Although he stayed on in office to complete the payment of troops, Morris expressly declared that he neither approved the Congressional plan providing for the public debts nor should his continuance in the Office of Finance be construed as even tacit support for that program. In fact, he made certain that his motive for remaining in office was carefully recorded in the *Journals* and broadcasted in a circular letter to the states.[36] About the plan itself he was apathetic.

. . . I have as you supposed consented to longer continuance in office but am very sorry to say that it is not from the reasons you suggest. There is indeed a plan adopted by Congress and if agreed to by the States it may procure to public creditors some temporary prospect of relief but in my poor opinion it is not well calculated to obtain a general adoption nor to give (when adopted) a perfect security[.] However I shall not impede tho I cannot in my conscience strongly recommend it.[37]

For the most part, funding, as the Financier conceived it, was dead. Defeat, it should be added, came in Congress, and thus at the hands of political compromise rather than because of long-term factors. There is considerable doubt whether the funding program of Morris, if adopted, would have succeeded, for the obligations assumed would have demanded a revenue which the nation, entering a depression, would have found difficult to provide. On the other hand, it is possible that the adoption of the funding measure would have "created" capital, and that the employment of these funds in land and commerce might have so stimulated economic activity as to produce prosperous conditions.[38]

The Financier was definitely stung by his defeat and by the growing criticisms against him and his actions. Although some of this criticism was not only bitter but deliberately falsified, other comment was more temperate and reasonable. Many persons felt that Morris had overstepped himself by his inordinate pressure to obtain the adoption of his funding plan. Samuel Osgood, although an affirmed opponent of Morris and therefore not a good representative of moderate opinion, wrote of Morris in December 1783:

He Judges well in almost all Money Matters; . . . He Judges generally for himself; and acts with great decision. He has many excellent qualities for a Financier, which however do not comport so well with Republicanism, as Monarchy. Ambitious of becoming the first Man in the United States, he was not so delicate in the Choice of Means, and Men for his Purpose, as is indispensably necessary in a free Government.

In reacting to these forces, the Financier, in the months immediately after the defeat of his measure, showed definite traces of personal bitterness in some of his letters, and his official correspondence is marked with a certain abruptness and sometimes ill humor. "There is such a disposition to traduce and vilify," Morris informed the Governor of Virginia, "that no prudent man will risk a fair reputation by holding an Office so important as mine." [39]

Although Morris' plan on funding had not been adopted, the army still had to be paid. When consulted about the possibilities in April—and this was a few days before the Congressional program on funding was passed—Morris declared that no money was available, nor did he foresee any avenue to obtain funds in the immediate future. Although the expenditures by May 1783 had exceeded revenue by $600,000, some $260,000 had been collected on requisitions; if the rate of increase in the collection of taxes should parallel that of 1782, this sum, together with the expected funds in Europe, would be adequate to meet current expenditures. But the problem of pay placed quite a different face on matters, for this would require an additional $750,000, a sum which would raise the total expenditure some 30 per cent. With no immediate funds at hand, any hope for meeting these demands rested mainly upon the available instruments of credit, the Bank and the Morris notes.[40]

The Bank of North America did not play as significant a role in the finances of the government in 1783 as it had in 1782. In the closing days of 1782, the government had relinquished its bank stock, some five hundred shares, in order to fulfill its obligations to the bank. Furthermore, the Financier did not borrow any additional money. Although the Bank continued to play a useful role in discounting those personal notes acquired by the government in payment for bills of exchange, such operations were not as extensive as in the previous year. As a private institution, the Bank certainly prospered. When a new subscription was opened, Thomas Willing, President of the Bank, in writing to his son-in-law, William Bingham, who had speedily left for England at the conclusion of the war, emphasized that only by extraordinary exertion had he been able to save Bingham some Bank shares in the "scramble" for them. "Our success increases daily," he continued. "Our circulation is widely extended. Customers are above 700 and our weekly rects [receipts] and payments one million at least. . . . Our stock has risen to 15% above the first cost. . . ." A month later, he wrote: "I'm in the Bank where we are really crowded with Business now and every hour in the day." Where the success of the Bank of North America was measured at the outset by the essential functions it performed for the Confederation, its success was now determined by its function as a private financial institution. In that role, the attractions of the Bank were largely responsible for the establishment of several deposit banks in the nation at this time.[41]

Despite its growing affluence, the Bank of North America could not lend $750,000 in specie, the sum necessary to pay the troops, without undermining its entire structure; some other method, therefore, had to be found. Although the Bank could possibly work out some arrangement with respect to a paper issue, the Financier decided that, if a paper anticipation were to be employed, the operation should be conducted by using Morris notes. "This is an operation of great delicacy, and it is essential to the success of it that my credit should be staked for the redemption," he asserted. "Do not imagine, gentlemen, that this declaration is dictated by vanity; it becomes my duty to mention truth. . . . In issuing my notes to the required amount it would be necessary that I should give an express assurance of payment, and in so doing I should be answerable personally for about a half a million when I leave this office. . . ." Morris conceived the payment for the troops to be vital, and he was "willing to risk as much for this country as any man in America," but he was scheduled to leave office on the thirty-first of May. This would mean that the redemption of Morris notes would depend on the arrangements of the person who followed him into office, and "it cannot be expected that I should put myself in so desperate a situation," affirmed the Financier. "Though I would sacrifice much of my property, yet I cannot risk my reputation as a man of integrity, nor expose myself to absolute ruin." This final thought led to the next logical step: Morris would stay on after his May deadline—that is, if he were asked. Congress, after some shifting and squirming, decided to go on record as requesting the Financier to stay in office until the payment to the army had been completed. Making such a payment now depended upon the Morris notes issued under the supervision of the Financier.[42]

Not until all of this had been finally decided did the Financier begin to carry out the plan of paying the troops in Morris "notes"—in reality warrants—with due dates in six months. The operation involved an anticipation of over one-half millions of dollars, which meant that the grand total of anticipations in Morris notes amounted to $1,000,000. According to the Financier, the first notes were in the hands of the Paymaster General by the 7th of June, a week after the operation was set in motion, and within a week he had signed personally some 6,000 notes totaling over $200,000. Morris' inevitable circular letter to the states accompanied the operation; it urged the fulfillment of the requisitions and explained that this was a golden opportunity to reward the army for its hardships—an object, said the Financier with more than a little bitterness, "which all affect to have so much at heart."[43]

While the Financier was signing the first notes, the soldiers were already leaving the cantonments on furloughs granted by Washington and approved by Congress, so that when the notes arrived at camp the main body of troops had already disbanded. After Congress discovered that the notes had not arrived in time, they passed a resolution asking Morris to report "immediately what measures he had taken relative to the pay of the army." Interpreting the resolution as a censure of his conduct, although it was rather mild, the Financier clearly revealed that the frustration caused by outspoken critics and by his disappointment over the results of his funding proposal was beginning to take its toll. With exaggerated care, he cited by chapter and verse a precise account of the actions suggested by him with regard to pay, beginning with April 9. Why did he present the report in such detailed form? "It is because I had rather bear the censure contained in the acts of the 11th of July [which asked the Financier to report on the implementing of pay], however painful, than place on the minutes of Congress anything which may hold up the idea of precipitancy on their part." Only the most naïve member of Congress could misinterpret that parting shot.[44]

It is almost impossible to trace the fate of the Morris notes throughout this period, but there is some indication that their credit was improved during the course of the year. In examining the reaction to the notes, it is difficult to know if the warrants (on time), or the notes (on sight), or the paper used to pay the army (six months) were the subject of discussion. In some respects, the situation seemed to parallel the development of 1782. The Morris notes circulated on a par with specie in Philadelphia, and, to judge from limited evidence, this credit extended into northern Virginia as before. Looking northward and eastward, however, one finds discounting being carried on. In March, Morris himself wrote to William Houston, Receiver of Taxes in New Jersey, that "I believe with you that my paper is purchased at a discount and brought in to you and others for payment." What remedy should be applied? "This is the inevitable consequence of our situation but speculation is among the evils which cure themselves and which admit of no other cure." Indeed, as late as August, this complaint was still acknowledged by the Financier. Although there were some intervening variations, the rate of discount definitely decreased by late fall. According to John Codman, the Boston merchant, the discount on the "Morris Notes"—and it is again impossible to know what species of paper he is talking about—did not amount to more than 3 or 4 per cent, "which is not an object."[45]

That the Morris notes in general were discounted in certain regions was accepted, but the discounting of the six months pay warrants, something which would normally be expected if sold before the due date, aroused some criticism. Morris thought that collectors who dabbled in this speculation carried on a "nefarious practice," but for others it was a legitimate avenue of business.

Pains are taken to cover with infamy all those who discount the public paper. The natural effect of this measure is to prevent those men from meddling with it who, from a regard of their own reputation, would do the business on moderate terms. Hence it follows, that the holders cannot obtain so much for their paper as they otherwise might. Hence again an additional clamor, and of course an additional loss to the possessors. On the basis of the depreciation is founded an argument to prevent the redemption. By these means the public credit is totally ruined, and the government becomes chargeable with flagrant injustice.[46]

It can be said in summary that the Financier, in looking for a way to make a payment to the soldiers, decided to use a note issue as the best method available. Before the operation was completed over one million dollars of various types of paper, issued under the signature of the Superintendent of Finance, were in circulation. There is every indication that the general value of such paper issues, despite the increase in the quantity of money, not only equaled their performance in 1782 but actually improved upon their previous record. Because the issues of Morris notes were an "anticipation" of revenue, their utilization as an instrument in reviving the public credit rested eventually upon some kind of revenue. The fate of revenue in 1783 as a complementary story is, therefore, highly important.

In preparing for the general requisitions of 1783, the Financier initiated a major reform in the nation's financial administration by introducing a budget system under the supervision of the Office of Finance. Estimates of each department's need, including the expenses of envoys abroad, were presented to the Office of Finance where the figures were correlated; recommendations were then transmitted to Congress as a guide for legislation upon requisitions. After Congress passed upon the "budget," disbursements were to proceed in the normal fashion, from the whole to parts with specific appropriations for various objects. Morris had submitted a budget of some $9,000,000 for 1783—this estimate was figured on the basis of the continuance of the war—but Congress had pared the total down to $6,000,000. Moreover, they had stipulated that only one-third of the total would be requested until more definite information was received on the prospect of additional foreign loans. Of course the incorrigible Franklin, upon learning of this new administrative measure, agreed to its merits; but he had taken a quarter's advance in salary anyway, "supposing it not intended to *muzzle* immediately *the mouth of the ox that treadeth out the corn.*"[47]

In his attempt to obtain the fulfillment of the requisitions levied, the Financier, utilizing his technique of receivers of taxes in each state with some effect while practically discarding the use of the familiar circular letters, experienced varied but, on the whole, reasonably good success. Basically, Morris' attitude was somewhat more pessimistic in this period than before, although the tone of his observations, quite naturally, corresponded to the increase or decrease of revenue. In the first six months, the delay in tax collection and the much-used device of appropriating money for state use designated originally for continental requisitions especially unsettled the Financier. "What grounds of reliance can be formed on grants liable to such operations?" he asked. In June, Morris was cheered by tax receipts which "look better than they have done for a long time past."

But such hopes "of wading thro the difficulties which now surround us" were soon displaced by the lament that states were "relapsing into their indolence." As the due dates of the Morris pay warrants loomed closer and closer, the pressure began to mount until even small remittances were welcomed as a "little shower" to help revive the public treasury "during its present emptiness." These comments of the Financier mirrored the trend of tax collection, which began very slowly but increased gradually, then spurted encouragingly in the third quarter of the year, and finally diminished quite sharply. In actual figures, $820,000 was received in the collection of taxes, a heartening increase over 1782, although it represented a smaller percentage of the total expenditures for the year.[48]

The coincidence of the flow of domestic revenue with the course of trade during the year is so remarkable that there can be little doubt that the two were intimately related, with the curve of tax collection, as might be expected, lagging slightly behind that of trade. Although it varied in different sections of the country, the general paralysis which gripped commerce late in 1782 and carried over into early 1783 swiftly relaxed under the impact of peace, for the two most important causal factors had been eliminated: the effective blockade by hostile cruisers, and the uncertainty in the market place over prospects for peace. Commerce in general quickened, and economic prospects appeared much more favorable, but this renewed economic activity was erected upon the sandy soil of uncertain markets and illusory anticipations.[49]

The unsettled state of mind resulting from a problematical peace settlement was, in the course of the year, replaced with new uncertainties, questions involving postwar trade connections, credit, and markets. In the lower South, for example, the production of rice and indigo, the basis of prewar trade, had suffered so severely in the latter stages of the war that it was an illusion to think that anything more than a precarious, limited commerce could be carried on, while the problem of the upper South is well represented by the quandary revolving around the marketing channels for tobacco. Moreover, many of the merchants who nominally would be instrumental in carrying on such a trade soon realized that a considerable amount of their resources were involved in what Mark Pringle, a Baltimore merchant, called "dead capital," and the entire credit structure of marketing was very uncertain. As for the grain region of America in the Middle states, their most promising market for flour and provisions lay in the West Indies, but they soon found themselves outside the sphere of the various mercantile empires in that area. The action of the Spanish authorities in excluding United States vessels caused William Constable, a Philadelphia merchant who became very well known in New York, to moan: "It has caused a stop to be put to our trade . . . and thereby cutt us off from the brightest prospects. . . ." It does not require any extended examination to know the difficulties arising in New England with its adjustment from a war-born economy to a peacetime one when such important prewar ingredients as fisheries and the carrying trade had been pretty thoroughly shattered. These conditions were aggravated by the attitude of the British who, after a momentary indecision about what policy would be to their advantage, were encouraged by such publications as Lord Sheffield's *Observations on Commerce* to restrict the Americans from trading with the remainder of the Empire. In short, although there was more economic activity in 1783 than in 1782, a fact which largely accounts for the increase in tax collection, the hopes for an extended commerce accompanied by a promising economic revival failed to materialize.[50]

The only possible source that remained to supply the revenue needed to meet current obligations was a loan from Europe. In the fall of 1782, Congress had ordered Franklin to ask the French Court for a loan of $4,000,000, largely intended, according to Morris, for peace-time purposes, to draw "by degrees the bands of authority together," to establish "the power of Government over a people impatient of control," and "confirming the Federal Union of the several States, by correcting defects in the general Constitution." France responded with a loan of 6,000,000 livres, a small part of which was shipped to the United States aboard the *Washington,* Captain Barney commanding, together with the important document containing the preliminary peace terms. This timely loan, combined with the income from taxes, provided the means to meet all current expenditures—except payments to the army. To fill this gap, recourse was once again made to the French Court, and Morris explained that he would "consider the obligation as being in some degree personal to myself, and I shall certainly exert myself for the repayment." But this request met a chilly response. "Our friend Morris I suspect is not a favorite at this court," observed Jay. "They say he treats them as his cashier, but refuse absolutely to supply more money." The Financier was not overly disappointed at the news—"indeed I should have been much surprised if you had been more fortunate"—partly because he hoped for assistance from the loan recently opened in Holland.[51]

The Financier had drawn some 300,000 florins ($120,000) on the foundation of the Dutch loan in the early months of 1783, but after April he relied on the requisitions, the sale of goods, and the money brought in by Captain Barney from France and by John Brown from Havana. As prospects of other income grew dim in the early fall, Morris began to look with favor on drawing additional bills on Holland, even though he was by no means certain the Dutch loan had filled sufficiently to satisy them. The favorable rate of exchange and the problem of meeting the pay warrants proved too tempting, and he decided to go ahead. Between August 5 and September 18 the Financier sold bills amounting to 500,000 florins ($200,000). It soon became apparent that he needed an additional $300,000 to comply with the anticipations for the year; so, anxious to fulfill his commitments, he ventured into a sale of three bills of exchange of 250,000 florins each —totaling approximately $300,000—at long sight, making careful agreements with the buyers—John Ross, Peter Whitesides and Company, and Isaac Hazlehurst—to give the Dutch bankers a maximum amount of time. Those acquainted with Morris' early career will immediately recognize that these firms were old friends and business partners of his, and that Morris, in this instance, was using his private connections to facilitate the measures of Morris in his public capacity. A final draft of 100,000 florins was made on December 12. In summary, Morris drew bills on Holland amounting to something like $540,000, in order to meet the obligation created by the warrants issued as payment to the troops. Indeed, Morris drew so extensively that the amount of anticipations—that is, regular Morris notes—was decreased by something like $150,000 over 1782. The Financier, therefore, balanced his budget, saved his engagements, and even eliminated some of the anticipations by drawing on the Dutch bankers.[52]

But were there funds in the hands of the Dutch bankers to satisfy these engagements? In a letter written on the last day of the year summarizing the transaction, it became obvious that the Financier had acted on hope rather than fact. According to simple arithmetic, it was possible that the loan would be overdrawn as much as 800,000 guilders ($320,000), although Morris optimistically thought 500,000 to be a maximum amount. Furthermore, the intelligence concerning the Dutch loan had not been promising. When the news reached Europe that the states were reluctant to collect taxes and that a meeting of the Pennsylvania troops threatened, in a rather mild way, the Continental Congress, the Financier hastened to reassure the bankers that it was a "trifling thing." Whether the subscriptions to fill the loan of the Dutch bankers would be at such a pace as to meet the bills of exchange drawn by Morris remained to be seen.[53]

★ ★ ★ ★ ★

In the course of the year, several parts of the Morris program operated with greater success than ever before. The troops were much better provisioned by means of the contracting system, the credit of the Morris notes improved, and the Bank, although acting largely as a private deposit bank, functioned so successfully that it encouraged the establishment of other banks. Even the soldiers had received a partial payment, and the obligation created as a result had, at least temporarily, been met. But the difficult issue of back pay for the troops, introduced at the very outset of the year, revived the question of funding the debts of the Confederation.

The struggle over the question of funding was accompanied by a concentrated effort on the part of the Office of Finance to put pressure upon Congress so that the Financier's plan as embodied in his detailed Reports on Public Credit would be adopted. When Congress was working out a solution to the problem, the assumption of state debts by the Confederation was introduced by Madison and immediately incorporated by the Financier into his plan in such a way that state debts would become a part of the public debt, to be paid for by permanent national revenues rather than by division among the several states. This policy completed Morris' plan on funding; and in its finished form it resembled in every significant detail the plan which Hamilton introduced during the Federalist decade.

Congress, in wrestling with the entire issue of funding, became deeply involved with important political questions that concerned the role of union in the future of the new Republic. Although some "ultranationalists" stood at one extreme and the "ultra-anti-nationalists" stood at the other, the ideas, opinions, and actions of most people fell within the extremes. That the struggle over funding resulted in a compromise was logical and reasonable, but it was not the kind of compromise which the Financier, for the most part, found acceptable.

Why was Morris so determined to obtain the approval of his plan to fund the debts of the Confederation? As he viewed the rapid movement of events in the spring of 1783—such as the prospects of peace, the clamor of the civil public creditors, the rising protest in the army as another group of public creditors—he saw it as an opportune moment to push through his measure on funding which he considered to be necessary to the preservation, during a time of peace, of a Union that had been created out of war. Although there can be no question that the Financier was not entirely satisfied with the Articles of Confederation, his entire program, as has been noted at pertinent places in this volume, was predicated on the continuation of the Articles as the constitutional basis of the new nation. As a "nationalist," Morris much preferred an imperfect union to no union at all. The program, in Morris' eyes, would restore the credit of the central government, and give it sufficient prestige and strength to enable it to carry out its powers in domestic and foreign affairs as designated in the Articles. Thus, funding the debts of the Confederation to complete the restoration of the public credit and to make the union more cohesive took on a crucial significance as far as Morris was concerned. It is plain, as the preceding material shows, that he was willing to go to dangerous lengths to reach his objective, and he tended to overreach himself in such a way that his case was unquestionably weakened before the nation and in the eyes of posterity. The means to the end were so intolerable to many that the end itself, however laudable, was nearly forgotten.

As for the end itself, the preservation and strengthening of the Union, it must be said that Morris was in the main stream of historical development. The most extreme "antinationalists" were looking backward, and their actions tended to reflect past fears while Morris, largely because his widespread mercantile and business interests naturally turned him in that direction, was looking forward, and his actions were guided by the fears of the future. Could the new nation survive internal frictions, could it meet its international responsibilities in trade, could it defend itself against the encroachments of powerful neighbors? Not until his plan of funding had been defeated did Morris' thoughts turn seriously to a complete replacement of the constitutional structure. Rhode Island would one day regret her "breach of our [?] union," Morris asserted, a union "which now secures to her an equal vote in disposing of the wealth and strength of states infinitely superior to her in both."[54] To George Olney, the Receiver of Taxes in Rhode Island, he stated his new views most clearly.[55]

I have my fears [with you] that the States will turn a deaf ear to all applications. Where all this is to end God knows. But it seems to me that one of the first effects must be to dissolve [sic] the Confederation. What will afterwards follow whether a new and better bond or total and absolute anarchy, time the great arbiter of human institutions must determine.

The Financier, for the most part, staked the future of his entire program on the outcome of his funding plan; as a result, its defeat marked the beginning of the end for most parts of that program. Criticism against Morris tended to become much sharper after the struggle over funding, and there was a renewed effort on the part of some members of Congress to destroy everything that he had constructed. Although a few members, like Stephen Higginson, continually expressed the fear that Morris had such enormous power that it would not be "an easy matter to set him aside," there was no sound basis for such an assertion. The fact that Morris' plan was defeated was proof enough of the limitation of his power; indeed, the arrangements he began to make for his return to private life and for resuming the management of his business affairs plainly indicate that he had no intention of continuing the exercise of those powers which he did possess. In Morris' final months in office, it was a time for closing of accounts in the Office of Finance; as for the Financier, it marked the reëmergence of Robert Morris, private entrepreneur.[56]

CHAPTER—TEN

The Superintendent of Finance
Reemerges as a Private Entrepreneur

THE FINAL YEAR OF ROBERT MORRIS' TENURE IN THE OFFICE OF FINANCE was a period of transition. It showed the Superintendent of Finance making arrangements to close the accounts of his administration, while at the same time it clearly marked the reëmergence of the Philadelphia merchant and businessman. As Financier, Morris abdicated his policy-making role and concentrated on fulfilling those tasks that had been initiated earlier; as a private entrepreneur, he gradually assumed a more active role in the management of his personal affairs, which had suffered some decline during his term of office. In making preparations to resume his position as the foremost merchant and businessman in the country, Morris erected a new business structure that included not only some of his former connections, but also a number of new associates. This shift of Morris' energies from public to private affairs had been completed by November 1784, when he formally vacated his position as Superintendent of Finance.

In the first two years of his administration, Robert Morris was so occupied with his public position that little time or attention was given to his private mercantile affairs. His concerns were carried on by others; and, of course, he suffered the impact of a declining commerce along with the rest of the community, a result which is clearly revealed in one of Morris' rare private letters during these burdensome years as Financier. Solicited for a loan by Colonel Richard Butler just at the time that the mercantile community was severely hampered by the British blockade, Morris responded with a candid note, though perhaps purposely tinged with gloom to discourage a borrower.

My property [he wrote] was then and is now very much out of my own power. A great part in the Hands of other People the Remainder in Lands. What I had afloat has all been lost and the amount of that loss I will forbear to mention as there might be in it an appearance of ostentation. I had

many pecuniary engagements which I found it difficult to comply with and
I had debts to pay which I was called on to discharge.[1]

The "other people" who carried on Morris' affairs were old business connections established before he became Financier. Morris' relationship with John Holker continued under the firms of William
Turnbull and Company and Benjamin Harrison and Company.
Samuel Inglis and Company—with Thomas Willing—managed Morris' interests in Philadelphia, while Jonathan Hudson still operated,
though rather feebly, out of Baltimore. It is not clear whether Morris
maintained his interest in some of the other firms, such as Isaac Hazlehurst, Peter Whiteside, and Morris, Beale, and May. The former connection with John Ross, however, seems to have been severed, although
Ross, Morris, and Holker were jointly concerned in several vessels and
voyages in this period. Naturally, the firms with which Morris was
associated promoted his interests, but there is no evidence indicating
that Morris purposely benefited these firms by his public actions, although he employed them on occasion, as has been observed. Morris
paid little more than scant attention to his private affairs, so that purchases, presumably made in his name, actually were made by his associates. Matthew Ridley, who had looked after Morris' sons in Europe,
sent goods to the United States for the joint account of Ridley and
Pringle, Holker, and Morris, for example, but it was Pringle and
Holker who managed the whole transaction.[2]

Only when peace hopes grew stronger did Morris begin to take a
more active interest in resuming his private business affairs. In fact,
Morris then seemed to act with unbecoming haste in reëstablishing
some old prewar connections. John Cruden, residing comfortably
under the British flag in New York City, sent a letter suggesting some
commercial schemes. At first Morris declared emphatically "No!";
their duties to their respective countries would not permit such plans.
But a few days later Morris changed his mind. "Circumstances have
so materially altered since the 5th Instant [August 1782] when my
former letter to you is dated, that I think there wou'd not be any im-
propriety in laying the foundation for a plan to be executed upon
the conclusion of Peace and if you will fix a time when you can be at
Elizabeth Town I will send a person to meet you for that purpose."
There is no evidence that the meeting took place. At first glance it
would appear that Morris, the private entrepreneur, was not completely submerged in the affairs of the Office of Finance, but Morris'
sudden change of mind coincided with two other developments which
strongly suggest that he was covering a necessary public transaction
under the guise of a private arrangement. The paralysis of trade had
stopped the sale of bills, and the Financier was desperate. In a coded
secret note dated a few days after the Cruden letter, the Financier informed Washington that the impossibility of obtaining money to meet
current public demands had forced him to engage in a transaction
whereby a sale of bills of exchange for the Continent would take place
in New York City. The money to be obtained from the sale of bills

would, so it appeared, be transported secretly to Washington. Although Washington agreed to the plan, it is questionable whether it was ever fulfilled.[3]

If it were a private rather than a public interest which prompted the letter to Cruden, Morris did not stand alone. Holker, among many others, was consumed with the desire to make the most of peace-time trade, and he was anxious to enlist Morris—and Morris' capital—in his enterprises. "Holker is full of schemes," observed Morris to Ridley as the peace loomed on the horizon. "I cannot pass much time with him nor enter into his Plans and Views, he will write everything you wish on those subjects and I shall ever be glad to promote his and your views as far as in my power." Some of the schemes evidently dealt with the normal channels of trade, but one plan in particular Holker pushed vigorously. "Mr. R. Morris knows that if he has [had] pursued a plan I had once brought him to adopt," Holker wrote in May of 1783, "instead of loosing [losing] each of us a fortune, we should by now have a China ship in this port. . . ." Indeed, Holker said he would have carried out the plan under his own power, but he did not possess the means.[4]

The hope of a China trade finally materialized, however, in the fall of 1783 with the voyage of the *Empress of China*. After long and elaborate preparations conducted by Daniel Parker—of Daniel Parker and Company—the *Empress* sailed for Canton in January 1784, loaded with ginseng, brandy, wine, tar, turpentine, and $20,000 in specie. The ownership was shared equally by Daniel Parker and Company, who were also the contractors for the army, and Robert Morris. With Morris' share of the cost alone amounting to nearly $60,000, it is obvious that the expedition was a major undertaking. Two other vessels, the *Columbia* and the *Comte de Artois,* were outfitted for Europe in another joint enterprise between Morris and Daniel Parker and Company, but by the time the voyages had been completed, the business relationship between the participants had splintered. Daniel Parker and Company faced bankruptcy, and Holker assigned their share of the vessels to the creditors, while the Holker-Morris dispute terminated the business connections between those two men.[5]

In many respects, the date of the China venture—December 1783, and January 1784—marked the reëmergence of Robert Morris, Philadelphia merchant, a development that began after Morris had been disappointed by the defeat of his funding program in April 1783, and gathered momentum throughout the months following. ". . . I am struggling through as well as I can to see the full performance of my engagements," the Financier wrote to Ridley about his public post, "and then [I shall] retire to my private pursuits which are infinitely more agreable and for which I am far better suited." Later he added, ". . . The neglect of my own affairs has injured me and deranged them very much." In the process of swinging back to his private affairs, Morris underwent a minor revolution in his mercantile concerns. A distinct transition was under way where some long familiar connections were severed to be replaced by new ones; some of this change was planned, but other parts of it occurred without forewarning.[6]

The first major change was precipitated by the death of Samuel Inglis. In casting about for someone to fill the vacancy in the firm, Morris and Willing decided upon John Swanwick, formerly a clerk in Morris' establishment and now Treasurer of the Office of Finance. With Thomas Willing engaged in the Bank of North America and Morris still busy as Superintendent of Finance, Swanwick made most of the decisions, carried on the correspondence, and for the most part conducted the business of the firm.[7]

The establishment of a new firm in Baltimore with Tench Tilghman, who had been an aide to Washington during the war and had entered into commercial affairs soon after the peace, figured importantly in Morris' new mercantile structure. The partnership was formed on January 1, 1784, and Morris supplied $12,000 as his share of the capital. The firm was immediately rewarded with a vast network of correspondents, owing to the far-reaching activities of Morris in the pre-war and war periods. In fact, a great number of letters, from Cadiz, Bordeaux, London, Genoa, Leghorn, Barcelona, Bristol, Gibraltar, Hamburg, Marseilles, Falmouth, and Lisbon, offering and requesting services, poured in. Seldom, indeed, did any mercantile firm enjoy such widespread connections at its inception.[8]

A major alteration in Morris' former business relationships, and an unforeseen one, took place when the Holker and Morris connection became entangled in a dispute concerning old accounts. As a result, Morris left Turnbull, Marmie, and Company of Philadelphia, while Holker withdrew from Benjamin Harrison and Company of Richmond. Later, Morris and Benjamin Harrison Jr. reorganized under the agency of a firm called Harrison, Nicholls, and Company.[9]

A share in the firm of Constable, Rucker, and Company, which was being set up in New York City in May 1784, rounded out Morris' new structure. "I am interested in that House," Morris informed Tilghman, "and it is the last that I shall be connected with having now compleated the plan which I have long had in contemplation." This firm was organized with a capital of 20,000 pounds (Pennsylvania currency) with the explicit intention of exploiting the opportunities presented by the port of New York which, they correctly predicted, would soon be the most important port on the Atlantic seaboard.[10]

When Robert Morris quit his public role, therefore, a complete structure of mercantile partnerships had already been erected. Was it prophetic that some of Morris' connections began to employ the Financier's notes as cash shortly after he returned to private life? Could the credit instruments used by Morris with such great effectiveness in his public role now be exploited in his private business? Those who viewed this framework of connections and witnessed the important business prestige of Robert Morris would find it hard to believe that the passage of a dozen years would find the Prince of Merchants so desperate and distressed in his personal business affairs that only a barricade in his country home would shield him, and then only momentarily, from his creditors. It is highly probable that the roots of Morris' decline, partly because of the lack of attention given to his personal affairs during a crucial period of transition that destroyed many fortunes, lay in these years when he acted as Superintendent of Finance.

During the final months of his administration, the Superintendent of Finance not only failed to give any attention to policy-making but also took special pains to refrain from giving any kind of advice to Congress or to the states. His time, with a few exceptions, was consumed in honoring old engagements, meeting the anticipations, straightening out administrative matters, and taking measures to deal with the overdraft on the Dutch bankers.

What remained of the army continued to be supplied by contracting. Daniel Parker and Company, which had been so successful in executing their contracts in 1783, was given a renewal of their agreement; but that firm found itself in dire straits and at the mercy of its creditors by May, 1784. Parker at this juncture suddenly decided to leave the country, but only a scant breath ahead of a writ from Duer and Holker, whose claims against him ranged upwards of $100,000. Among the creditors of the firm stood the United States, because the Financier had advanced $20,000 for rations that still needed to be delivered. Although Morris had taken preliminary steps to recover the advance by bringing suit, this incident had not been completely settled when the Financier retired from office. The contracting dispute between the government and Sands, Livingston, and Company also appeared and reappeared through the year, but it too remained unsettled. An arbitration committee had been set up, but the contractors refused to give the arbitrators permission to inspect their books, a stand which drew Morris' censure. Fortunately the matter of contracts during this period, the first months of 1784, was of minor consequence because of the modest size of the military establishment.[11]

Although the Financier's program on funding had not been adopted, a funding measure had been passed which continued to emphasize the importance of a settlement of accounts as a prerequisite of funding. All the tangled mass of accounts was inherited by the postwar period. The swelling volume of correspondence dealing with the settlements continued to reflect such trying problems as depreciation, the valuation of certain charges, and the validity of various types of documentary evidence. Were buildings or fences or trees that had been destroyed by troops to be allowed in claims? What if vouchers such as those of Virginia had been lost or destroyed because of the enemy? Whose word or what proof would be sufficient to satisfy the commissioners or Congress in these cases? How were claims for damages supported by forged signatures to be detected? What about those officers —and the commissary officers were apparently most deficient in this respect—who refused to submit to any settlement of account? It is perfectly understandable that commissioners like Edward Fox became so discouraged about the magnitude of the task that a "lump" settlement was urged. But the Financier replied that such an action would set a precedent which potentially would be exceedingly dangerous.[12]

As if the commissioners in settling accounts did not have enough problems, the Financier added an "important employment" to their duties, to act as elaborate census takers so that the condition and resources of the country could be appraised. Under the general heading of the "state of the country," Morris asked for information upon four topics—geographical, moral, political, and commercial. Under the first topic, the Financier was interested in receiving data on the rivers, the topography, the quality of soils, the natural advantages of the geographical location for husbandry, manufactures, or commerce; while the second category, the "moral state of the country" by which Morris meant the composition of society, called for information on the make-up of the population, the mode of life and kind of occupations, the types of husbandry practiced and the degree of improvement, the arts, "by which is not so much intended the fine as the useful arts," the kind and nature of buildings, and a list of the improvements in progress. In asking about political matters, the Financier requested that the constitutions of the governments be examined, but "not merely the paper form, but the practice under it—and that will depend much upon the tendency of the people towards aristocratical or democratical dispositions." He also wanted the names, powers, authority and reputation of the "magistracy," the interior police, the revenue methods employed within the state, and the extent of the public and private credit. Under the topic, the "commercial state of the country," Morris expected to learn about the produce of the country, the roads and navigation, the imports and exports, the value of lands, and the value of money and the facility of obtaining credit. Certain information which he thought would be valuable in case of war, such as the number of men available, the quantity of provisions and forage, and the means of transportation, was also requested. Although the plan to acquire this information was an intelligent one and greatly needed, it placed an added burden upon men already engaged in an overwhelming assignment.[13]

The only constructive suggestion made by the Financier in this period concerned the coinage. Thomas Jefferson had asked for his advice on the matter, and, in response, the report on a United States mint which had been submitted to Congress in January of 1782 was sent to the Virginian, together with an explanatory letter and a document that Gouverneur Morris had written somewhat later. Except for two points, the Financier thought that Jefferson and he were very much in agreement with respect to coinage. First, although they agreed on a decimal system, Morris insisted on a smaller base unit than one dollar; second, Morris thought gold should be undervalued in relation to silver, for he believed the bank notes could take the place of gold but not of silver. Such an undervaluation of gold, according to the Financier, would also halt the constant drain of silver to England that had continually plagued the colonies. Morris pointed up one omission in Jefferson's draft, the manner of defraying minting costs, and in this regard, Morris urged the minting procedure he had advocated in his report to Congress. Aside from this advice on coinage, the Office of Finance was almost strangely silent.[14]

Only in taking measures to meet the overdraft upon the Dutch bankers was the Financier's energetic activity reminiscent of his earlier years in office. His actions, some of which were rather urgent, were largely prompted by a natural personal motivation, to conclude his administration with a clean and favorable record. The bills of exchange, it will be recalled, had been drawn to meet the onrush of Morris warrants that had been issued to pay the troops. The fear that adequate funds would not be available in Holland to meet the bills was certainly realized when the Financier received word in March 1784 that slightly over $300,000 in bills of exchange had been protested for nonacceptance. But Morris had already taken some preliminary steps to meet this eventuality. Attempting to do the most important thing first, the Financier sought to strengthen the credit of the United States in Holland verbally by extolling the country's resources, and factually by sending remittances of tobacco and rice to the Dutch bankers. Some of these commodities, particularly tobacco, had been brought in as taxes, while a part of them had been specifically purchased by the Financier for these shipments. In the face of the nonacceptance of the bills, the tempo of Morris' actions was stepped up; at the same time, Morris urged Franklin to draw bills by a "circuitous" route, that is, "bill kiting," in order to postpone the fatal day of payment and thus allow time for commodity remittances to arrive. Such expedients had also been suggested by Morris to Le Couteulx and Company, the French bankers. Before any of these schemes materialized, however, the United States was able to meet the obligation. Because the credit of the new nation was good enough to command some degree of confidence, John Adams, the United States Minister to Holland, was able to borrow additional funds on a short-term loan—naturally at a higher rate of interest than the previous loan—and the bills, as a result, were saved from being protested for nonpayment.[15]

When the final accounts were drawn up for his entire administration, the Financier finished with a favorable balance of some $20,000. Morris completed his days as Financier in the unusual position of having balanced his budget, of having succeeded in much of his program, and yet of having failed to achieve the most cherished aim within his program, the complete restoration of the public credit by funding the debts of the Confederation.[16]

It is impossible to compress satisfactorily the life or career of Robert

Morris into a summary statement, but certain preëminent developments are apparent. By the eve of the Revolution, Robert Morris,
through the firm of Willing and Morris, had emerged as one of the
leading merchants in the colonies. He had acquired confidence in
himself in addition to making financial gains, and his management
of mercantile and financial affairs had given him an essential basis of
experience which he used to advantage during the Revolution. From
1776 to 1778, the firm of Willing and Morris thrived for the most part
on Revolutionary commerce, contracts, and privateers, but at the end
of that period Morris severed his long-time connections with his close
friend Thomas Willing. Operating individually for the first time in
his mercantile career, Morris embarked on a personal business expansion which reached out into at least nine major partnerships in addition to numerous temporary ventures based upon a single enterprise
or a lone voyage. Robert Morris was generally acknowledged as the
foremost merchant in America by 1781; and it was this reputation as
a highly successful merchant, above all other considerations, which
caused everyone to turn to him when the position of Superintendent
of Finance was created by Congress in the financial crisis of 1780-81.

Fortunately for Morris, the Revolution had introduced him to the
problems and political affairs of the youthful Republic. His early experience in the Continental Congress had been particularly important;
on occasion his enthusiasm and enormous energy were allowed relatively free rein, and his executive talents were given an opportunity
to develop. Although Morris' dual career of business and politics—
and they tended to become intertwined—aroused some justifiable criticism mixed with bitterness which lingered after he became Financier,
there can be little question that this political experience was essential
when he entered the Office of Finance.

When Morris accepted the position of Superintendent of Finance,
he inherited the major financial crisis of the war, the near collapse of
public credit. Morris, in analyzing the crisis, recognized that the economy was relatively prosperous and that private credit, as a result, was
available; to meet the crisis, therefore, he attempted to create financial instruments and policies that would utilize the existing private
credit to revive the public credit. Guided by this concept, Morris as
Financier was first compelled to employ short-term policies, but eventually he fashioned a long-term, far-reaching program with a powerful objective, the complete restoration of the credit of the Confederation. Administrative reform was instituted to clear the way for
policy-making; greater efficiency in expenditures was initiated, largely
by introducing a contracting system to supply the army; an attempt
was made to improve the collection of revenue by establishing Continental receivers in each state, by publishing tax returns, and by
appeals to the citizenry. But the heart of the program in utilizing
private credit to bolster the public credit was contained in the explicit
instruments of financial policy, the Bank of North America, the Morris notes, and the Financier's plan to fund the debts of the Confedera-

tion, the primary aim within his general program. This emphasis on the restoration of the public credit, the dynamic nature of that credit, and the combination of instruments to be used to achieve that objective, foreshadowed the Hamiltonian program as introduced under the new government.

Since an evaluation of this program in operation has been made at appropriate intervals throughout this volume, it seems unnecessary to recapitulate here in any great deal. General expenditures were curtailed and the contracting system, with some qualifications, supplied the troops more efficiently than any other previous method. Although the Financier's efforts in the collection of revenue were less successful, in part because of the limitations of the Articles of Confederation, but equally if not more important because of the decline in economic activity after 1781, the results were reasonable under the circumstances. The explicit instruments designed to revive the public credit by the use of private credit, the National Bank and the Morris notes, enjoyed remarkable success, especially in view of the depreciation which resulted from excessive issues of Continental currency before 1781. The fate of funding, the measure that began to assume an increasingly important position within the Financier's program over the years, was less fortunate. When acted upon by the Continental Congress, this measure, as Morris conceived it, was not adopted, although a compromise plan containing a few of his ideas was submitted to the states for approval.

If Morris' plan on funding had been adopted and implemented, it would have tended to sap the strength of any movement for a revision of the Articles of Confederation or certainly any movement for a new constitution. Assuming the thesis that security holders as public creditors acted as an important force in bringing about the establishment of the new constitution, it is apparent that a successful funding program would have satisfied this interest; logically, therefore, the Confederation would have enjoyed a much longer life. Whether the Confederation would have been able to satisfy other deep-seated interests which were powerful forces moving toward an alteration in the Articles—such as those involved in commerce—is less clear. Interestingly enough, those states and individuals who opposed Morris' program most vigorously, declaring that their security depended on the existing frame of government, were, in reality, defeating a program which had been designed, as far as the Financier was concerned, to preserve that instrument of union. But all this speculation overlooks a major factor, the course of trade. If Morris' program on public credit had succeeded in being adopted throughout the states, it would almost certainly have failed in actual operation at this time, for the decline in economic activity caused by a lethargic commerce made it almost impossible for the states to shoulder the obligations which would have been entailed. Indeed, trade, rather than security holders, probably holds the more important key in "an" economic interpretation to the Confederation period.

From what has been said, it is manifest that Hamilton, if he had held a position comparable to that of Morris at this time and had introduced the program he presented during the Federalist decade, would have failed as Morris failed. Although it is true that Morris was involved in the business community and, as a result, was inclined to be more actively partisan than Hamilton in terms of self-interest, it was precisely those qualifications of Morris as a private merchant with extensive connections and credit which commended him to Congress in the spring of 1781 and made his services as Superintendent of Finance so valuable. Hamilton had no personal credit to strengthen that of the Confederation; nor could he command the resources of others. He might have been able to match Morris' plan to reduce expenditures, but the New Yorker's scheme for a national bank, as he outlined it in 1780-81, was designed on such a grand scale that it would have failed dismally at this time. And Hamilton's experience in Congress and, for that matter, with practical government operations, was not extensive; anyone who has examined his writings cannot help but be impressed by the fact that the 1780's were tremendously influential in the development of the future Secretary of the Treasury. In brief, Morris was more successful as Financier than Hamilton could have been because of the nature of the financial crisis; each man was geared to his time.

Was Morris' program designed to enrich the wealthy at the expense of the whole community? The general theme of many phases of the program certainly was to "cement" the relationship between the monied interest of the country and the central government, for this alignment, from Morris' point of view, would best benefit the country. In examining the Financier's policies from this standpoint, however, certain reservations should be mentioned in order to place the program in its proper eighteenth-century setting when answering the question posed. In those parts of the plan which were devoted to the reduction of expenditures, and the increase of revenue, it can be assuredly stated that no practice of the Financier discriminated against the general populace in favor of a select group. The same judgment can be made with respect to the Morris notes, for it is evident that they benefited the country as a whole. The Bank of North America, in contrast, can be considered as an instrument intended, like most national banks, to attract the interest of the monied men of the country by handsome dividend returns based, at least in part, upon the profits made from the money transactions of the government. In the special case of the Bank of North America, with its effective service in making extraordinary loans to the government in the first year of its operation, an evaluation that the many were being exploited for the profits of a few must necessarily be qualified.

It was Morris' measure on funding that was most vulnerable to the charge that it was a policy designed to favor a restricted group, but when his measure is considered in its setting and compared with the alternatives offered at the time, it appears no more exploitative than

any other proposal. Funding of the public debt, as has been emphasized in the main body of this work, was a policy upon which there
was universal legislative agreement, and the issue arose solely on the
manner of funding. The debt would be the same in either case, but
the revenue to meet the obligations would, in the one instance, come
from the states by way of requisitions and, in the second, from national
sources of revenue. Within the total amount of the debt, however, an
important question was hidden: To whom was the debt owed? If speculators had purchased certain types of the debt at sizable discounts,
and this indebtedness were paid at face value, it would certainly benefit a few at the expense of the many. In this respect, it should be noted
that Morris' original suggestions for paying off the certificates of indebtedness for goods and services would have assured the original
holder of its full benefits, because Morris did not favor the forced
loans which, in his mind, these certificates represented. With respect
to the army, the second group of what might be called poorer public
creditors, Morris' counsel, if it had prevailed and been carried out
successfully, would have been beneficial and not in the least discrim-
inatory, for the funding measure would have been in operation when
their claims came to be settled. The value of these claims, therefore,
would have been good and their certificate of settlement would have
tended to remain at par rather than sell at the tremendous rates of
depreciation which marked this type of debt during the remainder of
Confederation period. The major share of the certificates involved in
the public debt, then, would not have been at the mercy of speculators. Only in dealing with loan office certificates would speculation
have full play, and in this type of indebtedness the practice was thoroughly approved by the Financier. It should be noted once again that
loan office certificates concerned only the wealthier classes, for they
were the only group who had enough money at hand originally to buy
them. As a result, speculation in this type of indebtedness, for the
most part, resolved itself into the question whether some people of
means might profit at the expense of other people of means.

When due consideration is given to those taxes that Morris conceived
to be necessary to meet the commitments of the funding program,
the thesis of the few benefiting from the toil of the many rests upon
much more solid ground, but once again there are important reservations to be made. An impost, a land tax, excises, and a poll tax were
proposed by the Financier, and in each case the incidence fell heavily
upon the general public. Thus the general public was being taxed to
pay a debt held by only a part of the community. It should be mentioned, however, that Morris' tax program, although not equitable in
twentieth-century terms, was fully as enlightened as any other
eighteenth-century tax program in the world. Moreover, even if the
obligations of the debt were met by revenue from state requisitions—
and everyone agreed that the public debt must be paid—the taxes
levied by the states to fulfill these questions would, in almost every
instance, be identical to those used by the Confederation; the inci-

dence of taxation, therefore, would be the same. In terms of the eighteenth-century setting and the alternatives presented at the time, therefore, important qualifications must be made concerning any judgment that the taxing program of the Financier was proposed in order to favor the few at the expense of the community.

If one wished, it would be easy to draw up a partial list of what might be called contributions made by Robert Morris as Superintendent of Finance. He initiated the settlement of accounts; his program for provisioning the troops supplied them more effectively than before; he introduced a regularity into financial accounting for his own administration unexampled during the Revolution; he was instrumental in setting up a national bank; his notes acted as an important instrument of credit at crucial junctures during the final years of the war; he advanced some ideas on funding the debts of Confederation, which for weal or for woe, were eventually adopted in the first administration of Washington; he had entered the Office of Finance at a time when the credit of the central government had almost collapsed and, although it had not been completely restored, his actions and policies had been important in helping to revive that credit to such a degree that the memory of the financial crisis of 1780-81 was largely erased. Even those men in and out of Congress, such as Samuel Osgood, who looked upon Morris with a jaundiced eye, readily admitted that he had performed important services.[17]

With respect to this office [Superintendent of Finance], I apprehend you doubt whether our sentiments are the same [Osgood wrote]. I will tell you very freely, that I am clearly in opinion, that, in mere money transactions, he has saved the United States a very large sum. I am of this sentiment, because a comparison of expenditures shows, that, since he has been in office, the expenditures have not amounted, annually, to half so much as they did before. I am also of opinion, that much more regularity has been introduced in keeping the accounts than ever existed before. This is a matter, in my mind, of very great importance; and, without the strictest attention to it, the several States ought not to trust Congress with a single farthing of their money. I lay it down as a good general maxim, that, when a person is to be attacked, it is wise not to endeavor to depreciate his real merit; because this puts into his hands an advantage. If he can clearly exculpate himself in part, it renders that which is really true liable to suspicion, and consequently less efficacious. If you suppose that person [Morris] has rendered the public no valuable services, I acknowledge there is a very considerable difference in our sentiments. If you suppose that he may have rendered valuable services, but that his notions of government, of finance, and of commerce, are incompatible with liberty, we shall not differ. I think, therefore, the fort to be raised against him ought to stand on this ground, if, in urging his dismission, or rather a new arrangement of the office, it shall become necessary to be personal. But I hope it will be generally agreed, that, if it was necessary to create an omnipotent financier in 1781, that necessity does not exist now. I am clearly against the office in its present form; and I am not sure any form will do.

Universal agreement on the character and relative purity of the

Financier's motives can scarcely be expected. It is apparent that Morris was inclined to exaggerate his own importance to the nation's finances, that he did not adjust to necessary compromises on some key measures, and that he became unduly bitter and almost petulant during the months immediately after the defeat of his funding plan. Morris, in stating his own feelings, would probably emphasize that the objectives, as he saw them, were so crucial that any deflection was undesirable. When he entered the Office of Finance, his motive was to save the Union by reviving the public credit from its nadir; by 1783, his motive, as he would state it, was to preserve that Union, based upon the Articles of Confederation, by the complete restoration of the public credit.

Although not all of the Financier's contemporaries could agree with his objectives and many would question his motives, one fact is certain. Morris attempted to incorporate a financial program into the Confederation which Hamilton later succeeded in incorporating into the new government; and after the Financier's program had matured during the course of his administration, the two programs were similar in every significant detail. If Hamilton and his program are considered to be sinister, some of the same opprobrium must be heaped on Morris as Superintendent of Finance; if, on the other hand, Hamilton is portrayed as the hard-headed financier, "the colossal genius of the new system," who "knew at first hand the stuff of which government is made," then Morris as Superintendent of Finance must be considered in the same light.[18] But when the precocious, colorful, youthful Hamilton held the spotlight on the Federalist stage and repeated the identical play line by line, the audience on the whole responded with an accolade which still echoes down through the decades. Why the difference in reaction to the two programs? Were the gesticulations of the leading actor the moving force? Was it the new theater in which he performed? Perhaps the acoustics lent resonance to his voice, or the lighting and the staging affected his audience. Or had the audience itself changed? The answer to these questions properly belong to a second book. But one conclusion is obvious. The play, in this case, is not the thing; only its reception is important.

NOTES ❖❖❖

CHAPTER ONE

1. Robert Waln, *Biography of the Signers to the Declaration of Independence* (Philadelphia, 1824), V. 190-91. Willing Letterbook, *passim*, 1755-56, Historical Society of Pennsylvania (hereafter cited as PHS). A series of letters tell the story. Thomas Willing to Robert Morris, 27 Feb. 1756. Willing to Thomas Willing of London, 1 Mar. 1756. Willing to Morris, 19 Mar. 1756. Willing to Morris, 6 Nov., 8 Nov., and 5 Dec. 1756. Willing to Thomas Willing in London, 30 Mar. 1757. All these are in Willing Letterbook, PHS. The concern was to begin on 1 May 1757. Willing to Nathaniel Sharpe, 17 Apr. 1757, *ibid.* Willing gives some indication of his firm's merit at the time. "I have been long in trade here, and am concerned in several vessels in the West India trade and can often command room for frt [freight] when many others cannot." Willing to Anthony Bacon, 12 Apr. 1757, *ibid.*

2. Robert Waln, *Biography of the Signers*, V. 189-90. *Pennsylvania Magazine of History and Biography* (hereafter cited as *PMHB*), XXVI, 153-54. Photostats of the birth certificates of Robert Morris, Sr., his wife, and Robert Morris, Jr., confirm the date. Morris Collection, Pennsylvania Archives (hereafter cited as PA). A certified copy of the will is in Morris Coll., PA. Morris' mother did not come to America. The unborn child became Thomas Morris, and he was eventually cared for by Robert Morris, his half-brother.

3. "Autobiography of Willing," printed in Thomas W. Balch (ed.), *Willing Letters and Papers* (Philadelphia, 1922), pp. 115-28. Also see Burton A. Konkle, *Thomas Willing* (Philadelphia, 1937). The PHS rather recently acquired a dozen or so personal letters of the Willing family. For first quote, T. Willing to R. Morris, 27 Feb. 1756, Willing Letterbook, PHS. Willing to Thomas Willing of London, 12 Apr. 1757, *ibid.* For second quote, Willing to Morris, 27 Apr. 1778, printed in Balch, *Willing Letters and Papers*, p. 85. See also p. 52.

4. This is based on an analysis of the Willing Letterbook. A characteristic letter is the instruction to Capt. David Stewart, 6 May 1757. There are some useful letters from one of the Captains hired by Willing and Morris in the Morris Papers, New York Public Library (hereafter cited as NYPL) for this period. See also, Willing and Morris to Anthony Bacon, 1 Oct. 1757, Willing Letterbook, PHS. For the insurance group, Willing and Morris to Lawrence Read, 13 Oct. 1757, *ibid.* Details on this insurance group are lacking. Willing was much displeased by Lord Loudon's embargo. "I'd rather pay 100 pounds sterling per year tax than have our trade sported with by a single man." Willing to Thomas Willing, 1 July 1757, Willing Letterbook, PHS. For earlier comment of Charles Willing, Charles Willing to John Perks, 2 Oct. 1754, Willing Letterbook, PHS. For example of attitude of Willing and Morris toward trade, Willing and Morris to Reade, 28 June 1759, and Willing and Morris to Samuel Bean, 28 June 1759, *ibid.* For position of each partner within the firm, see Willing Letterbook, *passim.* Also Willing and Morris to Thomas Willing of London, 6 May 1757, *ibid.* It is significant that in an address to John Penn upon the latter's arrival in Pennsylvania, Thomas Willing was the first signature, while that of Morris was among those in the second column. Address, 21 Nov. 1763,

Penn Papers, Addt'l Misc. Letters, I, 115, PHS.

5. For the quote, Morris to James Duff, 26 Feb. 1775, Morris Papers, NYPL (copy). Richard Champion's letters to Willing and Morris comprise part of this correspondence, but it is of interest chiefly for British merchant attitude toward the Revolution rather than Willing and Morris business. See part II of G. H. Guttridge (ed.), *American Correspondence of a Bristol Merchant, 1766-76* (Berkeley, 1934), *passim.* The firm had its ups and downs in ship ownership during this period, but it was definitely favorable in the long-term trend. They owned 5 ships in 1766, 10 in 1773, and the same number in 1775. I am indebted to Professor Anne Bezanson of the University of Pennsylvania and Mrs. Grace Larsen for providing me with this information.
The letters on the plantation from Willing and Morris to Pollock and James Willing, their correspondents in Louisiana, to Alexander Henderson, to Philip Francis, etc., are found in Morris MSS, Misc., PHS. They begin in 1774 and run up to the Revolution in 1776. Probably the most interesting letter is that to Henderson, as overseer, dated 12 Apr. 1774, where the complete instructions in laying out the plantation are outlined. Willing and Morris also enjoyed a balance of $42,000 in their favor in their dealings with Oliver Pollock just before the Revolution. James A. James, *Oliver Pollock* (New York and London, 1937), pp. 56, 82-83.

6. For Philadelphia merchants in the Revolutionary movement, A. M. Schlesinger's essential volume, *The Colonial Merchants in the American Revolution, 1763-76* (New York, 1917), pp. 79, 125-31, 191-94. For list on Non-Importation, John R. Young (ed.), *Memorial History of the City of Philadelphia* (2 vols.; New York, 1895-98), I, 369. See also *PMHB,* XXVII, 84-87.

7. Morris to James Duff, 26 Feb. 1775, Morris Papers, NYPL (copy). See also Edmund C. Burnett (ed.), *Let-*

ters of the Members of the Continental Congress (7 vols.; Washington, D. C., 1921-36), I, 271. Hereafter Burnett will be cited as follows: (Volume number) Burnett (Page number). To General Charles Lee, Morris wrote: "I think we cannot fail of succeeding in this most righteous cause. . . ." 21 Aug. 1775, Morris MSS, Misc., PHS. For the second quote, Morris to General Lee, 10 Jan. 1776, *ibid.* Final quote, Morris to General Lee, 24 Jan. 1776, *ibid.*

8. Morris to Joseph Reed, 21 July 1776, 2 Burnett 19. Reed had earlier urged Morris to bring a letter before Congress, written by Reed, that stressed reconciliation. William B. Reed, *Joseph Reed* (2 vols.; Philadelphia, 1847), I, 199-202.

9. Morris to General Lee, 24 Jan. 1776, Morris MSS, Misc., PHS. Morris wrote to Duff: "God forbid the sword of Civil war shoud e'er be drawn, but if it is none can tell when or on what terms it will be sheathed again." 26 Feb. 1775, Morris Papers, NYPL. Morris to General Gates, 6 Apr. 1776, 1 Burnett 416. See also letter to Joseph Reed, 20 July 1776, Reed Papers, IV, New York Historical Society (hereafter cited as NYHS). When Johnstone, the peace envoy from Britain, came to the United States in 1778 to discuss reconciliation, Morris wrote Gouverneur Morris: "No offers must tempt us; they ought not to have a hearing of one moment, unless preceded by acknowledgment of our independence, because we can never be happy people under their domination." 16 June 1778, 3 Burnett 294. A copy of the letter sent to Morris by Johnstone can be found in the Maryland Archives, Redbook, X, 78.

10. On his limited political experience previous to the Revolution, see Morris to James Duff, 26 Feb. 1776, Morris Papers, NYPL (copy).

11. I am indebted to Robert L. Brunhouse, *The Counter Revolution in Pennsylvania, 1776-1790* (Harrisburg, 1942), as any student of Pennsylvania during the Revolution must

7-11

be, for the background of details and leads to source materials. As is evident, however, I have some reservations about the thesis, and it appears that on occasion the author himself entertains moments of doubt (p. 91). I have found it very difficult to establish by specific correspondence or other materials Morris' positions on most happenings in Pennsylvania during this early period. In this respect the *Journals* of the Assembly are, of course, highly inadequate. The particular manuscript material which is useful (and it is fragmentary) is concentrated for the most part in the PHS, the NYHS, and the PA. Especially interesting on policy is Morris' letter to Reed, 29 Mar. 1779, Morris Coll., PA. For Morris' work on the Committee of Safety, see *Pennsylvania Colonial Records*, X, 280 ff. Also *Penn. Journals, passim*, but especially pp. 246-49, 311, 320-21, 562-63, 572, 600-601, 610-11, 658, 671.

12. *Journals of the Continental Congress, 1775-78, passim.* Hereafter to be cited as *Journals.*

13. Morris to the President of Congress, 16 Dec. 1776, printed in Peter Force (ed.), *American Archives*, 5 Series III, 1240. Hereafter the series and volume will not be cited, but merely the page. For second quote, Morris to President of Congress, 21 Dec. 1776, *ibid.*, 1332. Morris to President of Congress, 16 Dec. 1776, *ibid.*, 1240. *Journals*, VI, 1032 (21 Dec. 1776). It is not necessary to distinguish between Morris' actions before and after the appointment, for there was no real break. He merely carried on officially what he had been doing unofficially.

14. Morris to President of Congress, 13 Dec. 1776, *Am. Archives*, 1199.

15. Morris to President of Congress, 17 Dec. 1776, *Am. Archives*, 1254. Morris to President of Congress, 21 Dec. 1776, *ibid.*, 1332. Morris to President of Congress, 23 Dec. 1776, *ibid.*, 1372.

16. Committee in Philadelphia to Washington (signed by Morris), 9 Jan. 1777, 2 Burnett 212. Comm. in Phila. to Washington, 7 Jan. 1777,

printed in Jared Sparks (ed.), *Correspondence of the American Revolution* (4 vols.; Boston, 1853), I, 325. Comm. in Phila. to Washington, 22 Feb. 1777, 2 Burnett 272. Also letter of 26 Feb. 1777, 2 Burnett 284-85. Morris to Washington, 21 Dec. 1776, *Am. Archives*, 1330. Morris to Washington, 23 Dec. 1776, *ibid.*, 1374. Morris to Washington, 30 Dec. 1776, *ibid.*, 1485. Morris to Washington, 1 Jan. 1777, Sparks, *Corresp. of the Am. Rev.*, I, 316-17. Comm. in Phila. to President of Congress, 30 Dec. 1776, *Am. Archives*, 1483. For waste feed, Comm. in Phila. to President of Congress, 10 Jan. 1777, 2 Burnett 177 (footnote). Comm. in Phila. to Washington, 31 Dec. 1776, 2 Burnett 198. Comm. in Phila. to James Wilson, 9 Jan. 1777, *ibid.*, 213. Comm. in Phila. to President of Congress, 28 Dec. 1776, *Am. Archives*, 1458. Francis Wharton (ed.), *The Revolutionary Diplomatic Correspondence of the United States* (6 vols.; Washington, D. C., 1889), II, 231-38.

17. Comm. in Phila. to President of Congress, 30 Dec. 1776, *Am. Archives*, 1484. Morris to Washington, 1 Jan. 1777, Sparks, *Corresp. of the Am. Rev.*, I, 316. Care has been taken to cite the printed sources, but almost all these letters are conveniently available in the MSS volume of the "Committee in Philadelphia" in the Continental Congress Papers 133. In Cont. Cong. Papers 137, Appendix, there is a duplicate letterbook of letters sent to Congress. Copies of many of the letters, and some originals, are located in Morris Misc. MSS, PHS, and a few in Morris Coll., PA. The nature of the above quotes amply demonstrates that Morris was the major figure in the Committee. The letters, though cited as "Committee in Philadelphia" for accuracy, should read for the most part "Morris to —————." Many of the letters in the MSS letterbook are in Morris' own handwriting.

18. Hancock to Morris, 14 Jan. 1777, 2 Burnett 215. Hooper to Morris, 28 Dec. 1776, *ibid.*, 195. Morris to Wil-

liam Hooper, 18 Jan. 1777, Morris MSS, Misc., PHS. Mary Morris to her mother, 1 Apr. 1777, quoted in *PMHB*, II, 161.

19. *Journals*, III, 392 (29 Nov. 1775). *Ibid.*, IV, 104 (30 Jan. 1776). Morris to Commissioners in Paris, 21 Dec. 1776, Wharton, *Rev. Dipl. Corresp.*, II, 238 (entire letter 231-39).

20. Morris wrote: ". . . I see plainly it will be absolutely necessary for me to quit all other committees and business but that of the Secret Committee in order to have it well done and in that case I will most freely and chearfully devote my whole attention to it. As I wish most ardently to see our magazines, stores, and trade put on such a footing that we may tell Great Britain to kiss our B-h—— (excuse the expression)." Morris to Sec. Committee, 19 Feb. 1777, Morris MSS, Misc., PHS. The first record of the Committee's work is in the *Journals*, II, 253 (18 Sept. 1775) when they were to contract for field pieces, "muskets," arms, etc. On Oct. 6 they were given permission to export, to pay for ammunition. After that, the functions of the Committee "just grew." Morris joined the Committee December 13, 1775, replacing his partner, Thomas Willing. *Ibid.*, III, 426.

21. *Journals*, V, 659 (5 Aug. 1776). Also 739 (6 Sept. 1776). For a more detailed picture see III-IX, *passim*. In volume IV particularly Congressional orders came thick and fast.

22. See Morris' letter, "To the Public," 7 Jan. 1779, in NYHS *Collections*, 1888, 264 (the entire letter covers 259-66). There is a draft of this letter in Morris' handwriting in Morris Papers, LC. The five volumes of the NYHS *Collections* from 1886-90 are usually cited as *Deane Papers* with a corresponding volume number; hereafter these volumes shall be cited accordingly. For examples of authorizations, see *Journals*, II, 253 (18 Sept. 1775) and IV, 97 (27 Jan. 1776). See Morris to (Sec. Committee), Jan. 1777, Morris MSS, PHS. Cf. with Cont. Cong. Papers 143, 1-40, LC.

Specific cases in this contracting business varied. De Pliarne, Penet, and Company were to buy goods in France, transport them to available seaports where ships, sent by the Committee, were to pick up the goods. Once the goods were aboard, they were to be transported at the risk of Congress. Money was advanced in the case of De Pliarne, Penet, and Company although, according to some testimony, it was inadequate. Dubourg to Franklin, 10 June 1776, Paris, *Am. Archives*, 4 Series VI, 779. (The entire letter 771-82 is important.) The instructions to William Hodge were more confining. He was ordered to make contracts for a precise amount of powder, an exact number of "muskets," gun flints, etc. He was to contract for armed cutters and even instructed on the amount of goods to be sent on each vessel. Payment "in this country's produce" would be made to the firms with whom Hodge had contracted. Sec. Comm. to Captain William Hodge, 30 May 1776, *Am. Archives*, 4 Series VI, 618-20. A variety of people, including Washington and the Governor of Connecticut, recommended De Pliarne, and he eventually was directed to the Secret Committee. *Am. Archives*, 4 Series IV, 235, 261, 264, 310, 447.

For a careful exposition of another contract and its operation see James B. Hedges, *The Browns of Providence Plantations; Colonial Years* (Cambridge, Mass., 1952), pp. 225-39. When this important volume appeared, the present study was in finished form. In consequence, my use of Professor Hedges' book has, unfortunately, been limited.

23. Comm. of Sec. Corresp. to Deane, 3 Mar. 1776, *Deane Papers*, I, 123-26. Also letter of 2 Mar., *ibid.*, 119. The editor of these volumes of Deane Papers thoroughly confuses the two committees. John Brown to Morris, 18 Dec. 1777, York, Morris Papers, NYPL. Instructions to Bingham by Comm. of Sec. Corresp., 3 June 1776, Gratz Coll., PHS. Marine Committee to Capt. Stephen Cleve-

12-17

land, 30 July 1776, *Am. Archives,* 5 Series I, 670-71.

24. For Morris and Deane, see Section III and Section IV of this chapter. For Deane's brothers, *Deane Papers,* II, 133, 163, 181, 185-86, 193, 194-95, 209-10, 235, 293, 310, 332-34, 363. For partnership agreement between Silas Deane and his brother Simeon, Connecticut Historical Society *Collections,* XXIII, 124. Agreement between Sec. Comm. and John Alsop, Francis Lewis, Philip Livingston, Silas Deane, and Robert Morris, 19 Feb. 1776, *Deane Papers,* I, 117-18. Also the agreement between themselves, *ibid.,* 116-17. This agreement was authorized by Congress. *Journals,* IV, 97 (27 Jan. 1776) . Comm. of Sec. Corresp. to Deane, 3 Mar. 1776, *Deane Papers,* I, 124. Another good example of multiple representation is Oliver Pollock in Louisiana. He acted for the Secret Committee and for Willing and Morris. In this case, it is interesting to notice that the balance which Willing and Morris had built up in Pollock's hands was directed to Continental purposes. Pollock was also to draw bills on the credit of Willing and Morris in order to get supplies for the Continental expedition down the Mississippi River. The Secret Committee then owed this sum to Willing and Morris. Cont. Cong. Papers 50, *passim,* but especially Sec. Comm. to Pollock, 12 June 1777, pp. 29-36. For accounts, see Sec. Comm. to Bingham, 2 Sept. 1776, Gratz Coll., PHS (copy) . Accounts of mixed cargoes crop up quite frequently. See, for example, Morris to Sec. Comm., 6 Jan. 1777, Morris Coll., PA, or Sec. Comm. to Caesar Rodney, 15 Apr. 1777, Society Coll., Misc., PHS. However, more than once a zealous desire to get private remittances to Europe or to capitalize on incoming goods prompted mixed cargoes. For some effects of this time element, see Morris' letter "To the Public," 7 Jan. 1779, *Deane Papers,* III, 265.

25. See original instructions to Sec. Comm., *Journals,* II, 254 (18 Sept.

1775) . Also *Journals, passim,* for frequent reiteration. Also Comm. of Sec. Corresp. to Arthur Lee, 30 Nov. 1775, 1 Burnett 265-66. To see to what lengths this secrecy was carried at times, see 2 Wharton 151-52. For action on Paine, see *Journals,* XIII, 32-33 (7 Jan. 1779) . The reproof of Paine was, in part, a political maneuver.

26. The Committee was reorganized on July 5, 1777, and renamed the Committee on Commerce. *Journals,* VIII, 533-34. For an exploration of this relationship and these charges, see below, Section IV.

27. John Adams to Horatio Gates, 27 Apr. 1776, 1 Burnett 433.

28. For the quote, Morris to General Lee, 12 July 1775, Morris MSS, Misc., PHS.

29. *Journals,* IV, 257-59 (6 Apr. 1776) . According to Morris there were two contracts. The first was expressly for arms and ammunition and apparently made with Congress as a whole. Willing and Morris were advanced $80,000, but their ship captain (Capt. Wilson on the *Livre*) was unable to obtain such war goods from any European ports. When he returned with the money intact, Congress through the Secret Committee renewed the contract in February 1776. The second contract in September 1775 was made with the Secret Committee directly. One William Duncan, a young Philadelphia merchant, was jointly concerned (though not named in the contract) and the enterprise received an advance of $45,000. "An account of Certain Transactions of Willing and Morris and the Continental Congress," undated (probably 1779) , Morris Collection, Huntington Library (in Morris' handwriting) . Account of the first contract is on p. 1, the second p. 3. This document is not named by Morris, but the title given it by the author of this study seems appropriate. For criticism of contracts, see *Journals,* III, 473-74 (25 Sept. 1775) . A diligent search has failed to unearth the specific business papers to determine the profits. For guard,

Journals, III, 396 (2 Dec. 1775).
Willing and Morris also provided
600 bolts of sailcloth to the Continent for 3,000 pounds when, according to Morris, it could have brought
20,000 pounds in the general market. "An Account of Transactions,"
p. 3, Morris Coll., Huntington Library (hereafter cited as HL). Willing and Morris received permission
to send out almost 30,000 pounds
(probably Penn. currency) value in
commodities on behalf of the Continent during the prohibition of exports. "Account of Transactions,"
Morris Coll., HL. The vessels are
listed on p. 3.

30. This caution is evident throughout
much of the correspondence. See for
example, Deane to Morris, 23 June
1776, *Deane Papers,* I, 141, and Willing and Morris to Samuel Beale, 6
Mar. 1776, Morris Corresp., LC.

31. The reason Thomas Morris, Robert's half-brother, was sent to England (from France) in the early
summer of 1776 was to settle English accounts. Morris to Deane, 4
Oct. 1776, *Deane Papers,* I, 305.
Also, Morris to Deane, 29 Dec. 1777,
ibid., II, 296. According to Morris,
10,000 pounds sterling was tied up
in British hands. Morris to William
Bingham, 12 Jan. 1778, Morris Corresp., LC. For an example on ships
and shipping, see Willing and Morris to Bingham, 14 Sept. 1776, *ibid.*
Morris to Deane, 11 Aug. and 12
Sept. 1776, *Deane Papers,* I, 174, 235.

32. Harrison to Willing and Morris, 17
May 1776, Morris Corresp., LC.
Morris to Bradford, 27 Mar. 1777,
PHS. Braxton Papers, *passim,* PHS.
There are a series of letters from
Stephen Stewart in Morris Corresp.,
LC. All of these concern the buying
program. Morris definitely handled
the affairs of Willing and Morris at
this time. See Morris to Bingham,
14 Sept. and 20 Oct. 1776 in particular, but also Morris Corresp.,
passim, LC. Morris to Bingham, 12
Feb. 1777, *ibid.* The evidence indicates that most of the purchasing
was for Willing and Morris acting
on behalf of the Continent.

33. See Stephen Stewart's letters to Wil-

ling and Morris, 26 and 29 Sept., 17
and 24 Oct., and 6 and 22 Dec. 1776,
Morris Corresp., LC. Willing and
Morris to Bingham, 6 Dec. 1776,
ibid.

34. For first quote, Morris to Deane, 12
Sept. 1776, *Deane Papers,* I, 235.
Also Comm. of Sec. Corresp. to
Bingham, 3 June 1776, Gratz Coll.,
PHS. For final quote, Willing and
Morris to Bingham, 3 June 1776,
Morris Corresp., LC.

35. Morris to Deane, 12 Sept. 1776,
Deane Papers, I, 235. Willing and
Morris to Bingham, 20 Oct. 1776,
Morris Corresp., LC.

36. Willing and Morris to Bingham, 20
Oct. 1776, Morris Corresp., LC. Willing and Morris to Bingham, 25
Apr. 1777, *ibid.* The bulk of the
correspondence, as the foregoing
footnotes indicate, is in the Morris
Corresp., LC. Some of the letters are
very long and contain a tremendous
amount of information. There are
a few letters in the PHS and the
PA. Since this section was originally
written, Professor Anne Bezanson
has published her magnificent price
study of Pennsylvania during the
Revolution. Her authoritative work
confirms the suggestion of profitable
ventures in the West India trade,
for these goods were much in demand in the early years of the war.
Bezanson, *Prices and Inflation During the American Revolution: Pennsylvania, 1770-90* (Philadelphia,
1951), pp. 208 ff., 322. For forebod-
ing, Willing and Morris to Bingham, 27 Sept. 1776, Morris Corresp.,
LC. For Prejent, Willing and Morris
to Bingham, 12 Feb. 1777, in "Letters and Papers of Robert Morris,"
Dreer Coll., PHS. See also correspondence of Morris to Bingham,
passim, LC, from this date forward.

37. Willing and Morris to Bingham, 16
Feb. 1777, Morris Corresp., LC.

38. There is no biography of Deane
worthy of the name, but the five
volumes of letters in the NYHS *Collections* and the two volumes in the
Conn. Hist. Soc. *Collections,* both
cited previously, provide a wealth of
material. See Morris' sketch of
Tom's life in Morris to Henry Laur-

17-18

ens, 26 Dec. 1777, *Deane Papers*, II, 245-49. For quote, Morris to Deane, 11 Aug. 1776, *ibid.*, I, 174.

39. Morris to Deane, 11 Aug. 1776, *Deane Papers*, I, 174-6. The first two quotes come from p. 174 and the last from p. 176. Morris also advised that the cargoes be insured if possible.
Professor Thomas P. Abernethy has asserted that Morris realized that the American armies could not be supplied adequately except from Great Britain and consequently proposed to Deane that a company be organized to execute such importations. Its capital was to be 400,000 pounds sterling and it was to include a group of London merchants (particularly Thomas Walpole) and French merchants (particularly Chaumont) as well as Morris and his associates. T. P. Abernethy, "Commercial Activities of Silas Deane," *American Historical Review*, XXXIX, 478.
Professor Abernethy has based this assertion on a report of Paul Wentworth, a British intelligence officer (B. F. Stevens, *Facsimiles of Manuscripts in European Archives Relating to America, 1773-83* (London, 1889-95), No. 131), but he has read the Wentworth Report incorrectly. Wentworth writes that the plan was "a scheme for an extensive and very profitable commerce, to be carried on between the subjects of France and those of Great Britain now in rebellion"—in other words between France and the United States, *not* between England and the United States via France. Even when read correctly, the report of Wentworth is still shot through with inaccuracies and half truths. Professor Abernethy—as the body of the text also demonstrates—makes a considerable assumption in dismissing the plan with "this arrangement was carried into effect, and there is every reason to believe it was successful." (Abernethy, "Commercial Activities of Silas Deane," p. 479.)
I am inclined to feel that Robert East in his excellent book, *Business Enterprise in the American Revolu-*

tion (New York, 1938) oversteps a bit when he states that Willing and Morris' plan gave "the first clue to the formation of an international commercial and land-speculating group organized around Deane and Morris. . . ." (p. 131). It was a much more flexible instrument than East intimates and Morris-Deane were not always at the center. In addition, it was never consummated successfully during the Revolution. East also confuses the Wentworth letter and Morris' actual plan, and quotes Morris' approval to the plan sketched in the Wentworth letter while in reality he was urging his own trading plan in the letter of August 11, 1776. What East refers to as a separate agreement is in reality "the" agreement.

40. Silas Deane, in a letter to Morris dated September 30, 1776—and the date is crucial—stated his intention of sending out 100,000 pounds sterling in goods *(Deane Papers,* I, 286). It has usually been assumed that this intention concerned a private transaction with Willing and Morris which resulted in spectacular financial rewards. The evidence indicates, however, that Deane was speaking about *public* goods, for the remainder of Deane's letter concerns public affairs and refers to a letter of Morris, dated June 5, 1776 *(ibid.,* I, 136-40), which was also concerned with public affairs. Moreover, Deane did not receive Morris' letter about setting up a "trading plan," the private business arrangement with Willing and Morris, until the last of November, two months after Deane's letter of September 30 was written. Therefore, by process of elimination, the only possibility of the goods mentioned in the Deane letter of September 30 being private would be (1) that Morris had had a conversation with Deane before the latter's departure for France and at that time outlined a trading arrangement orally, or (2) that a second, and private, letter, dated June 5, 1776, was written by Morris to Deane but is now missing.

The first possibility seems unlikely and the second appears improbable. In late November, when Deane received Morris' letter of August 11, 1776, sketching the trading plan, he had to write Thomas Morris, Robert's half-brother, to relate Morris' instructions and to ask Thomas to return to France (*ibid.*, I, 400). This would have been unnecessary if Willing and Morris had presented a scheme to Deane orally before the latter's departure for France; Deane would have told Thomas Morris about any such plan immediately on arrival for there was an ample opportunity (*ibid.*, I, 196). With respect to a missing private letter, it appears unlikely that Morris would have found it necessary to write his extended letter of August 11, outlining "the" trading plan in detail, if he had submitted to Deane a proposal in a previous letter. Moreover, the tone of Morris' letter of August 11 clearly indicates that no mention had been made earlier about a trading arrangement and there is no reference to any previous intentions or operations. There is every reason to believe, therefore, that Deane in his letter of September 30, 1776 was speaking of public goods.

On the other hand, it should be noted that Morris, upon *receiving* Deane's letter of September 30, apparently interpreted it to mean the shipment of *private* rather than public goods for he replied that if they were "tolerably lucky in getting them in, great things will be done." (*ibid.*, I, 459). In view of the evidence, it appears that Morris confused his private and public letters which had been written five to seven months earlier, probably because he crowded so much public and private activity into this period —June 1776 to March 1777. This was the period when Morris acted as Congress' representative in Philadelphia and as an important force in the Committee of Secret Correspondence and Secret Committee of Commerce, in addition to attending his normal duties as a member of Congress while carrying out exten-

sive new private trading arrangements. Moreover, Morris' letterbooks had been moved in the late fall of 1776 because of Howe's threat to Philadelphia, and he did not have his records available when Deane's letter of September 30 arrived. Morris' recollection of his previous letters was dim, for the evidence shows that he had forgotten what he had written on the matter of insurance for shipments and contradicted his earlier letter unknowingly (*ibid.*, I, 458).

All of this reëmphasizes the fact that misunderstandings, inaccuracies, and mismanagement were almost unavoidable during the more hectic periods of the Revolution.

41. Deane to Morris, 12 Dec. 1776, Morris Corresp., LC. This is printed in part in *Deane Papers*, I, (13 Dec.), 419-21. However, the most important section has been omitted in the printed version. This venture, as the letters of Deane in December 1776 and early January 1777 indicate, was the first move to implement the instructions of Morris sent in the letter of August 11, 1776, and received by Deane in late November. This venture must be distinguished from any of Deane's previous promises to send out goods, because the evidence indicates that any earlier pledges were related to public goods (see previous footnote).

42. Deane to Morris, 6 Jan. 1777, *Deane Papers*, I, 448. Morris to Deane, 29 June 1777, *ibid.*, II, 82 (first quote), 83 (second quote). When European affairs between Willing and Morris and Deane were to be settled, Deane wrote John Ross, who had taken over the Willing and Morris affairs abroad, that the Chaumont adventure, a concern in a vessel with Delap (the *Timolean*, see *ibid.*, II, 307) which had been taken, and the concern in Captain Bell's privateer constituted the only adventures where the two had been jointly engaged (*ibid.*, I, 477). Deane to John Ross, 23 Mar. 1778, *ibid.*, II, 422-23. A careful study of the evidence bears out that this was substantially correct, although

18-23

Deane possibly forgot about the powder sent Willing and Morris (*ibid.*, I, 401). It is also possible that no joint adventure existed on this project. This summary by Deane is important, for there was no reason for him to deceive Ross or to lie; he would have had nothing to gain.

43. *Deane Papers,* I, *passim,* especially Deane to Delap, 14 Dec. 1776, *ibid.,* I, 421-22. Also *ibid.,* II, 307. France fairly seethed with ill-will between various representatives and agents of America in France.

44. Morris to Deane, 23 Oct. 1776, *Deane Papers,* I, 331 (first quote), 332 (second quote). Deane was to continue in his role as adviser to Thomas in the affairs of Willing and Morris.

45. Deane to Morris, 4 Dec. 1776, *Deane Papers,* I, 400. Morris to Deane, 31 Jan. 1777, *ibid.,* I, 475-76. Arthur Lee to Richard H. Lee, 6 Mar. 1777, *ibid.,* II, 22. Also *ibid.,* II, 152-6. Willing and Morris to Bingham, 16 Feb. 1777, Morris Corresp., LC. Thomas Willing to Morris, 3 Nov. 1777, in T. W. Balch, *Willing Letters and Papers,* p. 55.

46. The firm was known under various titles: De Pliarne, Penet and Gruel; Gruel and Company; Penet and Company; Morris, Penet, and Company. R. Morris later related: "He [Thomas Morris] readily fell into the proposals made by that house and became a party in it, but on what terms I do not know." *Deane Papers,* II, 249. De Pliarne had a contract with the Secret Committee to procure goods for Congress. See Section II of this chapter. For the quote, Morris to Henry Laurens, 26 Dec. 1777, *Deane Papers,* II, 250. Morris to Deane, 29 June 1777, *ibid.,* II, 77-84. See also Deane to Morris, 1 Oct. 1777, *ibid.,* II, 156-61. For the review before Congress, Morris to Henry Laurens, 26 Dec. 1777, *ibid.,* II, 243-54. Morris to Deane, 29 Dec. 1777, *ibid.,* 293-97.

47. "An Account of Transactions," Morris Coll., HL, p. 1 and p. 5. For contract preceding renewal see footnote 29. In the March contract, Congress

advanced $90,000. John Ross to Deane, 19 July 1777, *Deane Papers,* II, 94-97. Ross to Deane, 31 Jan. 1778, *ibid.,* II, 345.

48. Account Book of John Ross, p. 1, PHS. There are two account books. I am citing what appears to be the more finished account book. See Preliminary Account Book, p. 2, for the preliminary account mentioned. For indications of the Willing and Morris agreements with Congress, see Invoice Book, p. 17. Most of the goods that Ross was buying came from John Parish at "Hamburgh" with whom he had a gross account of over 200,000 pounds sterling. Account Book (preliminary), p. 7. Ross in his private capacity did engage with John and William Craig, Delap, and Conyngham in British trade—each ¼ share. Invoice Book, p. 59.

49. *Deane Papers,* I, 116-18, 420, 456-58. Also, *ibid.,* II, 84, 415. See also, Morris to Arthur Lee, 4 Oct. 1783, Cont. Cong. Papers 54, 13. Morris said he entered Indian goods contract "much against his inclination at that time." "An Acct. of Transactions," Morris Coll., HL, p. 5. Willing and Morris to Samuel Beale, 6 Mar. 1776, Morris Corresp., LC. Morris to J. H. Norton, 4 Feb. 1777, Morris MSS, Misc., PHS. Part of the story can be traced in Willing and Morris' letters to Bingham, 14 Sept. 1776, and 16 Feb. 1777, and 25 Apr. 1777, in Morris Corresp., LC. Council of Safety (of Md.) to Willing and Morris, 27 Sept. 1776, Morris Corresp., LC.

50. Morris to Deane, 12 Sept. 1776, *Deane Papers,* I, 233. Morris to Bingham, 4 Dec. 1776, Gratz Coll., PHS. Morris to Bingham, 25 Apr. 1777, Misc. MSS, NYHS. Morris to Pollock, 19 June 1777, Morris MSS, Misc., PHS. For Bell, Deane to Morris, 23 Aug. 1777, Morris Corresp., LC. Also *Deane Papers,* I, 477. Cf. East, *Business Enterprise and the Am. Rev.,* pp. 133-35. There is a tendency to distort when names are lumped together as participating in privateers without discriminating who engaged in each adventure.

Morris participated, for example, in Capt. Bell's adventure which was to function in the Mediterranean, but no evidence has been discovered that he was interested in the *Revenge*, as has sometimes been suggested.

51. Hudson to Morris, 19 July 1777, and 27 Aug. 1777, Morris Corresp., LC. Also Morris to Hudson, 26 Aug. 1777, Morris Papers, PA. Notice the distinction between Morris Collection and Morris Papers at the Pennsylvania Archives. The first consists of photostats of originals still in the hands of the Morris family. The second is separately boxed under Entry 128 and is valuable for business correspondence. Braxton Papers, *passim*, PHS. The connection began in August 1776. "Braxton's Reply to Morris," p. 1. The accounts between the two are confusing, but the evidence indicates that the gross business between the two amounted to upwards of 50,000 pounds (Penn. currency). "Accounts," Braxton Papers, PHS. Morris to Hudson, 20 May 1777, Morris Papers, PA. Also Braxton Papers, *passim*, PHS. On clothing — "expect there will be 8-10,000 pounds [presumably Penn. currency] made thereby." David Stewart to Morris, 27 Jan. 1778, Morris Corresp., LC. A series of letters found in Morris Corresp., LC, elaborate these activities. The Harrison connection can also be traced in Morris Corresp., LC. Apparently, the tobacco scheme was to total $40,000, a sizable sum in May 1776 before depreciation had set in. Harrison had to undergo a "fiery tryal [*sic*]" on the currency matter with a committee from Virginia. Harrison to Morris, 7 June 1776, Morris Corresp., LC. Willing and Morris to John L. Cripps of Charleston, 22 July 1777, Morris MSS, PHS. A purchasing program with John Langdon of Portsmouth (N. H.) failed to materialize because of price ceilings and social pressure. Langdon to Morris, 18 July 1777, Morris Corresp., LC. It was to Hudson that Morris wrote an oft-quoted letter: "It is well you will be so clear and distinct in your accounts. we have therefore nothing to do but make money fast as we can and wishing your honest endeavours may be crowned with success." 19 Aug. 1777, Society Coll., PHS. The original manuscript letter indicates that this note was written hurriedly. It is usually quoted beginning with "we" and ending with "can" which tends to throw it out of context. There can be no question, however, of Morris' zeal to make money.

52. Morris to Sec. Comm. of Congress (in Balt.), 19 Feb. 1777, Phila., Morris MSS, Misc., PHS. See Letter to Sec. Comm., 11 [?] Jan. 1777, Morris MSS, PHS. Also extract of letter, Morris to Carter Braxton, June 1777, quoted in "Morris' Account to the Auditors," Braxton Papers, PHS.

53. Burnett, *Letters*, III, and IV, "Preface," *passim*. Far better, of course, is to sample the letters themselves.

54. The material brought before the Congressional investigating committee at the time, the researches of David D. Wallace in his biography of Henry Laurens, and a letter of Morris to Deane, dated before the capture of the *Farmer* was known, stating the nature of the cargo, place beyond all question that the vessel was loaded on public account with the exception of the 50 hogsheads on Willing and Morris' private account. *Journals*, XIII, 46-47 (9 Jan. 1779), 49-50 (11 Jan. 1779), 65-66 (15 Jan. 1779), 79-86 (19 Jan. 1779), 164-76 (11 Feb. 1779). The dates on all the letters relating to the affair are particularly important. Documentary material which Morris submitted at the time of the investigation is found in Cont. Cong. Papers 19, 243-303. For the conclusions of Wallace, see his *The Life of Henry Laurens* (New York and London, 1915), pp. 329-34. Wallace mistakenly assumes that Morris was "the highest financial officer of the state" at the time. For letter to Deane, Morris to Deane, 31 Jan. 1777, *Deane Papers*, I, 479. According to Morris, his first information on the capture of the *Farmer* came early in February in a letter

23-27

from Richard Henry Lee. *Journals,*
XIII, 171 (11 Feb. 1779). Undoubtedly much of the original misunderstanding about this cargo resulted from the separation of members of the Secret Committee at the
time—they had been scattered because of Howe's threat to Philadelphia—plus the fact that the Committee books were neither in the
hands of Morris at the time nor in
those of his colleagues. *Am. Archives,* 5 Series III, 1241 (16 Dec.
1776).

55. A second dispute at the time is of
less importance intrinsically (the
accusation was circumventing public regulations rather than deliberate corruption such as the *Farmer*
affair), but it stirred up a generous
amount of passion. The dispute
centered on goods imported on the
French vessel *Victorious* and on
flour purchases for Bingham. It is
certainly a carryover, in part, of the
Deane dispute and the accusations
in Congress on the ship *Farmer.*
There are many accounts of this incident, but the best version by all
odds is that of Hubertis Cummings,
"Robert Morris and the Polacre
'Victorious'" in *PMHB,* LXX, 239-
57. He has skillfully used the new
material in the PA made available
by the descendants of the Morris
family. Among other interpreta-
tions of this incident one could ar-
gue the thesis that it was merchants
vs. merchants, those who did not
share in the French business against
those who did.

56. For the best single guide to archival
records for this period see the excellent typewritten "Preface to Prefederal Records" which is available
in the main reading room in the
National Archives in Washington,
D. C. See *American State Papers*
(38 vols.; Washington, D. C., 1832-
61), Misc., I, 241. See also, *ibid.,* II,
249-51. Painstaking efforts have
failed to unearth anything but fragmentary data on the firm and only
incidental letters of Thomas Morris.
What happened to the Thomas
Morris letters after Morris' death
remains a mystery. In Section III of

this chapter, see part on Bingham.
For Morris' own rough account, see
"An Account of Certain Transac-
tions," Morris Coll., HL.

57. See *Journals,* II, 254 (18 Jan. 1775).
For quorum in operation, see for
example, Sec. Comm. to William
Hodge, 30 May 1776, *Am. Archives,*
4 Series VI, 618 ff. or *Deane Papers,*
II, 94. For Morris' reports to Sec.
Comm., see for example, Morris to
R. H. Lee, Francis Lewis, William
Whipple, 21 Jan. 1777, Morris MSS,
Misc., PHS. Also that of Morris to
Sec. Comm., 19 Feb. 1777, in the
same collection. Also letter to the
Sec. Comm., 11 [?] Jan. 1777, in
Morris MSS, PHS. For William Lee,
Morris to (Sec. Comm.), 6 Jan.
1777, Morris Coll., PA, pp. 3 and 4
particularly. Wm. Lee (Alderman
Lee) never really fulfilled his func-
tion. On Dec. 5, 1777, Thomas Mor-
ris delegated what would normally
have been Lee's task to Jonathan
Williams, nephew of Franklin. T.
Morris to Williams, 5 Dec. 1777,
Nantes, Morris Corresp., LC (copy).
Morris to Jay, President of Congress,
28 Jan. 1779, Phila., Cont. Cong.
Papers 137, Appendix, 245-46.

58. James C. Ballagh (ed.), *The Letters
of Richard Henry Lee* (2 vols.;
New York, 1911-14), I, *passim.* Notice how gentle R. H. Lee is with
Deane in November 1777 and his
emphasis upon the "radical cures"
of taxation and economy rather
than price regulation (354-55).
Later, especially in early 1779, he
became thoroughly involved. For an
indication of the drift of complaint,
see Arthur Lee to Samuel Adams,
25 Nov. 1777, printed in Richard
Henry Lee, *The Life of Arthur Lee*
(2 vols.; Boston, 1829), II, 124-25.
Also John Ross to Arthur Lee, 6
Apr. 1778, *Deane Papers,* II, 455-57.
The incident which Ross discusses
on Lee's criticism of Willing and
Morris had occurred some six
months previously. Deane added
fuel to flaming tempers by implying
that Lee was incompetent. See for
example Benjamin Harrison to
Morris, 8 June 1778, in "Letters to
Robert Morris" in NYHS *Collec-*

tions, XI (1878), 436-37 (entire series of letters 399-488).

59. Lee's actions and thoughts are revealed in Cont. Cong. Papers 54, and Lee Papers, Widener Library. F. L. Lee to Arthur Lee, 10 Dec. 1778, 3 Burnett 531. The "great man" who appears to lend his influence "to this party" is probably Morris. For Ledgers, see Bibliographical note.

60. See for example, John Adams to James Lovell, 20 Feb. 1779, Charles F. Adams (ed.), *The Works of John Adams* (10 vols.; Boston, 1854), IX, 477. Also Joseph Reed's comments. For first quote, A. Lee to Sam Adams, 17 Feb. 1778, *Deane Papers,* II, 368-69. For second quote, A. Lee to Carter Braxton, 22 May 1779, *ibid.,* III, 466.
Lee's approach to the investigations reflected a man deeply embittered. After copying some passages from a letter of Morris to Jay, which he dates 14 July 1781, Lee writes: "I have copied these passages to shew the stupid vanity of the writer—to suppose the Court of Madrid which was issuing depretiated paper to carry on the war would lend us 5,000,000 in specie and to imagine that America could furnish 4,000,-000 was more like the dream of a madman than anything else." Lee Papers, VIII, 53, Widener Library. On a letter of Morris to Grand, 3 Dec. 1781, which Lee copied, Lee appended a sarcastic note: "There was no bad management in France, where many millions advanced to Dr. Franklin from year to year did not furnish in three years a single uniform to the army." *Ibid.,* VIII, 50, Widener Library. These examples are by no means isolated ones. See Lee Papers, *passim.*

61. It is interesting to notice that as late as 1783, Arthur Lee still did not believe that Deane had instructions to purchase goods for Congress, and he asked Morris to send any information he could to illuminate this point (A. Lee to Morris, 26 Sept. 1783, Cont. Cong. Papers 54, p. 7, LC). For quote, Arthur

Lee and Samuel Osgood to Congress, 12 Sept. 1788, Cont. Cong. Papers 143, 1-3. Much of this difficulty was accentuated because of the extended time lag between the placing of an order and its fulfillment. The delay was largely due to the hazards of the time. Some orders given in 1776 had not been completed by 1779. This meant that the accounts, through no one's fault, dragged on and became complicated further by the depreciation of currency.

62. Morris to Braxton, June 1777, quoted in "Morris' Account to Auditors," Braxton Papers, PHS (extract).

63. For the quote, Laurens to Morris, 11 Jan. 1779, 4 Burnett 27. See also memorandum of Henry Laurens, 4 Burnett 15-16, for the quarrel over settling accounts of the Secret Committee. Also, Tom Paine's insinuations printed in *Penn. Packet,* 5 Jan. 1779, and conveniently available along with a series of his articles in *Deane Papers,* III, 226 ff. Also, Paine's article of 12 Jan. 1779. See Morris' letter "To the Public," 7 Jan. 1779, printed in *Deane Papers,* III, 259-66. Printed in part in 4 Burnett 16-19. Original draft in Morris Corresp., LC. Laurens exaggerated the length of time the books were available for Morris, but Morris exaggerated the amount of work he accomplished in settling accounts. A second exchange between Laurens and Morris, 11 Jan. 1779, is found in 4 Burnett 25-30. The sharpness of feeling is clearly shown by Morris' closing remarks to Laurens, 11 Jan. 1779: "When I have received that acquittal which I am confident of and placed in that light which I know myself to deserve, it will be time enough to speak of private Friendships. I have a better opinion of you than to believe you would prostitute that term by a Connexion with me whom you seem to consider as a dishonest Man." 4 Burnett 30.

64. For the quote, Morris to Hudson, 19 Sept. 1780, Morris Papers, PA.

CHAPTER TWO

1. Morris to T. Wharton, 11 Nov. 1777, Lancaster, Morris Coll., PA (copy in Society Coll., PHS). See also Section IV of the first chapter for the dispute over the length of time Morris possessed the accounts. For army, *Journals*, IX, 972 (28 Nov. 1777), X, 18 (5 Jan. 1778). *Journals*, XI, XII, *passim* (from July-Oct., 1778).

2. Morris to Bingham, 1 Oct. 1778, Morris Corresp., LC (p. 2). *Penn. Packet*, 28 July 1778. Morris to Bingham, 12 Jan. 1778, Morris Corresp., LC (p. 1). First quote, Willing to Morris, 6 Feb. 1778, in Balch, *Willing Letters and Papers*, p. 61. Second quote, Morris to John Bradford, 9 Jan. 1778, Morris Coll., PA.

3. Balch, *Willing Letters and Papers*, pp. 49 ff., *passim*. Morris made certain Willing would not lack money by writing John Ross and Thomas Morris to give Willing credit. 13 Sept. 1777, Morris Coll., PA. First quote, Willing to Morris, 3 Nov. 1777, Balch, *Willing Letters*, p. 59. Second quote, Willing to Morris, 6 Feb. 1778, *ibid.*, p. 62. For final quote, Willing to Morris, 3 Apr. 1778, *ibid.*, p. 75.

4. Morris to Tench Tilghman, 22 June 1784, Morris Papers, NYPL. A report of these business affairs must of necessity be qualitative rather than quantitative. The important questions that one would like to answer—the lines of trade, the volume and character of the trade, the relative return from separate investments, the shift of capital from one type of enterprise to another, to mention a few — simply cannot be answered because of the available evidence. When there is a series of letters, for example, commenting that an investment in tobacco is excessive but where no figure or even hint is given indicating the amount of the purchase, it is impossible to report quantitatively the extent of the investment, what percentage of the whole business capital was concentrated in this particu-

lar investment, or the profits. Or again, when a letter mentions the purchase of a mill but fails to give the purchase price or the location, the conclusions that can be drawn are severely limited. And, of course, the letters which are available comprise only a small part of the original correspondence.

5. Morris to Bingham, 2 Jan. 1778, Morris Corresp., LC (draft). First quote, p. 1. Second quote, p. 5. For bills of exchange, p. 4.

6. Some of the old was arrival of medicines from southern France via Martinique, flannels to Norton and Beale, and the like. See, for example, Morris to Bingham, 12 Jan. 1778, Morris Corresp., LC. For Ord's adventures, "Account of Sales," 21 Nov. 1778, Gratz Coll., PHS. Another copy, Morris Corresp., LC. Also "Account of Sales," 24 Apr. 1780, Gratz Coll., PHS. Morris to Bingham, 10 Mar. 1778, Morris Corresp., LC. For quote, Morris to Bingham, 5 May 1778, *ibid*. Morris said that he had tried to purchase certificates in New England, but he had been unsuccessful.

7. Morris to Bingham, 1 Oct. 1778, Morris Corresp., LC (copy). Morris to Bingham, 21 Nov. 1778, *ibid.* (copy). For quote, Morris to Bingham, 10 Feb. 1779, Society Coll., PHS.

8. Margaret L. Brown, "William Bingham in Martinique" in *PMHB*, LXI, 79. (entire article 54-87). A series of good articles on Bingham by Miss Brown appear in successive issues of the *PMHB*. Bezanson, *Prices and Inflation during the American Revolution*, p. 21.

9. Morris to Hudson, 21 May 1778, Morris Papers, PA.

10. Morris to Hudson, 20 Oct. 1778, Morris Papers, PA. For the quotes, Morris to Hudson, 30 Nov. 1778, *ibid.* It would mean purchasing export goods at high prices and selling goods imported in a declining market, thus narrowing the margin of profit. As Morris asserted, "it puts our whole trade on a bad footing."

11. A series of letters in the Morris Papers, PA, amply document the scope of the business. For first quote, Morris to Hudson, 9 Feb. 1779, Morris Papers, PA. For second quote, Morris to Hudson, 25 Feb. 1779, *ibid.*

12. Morris to Hudson, 10 July 1778, Morris Papers, PA. See also the letter of 9 Feb. 1779, *ibid.* For quote, Morris to Hudson, 12 May 1779, *ibid.*

13. For quote, Morris to Hudson, 18 May 1779, Morris Papers, PA. Morris to Hudson, 21 June 1779, *ibid.*

14. Morris to Hudson, 15 Nov. 1779, Morris Papers, PA. For the first quote, Morris to Hudson, 23 May 1780, *ibid.* Morris to Hudson, 22 Aug. 1780, *ibid.* For second quote, Morris to Hudson, 6 Sept. 1780, *ibid.* Unfortunately, this correspondence does not provide definite clues to the location of the real property.

15. First quote, Morris to Hudson, 30 Nov. 1778, Morris Papers, PA. Second quote, Morris to Hudson, 11 Dec. 1780, *ibid.* (copy is in John Swanwick's handwriting).

16. See Bibliographical note. The dispute started in January of 1784. Morris delayed settling accounts because he was occupied with the Office of Finance.

17. "Observation on the State of the Facts," by Holker, Holker Papers, XL, 7736. Also 7769½ (the "½" refers to the reverse side of the page which is not numbered in the volumes). Early hopes were optimistic. See Holker to Chaumont, 25 Aug. 1779, *ibid.*, I, 103-04. For purchasing agent, see *Journals*, XI, 713 (23 July 1778). For introduction to Morris, Deane to Morris, 24 Dec. 1777, Paris, Morris Corresp., LC. Also Holker to Chaumont, 19 June 1778, Holker Papers, I, 64, LC. For series of quotes, see Morris to Holker, 26 Feb. 1784, *ibid.*, XXIV, 4758, LC (copy). See also, General Account, *ibid.*, XXIII, 4573. Hereafter all citations to Holker Papers will refer to the collection at the Library of Congress unless specifically stated to the contrary. It has been assumed that Morris' statement of the beginnings of the Morris-Holker relationship is an accurate representation. On the margin of the copied letter Holker has inscribed a running commentary embodying his own interpretation of events and transactions. But he has not contradicted this part of the letter. Furthermore, much of this material was apparently to be used by the referees in the dispute, and therefore Holker would certainly have corrected this version if he had thought it inaccurate.

18. For expenditures on D'Estaing's squadron, Holker Papers, V, 876-77. The extent of the Morris-Holker business may be judged from the fact that 41 separate accounts were delivered by Morris to Holker in June, 1780. See "List of Accounts," June, 1780, XL, *ibid.*, 7767. For quote, Morris to Holker, 18 Sept. 1779, *ibid.*, V, 981-2 (copy in Holker's handwriting). Morris employed others in procurement. Morris to (Robert) Smith, 10 Aug. 1778, *ibid.*, XL, 7772½ (copied extract) and Smith's purchases, *ibid.*, XIX, 3695-3706. For new company, see Holker to Turnbull, Marmie, and Co., 2 Apr. 1784, *ibid.*, XXV, 4871. Also Morris to Holker, 26 Feb. 1784, *ibid.*, XXIV, 4762½. Joseph Reed wrote to De Berdt, his brother-in-law in New England, that Turnbull's connection with "our" family "has laid the foundation of his fortune" in his partnership with Holker, "founded principally on my recommendation." Reed to De Berdt, 2 Apr. 1782, Phila., Reed Papers, 10, NYHS.

19. See "Questions [by Holker] and Answers [by Morris]," Holker Papers, XXVIII, 5545-48. It is easy to see why Morris entertained hopes that the currency would appreciate. The French Alliance, the appearance of the French Fleet, and the victory at Saratoga were hopeful signs. For follow-up, see "Observations of Holker before Referees," Holker Papers, XL, 7736-75. Also, *ibid.*, XXX, 5837-5948 and Morris to Holker, 28 Feb. 1784, *ibid.*, XXIV, 4765. Various methods of accounting—or more properly lack

33-38

of any uniformity in accounting
systems—were responsible for a large
number of disputes. It is apparent
that the complexities of business,
both governmental and otherwise,
had become so great in this period
that the conventional accounting
methods were no longer adequate
to keep a lucid and accurate record
of the multiple enterprises.

20. For quote, "Morris's answer to
    Questions," Holker Papers, XL,
    7773. Apparently, Morris had a
    fund of $300,000 (continental cur-
    rency) in his hands about the
    spring of 1780. A "View of Month-
    ly Balances" of John Holker with
    Morris indicates a very substantial
    sum employed in public business
    (French business) in 1778-79. Pri-
    vate funds of Holker, and those
    he represented, in the hands of
    Morris did not become substantial
    until well along in 1779. The pub-
    lic account also shows the French
    greatly in arrears to Morris. *ibid.,*
    VII, 1328-36. Again it should be
    emphasized that the materials
    which are available were brought
    together to support one side of a
    case, and therefore the assertions
    are not always reliable.

21. Morris to Holker, 25 Mar. 1784,
    Holker Papers, XXV, 4841.

22. Morris to Holker, 26 Apr. 1779,
    Holker Papers, XL, 7685 (copy).
    Morris to Stacey Hepburn, 26 Apr.
    1779, Society Coll., PHS.

23. See the series of letters to Hep-
    burn in Society Coll., *passim,* PHS.
    Especially important are those of
    23 Sept. and 10 Dec. 1779. Also 6
    Jan. and 17 Mar. 1780. For first
    quote, Morris to Hepburn, 10 Dec.
    1779, Society Coll., PHS. Second
    quote, Morris to Hepburn, 17 Mar.
    1780, Society Coll., PHS (copy).
    "Stacey Hepburn in Account with
    Morris," Morris Papers, PA.

24. An example of Deane's other en-
    terprises was a mast contract with
    William Duer of New York and
    James Wilson of Pennsylvania. Later
    Wilson wanted to interest Deane
    in a land scheme "carried into ex-
    ecution by gentlemen in Europe
    who have the command of money."
    Deane Papers, IV, 190, 271. First

quote, Morris to Deane, 31 Mar.
1780, *ibid.,* IV, 117. Morris to
Franklin, 31 Mar. 1780, *ibid.,* IV,
119-21. Deane replied to Morris'
gesture: "Had I no other testimon-
ials to produce, yours alone would
weigh down volumes of abuse written by my enemies." 15 Apr. 1780,
Morris Papers, NYPL. For the plan,
Morris to Deane, 31 Mar. 1780,
Deane Papers, IV, 117, and Deane
to Morris, 17 Apr. 1780, *ibid.,* IV,
124. Also, 126-27. For Deane in
France, Deane to Morris, 2 Sept.
1780, *ibid.,* IV, 213-18. Morris to
Deane, 3 July 1780, *ibid.,* IV, 173-
74. Also *ibid.,* IV, 400-02. When
Morris later received letters from
Deane where the latter clearly indicated that he was wavering with
respect to the Revolutionary cause,
Morris immediately turned the let-
ters over to Congress.

25. Morris to [?], 4 Nov. 1779, Dreer
    Coll., "Unbound," PHS (copy).
    See also a few Inglis to Morris let-
    ters in the Morris Corresp., LC.
    Agreement between Isaac Hazle-
    hurst and Robert Morris, 30 Oct.
    1780, Richard Ashhurst Coll., PHS.
    Articles of Agreement between Mor-
    ris, Beall and May, Feb. 1780, Mor-
    ris Coll., HL.

26. Braxton Papers, *passim,* PHS. Also
    see bibliographical note. For Ross,
    "Account Book," p. 16, PHS. "In-
    voice Book, 1776-79," pp. 162-63,
    PHS. On one occasion, dishes, leath-
    er stirrups, bridles, etc., were sent
    from England on account of Mor-
    ris. "Invoice Book," 30 June 1778.
    It was for personal use, for the
    purchase only amounted to 845
    livre. It is not stated whether Mor-
    ris authorized a purchase in this
    manner. For privateers, Morris to
    Bingham, 1 Oct. 1778 and 14 Dec.
    1778, Morris Corresp., LC. Charles
    I. Landis (ed.), "Letters of Col.
    Matthias Slough to Robert Morris"
    in *Lancaster County Historical So-
    ciety Papers,* XXIV, 59-65. Also
    Morris to William Heyshaw, 18
    June 1779, Morris Coll., PA. Morris
    to Thomas Mumford, 29 June 1779,
    Morris Papers, NYPL. Also Morris
    to Mumford, 17 and 25 Apr. 1780,
    and 1 Feb. 1781, *ibid.* For Russell,

Morris to Bingham, 10 Apr. 1779, Morris Corresp., LC (copy). Morris to Bradford, 9 Jan. 1778, Morris Coll., PA. Morris was interested in shipping to Sweden. This list could easily be extended, but with little profit. For example, Morris was connected with Juan de Miralles, Spanish observer in the United States, in some shipping, but its extent is indeterminable.

27. Morris to John Rowe of Boston, 10 July 1778, Holker Papers, XL, 7738 (copied extract).

28. Morris to Matthew Ridley, 6 Feb. 1781, Ridley Papers, Massachusetts Historical Society (hereafter cited as MHS).

29. Thomas Willing to Thomas Willing in London, 1 Mar. 1756, Willing Letterbook, PHS. Again and again one reads comments such as that of Matthias Slough: "Perhaps our friend Mr. Morris would be concerned in a scheme of this kind." Slough to Holker, 23 Mar. 1781, Holker Papers, LC.

30. This is a composite judgment, but see individual items such as "Anecdote of Richard Peters," undated, Peters Papers, PHS. Charles Thomson to Mrs. Robert Morris, 24 Dec. 1817, Letters of Charles Thomson, PHS. See also Redwood Fisher, *Revolutionary Reminiscences Connected with the Life of Robert Morris*. [?] to Morris, Nov. 1777, Pemberton Papers, PHS. It is interesting to see Deane criticizing Morris for asserting that the measures taken by Congress were meant by its members for the best even though he (Morris) apparently disagreed with their solution. Deane to R. Morris, 15 Apr. 1780, York, Morris Coll., NYPL.

31. Quote comes from Morris to Hudson, 9 Apr. 1779, Morris Papers, PA. Morris to Harrison, 29 Dec. 1776, *Am. Archives*, 5 Series III, 1472 (this is Harrison, Sr.).

32. Charles H. Hart, "Mary White—Mrs. Robert Morris," *PMHB*, II, 158 (entire article 157-84). Jay to Morris, 26 Dec. 1777, Morris Corresp., LC. Charles Hart, "Mary White," *PMHB*, II, 162. Mary Morris wrote very well for a young lady

of the Revolutionary generation. The existing letters are concentrated in the Ridley Papers, *MHS*, and the Morris Coll., HL. There is also an interesting copy of what is supposed to be an autobiographical fragment of Mary Morris in the Edward C. Gardiner Coll., Misc., *PHS*. It was probably written before she married.

33. Mary Morris to her mother, 14 Apr. 1777, quoted in Hart, "Mary White," *PMHB*, II, 161.

34. See Mary Morris to Kitty Livingston, [?] 1780, Ridley Papers, MHS, or Mary Morris' letter of 16 Jan. 1781, in the same collection. Morris to Peters, 27 Dec. 1777, Peters Papers, PHS. The quote comes from Jay to Kitty Livingston, 18 Sept. 1780, in H. P. Johnston (ed.), *Correspondence and Public Papers of John Jay* (4 vols.; New York, 1890-93), I, 409-10. There are a series of letters in the Ridley Collection which show the close friendship between the Jays and the Morrises and to some extent the Livingstons. The beautiful Mrs. Jay was Kitty Livingston's sister. Morris wrote on one occasion to Kitty: "We have travelled your journey with you, sometimes laughing, sometimes fretting at the route to Brunswick, and sometimes pitying and blaming the G——l." 6 May 1780, Ridley Papers, MHS. Jay's attachment to Morris was strong. "I am content to go on writing two or three for one [letters], but really you must let us hear sometimes of you and Mrs. Morris. There are some hearts which, like feathers, stick to everything they touch, and quit each with equal ease. Mine is not one of this kind; it adheres to few, but it takes strong hold; you must therefore, write to me. . . ." 19 Nov. 1780, Johnston, *Corresp. of Jay*, I, 446.

35. For the greatest accuracy, it is necessary to confine this analysis of Morris' ideas to the period before his entrance into the Office of Finance in order to determine what "intellectual baggage" he carried with him into the Office. Thus the

limits of this analysis are based on materials in the years 1776-81. Perhaps Morris held to an idea which he expressed, say, in 1770 without any change, but it would be foolish merely to assume so. Morris' ideas on questions while Financier are considered in later chapters.

36. Morris to [Wm. Hooper], 18 Jan. 1777, Philadelphia, Morris *MSS*, Misc., PHS.

37. Morris to Deane, 29 June 1777, *Deane Papers*, II, 82. Morris to Stacey Hepburn, 12 May 1779, Society Coll., PHS. Morris to Bingham, 14 Sept. 1776, Morris Corresp., LC.

38. Morris to (Necker), Morris Coll., 15 June 1781, PA. (In Morris' handwriting). "An Address to Citizens of the State," read on 10 Apr. 1781, Morris Corresp., LC. It is not clear whether Morris delivered it, however.

39. On nature of God, Morris to [Hooper], 18 Jan. 1777, Morris *MSS*, Misc., PHS. Also Morris to Kitty Livingston, 6 May and 17 Oct. 1780, Ridley Papers, MHS. Harold W. Thatcher, The Social Philosophy of William Livingston, (unpublished Doctoral Dissertation for the Department of History, University of Chicago, 1935), p. 217. For quote, Morris to Hepburn, 23 Sept. 1779, Society Coll., PHS. For liberty, see Section II of Chapter One on Declaration of Independence. For quote on property, Morris to Deane, 7 June 1781, *Deane Papers*, IV, 402.

40. Morris to Jay, 23 Sept. 1776, Johnston, *Corresp. of Jay*, I, 85.

41. Morris to (Hooper), 18 Jan. 1777, Morris *MSS*, Misc., PHS.

CHAPTER THREE

1. *Journals, passim* (1781). 5 Burnett *passim*. Paine's *The Crisis Extraordinary* was published 4 Oct. 1780. Although he was no longer an integral part of Congress, Tom Paine was still closely associated with official proceedings.

2. Although modern scholars have changed their point of view with regard to some important phases of Revolutionary finance—for example, the role of paper money—this summary owes a great debt to those scholars who have pioneered in the study of American finances in this period. Among the most significant are: Charles Bullock, *The Finances of the United States from 1775 to 1789, with Especial Reference to the Budget* (Madison, Wisconsin, 1895); W. G. Sumner, *The Financier and Finances of the American Revolution* (2 vols.; New York, 1891); Albert S. Bolles, *The Financial History of the United States from 1774 to 1789* (New York, 1884). Much of their work, of necessity, was based upon the volumes of the *American State Papers* relating to finance, a source work of importance. The *Journals of the Continental Congress* and E. C. Burnett's *Letters of Members of the Continental Congress*, both cited previously, are essential modern works. It seems unnecessary to note in detail the numerous lesser works which have contributed useful information respecting the national finances in the period from 1775 to 1780.

3. For the first emissions, *Journals*, II, 103 (22 June 1775). *Ibid.*, II, 207-8 (25 July 1775). *ibid.*, III, 390 (29 Nov. 1775). For summary of emissions, Bullock, *Finances of the United States from 1775 to 1789*, p. 135.

4. For first certificates, *Journals*, V, 845-46 (3 Oct. 1776).

5. See Bullock, *Finances of the United States*, pp. 143-44.

6. For a summary and analysis of all the intricate maneuverings with relation to finance in foreign affairs, see Samuel F. Bemis, *The Diplomacy of the American Revolution* (New York and London, 1935), pp. 87-93.

38-48

7. For first requisitions, *Journals*, IX, 955-56 (22 Nov. 1777).

8. The summary figures have been taken, for the most part, from Bullock, *Finances of the United States*, whose calculations are based on an examination of the volumes on finance in the *American State Papers*. For foreign loans, Bullock, p. 147; for requisitions, *ibid.*, p. 163; for domestic loans, loan office certificates, p. 143; for domestic loans, other certificates, Morris to the President of Congress, 29 July 1782, 5 Wharton 625-26; for bills of credit, Bullock, p. 136.

On domestic loans, there is some discrepancy between the figure given by Bullock and the one included in the text. The difference does not arise over loan office certificates, but rather over the other certificates such as commissary and quartermaster certificates. The figure noted by Bullock—$16,000,000 —is based on Hamilton's later estimate and includes the entire period up to 1789. The figure taken for this summary as the more accurate for the period up to 1781—approximately $8,000,000 — is that presented by Morris to Congress in 1782. It was based on the best available estimates at the time. This $8,000,000 plus the $11,000,000 in loan office certificates amounts to approximately $20,000,000.

Another way to determine the importance of the bills of credit is to compare the figure which Bullock gives as the total cost of the war from 1775 to January 1781—$52,000,000—with the total amount of bills of credit—$37,000,000. This comparison also demonstrates that the Americans supported a larger burden of the war's expenditures than many historians have noted.

9. Anne Bezanson, *Prices and Inflation during the American Revolution: Pennsylvania* (Philadelphia, 1951). The entire book is essential, but see particularly Chaps. i-iv, xviii-xix. There are many accounts of these meetings on price control, but see R. B. Morris, *Government and Labor in Early America* (New York,

1946), pp. 92-135, or a more general account in John C. Miller, *The Triumph of Freedom* (Boston, 1948), pp. 440-46.

10. *Journals*, XVI, 262-67 (18 Mar. 1780).

11. Bullock, *Finances of the United States*, pp. 142-43. Albert S. Bolles, *Financial History*, pp. 259-64. These volumes are disappointing with respect to these certificates. An adequate knowledge can be obtained only in working through the correspondence of the period and the Congressional reports of the period.

12. For requisitions, see Bullock's summary, *Finances of the United States*, p. 163. Vergennes to Luzerne, 14 Feb. 1781, 4 Wharton 256.

13. For a summary of the states, Allan Nevins, *The American States During and After the Revolution, 1775-1789* (New York, 1924), pp. 478-515.

14. Reed to Washington, 24 Apr. 1781, *Penn. Archives*, 1st Series, IX, 99.

15. Lloyd A. Brown and Howard H. Peckham (eds.), *Revolutionary War Journals of Henry Dearborn, 1775-83* (Chicago, 1939), pp. 209-10. Hereafter cited as Dearborn, *Journals*. Pickering to President of Congress, 30 Oct. 1780, Pickering Letterbook, National Archives. See bibliographical note on this entire twelve volume set of manuscript letterbooks. National Archives will be cited hereafter as NA. First quote, Heath to Washington, 24 Oct. 1780, Heath Papers, published in Mass. Hist. Soc. *Collections*, Series 7, V, 117. There is a vast amount of important material in the Heath MSS which is not included in these published volumes. Second quote, Heath to Washington, 9 Dec. 1780, *ibid.*, 140. Washington to Governor George Clinton, 27 Nov. 1780, printed in John C. Fitzpatrick (ed.), *The Writings of George Washington . . .* (39 vols.; Washington, D. C., 1931-44), XX, 413. Hereafter this will be cited as follows: (volume) Fitzpatrick (page). James Thatcher, *A Military Journal During the American Revolutionary*

48-51

War (Boston, 1823), p. 242. See also Samuel Parsons to Jeremiah Wadsworth, 14 Jan. 1781, printed in Charles Hall, *Life and Letters of Samuel Holden Parsons* (Binghamton, N. Y., 1905), pp. 321-22. Also the comments on the army by a British informer, *New York Colonial Documents*, VIII, 804-08. Thomas Boyd, *Mad Anthony Wayne* (New York, 1929), pp. 173-74. The quote, which is an excerpt of a letter to Joseph Reed, is on p. 173. There was no danger, however, that the troops would desert to the British in any large numbers. Stories that Philadelphia was having a gay time might have influenced the soldiers; at least Heath thought so. William Abbatt (ed.), *Memoirs of Major General Heath* (New York, 1901), Entry of 11 Jan. 1781. Washington to Gouverneur Morris, 10 Dec. 1780, 20 Fitzpatrick 458. Also to Jonathan Trumbull, 19 Dec. 1780, *ibid.*, 495.

16. Daniel Brodhead to Richard Peters, 22 Jan. 1781, Cont. Cong. Papers 148, I, 317-19. Greene to Washington, 7 Dec. 1780, printed in Sparks, *Corresp. of the Am. Rev.* III, 166. Gates to the Board of War, 12 Nov. 1780, Gates Letterbook (Box 19d), Gates Papers, NYHS.

17. Pickering to Charles Pettit, 1 Dec. 1780, Cont. Cong. Papers 148, I, 257-60, LC. The first quote is on p. 257, the second on p. 260. This letter is included in that of Charles Pettit to the Board of Treasury, 9 Dec. 1780, p. 249 of the same volume.

18. Germain to Clinton, 7 Feb. 1781, Whitehall, "American Dispatches," Shelburne Papers, Clements Library (extract).

19. Peletiah Webster, *Political Essays on the Nature and Operation of Money, Public Finances, and Other Subjects* (Philadelphia, 1791), p. 50.

20. The most powerful and readable presentation of this impact is in John C. Miller, *The Triumph of Freedom*, Chap. xxii. Although the book is not specifically documented, it is based on a very broad and judicious reading of the literature of the period.

21. Anne Bezanson, *Prices and Inflation*, p. 321. The material that follows has been carefully documented for two reasons: one, the analysis presented here for the general economic situation in 1780-81 does not agree completely with views of every other scholar; and two, it is absolutely essential that a base be established from which economic trends can be traced, so that the interaction between the Morris program and the economic developments can be properly analyzed.

22. H. J. Carman (ed.), *American Husbandry* (New York, 1939), Chaps. v, vi, viii, and particularly pp. 37-42. Also Percy W. Bidwell and John I. Falconer, *History of Agriculture in the Northern States, 1620-1860* (Reprint; New York, 1941), pp. 84-132. As late as the turn of the century, the prominent theme was self-sufficiency. P. W. Bidwell, "Rural Economy in New England at the Beginning of the 19th Century" in *Transactions* of Connecticut Academy of Arts and Sciences, XX, 354-67. For export, Carman, *American Husbandry*, pp. 44-45. Also Bidwell and Falconer, *Agriculture in Northern States*, p. 135. For observations of cattle drives, Marquis de Chastellux, *Travels in North America in the years 1780, 1781, and 1782* (2 vols.; Dublin, 1787), I, 58 ff., also 39-40. Charles J. Taylor, *History of Great Barrington, Massachusetts* (Great Barrington, 1882), p. 262. Daniel Parker Letterbook, Baker Library, *passim*. Robert East, *Business Enterprise*, pp. 88-94. For lack of agrarian complaint, Ralph Harlow, "Economic Conditions in Massachusetts, 1775-83" in Colonial Society of Massachusetts *Collections*, XX, 176-77. My conclusion differs slightly from that of the article. Also Chastellux, *Travels*, I, *passim*, and W. Duane and T. Balch (eds.), *The Journal of Claude Blanchard* (Albany, 1876), pp. 41-85, *passim*. Lee Newcomer in his study "Central and Western Massachusetts during the Revolution" supports the general conclusion of agricultural prosperity up to 1781. (Dissertation to

be published, Columbia, 1949), pp. 193-207, *passim*.

23. E. R. Johnson (et al), *History of Domestic and Foreign Commerce* (2 vols.; Washington, D. C., 1915), I, 169-71. William B. Weeden, *Economic and Social History of New England* (2 vols.; Boston and New York, 1894), II, 782. Raymond McFarland, *A History of New England Fisheries* (New York, 1911), p. 121. For a chart on the extent of pre-Revolutionary cod fisheries (by all odds the most important), see Lorenzo Sabine, *Report of the Principal Fisheries of the American Seas,* Exec. Doc. 23, 32nd Congress, 2nd Session, p. 350. For shipbuilding, Johnson, *Domestic and Foreign Commerce,* I, 125. R. F. Upton, *Revolutionary New Hampshire* (Hanover, New Hampshire, 1936), p. 150. Edgar S. McClay, *A History of American Privateers* (New York and London, 1924), traces origins of this war commerce, pp. 3-42. As does Weeden, *Economic and Social History,* II, 598-605, 655-64.

24. Whipple to Josiah Bartlett, 12 July 1778, *Historical Magazine,* VI, 74-75. *Rhode Island Colonial Records,* IX, 144. C. F. Adams (ed.), *Familiar Letters of John Adams and His Wife Abigail Adams* (New York, 1918), p. 320. These quotes could be multiplied many times. See Gardner W. Allen, *Massachusetts Privateers of the Revolution* (Boston, 1927), Introduction. "The Privateer General Sullivan" in *New England Historical and Genealogical Register,* XXIII, 291. For *Brutus,* William Knox to Henry Knox, 26 June 1781, Knox Papers, MHS.

25. The fact that the number of privateers increased in 1781 and decreased in 1782 in itself suggests that 1780 was a peak year for profits. McClay, *History of Privateers,* p. 113. For various fragments of New England privateering story see the following: O. T. Howe, "Beverly Privateers in the American Revolution," in Col. Soc. of Mass. *Collections,* XXIV, 421-3. Note that the ship tonnage of Beverly was greater in 1780 than 1772, p. 320,

p. 422. Robert E. Peabody, *Merchant Ventures of Old Salem* (Boston and New York, 1912), p. 48. Also, Peabody, "The Derbys of Salem" in *Essex Institute Collections,* XLIV, 217, says Derby begins withdrawing in 1780-81. Thomas S. Collier, "Revolutionary Privateers of Connecticut" in *New London County Historical Society Records,* I, Part iv, 9-26. A vast amount of information about Connecticut privateers is scattered through Louis F. Middlebrook, *Maritime Connecticut in Revolutionary Times* (2 vols.; Salem, Massachusetts, 1925), but it is not presented in usable form. Rhode Island seems to be an exception to the general trend. W. R. Sheffield, *Privateersman of Newport* (Newport, 1883), pp. 58-63. However, W. B. Weeden in *Early Rhode Island* (New York, 1910), says that "Revolutionary commerce had assumed large proportions" in 1779-80, although he concludes that the main current of business was injured. Chastellux and his translator both comment favorably on Providence trade. *Travels,* I, 8. For privateers sent out, see the following: According to Justin Winsor (ed.), *Memorial History . . .* (4 vols.; Boston, 1880-81), III, 118, Boston sent out 365. Freeman Hunt, "Elias Hasket Derby," in *Lives of American Merchants* (2 vols.; New York, 1856), II, claims 158 were fitted out from Salem with 445 captures. He probably secured his data from Joseph B. Felt, *Annals of Salem* (2 vols.; Salem, 1845), II, 277, where it is given as an approximate figure. For Beverly, Howe, "Beverly Privateers," pp. 405 ff. Governor Robertson of New York in writing to Germain testified as to the effectiveness of American privateers about 1780. *N. Y. Col. Doc.,* VIII, 811. See also the reactions of Parliament in *Parliamentary History of England,* XIX, 710 ff.

My compilation of numbers of men involved was made from Gardner W. Allen's excellent *Massachusetts Privateers of the Revolution.* Caution was exercised by the pres-

51-54

ent writer to eliminate double
counting—that is, ships which made
several voyages during the year
were, of course, only counted once.
For figures on population, see E. B.
Greene and Virginia Harrington,
*American Population Before . . .
1790* (New York, 1932), pp. 31-40.
The year used in making my esti-
mate was 1777. The ten ports used
were: Boston, Salem, Beverly, Mar-
blehead, Newburyport, Plymouth,
Gloucester, Ipswich, Yarmouth, and
Chatham. For arms quota, Acts
and Laws of Massachusetts, October
Session, 1780, chapter 104, passed 2
Dec. 1780, in *Acts and Laws of the
Commonwealth of Massachusetts*
(Boston, 1890).

Freeman Hunt, *Lives of American
Merchants*, II, 50, estimates that
at least 6,000 men sailed from Salem
and 30,000 from Massachusetts during the War. Chastellux finds the
fishing industry declining in Ipswich in later years, but says seamen turned to farming because of
the plentiful pasturage. He states:
"They have no want of subsistence,
which may account likewise for the
very considerable population. . . ."
Travels, II, 250-51.

26. Williams quoted in James D. Phillips, *Salem in the Eighteenth Century* (Boston and New York, 1937),
p. 426. This volume is one of the
best town histories for New England. Chastellux, *Travels*, II, 249,
252, 255. Data for Salem confirms
these observations. Felt, *Annals of
Salem*, I, 426. Chastellux, *Travels*,
II, 257 ff., 244 ff. Eliot to Jeremy
Belknap, 29 Mar. (1780), Mass.
Hist. Soc. *Collections*, Series 6, IV,
177, 184. Claude Blanchard, French
Commissary, recorded in his *Journal*, "The people [of Boston] seemed
to be in easy circumstances" though
he thought the shops "poorly
stocked" and the concentration of
prayerbooks at the bookstores dis-
maying, p. 51. For instructions, *Boston Town Records*, XXVI, 214. The
instructions also show that the citizens of Boston fully realized that
privateering was a temporary expedient and that they must look
to normal channels of trade and

fisheries for enduring commercial
success.

27. For commerce see the following:
Edward Channing, "Commerce dur-
ing the Revolutionary Epoch" in
Mass. Hist. Soc. *Proceedings*, XLIV,
369-74. East, *Business Enterprise*,
Chapters iii, iv. "Commerce of
Rhode Island" in Mass. Hist. Soc.
Collections, Series 7, X, 83-129,
passim. Notice the list of goods
p. 100. Kenneth Porter, *The Jacksons and the Lees* (2 vols.; Cambridge, Mass., 1937), I, 340-46. J.
F. Jameson, "St. Eustatius in the
American Revolution" in *Amer.
Hist. Rev.*, VIII, 685-86, 699-701.
When the island was captured, the
richness of the trade was clearly
revealed. Gaston Martin, ". . .
Nantes and the American Colonies"
in *Journal of Economic and Business History*, IV, 828. Meredith,
Jonathan Amory, passim. Jarvis of
Newburyport was astonished at the
amount of trade between his section of the state and Spain. Jarvis
to [?], 12 Feb. 1781, Boston Merchants in the Revolution, Boston
Public Library. See MSS sources in
Footnote 25. For the vigorous trade
of certain mercantile families,
Hedges, *Browns of Providence*, 240-
86.

J. Scallany in writing to Sam Adams
lamented that the days of the
"Bradfords, Winslows, and Win-
throps" had passed. "As to balls
and assemblys and public amuse-
ments I think with you that they
ought to be discontinued by every
virtuous community. . . . It is with
grief of heart that I see vice so
prevalent in this town especially
among the common people." 17 Jan.
1781, Boston, Adams Papers, NYPL.

28. Commerce of Rhode Island MSS
and Caleb Davis Papers in MHS.
Amory Papers, Codman and Smith
Letterbook, and Autograph Letters
of Boston Merchants in the Baker
Library. The papers at the Essex
Institute are not too helpful in
this regard. One Bostonian remarked, "Had I employed my
money in trade instead of advancing of it to procure supplies for
the army, I should have made my

fortune. Instead of that my family are suffering for want of many necessaries; while I behold the scum of the creation riding in state." Thomas Chase to Samuel Adams, 26 Jan. 1781, Boston, Samuel Adams Papers, NYPL.

29. The recovery of Newport is implicit in Mary E. Loughrey, *France and Rhode Island, 1636-1800* (New York, 1944), pp. 26-31. Also "French in Rhode Island" in *Magazine of American History*, III, 393-418. Note quoted description of Newport, p. 403. Blanchard does not mention any striking destruction. *Journal*, pp. 41-55, *passim*. Nor does De Fersen, an aide to Rochambeau. "Letters," in *Mag. of Am. Hist.*, III, 300 ff. For collapse of shipbuilding, S. E. Morison, *The Maritime History of Massachusetts, 1783-1860* (Boston and New York, 1921), p. 29. For domestic manufactures, Weeden, *Economic and Social History*, II, 789-94.

30. Samuel Cooper, *A Sermon preached before his Excellency John Hancock . . . 25 Oct. 1780*, p. 3. Psalm 65.

31. The favorable harvests are generally known, but see *Journals of the Cont. Cong.*, XIV, 953-54. John Cadwallader could write in the *Penn. Packet and General Advertiser* on 31 July 1779, that "a plentiful harvest has filled the country with an abundance of those articles." Though the extreme cold in the winter of 1779-80 and the late spring which followed threatened the crops, all turned out well. The county histories indicate this as well as other materials. See particularly, I. D. Rupp (comp.), *History and Topography of Northumberland, Huntingdon, Mifflin, Centre, Union, . . . Counties, Pennsylvania* (Lancaster, Penn. 1847), pp. 139-40. See also "John Hunt's Diary" in New Jersey Historical Society *Proceedings*, LIII, 27 Apr. (1781). For the favorable upturn in prices of agricultural goods after 1778, see Anne Bezanson's indispensable *Prices and Inflation*, pp. 20-21, 84-93, 323. Embargo lifted in New York, 21 Sept. 1780, but there are

signs that considerable trading preceded the actual passage of the law. *Laws of NY*, 4 Session, Chap. ii. When complaints were heard that produce taken for the use of the army was paid far below current prices, the legislature responded with a law which compelled payment according to current prices. *Laws of NY*, 3 Session, Chap. xv (13 Oct. 1779). See also the act of the Penn. legislature printed in the *Penn. Packet*, 20 Apr. 1779.

On money notice the following. Repeal of such legal tender laws did not come until the spring of 1781. *Laws of NY*, 4 Session, Chap. lviii (1 July 1781). *Penn. Journals*, 21 June 1781. For payment of taxes in Continental currency, *Laws of NY*, 2 Session, Chap. xvi (2 Mar. 1779). For implementation of the laws, see the newspapers advertising goods and land for cash, loan office certificates, or continental currency. *Penn. Packet, passim*. Also *NY Packet and the General Adv (Poughkeepsie)*. This kind of advertisement tends to decrease towards the latter part of 1780. Also see the receipts signed by Gerard Bancker for lands sold to Duer, unquestionably in state currency. Morris Papers, NYPL.

32. Virginia Harrington, *The New York Merchant on the Eve of the Revolution* (New York, 1935) does not mention extensive agricultural imports, pp. 172 ff., *passim*. Also see Carman, *American Husbandry*, pp. 70-153. For self-sufficiency, Bidwell and Falconer, *History of Agriculture*, pp. 123-25. For goods, see Channing, "Commerce during the Revolutionary Epoch," p. 376. The cry of luxurious living was raised in New Jersey as well as New England. See William W. Scott, *History of Passaic and its Environs* (3 vols.; New York and Chicago, 1922), I, 240. For imports of New York City, see tables from David MacPherson, *Annals of Commerce*, in Rolla M. Tryon, *Household Manufactures in the United States, 1640-1860* (Chicago, 1917), pp. 58-59.

33. See particularly, Otto Hufeland, *Westchester County during the Re-*

54-56

volution, 1775-83 (Privately Printed, 1926), Chaps. ix-xii. 20 Fitzpatrick 409. As Philip H. Smith, in his *General History of Dutchess County* (Rawlings, New York, 1877), says in discussing the little village of Amenia, it was "singularly free from any disturbance. The people here it is said, heard the sound of the cannon at the battle of Long Island, and they saw the smoke of burning Kingston; but it 'did not come nigh unto them'." (p. 122). George R. Howell and Jonathan Tenny, *History of Albany County, 1609-1886* (New York, 1886), p. 327. See *NY Col. Doc.*, VIII, 797. Also, *The American Revolution in New York* (Albany, 1926), pp. 169-71.

34. Raids after 1779 into New Jersey were infrequent, and those that occurred (like that of General Knyphausen) were undertaken because they thought loyalists would flock to their banners. Even in the raid of Knyphausen less than 100 Americans were involved. William Nelson (ed.), *The New Jersey Coast in Three Centuries* (New York and Chicago, 1902), p. 176. When incidents in a county as close to the British as Bergen are isolated, little real devastation occurred. W. Woodford Clayton and William Nelson, *History of Bergen and Passaic Counties, New Jersey* . . . (Philadelphia, 1882), pp. 73-74. As county historian, Honeyman is forced to say about northwestern New Jersey, "Actual battles were hardly fought on the soil of the counties, but decisive battles of war were fought out on its borders. . . ." A. Van Doren Honeyman (ed.), *Northwestern New Jersey* . . . (4 vols.; New York and Chicago, 1927), I, 115.

35. For Philadelphia, see J. Thomas Scharf and Thomas Wescott, *History of Philadelphia* (3 vols.; Philadelphia, 1884), I, 384, for a list of claims for damages. See J. Smith Futhey and Gilbert Cope, *History of Chester County, Pennsylvania* (Philadelphia, 1881), pp. 104-08, for claim lists from that county. They total something like $100,000

in the latter. See also Chastellux, *Travels*, I, 174, 176. The historian of Northampton County might well speak for the rest of Pennsylvania. "Northampton's soil had never felt a hostile tread, other than that of the stealthy savage, nor shook under the tramp of an army except that of Sullivan. But her record was a good and creditable one; her people . . . cheerful in patriotic sacrifices." Capt. F. Ellis, *History of Northampton County, Pennsylvania* (Philadelphia and Reading, 1877), p. 72. On market in Philadelphia during the occupation, see Joseph Borden to Robert Morris, 26 Jan. 1778, Bordentown, Morris Corresp., LC. Borden wrote: "Enormous quantity of provisions is carried in [to Philadelphia] openly. It is a fact." See also W. Woodford Clayton, *History of Union and Middlesex Counties, New Jersey*, pp. 81-82. This is a good county history. An officer wrote: "Almost open trade is carried on here with the rebels; at least both sides close an eye." Ray W. Pettengill (trans.), *Letters from America, 1776-79* . . . (Boston and New York, 1924), p. 232. "John Hunt's Diary" in NJHS *Proceedings*, LII, 232. Hunt was writing in New Jersey.

36. "Travel Diary of Bishop and Mrs. Reichel and their company . . . in 1780" in Newton D. Mereness (ed.), *Travels in the American Colonies* (New York, 1916), pp. 586-99. Amandus Johnson (trans.), *Journal and Biography of Nicholas Collin* (Philadelphia, 1936), pp. 243-49, 252-56. Also see Chastellux, *Travels*, I, 364, 366 on the state of New York.

37. Leonard Lundin, *Cockpit of the Revolution* (Princeton, 1940), pp. 403-04. East, *Business Enterprise*, p. 149. Peletiah Webster, *Political Essays*, p. 42. Much of my opinion rests on an examination of various merchant papers at the PHS, notably the Hollingsworth Papers, Chaloner and White Papers, Chevalier Papers, and various merchants dealing with Robert Morris (See Chap. ii, Section V). When the economic sky darkened at one time

Sam Hollingsworth stated that "our profits are only nominal." Yet there *were* profits.

38. Hanson (in Philadelphia) to Philip Thomas (in Maryland), 4 Aug. 1780, printed in J. Bruce Kremer, *John Hanson of Mulberry Grove* (New York, 1938), p. 134. See Kathryn Sullivan, *Maryland and France, 1774-89* (Philadelphia, 1936), Chap. iii. This volume also reveals the difficulties involved in the French market. See Holker Papers, LC, *passim* (1780). Examining merchant records reinforces this opinion. When a land office was opened in Virginia they required 40 pounds (apparently Virginia currency) per 100 acres as payment. *Laws of Va.*, General Assembly (beginning 3 May 1779), Chap. xiii. For payment in Treasury certificates, *Laws*, General Assembly (beginning 4 Oct. 1779), Chap. xiv. Tobacco also passed as currency if one wished to use it for this purpose. *Virginia Gazette* (Williamsburg) has advertisements of commodities and land for certificates and currency. For tobacco prices, Bezanson, *Prices and Inflation*, pp. 247-57.

39. For the general story see H. J. Eckenrode, *The Revolution in Virginia* (Boston and New York, 1916), Chap. viii. For indications of plentiful resources in Virginia during 1779 and 1780, see p. 209. County histories of Virginia have been examined for this period, but they yield little of value. The exception is the excellent regional study of Freeman Hart, *The Valley of Virginia in the American Revolution* (Chapel Hill, 1942). For continued crops and success in general during this period, see pp. 4-5. Lewis C. Gray has a chapter on agricultural conditions during this period, but some of its value is lost by merely comparing 1775 with 1783 rather than tracing the actual development. Gray, *History of Agriculture in the Southern United States in 1860* (Reprint: 2 vols.; New York, 1941), II, Chap. xxv.

40. East, *Business Enterprise*, p. 164. See also Woolsey and Salmon Let-

terbook, Sept.-Dec. 1780, *passim*, LC. Also the correspondence of the firm of Ridley and Pringle with Holker, Holker Papers, *passim* (1780), LC. See also Chap. ii, Section I of this book. Bernard C. Steiner, "Maryland Privateers in the American Revolution" in *Maryland Historical Magazine*, III, 101 (entire article, pp. 99-103).

41. For general story on North Carolina, see R. D. W. Conner, *History of North Carolina* (6 vols.; Chicago and New York, 1919), I, 389-475. Little attention is given to the economic affairs of the state, an important fact in itself because signs of distress are seldom unchronicled. None of the county histories speak of want or suffering. See for example, J. K. Turner and J. L. Bridgers, *History of Edgecombe County, North Carolina* (Raleigh, 1920), Chap. iii. Also D. A. Tompkins, *History of Mecklenburg County* (2 vols.; Charlotte, 1903), Chaps. iv, x, xi, xii. Also Clarence W. Griffin, *History of Old Tryon and Rutherford Counties* (Asheville, 1937), pp. 51-52. The excerpts printed in this volume of Lt. Allaire's Diary do not mention any general suffering or want, pp. 75-80. Even the "Revolutionary Incidents" of Rowan county, a section which usually covers the most disastrous events, appear of small moment. Jethro Rumple, *History of Rowan County* (Salisbury, N. Carolina, 1881), pp. 155-68. *The State Records of North Carolina* are very disappointing for information on internal affairs, except the militia. See Vols. XIV, XV. For early commerce, see Robert Mills, *Statistics of South Carolina* (Charleston, 1826), p. 161. I am indebted to Edward McGrady, *The History of South Carolina in the Revolution, 1775-80* (New York, 1901), for much of the detailed background on military movements, but this volume is very disappointing for economic and political matters. A more balanced survey is D. D. Wallace, *History of South Carolina* (4 vols.; New York, 1934), II, 109-307. For the killing off of trade, see Charles Gregg

57-67

Singer's useful monograph, *South Carolina in the Confederation* (Philadelphia, 1941), pp. 13-14. For a contrary view, see Gray, *History of Southern Agriculture*, II, 581. David Ramsay, *History of South Carolina* (2 vols.; Charleston, 1809), I, 318 ff.

42. There is one omission in this analysis, the artisan. Data on this subject is so elusive and fragmentary that it is a special topic in itself. My assumption—and it is subject to criticism—is that the circumstances of the artisan would parallel the economic outlook in general. In this analysis I have also subordinated the well-known spurt in manufacturers for fear of overemphasizing this development. Some may criticize this analysis because it fails to mention the fur trade. In reality, the fur trade was unimportant to the colonial economy at the outbreak of the Revolution. New York may be considered as a possible exception, but even there furs constituted only 2 per cent of that colony's exports in 1775. See Murry G. Lawson, *Fur: A Study in English Mercantilism, 1700-1775* (University of Toronto Studies, History and Economic Series, IX), 70-72.

43. Jennings B. Sanders' essential *Evolution of Executive Departments of the Continental Congress, 1774-89* (Chapel Hill, 1935) tells this story. See especially pp. 3-92.

44. *Ibid.*, 50-74. *Journals*, IV, 156-57 (17 Feb. 1776). *ibid.*, XIV, 903-8 (30 July 1779).

45. *Journals*, XIX 125-28 (7 Feb. 1781). Creation of Executive Departments had been considered very early in the winter of 1776-77. Morris then commented: "I will not enter into any detail of our conduct in Congress, but you may depend on this, that so long as that respectable body persists in the attempt to execute, as well as to deliberate on their business, it never will be done as it ought, and this has been urged many and many a time, by myself and others, but some of them do not like to part with power, or to pay others for doing what they cannot do themselves." Morris to Commissioners at Paris, 21 Dec. 1776, 2 Burnett 184.

46. *Journals*, XIX, 180 (20 Feb. 1781).

47. G. Morris to R. R. Livingston, 14 Mar. 1781, Philadelphia, R. R. Livingston Coll., NYPL. In characteristic vein G. Morris writes: "The contest between the man, the husband the father and the citizen is continual and each by turns predominate. The weight of the office presses sore upon his consideration. I behold him with anxiety about to be sacrificed to the indolence of his sovereign, the prejudices of his fellow citizens, the arduousness of affairs. . . ." For quotes of Robert Morris, Morris to the President of Congress, 13 Mar. 1781, 4 Wharton 298 (entire letter pp. 297-99). Almost all the letters of Morris as Financier which Wharton prints can also be found in Jared Sparks, *Diplomatic Correspondence of the American Revolution* (12 vols.; Boston, 1829-30), XI and XII. Although Wharton is reputed to be much more accurate than Sparks, he omits many of the same passages that Sparks deleted. Sometimes omissions are the result of two different copies of the same letter. In the remainder of this volume Wharton will be cited.

48. Morris to the President of Congress, 13 Mar. 1781, 4 Wharton 298. For charges, see Chap. i, Section IV.

49. *Journals*, XIX, 288-89 (20 Mar. 1781). Adams and Ward of Massachusetts, Huntington and Root of Connecticut, Bland of Virginia, and Sullivan of New Hampshire, voted against giving Morris permission to continue his private business affairs.

50. Morris to President of Congress, 13 Mar. 1781, 4 Wharton 299.

51. Morris to Burke, Houston, and Wolcott (Committee of Congress), 26 Mar. 1781, 4 Wharton 330-33. This letter is in Cont. Cong. Papers, 137, I, 5-7.

52. *Journals*, XIX, 432-33 (21 Apr. 1781), XX, 455-56 (27 Apr. 1781). The vote on these resolutions is not recorded. Morris to President of

Congress, 14 May 1781, 4 Wharton, 412-14.

53. Joseph Jones to Washington, 21 Feb. 1781, 5 Burnett 579. Mrs. John Jay to Mary Morris quoted in *PMHB*, II, 165. Luzerne quoted in W. G. Sumner, *Financier and the Finances of the American Revolution*, I, 262. Washington to John Mathews, 7 June 1781, 22 Fitzpatrick 177. Washington, however, felt that a Minister of War was more essential. Washington to Joseph Jones, 24 Mar. 1781, 21 Fitzpatrick 374.

54. Houston to McKean, 31 Mar. 1781, 6 Burnett 39-40.

55. For Adams' point of view on the entire matter of the Executive Departments, see William V. Wells, *The Life and Public Service of Samuel Adams* (3 vols.; Boston, 1865), III, 128 ff., but especially 130. John Armstrong to General John Armstrong, 10 May 1781, Society Coll., PHS (copy).

56. Franklin to Morris, 26 July 1781, 4 Wharton 605. It is also printed in John Bigelow (ed.), *The Complete Works of Benjamin Franklin* (10 vols.; New York and London, 1887-88), with an additional postscript which indicates that Franklin intended it to be a personal letter. The letter is in reply to Morris' of 6 June 1781 in Franklin Coll., PHS.

57. Morris to Schuyler, 29 May 1781, 4 Wharton 458.

58. Robert Morris' Official Diary, Morris Papers, LC. Hereafter cited as Official Diary. See bibliographical note on this source. For the story of these documents, see Ellis Oberholtzer, *Robert Morris: Patriot and Financier* (New York, 1903), Preface.

59. Morris, in a letter to a Committee of Congress, declared that he was concerned with the easiest means to collect revenue and the most frugal manner of spending it, but this is scarcely enlightening. 26 Mar. 1781, Letterbook A, LC. This Letterbook is one in a series of Letterbooks of the Office of Finance which can be found at the Library of Congress. Hereafter these volumes will be cited merely by the Letterbook.

60. Morris to Necker, 15 June 1781, Morris Coll., PA. This letter is in Morris' handwriting. It is incomplete and probably was never sent.

61. Morris to the President of Congress, 14 May 1781, Letterbook A.

CHAPTER FOUR

1. Proceedings and Observations of Committee of Finance, Nov. 1780, 5 Burnett 464-72. The familiar letter of Hamilton is in Henry Cabot Lodge (ed.), *The Works of Alexander Hamilton* (9 Vols.; New York, 1885-86), III, 82-125. See also 61-82. For Bank of Pennsylvania, *Journals*, XVII, 542, 548-50.

2. The "Plan of the Bank" is in Letterbook A, following Morris' letter to Congress of 17 May 1781. This version correlates with the printed version in 4 Wharton 565-66. However, there is a slight discrepancy between these versions and the copy in Morris' handwriting which was submitted to Congress. The important Article Twelve calling for bank notes is inserted in the margin of the Morris draft. In short, it is possible that this important Article was inserted later. See Cont. Cong. Papers, 137, I, 20-23. Although the help of Gouverneur Morris was enlisted in formulating the bank proposal, the plan was not only written by the Financier, but the style of the document was quite assuredly his own.

3. The quotes come from Morris' "Observations" on the "Plan of the Bank" which follow the plan itself in Letterbook A. The printed version can be located in 4 Wharton, 566-68.

4. These quotes are also found in Morris' "Observations" on the "Plan of the Bank." See preceding footnote.

67-76

5. *Journals*, XX, 545-48 (26 May 1781). 6 Burnett 89-105, *passim*.
6. "To the Public," 28 May 1781, Papers of James Wilson, PHS.
7. The first quote comes from letter of 13 July 1781, printed in 4 Wharton 568-69. The second from a letter of 14 July 1781, *ibid.*, 574.
8. Morris to Jay, 13 July 1781, 4 Wharton 562-63.
9. *Boston Gazette and Country Journal*, 18 June 1781. See also *New York Packet and the American Advertiser*, Fishkill, 14 June 1781. Rendon to De Galvez, 15 July 1781, Sparks Coll., 98, Widener Library.
10. Morris to President of Congress, 21 June 1781, Letterbook A. *Journals*, XX, 688-89 (22 June 1781). The Bank of Pennsylvania had been organized in 1780 to purchase foodstuffs for the army.
11. The whole series of letters dealing with this incident are in Letterbook A. Morris to the Governor of Havana, Morris to Captain James Nicholson, and Morris to Robert Smith, all dated 17 July 1781. Also Morris to Robert Smith, 21 July 1781. Jay, America's minister to Spain, was informed of the plan. Morris to Jay, 29 July 1781, Letterbook A. In May, Morris had requested a wide latitude in importing and exporting money, but there is some question whether or not he received it. See Morris to the President of Congress, 23 May 1781, *ibid.* Also *Journals*, XX, 548 (26 May 1781). For quote, Morris to Gates, 15 Sept. 1781, Philadelphia, Gates Papers, NYHS.
12. Morris to Jay, 4 July 1781, 4 Wharton 531-39. For the quote, Morris to Jay, 7 July 1781, *ibid.*, 552.
13. For the strength of his feelings, see Morris to Washington, 15 June 1781, 4 Wharton 505-06. General Irvine to General Wayne, 6 June 1781, Wayne Papers, PHS. By taking the oath of office as Superintendent of Finance, Morris would have been automatically disqualified to sit in the Pennsylvania Assembly.
14. *Journals of the Penn. Assembly*, 680 (25 June 1781). Morris was authorized to draw up to 500,000 pounds (Penn. currency). The only

exception to the warrants of Morris was the 30,000 pounds provided for the President of the Executive Council for exigencies. For Morris' letter of acceptance, *ibid.*, 681 (26 June 1781). For funding measure of March 18, 1780, see discussion in Chap. iii, Section I.

15. Morris to President of the Executive Council, 9 July and 14 July 1781, Morris Papers, PA. The story can be followed pretty well in letters between Morris and the Executive Council which are printed in the *Penn. Archives*, Series 1, IX, 244-45, 250-51, 262-63, 264-65.
16. For the most complete account, Morris to Franklin, 21 July 1781, 4 Wharton 598-600. For Reed's comments, Reed to Morris, 27 July 1781, printed in *Penn. Archives*, Series 1, IX, 312. Morris to Franklin, 28 Aug. 1781, 4 Wharton 666.
17. Morris to the President of Penn., 23 Aug. 1781, Letterbook A. For comment on bills, Morris to the Governor of Md., 28 Aug. 1781, 4 Wharton 678.
18. For the quote, Reed to [?], Militia Hdqts., Trenton, 25 Aug. 1780, Reed Papers, VIII, NYHS. For the general story: Morris to the President of Penn., 12 Sept. 1781, Letterbook A. President Reed to Morris, 20 Sept. 1781, and Morris' reply on the same date printed in *Penn. Archives*, IX, 414. Morris was asked to take charge of contracting for the militia, however. Reed to Morris, 22 Sept. 1781, *ibid.*, 417. For implementation, see Morris to President of Penn., 24 Sept. 1781, Letterbook A. For Morris' continual pressure to dismiss the militia, 1 Oct. 1781, Letterbook B. For warrants to pay engagements, see Morris to the President of Penn., 10 Oct. 1781, *ibid.*, and Morris to the Vice-President of Penn., 10 Nov. 1781, *ibid.*
19. The settlement of the accounts on specific supplies for 1781 carried over into 1782. See Morris to President of Penn., 9 Feb. 1782, Letterbook B. Morris to the Comptroller 28 Feb. 1782, Letterbook C. Morris to the Quartermaster General, 7 Mar. 1782, *ibid.* Morris to the Presi-

dent of Penn., 8 May 1782, *ibid.*
Morris actually submitted his accounts in November of 1782. Morris to the President of Penn., 9 Nov. 1782, Letterbook D. Also Morris to the Comptroller of the Treasury, 3 Dec. 1782, *ibid.*

20. *Journals*, XIX, 127-28 (7 Feb. 1781). *Journals*, XXI, 943 (7 Sept. 1781). For McDougall, see Charles O. Paullin, *The Navy of the American Revolution* (Cleveland, 1906), pp. 217-18. This little volume is still very useful for the administrative side of naval affairs during the Revolutionary period.

21. For Morris' acceptance, Morris to the President of Congress, 8 Sept. 1781, Letterbook A. For Morris' actions: Morris to Navy Board, 4 Aug. 1781, *ibid.* Morris to the Governor of Mass., 4 Aug. 1781, *ibid.* Paullin, *The Navy of the Am. Rev.*, p. 220. For quote, Morris to the President of Congress, 10 Sept. 1781, Letterbook A. *Journals,* XXI, 953 (12 Sept. 1781).

22. The Letterbooks "A" and "B" are sprinkled with these orders. For the most important, see the elaborate instructions to John Brown, 19 Sept. 1781, Letterbook A. Also to Governor of Mass., 21 Sept. 1781, *ibid.* Morris to Barry, 21 Sept. 1781, *ibid.* Barry did not go out as soon as Morris expected, however. Morris to Barry, 17 Oct. 1781, Letterbook B. For accounts, Morris to Bradford, 21 and 22 Sept. 1781, Letterbook A. Also, Morris to Warren and Vernon, 21 Sept. 1781, *ibid.* For troubles, Morris to John Brown, 14 Nov. 1781, Letterbook B.

23. There is an Agent of the Marine Letterbook but it does not become useful until 1782. See bibliographical note.

24. Morris to the President of Congress, 14 May 1781, Letterbook A. Official Diary, 18 May 1781.

25. David Duncan to Colonel Blaine, 5 May 1781, Ephraim Blaine Papers, III, LC. Washington to President of Congress, 8 May 1781, 22 Fitzpatrick 60-61. Washington to General Heath, 9 May 1781, *ibid.*, 64.

26. *Journals*, XX, 555-56 (28 May 1781).

Morris to Sullivan, Houston, and Mathews, 29 May 1781, Letterbook A. Morris to Thomas Lowrey, 29 May 1781, *ibid.* Morris to Schuyler, 29 May 1781, *ibid.* Morris to Washington, 29 May 1781, *ibid.*

27. Official Diary, 31 July 1781, also 7 Aug. 1781. Morris and Peters to Washington, 13 Aug. 1781, Letterbook A. Washington to Morris, 17 Aug. 1781, 23 Fitzpatrick 11-12.

28. Morris to Matthew Ridley, 21 Aug. 1781, Letterbook A. Morris to Ridley, 28 Aug., and Morris to Donaldson Yeates, 28 Aug. 1781, *ibid.*

29. Morris to Ridley, 27 Aug. 1781, Letterbook A.

30. Morris to Governor of Md., 21 Aug. 1781, Letterbook A. Morris to Governor of Del., 26 Aug. 1781, *ibid.* Morris to James Calhoun (Agent of Maryland), 28 Aug. 1781, *ibid.* Morris to Governor of Del., 1 Sept. 1781, *ibid.* Morris to Stephen Stewart, Jonathan Hudson, David Stewart, and Smith, 28 Aug. 1781, *ibid.*

31. Morris to Luzerne, 2 Aug. and 4 Aug. 1781, Letterbook A. Official Diary, 7 and 21 Aug. 1781.

32. Official Diary, 30 and 31 Aug. 1781. *Ibid.,* 7 and 21 Aug. 1781. For quote, *ibid.,* 1-5 Sept. 1781. Wayne to Morris, 14 Sept. 1781, Wayne Papers, PHS.

33. See Letterbook A, Aug. and Sept., *passim,* for Morris' efforts toward the Virginia campaign. Heath to Morris, 20 Sept. and 4 Oct. 1781, Heath Papers, MHS. Morris to Duer, 16 Oct. 1781, Letterbook B. For implementation, see the series of letters between Duer and Heath, Nov. and Dec., Heath Papers, *passim,* MHS. Duer had written Morris earlier: "I flatter myself our Friendship will not debar you from Employing me in this Line [that is, purchasing flour]. It is neither my Disposition to Ask, or yours to grant any Advantages from it to the least detriment of the Public. But I may venture to say that I have thrown my Business into such a channel that it is in my power to Contract with you for any Supplies for the Army on as reasonable terms, and to perform it with as

76-84

much Punctuality as any person in this State." 11 July 1781, Morris Corresp., LC. For the confidence which actions of Morris infused into many department heads, see Pickering to Hughes, 17 July 1781, Letterbook of the QMG, 1781-82, LC.

34. Official Diary, 11 Sept. 1781. See also 15 Sept. 1781.

35. Franklin to the President of Congress, 12 Mar. 1781, 4 Wharton 281. Luzerne to the President of Congress, 24 Mar. 1781, *ibid.*, 329-30. Franklin to the President of Congress, 14 May 1781, *ibid.*, 409. Franklin wrote Morris that expenditures in France had already swallowed up the new funds. "By these means you have really at present no funds here to draw upon." 26 July 1781, *ibid.*, 606.

36. Luzerne to the President of Congress, 28 Feb. 1781, 4 Wharton 270. Also Luzerne to the President of Congress, 25 May 1781, *ibid.*, 435. Luzerne later told Congress that Vergennes had instructed him to hold Morris to the original 500,000 livres because of the money which was being shipped to the states under the care of Laurens. Communications of Luzerne to Congress, 24 Sept.

1781, *ibid.*, 726. By this time Morris had already drawn bills up to one million livres. Morris argued that he had been so successful in raising the discount on bills that it was just as cheap as transporting the specie. Morris calculated the discount at this time at about 16½ per cent. For accounts of 1781, see Cont. Cong. Paper 137, III, 319. Another account, in which some general discrepancies appear from the one already cited, is in Michael Nourse, "The Accounts of Robert Morris, Superintendent of Finance" in *The Bankers' Magazine and Statistical Register*, 1860, p. 581. *The Statement of the Accounts of The United States of America during the Administration of the Superintendent of Finance* which was published in 1785 is unsatisfactory for annual receipts and annual balances. For the specie from France, Morris to Franklin, 7 Sept. 1781 (addenda), 4 Wharton 667. An additional $300,000 was to be sent from Amsterdam, but Franklin had to detain it to meet bills of Congress.

37. Communications of Luzerne to Congress, 24 Sept. 1781, 4 Wharton 725-26.

CHAPTER FIVE

1. Official Diary, Oct., Nov., Dec., *passim*. Also Morris to Honorable Mr. Sullivan, 15 Dec. 1781, Letterbook B. For the final quote, see Hughes to Miles, 8 Nov. 1781, Letterbook of QMG of Penn., LC.

2. There is a great deal of correspondence on the Ross and Bingham payments. See, however, Morris to Franklin, and Morris to Messrs. Le Couteulx and Co., both 4 Dec. 1781, Letterbook B. Also Official Diary, 5 Dec. 1781. Also Journal (16 Apr. 1776, 20 Sept. 1781), entry 13 July 1781, Fiscal Section, NA. For Bean-Morris exchange, see Bean to Morris, 15 Dec. 1781, and Morris to Bean, 24 Dec. 1781, both in Morris Papers, PA. There is a considerable correspondence in preparation for

the departure of the Morris sons for France. See excerpt of Morris to Washington letter, 19 Oct. 1781, in Stan V. Henkel, *This Confidential Correspondence of Robert Morris* (Number 53). Also, Morris to Jay, 19 Oct. 1781, H. F. Johnston, *Correspondence of Jay*, II, 136-37, Morris to Matthew Ridley, Oct. 1781, Morris Corresp., LC. For Mary Morris' fears, see Kitty Livingston to Mrs. Jay, 18 Oct. 1781, Johnston, *Correspondence of Jay*, II, 135.

3. For "general arrangements" see Morris to Governor of Mass., 15 Sept. 1781, Letterbook A.

4. Quote from Morris to the President of Congress, 24 Aug. 1781, Letterbook A.

5. *Journals*, XIV, 903-08 (30 July

1779). For the animosity, Sanders, *Evolution of Executive Departments,* pp. 73-74.

6. Morris to President of Congress, 24 Aug. 1781, Letterbook A. Official Diary, 27 Aug. 1781. Morris to Governor of Mass., 15 Sept. 1781, Letterbook A. *Journals,* XXI, 948-50 (11 Sept. 1781). Jennings B. Sanders, *Evolution of Executive Departments,* p. 133.

7. See Official Diary, 8 June 1781. In the treasury records, Swanwick is consistently referred to as "Treasurer to the Superintendent of Finance." See Journal, Blotters, etc. for this period in Fiscal Section, NA.

8. My information about the early life of Swanwick is gleaned largely from petitions of Swanwick or some members of his family to the Executive Council of Pennsylvania. Richard Swanwick to (Robert Morris), 1 Apr. 1778, Morris Corresp., LC. John Swanwick to the President and Executive Council, Rev. Papers, XXXVI, 50, PA. Another petition in XXXVIII, 10. Another in XXXVI, 52 (dated 9 June 1780). Also XL, 59. There is an exchange of letters between Morris and Laurens in April 1778. See Cont. Cong. Papers 137, Appendix, 225-26, 229, LC. See T. Matlack to the Committee for Seizing Tory Property, 11 Nov. 1777, Provincial Papers, XLV, 83, PA.

9. Morris to the President of Congress, 28 June 1781, Cont. Cong. Papers, 137, I, 61. *Journals,* XX, 724 (6 July 1781). Official Diary, 4 Aug. 1781.

10. The best source of information on the pre-revolutionary and revolutionary career of Gouverneur Morris is still Jared Sparks, *The Life of Gouverneur Morris* (3 vols.; Boston, 1832). Theodore Roosevelt's biography of Gouverneur in the *American Statesmen* series belittles Sparks, but his book indicates that all he did was to consolidate Sparks' work into fewer pages. Anne Carey Morris, *Diary and Letters of Gouverneur Morris* (2 vols.; New York, 1888), concentrates on his career as Minister to France and contains absolutely nothing of value

for his important earlier career. I have searched with care for new manuscript material, but for the most part unsuccessfully. The relatively new papers in the Library of Congress — the single major collection—contribute nothing new to the earlier period. My discoveries have been confined to isolated letters in other collections, such as the Ridley Papers, MHS. A recent biography, Howard Swiggett's *The Extraordinary Mr. Morris* (New York, 1952), is, from the scholar's point of view, very disappointing.

11. Robert Morris to R. Peters, 25 Jan. 1778, Wayne Papers, PHS. Robert Morris to Jay, 19 Oct. 1781, in Johnston, *Correspondence of Jay,* II, 137. Kitty Livingston to R. Vaughan [1784], Ridley Papers, MHS.

12. For Luzerne and Lee, see extract of Luzerne letter, 11 Aug. 1781, Sparks MSS, 32, I, 61-62, Widener Library. Also Sanders, *Evolution of Executive Departments,* pp. 108-11. And *Journals,* XXI, 851-52 (10 Aug. 1781). Sanders, *Evolution,* pp. 98-101. *Journals,* XXI, 1087 (30 Oct. 1781).

13. Official Diary, 3 Dec. 1781. These meetings are appropriately noted in Morris' Official Diary after this initial meeting. For example, on 17 December, Morris notes the meeting on public business "tending to promote system and economy in the management of public business."

14. The quote comes from General Greene to Morris, 18 Aug. 1781, printed in George Washington Greene, *The Life of Nathanael Greene,* III, 370. See first subscription list in Lawrence Lewis, *A History of the Bank of North America,* Appendix iv. Notice that this subscription list runs to 25 July 1783. The original is in the Bank of North America Papers, 1781-92, PHS. For Morris' urging to friends, see Letterbook A, *passim.* Lawrence Lewis, *Bank of North America,* p. 33. The news of Laurens' arrival reached Philadelphia on the same day that information arrived of De-Grasse appearing at the Capes. Nixon and Clymer to Thomas Sen-

85-94

nickson, 4 Sept. 1781, Society Coll.,
PHS.
Duer responded enthusiastically to
the plan of the Bank: "I can only
say without flattery that the Plan
you propose, is in my opinion the
only Rational Plan I have seen for
restoring the Credit and Circulation of a Paper Currency. I will subscribe you may be assured as soon
as I can Command the Specie and
will Endeavor amongst all my
Friends to Explain the advantage
to the Proprietors, in order that
private interest may unite with public Zeal in promoting the plan. I
observe in your Address to the Public, that you do not Enter into a
Detail of the Advantages to be derived to the Proprietors; perhaps it
was most prudent not to do it in a
public Way; but I suppose you
have been more minute in your Explanations in Circular Letters written to the principal Gentleman of
Monied Interest in the different
States. The Knowledge of Banking
is scarcely familiar to the merchants
in America, however skilful in other
Branches of Business—and indeed
there are some advantages to be derived by an American Bank which
cannot Result from those Established in Europe." Duer to Morris,
11 July 1781, Morris Corresp., LC.

15. Official Diary, 10 Sept. 1781. Morris
to Tench Francis, 11 Sept. 1781,
Letterbook A. Morris to the Board
of War, 10 Sept. 1781, *ibid.* Morris
to Governor of Mass., 11 Sept. 1781,
ibid. Morris to Heath, 11 Sept. 1781,
ibid. Heath to Morris, 15 Sept. 1781,
Heath Papers, MHS. Official Diary,
6 Nov. 1781. Payment to Francis
dragged on for two years.

16. Official Diary, 30 Oct. 1781. Entries
of 1 and 2 Nov. in "Minutes and
Letterbook, 1781-92" in the Bank of
North America Papers, PHS. The
directors elected were: Thomas Fitz-
simmons, James Wilson, John M.
Nesbitt, Thomas Willing, Henry
Hill, Samuel Osgood, Cadwallader
Morris, Andrew Caldwell, Samuel
Inglis, Samuel Meredith, William
Bingham, and Timothy Matlack.
Although elected, Inglis, a partner

of Willing and Morris, was apparently not present. For Willing letter,
13 Nov. 1781, Wallace Papers, 4,
PHS. For bank notes, Morris to Pen-
nell, 16 Oct. 1781, Letterbook B.
See Official Diary, 12 Nov. 1781.
Also Entries of 10 and 20 Nov. and
22 Dec. 1781 in "Minutes and Letterbook, 1781-92" in the Bank of
North America Papers, PHS.

17. Official Diary, 29 Dec. 1781. Va.
Delegates to Governor of Va., 8 Jan.
1782, 6 Burnett 288-89. The quote
is on 289. *Journals,* XXI, 1185 (29
Dec. 1781).

18. Official Diary, 27 and 28 Dec. 1781.
Madison to Edmund Pendleton, 8
Jan. 1782, 6 Burnett 290. Official
Diary, 29 Dec. 1781.

19. *Journals,* XXI, 1187-90 (31 Dec.
1781).

20. Va. Delegates to the Governor of
Va., 8 Jan. 1782, 6 Burnett 289.
Madison to Pendleton, 8 Jan. 1782,
ibid., 290. If the vote were recorded
it would be possible to analyze this
issue with more assurance. *Journals,*
XXI, 1190 (31 Dec. 1781). Madison
to Pendleton, 8 Jan. 1782, 6 Burnett
290.

21. Official Diary, 7 Jan. 1782. Morris
to Governors of States, 8 Jan. 1782,
5 Wharton 94-95.

22. Morris to Harrison (in private capacity), 15 Jan. 1782, Morris Corresp., LC. He crossed out the following phrase: "I need not mention . . .
how useful it has been."

23. For the description, see Morris to
Receivers of Taxes (Circular), 15
Apr. 1782, Letterbook C. For first
signs of their use, Morris to Ridley
and Pringle, 13 Nov. 1781, Letterbook B. For preparations on a more
elaborate scale, see Official Diary,
26 Dec. 1781, and 9 Jan. 1782. The
letters to those employed in the departments begin to mention the
notes more frequently early in 1782.

24. For the connection between the tax
burden and circulating medium, see
Morris to Governors, 4 Sept. 1781, 4
Wharton 693.

25. Morris to William Gordon, 5 Sept.
1781, Letterbook A. Morris to Dudley, 5 Sept. 1781, *ibid.* Also follow
up letters to both men dated 11

Sept. 1781, *ibid.* In addition, see Official Diary, 23 and 31 Oct., 12 and 16 Nov., all in 1781. *Journals,* XXII, 9 (7 Jan. 1782). For Gouverneur's assistance, Official Diary, 18 Jan. 1782.

26. The letter is dated the 15th even though it was actually sent the 18th. Official Diary, 18 Jan. 1782. Morris to the President of Congress, 15 Jan. 1782, printed in 5 Wharton 103-110. The original is in Cont. Cong. Papers 137, I, 300. This information was used later in reference to the Jefferson plan on coins. Though the printed version is readily available, it might be well to summarize the positive suggestions made in the mint message. A monometalist standard was recommended with silver rather than gold as the standard of value. The only real reason given for this preference was the susceptibility of gold to "fraudulent practices" because it was more valuable than silver. There was the question, of course, of changing values and the consequent danger of exportation of coins which would cause a stringency and possibly hardship. This they hoped would be avoided by making it more profitable to export the bullion rather than the coin. "Hence, then, it appears proper that the price of coining should be defrayed by the coinage." Thus the money would receive a value distinct from that of bullion as a commodity. Insofar as the actual coins were concerned, "it must have some affinity to the former currency" so that it would be "intelligible to the whole people." Also, it should have very small units with a decimal system desirable to make such units and multiplications thereof "simple and accurate." When this system was finally decided upon, it should be designated as "legal money."

27. Official Diary, 16 Feb. 1782. *Journals,* XXII, 87 (21 Feb. 1782).

28. Morris to Luzerne, 3 Nov. 1781, 4 Wharton 818.

29. Professor Merrill Jensen, in his recent book, the best single comprehensive volume on the Confederation, takes a different point of view.

Jensen, *The New Nation,* pp. 45-46, 56-57.

30. An examination of some of the existing material in the National Archives or the General Accounting Office gives the modern scholar the best insight into these perplexing problems. See also Chap. i, Section II, on the Secret Committee. For an excellent summary, Jensen, *The New Nation,* pp. 375-76.

31. This paragraph and the ones to follow are based on a letter of Morris to the President of Congress, 28 Aug. 1781, except where noted; and then the quotes are taken from his accompanying letter of 5 Nov. 1781. These letters are published in 4 Wharton 667-77 and in Sparks, *Diplomatic Correspondence,* XI, 442-59 with changes. However, it is important to consult the original, which differs a great deal from the Sparks and slightly from the Wharton. It is located in the Cont. Cong. Papers 137, I, 121-9, LC. The difference in the Sparks and Wharton versions is largely accounted for by the source from which each copied. Sparks evidently took his from the Letterbooks of the Office of Finance, and Wharton from the original submitted to Congress.

32. The Financier's comments are from the letter which accompanied the funding message. Morris to the President of Congress, 5 Nov. 1781, 4 Wharton 824.

33. The Financier claims a triple credit, but the present writer is unable to follow his reasoning.

34. The Morris letter of July is to the Governors of Mass., R. I., N. Y., Del., Md., and N. C., 27 July 1781, 4 Wharton 608-09. The latter quotes are from the 28 of Aug. letter. The quote on the rich and poor is sometimes presented completely out of context. It is implied that Morris was talking about holders of loan office certificates rather than about the states. When the phrase is placed in its proper setting, its meaning obviously refers to the states.

35. Morris to President of Congress, 28 Aug. 1781, 4 Wharton 675-77.

94-104

36. For previous inspection, Official Diary, 28 Sept. 1781. For committee report, *Journals*, XXI, 1112 (12 Nov. 1781). Some of the delay probably arose because representation in Congress was a little "thing."

37. *Journals*, XXI, 1132 (23 Nov. 1781). Report to Congress, 10 Dec. 1781, Letterbook B. Also printed in *Journals*, XXII, 14-17 (9 Jan. 1782).

38. *Journals*, XXII, 12-15 (9 Jan. 1782). *Journals*, XXII, 34, 36, 68. For consultations, Official Diary, 15 and 16 Feb. 1782. *Journals*, XXII, 102-4 (27 Feb. 1782).

39. For Morris' letter, see Morris to President of Congress, 18 Feb. 1782, 5 Wharton 172-73. *Journals*, XXII, 102-04. Morris urged that "adequate rewards" be given to the peo-

ple who settled accounts because it would require men of "such uncorrupted and uncorruptible integrity as will give security to the United States." He had heard "that many fraudulent practices have happened."

40. Morris to the Governors, 9 Mar. 1782, 5 Wharton 230. Morris to Governors, 15 Apr. 1782, *ibid.*, 309-10.

41. See Conn. Delegates to the Governor of Conn., 21 Jan. 1782, 6 Burnett 293. Also Madison to Pendleton, 7 Feb. 1782, *ibid.*, 299-300. For quote, Va. Delegates to Harrison, 25 Feb. 1782, *ibid.*, 305.

42. Morris to the President of Congress, 27 Feb. 1782, Letterbook C.

CHAPTER SIX

1. For quote, Morris to Matthew Ridley, 27 Aug. 1781, Letterbook A.

2. *Journals*, XIX, 112-13 (3 Feb. 1781). The exceptions included a few articles of war, woolen cards and cotton cards, and salt. The impost was passed with some reservations, for the *Journal* indicates indecision and opposition.

3. Morris to Governors of Mass., R. I., N. Y., Del., Md., and N. C., 27 July 1781, 4 Wharton 606-09. Morris apparently did not find his views on free trade in conflict with his advocacy of the impost. When Morris spoke of free trade, he meant freedom of restriction on trade. The impost was a matter of revenue, and it would not discriminate between sellers; for it would apply to everyone. Thus, it followed, all the essential elements of free trade would still enjoy full play.

4. Morris to Glover, 22 Oct. 1781, Letterbook B. See also Morris to Smith, 26 Sept. 1781, and to John Lloyd, 18 Sept. 1781, Letterbook A. Also Official Diary, Oct. and Nov. *passim*. Morris to Governors, 19 Oct. 1781, 4 Wharton 793-94. Also Morris to Loan Officers, 13 Oct. 1781, *ibid.*, 772.

5. Morris to Governors, 3 Jan. 1782,

5 Wharton 85. Morris to Franklin, 27 Nov. 1781, *ibid.*, 16. There was considerable comment on the insufficiency of the revenue which could be expected from the impost when the measure was under consideration by Congress. See for example, John Mathews to Governor of N. J., 29 Jan. 1781, 5 Burnett 550. Morris to Franklin, 27 Nov. 1781, 5 Wharton 16. Morris to Governors, 3 Jan. 1782, *ibid.*, 84-85.

6. *Journals*, XXI, 1091 (2 Nov. 1781).

7. Morris to Receivers (Circular), 12 Feb. 1782, Letterbook C.

8. For data on tax situation see Morris to Washington, 12 June 1782, Letterbook C, and Morris to Greene, 20 Jan. 1783, Letterbook E. The matter of collectors can be traced in almost every state. New York is a good example where collectors were elected from their own counties — a "freeholder and inhabitant of the district, in which he is so elected a collector." *Laws of N. Y.*, Third Session, XLV, (1 Mar. 1780). See index, under revenue in *Collection of Laws of Va., 1768-83* for these years.

9. The tax requisition for 1782 which was passed in November 1781 recommended separation of continen-

tal from state taxes. Morris explained some of his views when Pennsylvania passed a tax law which tended to restrict the availability of the funds to be collected. Morris to the Speaker of the Assembly of Penn., 13 Feb. 1782, Letterbook C. See also Morris to George Olney, 2 July 1782, and Morris to Merrill, 13 Aug. 1782, Letterbook D. When New Jersey passed a tax law which conformed with Morris' wishes and made the collectors "liable to the Receivers," the Financier sent it to the other Receivers as an example. See Morris to Governor of Conn., 5 Nov. 1782, *ibid.*

10. There are many expressions of these ideas, but the letter quoted at length best describes it in one piece. Morris to Houston, 29 Oct. 1782, Letterbook D.

11. See Morris to Hall, 18 Jan. 1782, Letterbook B, in particular, but this was repeated to most of the receivers when they were appointed. See also Morris' circular to the receivers, 15 Apr. 1782, Letterbook C. A long search for the full complement of letters which Morris received from these observers has yielded little success; only an occasional miscellaneous letter has turned up.

12. The complete list, together with their fees, is as follows: William Whipple, N. H., 1/6; James Lovell, Mass., 1/8; George Olney, R. I., 1/4; Hezekiah Merrill, Conn., 1/8; Alexander Hamilton, N. Y. 1/4 (Thomas Tillotson took over in September) ; William C. Houston, N. J., 1/8; John Swanwick, Penn., 1/8; John Read, Del., 1/8; Benjamin Harwood, Md., 1/8; George Webb, Va., 1/8; George Abbot Hall, S. C., 1/2. This has been compiled from Letterbooks C and D. For the offer to Rittenhouse, 16 Feb. 1782, Letterbook C. For the quote, A. Lee to S. Adams, 29 Jan. 1783, Samuel Adams Papers, NYPL.

13. Official Diary, 24 Nov. 1781, 14 and 15 Dec. 1781. Morris to the Governors of N. C., S. C., and Ga., 19 Dec. 1781, 5 Wharton 56-59.

14. On taxes Morris wrote: "The ob-

jection that those who have land only will be distressed by the sale of it will have just as much weight as the legislature may choose to give it; for if no taxes are raised on land the objection will vanish, and certainly the legislature will be in capacity to determine whether any tax should be laid on it and what that tax should be.

"But, further, it appears that the objection is calculated to favor the rich, who are great land holders, in preference to the poor, who labor on a small plantation; and how far this may be either wise or just is not for me to determine. I will, however, suggest an expedient, that, as the taxes are payable quarterly, the first two quarters tax should be raised on the polls, the slaves, and other personal property in the State, and the land tax be paid on the last quarterly installments. This will give the several land holders room to turn themselves so as to provide for their several appropriations in season. I will just add under this head, that if (as there is some reason to hope) the southern States should be totally evacuated, the extension of their commerce will soon obviate every objection which can possibly be in the way of taxation." *ibid., 58.*

15. Official Diary, 15, 18, and 19 Dec. 1781. Morris to the Governors of N. C., S. C., and Ga., 19 Dec. 1781, 5 Wharton 57-59. Morris, however, was not quite as outspoken on price ceilings in action. He wrote Greene that the purchasing agents for the Southern army should be prohibited to pay above a certain stated reasonable price. Morris to Greene, 19 Dec. 1781, Letterbook B.

16. Morris to John Langdon (Speaker of the N. H. Assembly) , 28 Sept. 1781, Letterbook A. Morris to the Governor of Va., 16 Oct. 1781, Letterbook B.

17. Morris to the Governors, 19 Oct. 1781, 4 Wharton 790-94. Morris to Franklin, 27 Nov. 1781, 5 Wharton 26.

18. Morris to Luzerne, 3 Nov. 1781, 4 Wharton 818. See also Morris to

104-115

Franklin, 27 Nov. 1781, 5 Wharton 26-27.

19. Morris to Luzerne, 3 Nov. 1781, 4 Wharton 818-20.

20. Morris to Franklin, 27 Nov. 1781, 5 Wharton, 15-16, 17, 27, 28. Congress had also requested Livingston, Secretary for Foreign Affairs, to send dispatches along with Lafayette describing the needs of the Confederation. It is obvious that much of the approach was worked out in the Committee which Morris had organized, for Livingston's letter closely parallels and bolsters that of Morris. It was the letter of the Superintendent of Finance which took precedence over Livingston's letter, for the Secretary for Foreign Affairs usually ends an argument by directing Franklin to Morris' letter. Morris also came in for some fine — and possibly self-approved — compliments. "You will therefore show the necessity of setting our credit upon a firm basis, the prospect we have of accomplishing it from the great confidence in the integrity and abilities of the Financier, from the economy which is introduced into our departments, from the industry which money excites and which a fluctuating medium had destroyed, and from the total debility which must attend another shock to public credit."

21. The entire letter is Morris to Franklin, 27 Nov. 1781, 5 Wharton 12-29. For the first quote, p. 27; for the second, p. 29. For Franklin's previous use of this argument see Franklin to Vergennes, 13 Feb. 1781, 4 Wharton 255.

22. The quote comes from Morris' letter to the Southern States, 19 Dec. 1781, 5 Wharton 59.

23. For example, in the civil branch, economy was one of the major motives for fixing a stated salary for the President of Congress. Morris to the President of Congress, 9 Nov. 1781, Letterbook B.

24. Circular to the States, 22 Jan. 1782, 23 Fitzpatrick 460. There is abundant evidence of the difficulties and expense of the specific supplies in the letters of the Generals Heath,

Greene, and Knox, and in the Pickering Letterbooks in the NA. For a short cut, see Victor L. Johnson, *The Administration of the American Commissariat During the Revolutionary War* (Philadelphia, 1941), pp. 168-75, and Louis C. Hatch, *The Administration of the American Revolutionary Army* (New York, 1904), pp. 104 ff.

25. For quote, Morris to General Heath, 23 Oct. 1781, Letterbook B.

26. The quote comes from Morris to Oliver Phelps, 30 Mar. 1782, 5 Wharton 286. However, this discussion is based on Morris' numerous letters written in the fall of 1781 on contracting. See particularly Morris to General Heath, 13 Nov. and 22 Dec. 1781, Letterbook B. Also the very long and comprehensive letter to General Greene, 19 Dec. 1781, *ibid*.

27. For quote, Morris to Heath, 22 Dec. 1781, Letterbook B.

28. Morris to Schuyler, 29 May 1781, 4 Wharton 459. *Journals*, XX, 734 (10 July 1781).

29. Contract between the Superintendent of Finance and Jonathan Lawrence and Melancton Smith, dated 21 Dec. 1781, Jonathan Lawrence Papers, Misc. MSS, NYHS. Another copy, Heath Papers, XXVI, 162, MHS. See also contract between the Financier and Comfort Sands and Co., dated 6 Dec. 1781, Heath Papers, XXIII, 37, MHS. Another copy in McDougall Papers, NYHS. Such details as defining what area was covered by the West Point contract were left to the General in command and the contractors. Morris to Heath, 12 Dec. 1781, Letterbook B. Also agreement between Heath and Comfort Sands, 25 Dec. 1781, Heath Papers, MHS. Heath approved contracting but was skeptical of its operation. See Heath to Morris, 19 Nov. 1781, *ibid*.

30. Morris to Schuyler, 29 May 1781, 4 Wharton 459. Morris to Duer, 6 Nov. 1781, Letterbook B.

31. See footnote *ante* 7 for the location of some of the contracts. See also Official Diary, 15 Nov. and 31 Dec. 1781, *passim*. See also Morris to Schuyler, 3 Dec. 1781, Let-

terbook B. See also, Morris to Duer, 3 Dec. 1781 and 29 Dec. 1781, *ibid.*

32. Morris to General Greene, 19 Dec. 1781, Letterbook B. Morris to Greene, 2 Nov. 1781, 4 Wharton 816-17. Morris to Greene, 10 Sept. 1781, Letterbook A. A careful examination of the evidence clearly indicates that the decision to withhold contracting from the South was based upon the factor of economic disruption in the South rather than upon any deep hidden political motive, as has sometimes been intimated.

33. For the hospital department, see Morris to the President of Congress, 21 Sept. 1781, Letterbook A. Also the series of reports on the hospitals which were sent to the Superintendent of Finance earlier which are in the Cont. Cong. Papers 137, I, 147-68. Morris explained his skepticism to Greene in his comprehensive letter of 19 Dec. 1781, Letterbook B. For the act of reorganization, see *Journals*, XXI, 1093-98 (3 Nov. 1781). For Clothier General, see *Journals*, XX, 667 (18 June 1781). For reduction of forces, see Official Diary, Nov. and Dec., *passim*. For Navy, Official Diary, 22 Nov. and 24 Dec. 1781.

34. Morris to the Governor of R. I., 29 Dec. 1781, 5 Wharton 77. Morris to the Governors of the Southern States, 19 Dec. 1781, *ibid.*, 58. Morris to Greene, 3 Oct. 1781, 4 Wharton 765.

CHAPTER SEVEN

1. Morris to Marinus Willet, 11 Mar. 1782, Letterbook C.
2. Ralph George Vaccaro, "The Politics of David Howell of Rhode Island in the period of The Confederation" (unpublished M.A. thesis, Department of History, Columbia University, 1947), traces this development.
3. Joseph Reed to General Greene, 1 Nov. 1781, printed in Reed, *Joseph Reed*, II, 370-76. For quote, p. 375. There is a copy of this letter in the Reed Papers, NYHS. William Livingston to Robert Livingston, 17 Dec. 1781, printed in Theodore Sedgwick, *Memoir of William Livingston* (New York, 1833), p. 369.
4. Reynolds to James Eyma, 27 Oct. 1781, Reynolds Letterbook, LC.
5. Morris to Schuyler, 29 Aug. 1781, Letterbook A. For quote, Morris to Matthew Ridley, 27 Aug. 1781, *ibid.* "John Hunt's Diary" in NJHS *Proceedings*, Vol. LIII, 29 (Nov. 1781). Bezanson, *Prices and Inflation*, pp. 93-94.
6. This analysis is built on a continuation of the same materials cited in detail in Chap. iii, Section II.
7. Morris to Luzerne, 22 Nov. 1781, 4 Wharton 855. The letter was not actually sent until the 24th. Official Diary, 24 Nov. 1781. Luzerne agreed with Morris, apparently, but he was a bit skeptical about such a disposition. Official Diary, 4 Dec. 1781.

8. Jay to Franklin, 21 Feb. 1781, 4 Wharton 262-64. Jay to President of Congress, 3 Oct. 1781, *ibid.*, 751. Jay to President of Congress, 20 Sept. 1781, *ibid.*, 716-18. The quote is taken from Frank Monaghan, *John Jay*, p. 165. Vergennes to Luzerne, 7 Sept. 1781 (extract), 4 Wharton 860. Franklin to Morris, 5 Nov. 1781, *ibid.*, 829-31. Franklin to Congress, 5 Nov. 1781, *ibid.*, 828. Official Diary, 22 Nov. and 25 Nov. 1781. Franklin to Morris, 28 Jan. 1782, 5 Wharton 136-37.

9. Adams to the President of Congress, 4 Jan. 1781, 4 Wharton 226. Adams to the Pres. of Cong., 15 Jan. 1781, *ibid.*, 235. Franklin to Dumas, 6 and 10 Aug. 1781, *ibid.*, pp. 625, 627, provides the best source to follow the ups and downs in these negotiations. S. F. Bemis, *The Diplomacy of the American Revolution*, p. 169.

10. Morris to Grand, 3 Dec. 1781, 5 Wharton 35-36. Morris to Minister to France, 28 Jan. 1782, Letterbook B. Franklin to Morris, 5 Nov. 1781,

116-129

4 Wharton 829-31. Franklin to Jay, 19 Jan. 1782, 5 Wharton 120.

11. Morris to Directors of the Bank, 7 Jan. 1782, Letterbook B. Morris to Register of the Treasury, 16 Jan. 1782, *ibid.* Morris to Comptroller, 16 Jan. 1782, *ibid.* Morris to Register of the Treasury, 7 Mar. 1782, Letterbook C. Official Diary, 7 and 15 Jan., 1 and 5 Feb. 1782.

12. The quote comes from "Minutes and Letters of the Bank, 1781-92 (4 Nov. 1782)" in Bank of North America Papers, PHS. For circulation of Bank Notes, see Morris to John Wendell, 25 Mar. 1782, Letterbook C. In May, Morris predicted a 6 per cent dividend. Morris to Langdon, 2 May 1782, *ibid.*

13. For securities quote, see Official Diary, 17 Jan. 1782. Also Morris to Colonel Thomas Proctor, 18 Jan. 1782, Letterbook B. For Penn., Official Diary, 15 Apr. 1782. Morris to Jenifer, 10 and 12 July 1782, Letterbook D. For private discounting, see such letters as Morris to John Wendell, 25 Mar. 1782, Letterbook C. For temporary halt on private discounting, Morris to Duer, 12 June 1782, *ibid.* For halt on public discounting, Official Diary, 23 May 1782. For discounting notes for the government, see Morris to Register, 8 Apr. 1782 and to Michael Hillegas, 9 May 1782, Letterbook C. Official Diary, 3 and 12 Sept. 1782.

14. Pickering to Hughes, 8 Mar. 1782, Phila., Letterbook of the QMG, LC. The Connecticut delegates wrote somewhat later: "The Financier's notes and bank bills are in full credit and paid on sight, and are rather preferred to money by the merch'ts here. . . ." 29 July 1782, 6 Burnett 395. Pickering to Hughes, 2 Apr. 1782, Phila., Letterbook of the QMG, LC. Hughes replied the 17th of April, "It is with greatest difficulty that anything can be obtained from the inhabitants now without cash. They say that it (their property) may as well remain in their custody as ours till money arrives, since they cannot depend on our engagements." *ibid.*, p. 246. Morris to Yeates, 10 Apr.

1782, Letterbook C. For Mass., Official Diary, 26 Mar. 1782. See also Morris to Hamilton, 5 Oct. 1782, 5 Wharton 798. For South, Morris to Hall, 18 Jan. 1782, Letterbook B.

15. Morris to James Lovell, 1 June 1782, Letterbook C. A month later Morris again used the same argument, which reflects the persistence of the depreciation in that area. Morris to Lovell, 10 July 1782, 5 Wharton 605. Lovell was instructed to sell bills of exchange and take notes and warrants in payment. In this way Morris hoped to bring their value in circulation up to par.

16. Cornell to Morris, 5 Oct. 1782, Cont. Cong. Papers 137, I, 850-53. Hamilton to Morris, 9 Oct. 1782 (Albany), Lodge, *Works*, VIII, 83. Morris to Receivers, Circular, 29 Aug. 1782, Letterbook D. Parker to Sands, Livingston, and Company, 10 Oct. 1782, Parker Letterbook, Baker Library. Morris to Lovell, 11 Dec. 1782, Letterbook D.

17. Hamilton to Morris, 21 Sept. 1782, Lodge, *Works*, VIII, 79-80. Madison wrote: "Soon after I was shewn by Lee . . . instructions for peace. The plan is to exclude F———n and J———y [Franklin and Jay] and to withdraw the others from the direction of France. The notes of M———s [Morris] are also to be attacked." Madison to Randolph, 23 July 1782, 6 Burnett 388. See also Madison to Randolph, 30 July 1782, *ibid.*, 405. For collectors, Parker to Sands, Livingston, and Company, 10 Oct. 1782, Parker Letterbook, Baker Library. Also Morris to Lovell, 17 Dec. 1782, Letterbook E.

18. For the quote, Morris to Ralph Pomeroy, 25 Sept. 1782, Letterbook D.

19. The figure for expenditures is taken from "A State of the Receipts and Expenditures of Public Monies upon Warrants from the Superintendent of Finance from the 1st of January 1782 to the 1st of January 1783" found in the Cont. Cong. Papers 137, III, 337. It is labeled "Excess of payments beyond the receipts, being an anticipation on the public credit."

20. Morris to President of Congress, 3

Dec. 1782, Letterbook D. For quote, Morris to Rutledge, 2 Mar. 1782, Letterbook C. Appointments were as follows: Benjamin Stelle, Penn.; Henry Sherburne, N. Y.; Samuel Gridley, N. H.; Edward Chinn, R. I.; William Winder, Del.; Daniel De Laussure, Md.; Lewis Pintard, N. J.; Zephaniah Turner, Va.; Melancton Smith, Conn.; Jerman Baker, N. C. The appointments for the various departments were as follows: William Denning, Quartermaster; Jonathan Burrell, Commissary; Edward Fox, Hospital; Joseph Bindon, Clothier. This list has been compiled from Letterbooks C, D, and part of E.

21. For quotes, Morris to Commissioners of States, 7 Sept. 1782, Letterbook D. Also Morris to the Commissioners of the Departments, 19 Sept. 1782, *ibid.*

22. For a preliminary view, see Morris to Commissioners, 3 Oct. 1782, Letterbook D. Morris to the Governor of Md., 30 Nov. 1782, *ibid.* Burrell is quoted in a letter of Morris to the President of Congress, 18 Apr. 1782, Letterbook C.

23. Report of Morris, 12 June 1782, Letterbook C. *Journals*, XXII, 328-29 (13 June), 376 (1 July), 384 (12 July 1782).

24. Morris to the President of Congress, 8 May 1782, 5 Wharton 400. *Journals*, XXII, 305-06 (28 May 1782). *ibid.*, 421 (29 July 1782). See also 6 Burnett 396-97 on the same day. For the difference of opinion between the Committee and Morris, see particularly *Journals*, XXIII, 729-31 (18 Nov. 1782), and Morris to the Committee, 26 Aug. 1782, Letterbook D. For the final Congressional resolution, *Journals*, XXIII, 728 (18 Nov. 1782).

25. *Journals*, XXIII, 744 (20 Nov. 1782). For the initiation of the firm of Barclay, Moylan, and Co., in which Thomas Barclay was a partner, see T. Barclay to Cadwallader and Samuel Morris, 24 Jan. 1782, Provincial Delegates, I, 13, PHS. There is quite a bit of material here on their transactions. See also John Barclay to Thomas Barclay, 23 Mar. 1784, Etting Papers, Misc. MSS, II,

24, PHS. For the instructions to Barclay, Morris to Barclay, 5 Dec. 1782, 6 Wharton 115-19.

26. For an example of directing those who pleaded for settlements, see Morris to General Hazen, 15 Jan. 1782, Letterbook B. For quote, Morris to Speaker of the Assembly of Penn., 13 Feb. 1782, Letterbook C.

27. Morris to the President of Congress, 27 Feb. 1782, Letterbook C. He thought the excise tax might be a bit high, but this would be beneficial.

28. *Journals*, XXII, 115 (4 Mar. 1782). Report of Morris, 12 June 1782, Letterbook C.

29. Official Diary, 26 June 1782.

30. *Ibid.*, 9 July 1782.

31. This message is printed in several places, but its importance has been completely overlooked. See 5 Wharton 619-34, or 12 Sparks 211-38, or *Journals*, XXII, 429-46. Also in Letterbook D. The copy sent to Congress is in the Cont. Cong. Papers 137, 677-704. Apparently the letter was not sent in until August 5 and then it was referred to a "Grand Committee" which had been set up July 22. The paper was considered sufficiently important by the British to forward home. "American Dispatches, 1780-82," Shelburne Papers, Clements Library. Compare Hamiltonian arguments in his First Report on Public Credit printed in Samuel McKee, Jr. (ed.), *Papers on Public Credit, Commerce, and Finance by Alexander Hamilton*, pp. 1-50.

32. Morris to Appleton, 16 Apr. 1782, 5 Wharton 311-12. What Morris wrote to General Parsons in the period previous to his Report is typical. "But grant me solid permanent revenue to enable a punctual discharge of interest and I am confident that monied men will soon purchase all the funded debts and lend the remainder of their money to the public. For these reasons every public creditor should urge the several legislatures to grant revenue." Morris to Parsons, 1 Feb. 1782, Letterbook B. See also Morris to John Reynolds, 18 Jan. 1782, *ibid.* Also

129-137

Morris to Appleton, 22 Jan. 1782, *ibid.*

33. *Journals*, XXII, 447 (5 Aug. 1782). For the appointment of the Grand Committee, *ibid.*, 407-08 (22 July 1782). For report, *Journals*, XXIII, 545-46 (4 Sept. 1782). What happened in the committee or to the report is unintelligible in the *Journals* themselves, but the letter of the delegates of North Carolina to the Governor, dated 22 Oct. 1782, is enlightening. It is printed in 6 Burnett 516-19. Hugh Williamson of North Carolina said if the land tax should be adopted their state would "be charged with near double the quota of public Debt that should in Justice fall to our share." Williamson to Governor Martin, 2 Sept. 1782, printed in 6 Burnett 462. For some of the obstacles concerning western land claims and their ramifications, see Madison to Randolph, 10 Sept. 1782, printed in 6 Burnett 468-69. *Journals*, XXIII, 564-71 (10 Sept. 1782), 553-55 (9 Sept. 1782). Morris to Governor of R. I., 24 Oct. 1782, 5 Wharton 831.

34. See Official Diary, 2 July 1782, for Morris' assumption on Howell. See Howell's letter to Governor Greene of R. I., 30 July 1782, printed in 6 Burnett 399 ff.

35. Howell to Governor of R. I., 30 July 1782, 6 Burnett 399-403. Morris to Governor of R. I., 2 Aug. 1782, 5 Wharton 639-42.

36. Madison to Randolph, [17] Sept. 1782, printed in 6 Burnett 479. For the resolution of Congress, *Journals*, XXIII, 643-45 (10 Oct. 1782). The only friend which the Rhode Island delegates had when it came to a vote was Georgia. Frank G. Bates, "Rhode Island and the Impost of 1781," in *Report* of the Amer. Hist. Assoc., 1894, 355. *Journals*, XXIII, 771-72 (6 Dec. 1782). See also p. 863. Official Diary, 7, 9, 10, and 19 Dec. 1782. For news from Va., *Journals*, XXIII, 831 (24 Dec. 1782).

37. Howell to the Governor of R. I., 30 July 1782, 6 Burnett 402.

38. Hillman Metcalf Bishop, "Why Rhode Island Opposed the Federal Constitution: The Continental Impost" in *Rhode Island History*, VIII, No. 1, 1-10 (Jan., 1949). This is one in a series of articles. The author is indebted to Mr. Donald R. Raichle for calling these articles to his attention when they first appeared.

CHAPTER EIGHT

1. Morris to the President of Congress, 11 Feb. 1782, 5 Wharton 152-59.

2. Morris to the Governors of the States, 15 Feb. 1782, 5 Wharton 164-69 (final quote, page 169). Those familiar with the style of Gouverneur Morris, the Financier's assistant, will recognize his touch in these letters.

3. For consultation, see Official Diary, 8 Feb. 1782. Tom Paine might have had a hand in the writing of these letters but it is doubtful. Though Paine began to write for Morris in February (5 Wharton 134-35), he must have started after the 19th. According to the Official Diary, Livingston, Paine, and Morris met at the Office of Finance and agreed on a plan "for supporting and promoting the cause of America by rousing the people to spirited exertions. . . ."

4. Morris to Livingston, 8 Mar. 1782, Franklin Papers, VI, Misc. PHS. Morris inscribed at the end of this letter: "The contents of this letter are such, that I must pray your excuse for requesting the most profound secrecy, and that your communication to Doctor Franklin be all in cyphers."

5. Morris to the Governors of the States, 16 May 1782, 5 Wharton 423-24. In the copy of the letter which was submitted to Congress the final flourish does not appear. "Congress may dismiss their servant, and the States may dismiss their Congress, but it is by rectitude alone that man can be re-

spectable." Cont. Cong. Papers 137, I, 468-69. It is included in the version in Letterbook C, however.

6. Morris to the President of Congress, 17 May 1782, 5 Wharton 426. Official Diary, 20 May 1782. *Journals*, XXII, 279-80 (20 May 1782). *ibid.*, 289 (22 May 1782). Official Diary, 22 May 1782. Morris to Secretary at War, 7 May 1782, Letterbook C.

7. Morris to John Wendell, 25 Mar. 1782, Letterbook C. Morris to Oliver Phelps, 30 Mar. 1782, 5 Wharton 286.

8. Every effort to locate these reports has been unsuccessful. Their contents can only be surmised by indirection in the letters sent out from the Office of Finance in reply to the reports.

9. Morris to Greene, 18 Jan. 1782, Letterbook B. Morris to Hall, 18 Jan. 1782, *ibid.* Morris to the Governor of S. C., 10 June 1782, Letterbook C. See also Singer, *South Carolina in the Confederation*, pp. 52-54.

10. The figure for taxes received is taken from Cont. Cong. Papers, 142, II, 159-60. The figure for expenditures is taken from a printed copy of "Receipts and Expenditures of Public Monies upon Warrants from the Superintendent of Finance from the 1st of January 1782 to the 1st of January 1783," dated 31 Jan. 1783, Register's Office, Joseph Nourse, and found in Cont. Cong. Papers 137, III, 337. (The full title has been included, for it is obvious that the account did not include some of the expenditures which occurred in Europe such as paying interest on past foreign loans, paying Beaumarchais, etc. These transactions were largely in the hands of Franklin.) The figure taken, which is really an account of current expenditures, differs about one million dollars from the account published by Michael Nourse entitled "The Accounts of Robert Morris, Superintendent of Finance . . ." in the *Bankers Magazine and Statistical Register*, 1860. The discrepancy occurs because, in the Nourse account, the loans from

the bank and the repayments to the bank are included in the accounts. However, the only actual expenditure involved was, of course, the interest on the loans. Consequently, the lower figure has been accepted as a better approximation.

11. There is no single report of the total monthly revenue coming in from all the states. I have compiled these figures from the record of the contributions by the individual states which are found in Cont. Cong. Papers 142, II, 162-231. The usefulness of the material in the *American State Papers* is limited with respect to this study, for most of the figures presented represent a summary for the Revolutionary period rather than an analysis of the finances year by year. In addition, much of the *American State Papers* material is based on figures and estimates compiled by the Treasury under Joseph Nourse now available in the Continental Congress Papers in the Library of Congress.

12. For Franklin's troubles, see Franklin to Morris, 9 Jan. 1782, 5 Wharton 95-96. Franklin to Jay, 19 Jan. 1782, *ibid.*, 119-20. Franklin to Morris, 28 Jan. 1782, *ibid.*, 136-37. For the quote, Franklin to Adams, 12 Feb. 1782, *ibid.*, 159. Lafayette to Washington, 30 Jan. 1782, *ibid.*, 140-41. Also Livingston to Franklin, 13 Feb. 1782, *ibid.*, 160.

13. Franklin to Morris, 4 Mar. 1782, 5 Wharton 218-19. Morris to Franklin, 17 Apr. 1782, *ibid.*, 312.

14. Franklin to Jay, 16 Mar. 1782, 5 Wharton 244. Morris to Franklin, 23 May 1782, *ibid.*, 437-38. Also Morris to Franklin, 29 May 1782, *ibid.*, 445-46. Morris to the President of Congress, 23 May 1782, *ibid.*, 438. *Journals*, XXII, 290-3 (24 May 1782). Franklin to Morris, 12 Aug. 1782, 5 Wharton, 657-59.

15. Adams to Franklin, 25 Jan. 1782, 5 Wharton 130-31. Adams to Livingston, 14 Feb. 1782, *ibid.*, 162-3. Adams to Livingston, 16 May 1782, *ibid.*, 420. Adams to Livingston, 5 July 1782, *ibid.*, 594-95. Adams to Livingston, 18 Aug. 1782, *ibid.*,

138-144

665. Adams to Lafayette, 29 Sept.
1782, *ibid.*, 786.
16. Salmon to James Moore and Co.,
9 May 1782, Salmon and Woolsey
Letterbook, LC. Pringle to Holker,
26 May 1782, Balt., Holker Papers,
LC. For contemporary comments,
see Ridley to Turnbull and Co., 10
July 1782, Amsterdam, Letterbook
(May to Aug. 1782), Ridley Papers,
MHS. For the quote, Constable to
B. Moylan and Co. [July 1782],
Constable Letterbook, 1782-90, Constable-Pierrepont Papers, NYPL.
"I perceive the Philadelphians are
much frightened and dismayed by
the misfortunes they have lately
experienced," Pringle wrote Holker.
18 June 1782, Holker Papers, XVIII,
LC. He hoped, however, the promise of the Havana trade would "encourage the underwriters to go on."
For final quote, Codman and Smith
to T. Fitzsimmons, 30 May 1782,
Codman and Smith Letterbook,
Baker Library.
17. Official Diary, 9 Apr. and 1 May
1782. *Journals*, XXII, 237-38 (4
May 1782). Report to Congress on
Memorial of Philadelphia Merchants, 4 May 1782, 5 Wharton
395-96. State of the American Commerce, Agent of the Marine Letterbook, 64-71, Annapolis Naval Academy. Also published in *Journals*,
XXII, 264-74 (14 May 1782).
18. *Journals*, XXII, 238 (4 May 1782).
Morris to De Grasse, 16 May 1782,
Agent of Marine Letterbook, Annapolis. Morris to Don Solano, 16 May
1782, *ibid.* See also the letter to
Robert Smith of the same date,
ibid. The letter to Barney is printed in Ralph D. Paine, *Joshua Barney*, pp. 199-200. The voyage is
described pp. 197-205. Paine states
that the amount of money carried
back by Barney was $600,000, which
is an error. Official Diary, 17 July
1782.
The specie which the Financier
planned to obtain was really the
accumulation of private merchants
who had been exporting to the
West Indian ports. It appears in-
admissible that a vessel outfitted
by the government should carry
private monies. But here again is

an example of Morris' conception
of the compatibility of public and
private interest. He could not sell
the bills of exchange because of the
condition of trade. If the government could aid in getting the
money of the merchants into the
hands of each merchant, then those
enterprisers would be in a position
to purchase the bills of exchange
which the government was trying
to sell.
19. For the turn to West Indian commerce, see Constable to Barclay,
Moylan, and Co., [July 1782], Constable Letterbook, 1782-90, Constable-Pierrepont Papers, NYPL. Also Reynolds to Webb and Holston,
20 July 1782, Reynolds Letterbook,
LC. Also Pringle to Holker, 12
June 1782, Holker Papers, XVIII,
LC. Also Pringle to Holker, 5
June 1782, *ibid.* For quote, Salmon
to Williams, Moore and Co., 21
Aug. 1782, Woolsey and Salmon
Letterbook, LC. For rescinding
order, 3 Nov. 1782, *ibid.*, Pringle to
Ridley, 31 Oct. 1782, Ridley Papers,
MHS. Also Pringle to Holker, 28
Dec. 1782, Balt., Holker Papers,
XIX, LC. John Welsh Letterbook,
Codman and Smith Letterbook,
Daniel Parker Letterbook, Boston
Merchants volume, all in Baker Li-
brary. For final quote, Ridley to
Holker, 14 Oct. 1782, Holker Papers,
XVIII, LC. The merchant correspondence fairly seethes with post
war schemes. As late as December,
Digby, British Naval Commander
in American waters remarked, "The
Rebel Privateers have suffered so
much that there are but few out.
. . . I am in hopes this winter will
pretty well knock up their trade.
. . ." Report to Townshend, 15 Dec.
1782, "American Dispatches," Shelburne Papers, Clements Library.
20. Official Diary, 8 May 1782. Morris
to Grand, 18 May 1782, 5 Wharton
429.
21. Morris to Barry, 24 May 1782, Agent
of Marine Letterbook, Annapolis.
Another copy in Morris Papers,
PA. Morris to Smith, 25 May 1782,
Letterbook C. Morris to Messrs.
Harrison and Co. at Cadiz, 25 May
1782, *ibid.* Morris to Grand, 18

May 1782, 5 Wharton 430. The makeshifts can best be followed in the Official Diary, *passim*, but see particularly 30 May, 1 and 15 July. For the quote, 26 Aug. 1781. See also Morris to Lovell, 4 May and 13 June 1782, Letterbook C.

22. Morris to Lovell, 7 Sept. and 27 Nov. 1782, Letterbook D. Morris to John Brown, 23 Nov. 1782, *ibid.* See also Morris to Luzerne, 25 Nov. 1782, *ibid.* Also Morris to Captain John Greene, 27 Nov. 1782, Agent of Marine Letterbook, Annapolis. The Financier also borrowed some money from individuals in this period. See Official Diary, 30 Aug. 1782. Brown to Morris, 4 Mar. 1783, Cont. Cong. Papers 137, II, 271. See also 275. For the general story, see William B. Clark, *Gallant John Barry,* pp. 287-303.

23. There is a relatively complete series of letters to support the statement on the minor contracts, but see Morris to Colonel Rawlings, 20 Mar. 1782, and Morris to General Irvine, 29 May 1782, Letterbook C. Morris to Tench Francis, 21 Feb. 1782, *ibid.* Washington to the Superintendent of Finance, 28 Mar. 1782, 24 Fitzpatrick 93-94. Morris to Francis and Slough, 2 Apr. 1782, Letterbook C. For quote, Morris to Washington, 22 Apr. 1782, *ibid.* Morris to Washington, 9 Sept. 1782, Letterbook D. Morris to Colonel Richard Butler, 16 Sept. 1782, *ibid.*

24. The major sources for my material are as follows: For the West Point contract, Heath Papers, MHS; Duer Papers, NYHS; Holker Papers and Morris Papers and Letterbooks, LC. For the early contract of posts north of Poughkeepsie, Jonathan Lawrence Papers, NYHS. For the later contract, Duer Papers, NYHS; Daniel Parker Letterbook, Baker Library; Holker Papers and Morris Letterbooks and Papers, LC; and Andrew Craigie Papers, Am. Antiq. Soc. In all the contracts the extensive letterbooks of Timothy Pickering in the War Department Records at the National Archives have been enlightening. Part of the foregoing material has been used by

Robert East in his important *Business Enterprise and the American Revolution,* but his approach was to trace business connections, while my interest is in the relationship to the program of the Financier.

25. Temple Prime, *Descent of Comfort Sands and of his Children* (New York, 1897).

26. Heath to Comfort Sands and Co., 20 Dec. 1781, Heath Papers, MHS. Instructions of Heath, 18 Jan. 1782, *ibid.* Morris to Comfort Sands, 19 Jan. 1782, Letterbook B. Morris to General Heath, 19 Feb. 1782, Letterbook C. On hospital contract, Morris to Comfort Sands, 2 Jan. 1782, Letterbook B. The two quotes come from Morris to Sands, 28 Jan. 1782, and Morris to Heath, 7 Feb. 1782, *ibid.*

27. For quote, Comfort Sands to Heath, 24 Feb. 1782, Fishkill, Heath Papers, MHS. For the exchange, see Sands to Heath, 24 Feb., Heath to Sands and Co., 1, 8, and 18 Mar., and Sands to Heath, 7, 15, and 20 Mar., all in 1782, Heath Papers, MHS. Heath to B. Lincoln, 26 Mar. 1782, *ibid.*

28. Morris to Comfort Sands, 11 and 18 Mar. 1782, Letterbook C. Official Diary, 27 and 30 Mar. 1782. George Clymer, Charles Carroll, and Samuel Osgood composed the committee of Congress. Official Diary, 2 and 3 Apr. 1782. Morris to the President of Congress, 3 Apr. 1782, Letterbook C. Morris to Duer, 3 Apr. 1782, *ibid. Journals,* XXII, 173 (5 Apr. 1782). Official Diary, 4, 5, 6, and 11 Apr. 1782. At least part of the delay in drawing up the contract was the dispute between the various contractors. Morris to Washington, 15 Apr. 1782, Letterbook C. Washington to Morris, 23 Apr. 1782, 24 Fitzpatrick 159. He also wrote: "I am pleased to find, that saving the Complaints which have arisen in their Execution, they [the Officers] are generally inclined to acquiesce and promote the Contracts."

29. Morris to the President of Congress, 20 Apr. 1782, Letterbook C. The contract is found in Cont. Cong. Papers 137, I, 408-11.

144-151

30. Agreement with Livingston and Duer, 23 Apr. 1782, Doc. 43, Holker Papers, Clements Library. Agreement Duer and Holker, 4 May 1782, Holker Papers, XVII, 3320, LC. For Holker's acceptance of a share in the contract, Holker to Duer, 25 May 1782, Holker Papers, XVII, 3354-56. After reviewing their general business operations, Holker wrote: "I advise you not to lay in too large stores, on accot of Contracts, otherwise you may be taken in too deep — Be cautious though not mistrustfull." For Lawrence & Smith, see their papers in the NYHS. The subcontracts, though incomplete, shed some light on their mode of carrying out their contract with the Financier. Enoch Leonard, Thomas Foulger, William Goodrich, and Joseph Klingman figured in these contracts. Sometimes the subcontracts covered an entire post and at other times they involved specific commodities.

31. According to Duer, the partners under the firm of Sands, Livingston, and Co. were: Comfort Sands, Joshua Sands, Richardson Sands, Walter Livingston, Thomas Lowrey, Charles Stewart, Daniel Parker, and William Duer. Duer to Holker, 8 Jan. 1785, Holker Papers, XXIX, LC.

32. My own appraisal has been based largely on the William Duer Papers, NYHS; the Holker Papers, LC; Daniel Parker Letterbook, Baker Library; Andrew Craigie Papers, Am. Antiq. Soc.; with some help from Holker Papers, Clements Library. Joseph Davis' *Essays* has been helpful for leads, but the story of Duer's early career can now be supplemented by the new material available. For listing of Holker-Duer connections, see Brief of Holker v. Duer, (no date), Doc. 63, Holker Papers, Clements Library. See also Duer's pleas before the Circuit Court of the United States in the District of Pennsylvania, in Duer Papers (Misc. MSS, Box 7, Enclosure 8), NYHS. For agreement of pay certificates, dated 14 Nov. 1781, Holker Papers, XVI, 3020, LC. Deane obtained the mast contract for them. Duer to Holker, 5 Mar. 1781, Holker Papers, LC.

33. Duer Papers, 1779-80, *passim*. For quote, Morris to Kitty Livingston, 6 May 1780, Ridley Papers, MHS. See also in the same collection, Mrs. Morris to Kitty [1780]. For French Contract, see Duer to William Alexander, 15 June 1781, Alexander Papers, V. NYHS. Also, "Proposal of a Contract with Morris, Duer, and Schuyler," 12 Oct. 1780, Morris Corresp., LC. Duer had also borrowed money from Morris for a land purchase. Morris to Duer, 27 Dec. 1780, and Morris to Duer, 29 May 1781, Duer Papers, I, NYHS. For the official notice of Duer's successful bid for a contract, Morris to Duer, 7 Feb. 1782, Letterbook B. For the private letter, Morris to Duer, 7 Feb. 1782, Duer Papers, I, NYHS (private). Another draft in Morris' handwriting, Morris Papers, NYPL. Duer's bid for the Posts Northward of Poughkeepsie were apparently sent via Holker. Duer's hopes were high on the possibilities. "If there should be a campaign to the Northward, it can be made a clever thing. I cant enter at present into a detail of the advantages." Duer to Holker, 23 Jan. 1782, Holker Papers, XVIII, 3430-31. Part of the records of Duer's contract can be found in Misc. MSS, Duer Papers, NYHS. Duer set up subordinates who were actual employees rather than subcontractors. The framework by which Duer carried out his contract ran pretty much as follows: Enoch Leonard, Saratoga; John Wendell, Schenectady; J. Smith, Ft. Herkimer; Ketchum, Red Nook; T. Leonard, Ft. Rensselaer; and Elisha Crane acting as an itinerant agent. Duer to Heath, 1 Mar. 1782, Heath Papers, MHS. Morris to William Duer, 22 May 1782, Letterbook C.

34. Washington to Sands, 25 May 1782, 24 Fitzpatrick 285. Washington to Morris, 17 May (But actually sent the 25th according to the postscript), 1782, *ibid.*, 287-91. For the quote, 289. General Knox also reported a considerable discontent among the officers about their issues.

144-151

Knox to Lincoln, 29 May 1782, Newburgh, Knox Papers, MHS.

35. Heath to Washington, 24 and 27 May 1782, Heath Papers, MHS. Morris to Comfort Sands, 4 June 1782, Letterbook C. For first quote, Heath to Comfort Sands and Co., 21 June 1782, Heath Papers MHS. For the second, Heath to Sands, 25 June 1782, *ibid.* Sands and Heath were on good enough terms, however, for Heath to ask the contractor to secure him a coat. But the contractors had to delay it when all they could find in Philadelphia was French cloth and Heath wanted fine blue English cloth. Comfort Sands to Heath, 19 June 1782, Fishkill, *ibid.* For some evidence of Heath's action to obtain evidence see his letters of 8 and 23 July 1782 to Col. Nicolas and Henry Jackson, respectively, *ibid.* For Sands quote, Sands and Co. to Heath, 27 June 1782, *ibid.* For some of contractor's complaints, see Sands, Livingston, and Co. to Heath, 18 and 28 July 1782, *ibid.*

36. Morris to Washington, 4 June 1782, Letterbook C. Some of this letter is printed in 5 Wharton 473-4, but at least one-half of it is omitted.

37. Duer to Holker, 8 June 1782, Holker Papers, XVIII, LC. Morris to Duer, 23 July 1782, Letterbook D. I. Geary to Duer, 15 Aug. 1782, Duer Papers, Misc. MSS, NYHS. Morris to Sands, 22 June 1782, Letterbook C. Morris to Washington, 22 June 1782, *ibid.*

38. Morris to Livingston, 12 July 1782, Letterbook D. J. McCall to Swanwick, 19 July 1782, *ibid.* Washington to Morris, 30 July 1782, 24 Fitzpatrick 440.

39. Morris to Washington, 5 Aug. 1782, Letterbook D. See also the Issues for the Moving Army and West Point, p. 104.

40. Morris to Washington, 20 Aug. 1782, Letterbook D. See also Morris to Henry Remsen, 21 Aug. 1782, and Morris to Walter Livingston, 29 Aug. 1782, *ibid.* Morris to the Quartermaster General, 30 July 1782, *ibid.*

41. See Official Diary, 30 Aug. to 10 Sept. 1782, *passim.* Morris to Washington, 29 Aug. 1782, 5 Wharton 676. Also Morris to Washington, 30 Aug. 1782, *ibid.*, 679. Morris to Washington, 9 Sept. 1782, *ibid.*, 714-15 (quote from 715).

42. Washington to Duer, 18 Sept. 1782, 25 Fitzpatrick 175. When Washington did receive the messages from Morris, he wrote: "I am really more alarmed at the Contents of your letters . . . than at any occurrence which hath lately happened. . . ." Washington to Morris, 22 Sept. 1782, 25 Fitzpatrick 187. Sands, Livingston, and Co., 11 Sept. 1782, Cont. Cong. Papers 137, I, 824-30.

43. Sands, Livingston, Duer, and Parker, to the Superintendent of Finance, 11 Sept. 1782, Cont. Cong. Papers 137, I, 824-30.

44. Morris to Cornell, 20 Sept. 1782, Letterbook D. For the quote, Morris to Cornell, 23 Sept. 1782, *ibid.*

45. Cornell to Morris, 5 Oct. 1782, Cont. Cong. Papers 137, I, 850-53. First talks with Wadsworth and Carter about taking over contracts was September 18. Official Diary, 18 and 19 Sept. 1782. Agreement between the Superintendent of Finance and Wadsworth and Carter, Cont. Cong. Papers 137, I, 868-70. Morris to President of Congress, 21 Oct. 1782, Letterbook D.

46. Morris to President of Congress, 21 Oct. 1782, Letterbook D.

47. Morris and General Cornell both commented on the disputes among the contractors. The controversy over the "vacated" contract persisted over the years and apparently was finally settled in 1826. See Duer to Holker, 29 Nov. 1784, Holker Papers, XXVII, LC. Sands, Livingston, and Co. to Congress, 28 Feb. 1785, Cont. Cong. Papers 137, I, 881-3. Also their letter of 7 Oct. 1784, *ibid.*, 885. They gradually adopted the position that they did not make the move to vacate the contract but rather that the government initiated the action. See "Statement of the Claim of the Executors of the Estate of Walter

152-163

Livingston," dated 1826, in the Boston Public Library.

48. For high prices of specific supplies, see Morris to Hall, 10 June 1782, Letterbook C. Also Morris to Hall, 11 Sept. 1782, Letterbook D. Also Morris to Carrington, 17 Oct. 1782, *ibid.* Gist to John Herett, 22 Apr. 1782, Gist Papers, III, 77, Md. Hist. Soc. Green to [?], August [1782], printed in George Washington Greene, *The Life of Nathanael Greene* (3 vols., Boston, 1878-90), III, 445.

49. For the aid of the Financier, *Journals*, XXII, 201-02 (20 Apr. 1782), 342-43 (21 June 1782). Morris to Carrington, 25 Apr. 1782, Letterbook C. Morris to Greene, 10 June 1782, *ibid.* For Virginia posts, Morris to Bland, 18 June 1782, *ibid.* Greene apparently wrote to the Financier in August that "was I at liberty or had I the means to pay I could contract for the subsistence of the Army at the same rate as your contracts are at the Northward." But Greene's optimism, as later events demonstrated, was not warranted. Greene to Morris, 13 Aug. 1782, Osgood Papers, NYHS (copied extract).

50. Pickering to Morris, 19 Feb. 1782, Pickering Letterbook, War Dept. Records, NA. See also 5 Wharton 167-68. Washington to Morris, 8 Jan. 1783, 26 Fitzpatrick 20. Morris to Duer, 29 Aug. 1782, Letterbook D (another copy in Duer Papers, I, NYHS). Also Morris to Duer, 13 Sept. 1782, *ibid.* James Lovell to Duer, 14 Sept. 1782, Duer Papers, NYHS. Morris to Duer, 20 Oct. 1782, Letterbook D. For clothing, Morris to the Paymaster General, 1 Feb. 1782, Letterbook B. Morris to John Moylan, 25 July 1782, Letterbook D. Also Morris to Otis and Henley, 23 Oct. 1782, *ibid.* For final quote, Washington to General Heath, 5 Feb. 1783, 26 Fitzpatrick 97.

51. Morris to De Grasse, 16 May 1782, Agent of the Marine Letterbook, Annapolis. In this general connection of trade and taxes, see Pringle to Ridley, 19 May 1782, Ridley Papers, MHS. Morris to Duer, 2 Oct. 1782, Letterbook D.

52. Morris to Greene, 24 Apr. 1782, 5 Wharton 327. Morris to Varnum, 16 July 1782, Letterbook D. Morris to Hamilton, 28 Aug. 1782, 5 Wharton 674. By this time, the "partial, private, or interested views" had become "weak or wicked minds," and "vulgar souls." Morris to Lovell, 3 Oct. 1782, Letterbook D.

53. Morris to Hamilton, 16 Oct. 1782, Letterbook D. Heath to Lincoln, 19 Aug. 1782, Heath Papers, MHS. Washington to Lincoln, 2 Oct. 1782, 25 Fitzpatrick 227-28. Washington to James McHenry, 17 Oct. 1782, *ibid.*, 269-70.

54. Knox to Lincoln, 25 Nov. 1782, Knox Papers, MHS. Knox to Lincoln, 20 Dec. 1782, *ibid.* (private). Morris to the Governors of the States, 21 Oct. 1782. 5 Wharton 828. Morris to the President of Congress, 3 Dec. 1782, Letterbook D. Tench Tilghman had written to Morris asking for two months' pay for troops before going into winter quarters. At that time Tilghman stated that two months' pay would be adequate. ". . . That would serve them to amuse themselves, and that is all the use that a well fed and well clothed soldier has for money." Tilghman to Morris, 5 Oct. 1782, Cont. Cong. Papers, 137, I, 855-56.

55. Lincoln to John Lowell, 24 Sept. 1782, Sparks MSS 12, Widener Library, Harvard 495-96. The context of the letter indicates that Lincoln was not talking primarily about the army but about the states and taxes. He did not believe that the Confederation needed to be altered, but rather that the existing powers should be more strictly enforced, such as complying with requisitions. Morris to Gouverneur Morris, 3 Apr. 1782, Letterbook C. Gouverneur was engaged in settling an agreement on exchange of prisoners with the British at the time.

152-163

CHAPTER NINE

1. Official Diary, 11 Nov. 1782. Contract between John Hazlewood and Superintendent of Finance, dated 18 Dec. 1782, is in Irvine Papers, PHS. The other men concerned with Hazlewood were Blackiston, Dering, Par, and Millar.

2. Official Diary, 12 Nov. 1782.

3. Duer to Daniel Parker, 14 Nov. 1782, Duer Papers, Misc. MSS, NYHS. Holker "Observations," Holker Papers, XXX, 5909-10. These observations were made some time after the event when Holker was trying to recover damages from Parker who had absconded.

4. Official Diary, Nov., *passim*. The contract is in the Duer papers, dated 29 Nov. 1782, NYHS. Another copy, Holker Papers, XVIII, LC. Morris to Washington, 19 Dec. 1782, Letterbook E. The day the contract was issued Holker signed a security bond for the group for $200,000. Duer Papers, Misc. MSS, NYHS.

5. The actual contract for the New England area has not been located, perhaps because the contract was never fully executed. "Enclosed you have the papers which relate to Messrs. Parker and Co. contract for the Eastern States. The terms offered by Mr. Parker must be considered as accepted of altho the Contract was (by accident) not executed; and his account is to be settled accordingly." Morris to the Comptroller, 10 Oct. 1783, Letterbook F. For its terms, however, see Holker Papers, XIX, 3661, LC. Also Morris to Lovell, 17 Dec. 1782, and 3 Mar. 1783, Letterbook E. For the role of each partner, see Holker Papers, XXIX, 5769-70, LC. For the upper South, Morris to Samuel Patterson, 24 Feb. 1783, Letterbook E. Morris to Webb, 10 Jan. 1783, *ibid*. Morris to Lee, 20 Feb. 1783, *ibid*. Morris to Rawling and Nichols, 20 Feb. 1783, *ibid*.

6. For a brief survey of the letting of the contract, see William Johnson, *Sketches of the Life and Correspondence of Nathanael Greene* (2 vols.; Charleston, 1822), II, 374-75. For the first quote, see p. 375. Contract between John Banks and the Superintendent of Finance, 15 Feb. 1783, Gist Papers, III, 93-94, Md. Hist. Soc. (copy). This is signed by Carrington. Morris to Greene, 14 Mar. 1783, Letterbook E. There are some printed versions of this letter (6 Wharton 299 and 12 Sparks 338-39), but they have omitted the section of the letter that is quoted in the text.

7. My material on the Banks contract is disappointingly scanty. Why Banks failed financially is not at all clear. Greene's biographers claim that the depreciation of the warrants of Morris — they call them Morris notes but they were probably warrants—was responsible for the bankruptcy of John Banks, but such an explanation is hardly plausible. First, the warrants were sent by Banks to his agent in Philadelphia, a person named Stanley, and in Philadelphia such warrants met cash payments when they became due. If Morris notes were involved, then, no difficulty would have been encountered. Second, the contract called for a credit of four months— that is, the February issues were to be paid in June, the March issues in July—and under this agreement, therefore, no payment was due until July, and yet the collapse of Banks came before that date. This would indicate that the seat of the difficulty lay in the financial instability of the contractor. One gets a hint of this in Johnson, *Greene*, II, 383. For the evacuations, see the following: Morris to Carleton and Digby, 24 Apr. 1783, Morris to John Nicholson, 25 Apr. 1783, Morris to Benjamin Harwood, 18 May 1783, Morris to Carrington, 11 July 1783, all in Letterbook E. Also Morris to Comptroller, 26 Aug. 1783, Letterbook F. Also see Parker to Flint, 25 May 1783, New York, Holker Papers, XXI, 4022-23.

8. Parker to Duer, 25 Nov. 1782, Duer Papers, Misc. MSS, NYHS. Parker to Duer, Boston, 1 Dec. 1782, Holker Papers, XVIII, 3546 (copy). Parker's

exchange operation was a success. Parker to Holker, 13 Jan. 1783, Holker Papers, XIX, 3693.

9. For the subcontracts, see the following: Contract with Phelps, Edward, Reed, Davis, Skinner, Champion, Isham, and Day, 17 Dec. 1782, Holker Papers, XVIII, 3584-86, LC. Contract with Hugh Walshand, 2 Jan. 1783, Holker Papers, XIX, 3668-69. Contract with Christopher Below, 9 Jan. 1783, *ibid.*, 3686. Contract with Joshua King, 1 Mar. 1783, *ibid.*, 3800-01. There are a series of contracts with the officers and the various regiments in the Chamberlain Collection, Boston Public Library, dated 3 Jan., 9 Jan., and 13 Jan. 1783. Also one of 16 Jan. 1783, Holker Papers, XIX, 3710. For the stores under the direction of Melancton Smith, see "Agreement," *ibid.*, 3660. Also 3712. For the quote, Parker to Holker, 13 Jan. 1783, *ibid.*, 3693.

10. Washington to Morris, 29 Jan. 1783, 26 Fitzpatrick 78-80 and Morris's reply 5 Feb. 1783, Letterbook E. Washington to Morris, 25 Feb. 1783, 26 Fitzpatrick 161-62 and Morris' reply, 3 Mar. 1783, Letterbook E. For the quote, Washington to Morris, 12 Mar. 1783, 26 Fitzpatrick 212-13. For the general lack of complaint, see Heath Papers, *passim*, MHS and 26 Fitzpatrick, *passim*. For the passing complaint, Washington to Duer and Parker, 29 May 1783, 26 Fitzpatrick 459-60.

11. Duer to Holker, 20 Jan. 1783, Holker Papers, XIX, 3720, LC. Elisha Crane, who worked for Duer, had not received any answers to previous letters requesting money. This was a circumstance, said Crane, "I little expected from a man of your character and abilities. If you imagine a man in low circumstances can be able to be used as I am I must impute it to your want of knowledge of the necessities of poor men." 28 June 1783, Duer Papers, Misc. MSS, NYHS. For the quote and for Duer's suspicion with respect to the bills of exchange, see Duer to Holker, 2 May 1783, Dobbs Ferry, Holker Papers, XX, 3972-74, LC. For

masts, Duer to Holker, 4 Mar. 1783, *ibid.*, 3810-11, LC. The material which explains the acquisition of the British contract is extensive. For the letter of Morris and Lincoln, see Parker to Duer, 26 Mar. 1783, Duer Papers, I, NYHS. For Washington's, Parker to Duer, 6 Apr. 1783, Duer Papers, Misc. MSS. For the actual contract, 13 June 1783, Holker Papers, XXI, 4088-89. John Ross, Morris' friend and partner, offered to help them fulfill the British contract, and his offer was accepted. Ross to Parker and Co., 5 June 1783, Holker Papers, Clements Library, and Ross to Parker and Co., 26 June 1783, Holker Papers, XXI, LC. "You may depend on it," Ross wrote Parker, "nothing will be wanting to facilitate our business." Parker received a general passport for all articles to the army, but the result was disappointing to him. "We have very small prospects of making any speculations here to a very great advantage, we shall however be attentive that no object of consequence pass us without notice." Parker and Co. to Holker, 16 Apr. 1783, New York, Holker Papers, XX, LC. If some of the bookkeeping resembled Duer's, trouble for the firm was inevitable. One of Duer's bookkeepers asserted: "You will I am assured readily allow that Wm. Washburn's accounts were complicated and perplexing and rendered in such a manner as made it almost impossible to form an accurate statement of them. I confess to have been never more embarrassed in adjusting any accounts in my life than I was with his—and Mr. Geary informs me that finding it out of his power to come at a true state of the deficiencies . . . he was obliged to close them finally on mere supposition." Amos Marshall to Duer, Fishkill Landing, 7 June 1783, Duer Papers, Misc. MSS, NYHS.

12. Account of Wm Duer and Daniel Parker (contractors for the NY and NJ) with the US, dated 30 Apr. 1784, Duer Papers, Misc. MSS, NYHS. For profits see following footnote.

13. "Accounts of Robert Morris," in *The Bankers' Magazine and Statistical Register* (New York, 1860), 583-84. For a general comparison for the early years, see C. J. Bullock, *Finances of the United States from 1775-89*, p. 174.

    The question of profits touches upon the effectiveness of the contract system. Holker, apparently, when preparing his claims against Parker, estimated the profits as upwards of $100,000. Holker Papers, XIX, 3661-63. Also 3755-56. Holker makes his calculation by taking the number of rations issued according to the warrants of the Treasury, calculating a profit per ration, and then multiplying. Before discovering the Holker estimate, the present writer had attempted to calculate the profits by using the average price paid for the commodities which went into the ration and subtracting that total from the amount received from the Financier per ration in accordance with the contractual agreement. According to these calculations, the gross profits—that is, without deducting contingent expenses — would amount to something like 20 per cent. When this is applied to the total value of the issues in the New York and New Jersey contract—about $425,000 in round numbers — it would indicate a profit of some $85,000. This would parallel Holker's figures because the New York and New Jersey contract was by far the most important. It should be pointed out, however, that this 20 per cent gross profit is calculated on the gross business, and also that such expenses as storage and service charges would have to be deducted in order to obtain a net profit. If the $100,-000 of Holker's estimate is compared with the amount of capital which the entrepreneurs originally invested—$50,000—then their return was 200 per cent on their original investment. Even if $50,000 be accepted as a correct figure for profits, it would be less than 10 per cent of the gross business but 100% on the amount invested. The lack of adequate records from Parker make any precise calculation impossible. "Observations on the Daniel Parker and Company Contract" by Holker, Holker Papers, XXVIII, 5554-57. Also 5564.

14. The Financier specified his order of needs to Washington and Greene. See letter to Greene, 19 Dec. 1781, and to Washington, 26 Jan. 1782, both in Letterbook B. Morris omitted the tending of the sick in the letter to Greene. Indeed, the Financier's attitude toward the Revolutionary hospitals was one of skepticism. The first quotes come from the Greene letter and the later quotes from that to Washington.

15. Quoted in L. C. Hatch, *The Administration of the Revolutionary Army*, p. 150.

16. Gouverneur Morris to Matthew Ridley, 6 Aug. 1782, Ridley Papers, MHS. This letter was received on September 27 and answered on October 10, 1782. Another copy of the letter signed by Gouverneur is in the Chamberlain Collection, Boston Public Library. The Assistant to the Financier commented on the growing strength of the state governments which he saw as a hopeful sign. ". . . The solidity which our governments are daily acquiring is of great Consequence. There are always some small matters which influence much and are frequently overlooked. During the Ferment of the Revolution like as in other Ferments the Dregs were uppermost. The Liquor is daily refining[.] In other words men of Sense and Property are getting into the Places which such men ought to fill. The People are beginning to be convinced that those men are alone fit to govern and in a very little Time.[,] The Rulers of America will be well obeyed if they pursue the Paths of Honesty which I hope they will do."

17. Office of Finance to Washington, 16 Oct. 1782, HL. This letter is not in the handwriting of Morris nor is it signed by him, but it is headed the Office of Finance. It is not certain that Washington ever received it; at

168-175

least, he makes no acknowledgment
of it in his future letters to the Financier. The only indication that
he might have received it, is the
reply which he sent to the Reverend William Gordon about the
probable peace. "I never was among
the sanguine ones, consequently
shall be less disappointed than People of that description, if our Warfare should continue. From hence
(it being the opinion of some Men
that our expectations have an accordance with our wishes) it may
be infered that mine are for a prolongation of the War. But maugre
this doctrine, and the opinion of
others that a continuation of the
War till the Powers of Congress, our
political systems, and general form
of Government are better established, I can say, with much truth,
that there is not a Man in America
that more Fervently wishes for
Peace, and a return to private life
than I do." Washington to Gordon,
23 Oct. 1782, 25 Fitzpatrick 287-88.

18. Morris to Ridley, 6 Oct. 1782, Ridley Papers, MHS. This letter is
signed by Morris and addressed by
him, although it is not in his handwriting except for the corrections
which he inserted as I have pointed
out in the body of the letter. This
is his first letter to Ridley since
July.

19. Morris to Gates, 28 Jan. 1783, Phila.,
Gates Papers, 16, NYHS. See also
Morris to Gates, 3 Dec. 1782, *ibid*.
It is sometimes inferred that the
Financier was connected with the
"monarchial" tendencies in this
period, but there is no hint in all
the correspondence of Robert Morris, either public or private, which
would connect him with such views.
In the case of Gouverneur Morris, it
is not always possible to ascertain
his positions. He enjoyed shocking
people and he savored a phrase—
usually Biblical—which would do
just that.

20. Gouverneur Morris to Ridley, 1 Jan.
1783, Ridley Papers, MHS. It should
be emphasized that the army as a
public creditor amounted to a considerable sum. According to an esti-

mate, some $11,000,000 was owed to
the soldiers, a sum which equalled
that of the loan office certificates.
Cont. Cong. Papers 137, II, 203a.

21. Morris to Washington, 25 Sept.
1782, Morris Coll., HL. Morris to a
Committee of Congress, 14 Apr.
1783, 6 Wharton 376.

22. James Madison, "Notes of Debates
in the Continental Congress," *Journals*, XXV, 846. Hereafter this
source will be cited as Madison's
Notes. *Madison's Notes*, p. 847. Morris to the President of Congress, 9
Jan. 1783, Letterbook E. *Journals*,
XXIV, 43-44 (9 and 10 Jan. 1783).
Madison's Notes, p. 848. Official Diary, 13 and 17 Jan. 1783. *Madison's
Notes*, p. 857. *Journals*, XXIV, 48-
49 (17 Jan. 1783).

23. Morris to the President of Congress,
24 Jan. 1783, 6 Wharton 229. In his
Official Diary Morris recorded:
"This day I wrote a letter to his
Excellency the President of Congress which was dictated by the
warmest attachment to the United
States a due sense of the Honor of
Congress, a strict regard to the principles of Justice a pure and compassionate feeling for the public
Creditors and a lively feeling of
what is due to my own character."
24 Jan. 1783. Three months later
Gouverneur wrote: "You will have
seen Mr. Morris's resignation. I
know not what effect it may have
on our Credit in Europe. Here it
was intended to stimulate exertions
for the support of credit, but I believe that such things must take the
course which nature has prescribed
for them." Gouverneur Morris to
Ridley, 17 Apr. 1783, Ridley Papers,
MHS.

24. *Madison's Notes*, p. 862 (24 Jan.
1783). *Journals*, XXIV, 95 (25 Jan.
1783).

25. Official Diary, 25 Jan. 1783. Hamilton to Washington, 7 Feb. 1783, 7
Burnett 33 (first quote), 34 (second
quote). For the change in the tenor
of Hamilton's letters, see Lodge,
Works, VIII, *passim*. When Hamilton was Receiver of Taxes in New
York, he asked Morris how much he
should press "the establishment of

permanent *funds."* 14 Sept. 1782, *ibid.,* 78.

In late February, Morris asked Congress for permission to lift the ban of secrecy on his resignation in order to make arrangements with those who had made agreements with the Office of Finance. His letter of resignation was published almost immediately and its content and timing caused a great deal of speculation. Merchants and friends like Mark Pringle worried about what the resignation would mean to public credit, and Greene wrote anxiously that if the report were confirmed "the contractors will not go on with the business." Morris' friend Jay was equally anxious, and even Arthur Lee complained that Morris' resignation placed the public credit in jeopardy. Madison and Hamilton thought that the publication of the letter was a misstep on the part of the Financier. The Financier probably hoped that all of this would increase the pressure on Congress to adopt his program on funding. For the quote, Greene to Pettit, 3 Apr. 1783, Charlestown, Reed Papers, 10, NYHS.

26. Gouverneur Morris to General Greene, 15 Feb. 1783, quoted in Jared Sparks, *Gouverneur Morris,* I, 251. G. Morris to General Knox, 7 Feb. 1783, quoted in Hatch, *The Administration of the Revolutionary Army,* p. 164.

27. Morris to Greene, 31 May 1783, Letterbook E.

28. Morris to Paine, 4 Feb. 1783, Letterbook E.

29. See *Madison's Notes,* Feb. and Mar., *passim.* Arnold to the Governor of R. I., 28 Mar. 1783, 7 Burnett 111. Lee to Samuel Adams, 29 Jan. 1783, *ibid.,* 28. *Madison's Notes,* p. 884 (29 Jan. 1783).

30. This summary paragraph represents my conclusions after a thorough reading of the debates and the letters of men in and out of Congress in connection with the interests of the areas they represented, and an examination of the actions of the various states. For specific citation to states mentioned, see

Richard P. McCormick, *New Jersey in the Critical Period,* p. 233-44. Freeman Hart, *The Valley of Va. in the Am. Rev.,* p. 117, p. 170. Rhode Island in the Confederation has been more expertly analyzed than ever before in a series of articles by Hillman Metcalf Bishop in *Rh. Is. Hist.* For his article on the continental impost, see Vol. VIII, 1-10 (January, 1949). Brunhouse, *The Counter Revolution in Penn.,* pp. 131-32.

For a different view of this entire issue, although based on a reading of much the same material, see Merrill Jensen, *The New Nation,* pp. 73-76. Professor Jensen's volume, in many places, contains conclusions somewhat different from those offered in the present work.

31. For the speech of Wilson, see *Madison's Notes* (29 Jan. 1783), pp. 879-81. Fitzsimmons, who had seen the Financier about the memorial of the Pennsylvania Assembly on behalf of the public creditors, wrote a strong report on general funding which was apparently adopted by Congress. Despite the discouraging obstacles which had been placed in their path, Congress "conceive it a duty to themselves and to their constituents, to persevere in their intentions, and to renew and extend their endeavours to procure the establishment of revenues equal to the purpose of funding *all* the debts of the United States." *Journals,* XXIV, 104 (30 Jan. 1783). Much of this report reflects the ideas and even the phrases found in the earlier communications from the Office of Finance.

32. For a choice example on consultation, Official Diary, 24 Feb. 1783. For quote, *Journals,* XXIV, 173 (6 Mar. 1783). Morris to President of Congress, 8 Mar. 1783, 6 Wharton 280. Irving Brant in the second volume of his masterful biography of James Madison does not highlight the difference between Morris' plan of funding (and later Hamilton's) and Madison's. Brant, *James Madison,* II, 233. Brant's blow-by-blow account of Congress in these months

176-182

is admirable, but he does fail to note the extended pressure of funding before this crucial period. Although the Financier had advocated limited assumption for some time, the extension of the idea properly belongs to Madison. It is logical, of course, that a Virginian should bring forward this proposition, for that state stood to benefit by assumption because of its extensive debts. It was quite another matter when assumption came up during Washington's administration under the new Constitution. Then Virginia had provided for much of her state debt, while some of the other states had reneged.

33. Knox to Lincoln, 12 Mar. 1783, Knox Papers, MHS. *Madison's Notes* (17 Mar. 1783), p. 926. With regard to Washington's action, Madison wrote: "This dissipation of the cloud which seemed to have been gathering afforded great pleasure on the whole to Congress; but it was observable that the part which the Gen had found it necessary and thought it his duty, to take, would give birth to events much more serious if they sd [should] not be obviated by the establishment of such funds as the Gen, as well as the army, had declared to be necessary." *Madison's Notes* (22 Mar. 1783), p. 938.

34. Washington to Hamilton, 4 Apr. 1783, 26 Fitzpatrick 293. The two other reasons which prompted Washington to write were: one, the army was a dangerous instrument to play with; and two, everything should be done to disband them peacefully and quickly. Washington definitely thought that the story of uneasiness in the army originated in Philadelphia and drifted — with careful direction by certain men in Philadelphia — toward the troops stationed in New York. Washington to Joseph Jones, 12 Mar. 1783, 26 Fitzpatrick 213-14. Hamilton's reply to Washington is interesting, and plays down the Financier's early position. Hamilton to Washington, 9 Apr. 1783, 7 Burnett 130. In that section of the letter which precedes

the part where he replied to Washington with respect to Morris, the New Yorker still emphasized that "the necessity and discontents of the army presented themselves as a powerful engine." For quote, Morris to Washington, 29 May 1783, 6 Wharton 454. Washington apparently sent a letter to Morris on the 8th, but it is not published in Fitzpatrick, and the present writer has been unable to locate it.

35. *Journals,* XXIV, 256-62 (18 Apr. 1783). For quote, p. 258.

36. Morris to the President of Congress, 1 May 1783, 6 Wharton 399-403. Morris to the President of Congress, 3 May 1783, *ibid.,* 405. *Journals,* XXIV, 283-85 (28 Apr. 1783), and 326 (2 May 1783). Also Official Diary, 29 Apr. 1783.

37. Morris to Edward Carrington, 19 May 1783, Letterbook E.

38. Dr. E. James Ferguson has written an important article showing the constructive steps taken by the states in solving the problem of public creditors during the whole of the Confederation period, 1781-89. His analysis of the early years does not in all respects agree with that presented in the text. Ferguson, "State Assumption of the Federal Debt During the Confederation" in *Miss. Valley Hist. Review,* XXXVIII, 403-24 (Dec., 1951).

39. Samuel Osgood to John Adams, 7 Dec. 1783, 7 Wharton 379. Morris to Governor of Va., 19 Aug. 1783, Letterbook F. Some of the criticism was vicious. Articles in the *Freeman's Journal* beginning with February 1783, were full of insinuations with regard to the Financier's motives. By April the articles became sharp personal attacks. Replies to these attacks upholding Morris were published at intervals.

40. Morris to Committee of Congress, 14 Apr. 1783, 6 Wharton 376. For tax collection, Cont. Cong. Papers 137, II, 455.

41. Official Diary, 24 Dec. 1782. Willing to Bingham, 12 Sept. 1783, Provincial Delegates, I, PHS. Willing to Bingham, 29 Nov. 1783, Provincial Delegates, V, PHS. The Bank Divi-

dends for 1783, according to the calculations of the author, amounted to 13 per cent. See also Lewis, *Bank of North America,* pp. 49-53. The Bank of Massachusetts and the Bank of New York were organized in 1784. There was a movement afoot to establish one in Baltimore. See Charles Carroll to Fitzsimmons, 28 Apr. 1783, Annapolis, Gratz Coll., PHS. It is interesting to notice that Carroll states he is in favor of a bank but he is financially unable to contribute much because of the "nature of my estate." "With a large landed estate," he continued, "and considerable sums at interest I can command but very little money."

42. Morris to Committee of Congress (Bland, Fitzsimmons, Hamilton, Osgood, Peters), 14 Apr. 1783, 6 Wharton 376 (first quote), 377 (second quote). Morris to Committee of Congress, 15 May 1783, 6 Wharton 429-32. *Journals,* XXIV, 284-85 (28 Apr. 1783).

43. Official Diary, 27 May and 7, 9, and 10 June 1783. Also, Morris to Washington, 5 June 1783, Letterbook E. Morris to Governors, 5 June 1783, 6 Wharton 476. Morris to Governors, 11 July 1783, *ibid.,* 534.

44. Hatch, *The Administration of the Revolutionary Army,* pp. 180-82. *Journals,* XXIV, 430-33 (11 July 1783). The quote comes from page 432. Morris to the President of Congress, 18 July 1783, 6 Wharton 563-66. The quote is on p. 566.

45. For Phila., see Pickering to Hodgdon letters in Pickering Letterbook, *passim* (No. 11—12 Dec. 1782 to 19 June 1783), NA. For Northern Va., see Reynolds to Hoe and Harrison, 19 Mar. 1783, York, Reynolds Letterbook, LC. For quote, Morris to Houston, 3 Mar. 1783, Letterbook E. Morris to Thomas Tillotson, 12 Aug. 1783, Letterbook F. See Royal Flint to Holker, 16 Apr. 1783, Newburgh, Holker Papers, XX, LC. Pickering to Hodgdon, 29 Apr. 1783, Pickering Letterbook (No. 11), NA. For some exceptions, see Morris to Hezekiah Merrill, 31 Mar. 1783, Letterbook E. Also Holker Papers, XX, 3937-38. For the Conn. area, see

John Dishon to Parker, 24 Aug. 1783, New London, Holker Papers, XXI, LC. For Codman's observations, see his letter to Fitzsimmons, Boston, 9 Oct. 1783, Codman Letterbook, Baker Library.

46. See Pickering to Richard Claiborne, 16 Aug. 1783, Pickering Letterbook (No. 12), NA. Morris to the Governors of the States, 28 July 1783, 6 Wharton 612.

47. Morris to the President of Congress, 30 July 1782, 5 Wharton 636-38. For the inclusion of the foreign service, Morris to President of Congress, 8 May 1782, *ibid.,* 400. Also Morris to Franklin, Adams, and Jay, 25 Sept. 1782, *ibid.,* 763. On the estimates, see Cont. Cong. Papers 141, I, 3-57 and Cont. Cong. Papers 144, 9-49. See C. J. Bullock, *Finances of the United States,* pp. 247-50. *Journals,* XXIII, 658-60 (16 Oct. 1782), 665-69 (18 Oct. 1782). Franklin to Morris, 12 Aug. 1782, 5 Wharton 659.

48. Morris to Benjamin Stoddert, 20 June 1783, Letterbook E. Morris to James Lovell, 22 June 1783, *ibid.* Morris to Lovell, 8 July 1783, *ibid.* Morris to Houston, 8 July 1783, *ibid.* Morris to the Governors, 28 July 1783, 6 Wharton 611. Morris to Houston, 16 Sept., 7 Oct., and 1 Dec. 1783, Letterbook F. Morris to George Webb, 19 Aug. 1783, *ibid.* Nourse, "The Accounts of Robert Morris" in the *Banker's Magazine and Statistical Register* (New York, 1860), 583. Cont. Cong. Papers 137, II, 449. In some of the Southern states Morris accepted specifics in payment of taxes. In fact, in Virginia, he introduced a tobacco-buying program partly with the intent of fulfilling some of the obligations on the Dutch loan, partly to stimulate taxation by providing a market, and partly to quiet the criticism from some states of the upper South which claimed that Morris' policies were draining specie from that region. There is a considerable correspondence on this but see Morris to Daniel Clark, 23 Sept. 1782, Letterbook D, and 17 Dec. 1782, Letterbook E. Also Morris to George

182-193

Webb, 17 Oct. and 11 Nov. 1782, Letterbook D. Morris to Webb, 12 May and 15 July 1783 in Letterbook E. Also Morris to Webb, 14 Oct. and 23 Dec. 1783, Letterbook F. For shipments, Morris to Webb, 17 Apr. 1783, Letterbook E. Morris to Daniel Clark, 23 Apr. 1783, *ibid.*

49. My analysis is based upon the same key mercantile materials which were used in my earlier sections on this subject. They are for the most part: Holker Papers, Ridley Papers, Woolsey and Salmon Letterbook, Beverley Welsh Letterbook, Constable Letterbook — 1782-90, Reynolds Letterbook, John Welsh Letterbook, and John Codman Letterbook. Also a few letters from Pierce Butler to Fitzsimmons reporting on Charleston have been helpful. Gratz Coll., PHS. Also *Commerce of Rhode Island*, II, 1783, *passim*. Only the quotes will be cited in the next few paragraphs.

50. Pringle to Holker, 24 Mar. 1783, Balt., Holker Papers, XX, LC. For Havana circumstances, Pollock to Morris, 10 Sept. 1783, Cont. Cong. Papers 137, III, 185-86, LC (copy). Constable to "Dear John," 30 Oct. 1783, Letterbook (1782-90), Constable-Pierrepont Papers, NYPL.

51. *Journals*, XXIII, 577-79 (14 Sept. 1782). Morris to Franklin, 27 Sept. 1782, 5 Wharton 771-75. For the quote, 774. In his usual fashion Morris provided the instructions for the disposition of the loan. He wanted $1,000,000 shipped from Havana, free of duty, through the intervention of the Spanish court, $500,000 put in the hands of Le Couteulx and the rest placed in the hands of Grand. Franklin to Morris, 14 Dec. 1782, 6 Wharton 134-36. Franklin to Morris, 23 Dec. 1782, *ibid.*, 159-60. Paine, *Joshua Barney*, p. 219. Official Diary, 12 Mar. 1783. Morris to Franklin, 26 May 1783, 6 Wharton 450. Franklin to Morris 27 July 1783, *ibid.*, 598-600. For the quote, John Jay to Gouverneur Morris, 17 July 1783, Sparks MSS 32, II, Widener Library, Harvard. Morris to Franklin, 30 Sept. 1783, 6 Wharton 708.

52. Morris to Messrs. Willink (et al), 29 Jan., 12 and 29 Apr. 1783, Letterbook E. For sale of goods, see particularly Morris to Carrington, 19 May 1783, *ibid.* See also Pickering Letterbooks, 1783, *passim*, NA. Morris to Willink etc., 5 Aug., 13 Aug., 18 Sept., Letterbook F. Morris to Messrs. Willink etc., 23 Oct. 1783, 6 Wharton, 712-13. Morris to Willink, 12 Dec. 1783, Letterbook F. Nourse, "The Accounts of Robert Morris," in *Bankers' Magazine and Statistical Register* (1860), 583. The excess of expenditures over payments is given as $230,000 (in round numbers) but he has carried the anticipations of 1782 which amounted to $380,000 as an expenditure item for 1783, and therefore he carried over a balance. The comparison indicates a paring down of anticipations for the year as a whole.

53. Morris to Willink etc., 31 Dec. 1783, Letterbook F. This letter is printed in 6 Wharton 749 but the most important part of the letter is omitted. The same is true of 12 Sparks 437-39. See particularly Morris to Willink etc., 31 Dec. 1783, 6 Wharton 750-51. This is the second letter for this date and should not be confused. Morris always pointed up the measures which he thought bolstered the American credit. For a good example, see Morris to Willink, etc., 5 Nov. 1783, Letterbook F. One of the constant problems which confronted Morris was the way in which old bills drawn before he came into office would turn up in France and be paid out of current loans. Indeed, the Financier seldom knew the precise state of the accounts in Europe. This was responsible for part of the deficiency of funds at this time. In order for Grand to meet his bills, Morris transferred some funds from the Dutch loan. See, for example, Morris to Grand, 9 May 1783, Letterbook E.

54. Morris to Olney, 20 Dec. 1783, Letterbook F.

55. Morris to Olney, 20 Aug. 1783, Letterbook F.

56. Stephen Higginson to Samuel Adams, 20 May 1783, 7 Burnett 167. The criticisms of Morris can always be found in the same group of letters, namely, those of Higginson, Arthur Lee, Samuel Osgood, and occasionally a person embittered by a personal event such as Andrew Gillon, who had not, according to his view, been treated properly by Franklin.

CHAPTER TEN

1. Morris to Richard Butler, 18 July 1782, Morris Papers, NYPL.
2. See Holker Papers, XXXI, 6115, LC. Also see Holker to Ridley, 21 Nov. 1782, *ibid.*, XVIII, and Pringle to Holker, 13 May 1783, *ibid.*, XX, LC.
3. Morris to John Cruden at New York, 5 Aug. 1782, Morris Papers, NYPL. Morris to Cruden, 13 Aug. 1782, *ibid.* Morris to Washington, 17 Aug. 1782, Morris's Coll. HL. Washington to Morris, 23 Aug. 1782, 25 Fitzpatrick 54. Also Washington to Morris, 2 Sept. 1782, *ibid.*, 108.
4. The Holker Papers fairly bristle with anticipations of post-war trade, as do the papers of many other businessmen in this period. For the first quote, Morris to Ridley, 6 Oct. 1782, Ridley Papers, MHS. For the second quote, Holker to Ridley, 28 May 1783, *ibid.*
5. The story of the preparations is scattered throughout the Holker Papers, for the most part, beginning with September 1783. Detailed citation would be too cumbersome. For key document, however, of Morris' investment in these ships, see Holker Papers, XXVIII, 5563. For cargo of *Empress*, *ibid.*, XXIV, 4695. For assignment of Parker and Company's share to creditors, *ibid.*, XXV, 4859. See Ver Steeg, "Financing and Outfitting the First United States Ship to China," in the *Pacific Historical Review*, XXII, 1-12.
6. Morris to Ridley, 5 Nov. 1783, Ridley Papers, MHS.
7. Printed note sent to Correspondents concerning Willing, Morris, and Swanwick, 15 Sept. 1783, in Morris Papers, NYPL. For some of the activity of Swanwick, see the extensive correspondence of the firm with Tench Tilghman and Company, Morris Papers, PA.
8. There is a comparatively full correspondence from Morris to Tilghman in the Morris Papers, NYPL. For capital invested, Morris to letters from correspondents acknowledging the firm are in Tench Tilghman, 30 Apr. 1784, *ibid.* The man Papers, Md. Hist. Soc.
9. See Chap. ii, Section I.
10. See the Constable Letterbook, 1782-90 (beginning in May 1784), Constable-Pierrepont Papers, NYPL. For the quote, Morris to Tilghman, 22 June 1784, Morris Papers, NYPL.
11. Morris to Daniel Parker, 22 Dec. 1783, Letterbook F. For Daniel Parker and Co. troubles, Holker Papers, 1784, LC, *passim*, and Duer Papers, 1784, NYHS, *passim*. The difficulties continued throughout the decade. For Duer alone, Morris to Duer, 12 Apr. 1784, Letterbook G. For Daniel Parker and Co. indebtedness to U.S., Morris to Parker and Co., 11 Aug. 1784, *ibid.* Morris tried to get the Sands, Livingston, and Co. dispute settled many times. Letterbook G, *passim*.
12. It would be too cumbersome to cite in detail the numerous correspondence upon which this paragraph is based. See Morris to Gorham, 15 Dec. 1783, Letterbook F. For the plea for lump settlements, Morris to Fox, 15 Oct. 1783, *ibid.* The *Journals* of Congress have substantial portions devoted to settlements (see index). See also, Cont. Cong. Papers 137, II, 783-800, and III, 141-44, 271-85. Also Morris' reply in reference to the question of settlements in 6 Wharton 726-33.
13. Morris to the Commissioners of Accounts (Circular), 4 Sept. 1783, 6 Wharton 671-73.
14. Morris to Jefferson, 1 May 1784, Letterbook G. For Jefferson's ideas

193-199

on coinage, Dumas Malone, *Jefferson The Virginian* (Boston, 1948), pp. 416-418.

15. Morris to the President of Congress, 17 Mar. 1784, 6 Wharton 787-88. There is a good bit of correspondence dealing with these purchases of the Financier, some of it (from Virginia) critical of the purchases. At first remittances were sent through private firms, and when this did not work out well, remittances were sent through Receivers of Taxes. See the letters to La Case from Sept. through Dec., 1783, Letterbook F, *passim*. Also those to Webb in Va. for the same period. Also Morris to John Fitzgerald, 7

Apr. 1784, Letterbook G. Morris to Franklin, 12 and 13 Feb. 1784, 6 Wharton 769-73, Morris to Le Couteulx, 12 Feb. 1784, *ibid.*, 767-68.

16. Nourse, "The Accounts of Robert Morris," in *Bankers' Magazine and Statistical Register* (New York, 1860), 58.

17. Samuel Osgood to Stephen Higginson, 2 Feb. 1784, 7 Burnett 431-32. For the entire letter, 430-36.

18. Charles A. Beard, *An Economic Interpretation of the Constitution* (1935 edition; New York, 1935), p. 100 (first quote), p. 114 (second quote). Hamilton is actually the hero of Beard's volume.

BIBLIOGRAPHY

The bibliographies of many of my predecessors in their studies of the Revolutionary Generation provided indispensable guideposts for this study. I made free use of four distinguished bibliographies in particular—Robert East's *Business Enterprise and the American Revolutionary Era* (New York, 1938); Evarts B. Greene's *The Revolutionary Generation* (New York, 1943); Joseph S. Davis' *Essays in Earlier American Corporations* (two volumes, Cambridge, 1917); and Allan Nevins' *The American States During and After the Revolution* (New York, 1924). It has not seemed necessary to duplicate their work, and therefore the following list of printed works is very selective; nothing is included which is not specifically cited in the footnotes. As a result, many secondary works and printed source materials which were examined and which unquestionably left sundry general impressions with me important to my work are not found in the bibliography that follows, because the material was not used in a specific manner. Among these omissions is a considerable list of town, county, and state histories; such a list, with an evaluation of each volume, would serve a worthwhile purpose, but this bibliography is not the place for it. Newspapers are also omitted, for only two newspapers were examined thoroughly, the *Pennsylvania Packet* and the *Freeman's Journal*. Other newspapers, occasionally cited in the footnotes, were explored with specific points in mind rather than inspected in a thorough and regular manner. No introductory paragraph to printed materials would be complete without paying profound tribute to the large number of scholars who have provided important and illuminating monographs and general works on the Revolutionary Generation. Without their contributions, this volume could not have been written.

With respect to manuscripts, an essay (Section A) is included on strictly Morris material. To the best of my knowledge, every group of Morris letters was exploited with one exception — the Morris Collection in the Huntington Library. Limited funds prohibited a trip to California, but negotiations produced a score of key letters on microfilm. For this success I am indebted to Dr. Sylvester K. Stevens, State Historian of Pennsylvania, who provided me with a list of Morris materials at the Huntington, and Professor Dwight C. Miner of Columbia University, who, on a research visit to the Huntington, conducted the final arrangements with consummate skill. Section B under manuscript sources includes the material outside of the immediate Morris circle, used either in tracing the operation of the Financier's program or in throwing light on the general career of Robert Morris. This introductory comment could not properly conclude without an expression of sincere gratitude to those individuals who in the last quarter of a century have compiled various invaluable "Guides to Manuscripts," for without such help the work involved in this book would certainly have been quadrupled.

I. MANUSCRIPT SOURCES

A. Morris Material

Morris was at times a prolific correspondent, but unfortunately his carefully husbanded papers began to disappear in the years after his death.

Consequently, the manuscript material on Morris is rich only for certain periods.

Except for birth certificates, a few isolated letters, and similar fragmentary data, the childhood and early youth of Morris is obscure. Anecdotes grew up in later years which have often been presented with authenticity since, but there is no way of proving — or disproving, for that matter — their validity. When the firm of Willing and Morris is established, the existing material assumes more encouraging proportions in the form of the Willing Letterbooks (Historical Society of Pennsylvania) covering the period 1754-61. From 1761 until the Revolution, however, only small patches of business and personal correspondence appear.

Beginning with the Revolution and ending with 1781, the Morris material takes on more substantial proportions. In the Historical Society of Pennsylvania, the Morris Papers contain a good many unpublished and neglected letters on both his public and private careers, especially among the miscellaneous and uncatalogued manuscripts. The correspondence of Morris' Pennsylvania contemporaries helps to provide an understanding of his world in addition to the specific letters of the Philadelphia merchant found in these collections. Among such collections must be cited the following: Franklin Papers, Wilson Papers, Read Papers, Wayne Papers, Peters Papers, Irving Papers, John Ross Invoice Books, and the enormous Dreer and Gratz collections. The Letterbooks of John Nicholson — with whom Morris later became involved in business — supposedly start with 1775, but they are of no value until the 1790's. Also, a ledger of John Hatkinson, with whom Morris was reportedly in partnership, is, for all intents and purposes, worthless. One business connection can be explored in the Carter Braxton Papers, although these documents have a limitation, for they were collected to settle a dispute between Braxton and Morris. In the Pennsylvania Archives, two sets of Morris material are significant: one, the Morris Papers (Entry No. 128) which have been completely neglected by students of the period; and two, material recently photostated from the remaining family papers in the hands of Robert Morris VI. The material from the family helps to fill gaps in the correspondence of other depositories; it also contains Morris' draft of a letter to Necker. The other papers at the Pennsylvania Archives comprise the major source of the Hudson-Morris connection. The Morris correspondence in the Library of Congress is extremely important. Here the informative and bulky letters to Bingham are located, which, together with a few letters in the Historical Society of Pennsylvania, tell the Morris-Bingham story. Here, too, are letters to numerous other business connections. In addition to the explicit Morris Papers, the Holker Papers are invaluable in tracing certain business and personal connections of Morris (see explanatory note in Section B).

In the Papers of the Continental Congress, 133, the Letterbook of the Committee at Philadelphia (1776) is found, and in the same vast collection (137, Appendix), those letters which were sent to Congress by the Philadelphia Committee are copied. The Letterbook of John Bradford illuminates the role of Morris in the Secret Committee of Commerce as well as in occasional business interests in New England. In contrast to the material in the Library of Congress, the Morris Papers in the New York Public Library are disappointingly thin in the period 1776-81. The correspondence does not really begin to swell until the 1780's, when it becomes particularly important in tracing the activities of the Morris-Tench Tilghman connection. There are some important letters in the Morris Papers at the New-York Historical Society, but a good many others are scattered through an assortment of collections. Figuring most prominently are the Gates Papers and the Duer Papers. The Morris Collection in the Huntington Library is most important for personal materials although there is some informative materials on other matters. Almost all the early mercantile correspondence of Willing and Morris with Richard Champion to be found in this collection is printed in George H. Guttridge (editor), *The American Correspondence of a Bristol Merchant, 1766-76.* Some of the personal material is available in Charles Hart's "Mary White — Mrs. Robert Morris," in the *Pennsylvania Magazine of History and Biography,* II.

The basic materials of Morris as Financier are the Letterbooks (A through G) and Diary (three volumes) of the Office of Finance. Only scraps of the Diary, but a substantial proportion of the letters, were published in the eleventh and twelfth volumes of Jared Spark's *The Diplomatic Correspondence of the American Revolution* (Boston, 1829-30), and republished — often with the precise omissions and errors — in Francis Wharton's *Revolutionary Diplomatic Correspondence* (six volumes; Washington, D. C., 1889). Those letters sent from the Office of Finance to Congress are found, for the most part, in Papers of the Continental Congress (137), at the Library of Congress. The Agent of the Marine Letterbook at Annapolis also provides important material for some phases of the Financier's program.

The fiscal records are so widely scattered that their utility was seriously reduced. Three sets of books were apparently involved in keeping accounts by the Register of the Treasury — blotters, wastebooks, and journals. Original entries amounting to a daily running record seem to have been made on a blotter. Then the entries were consolidated and transferred to a more comprehensive wastebook, and finally a finished account was transcribed into the Journals. At first glance, the blotters in the Fiscal Section, National Archives (Nos. 1 through 7), would indicate that a complete record was available of original entries during the administration of the Financier. However, blotter No. 1 begins with 16 January 1782; blotter No. 2 does not follow blotter No. 1, but is a series of incidental entries ranging from 1782 to 1787. Only with blotter No. 3 (beginning 10 December 1782) do the blotters, as preserved in the Fiscal Section, make up a full record. The wastebooks covering the period — "B," "C," "D," "E" — are located in the General Accounting Office, Records Section, Cameron, Virginia. In the third set of records — the Journals — Journal "A" is located at the Library of Congress, while Journals "B" and "C" are found in the Records Section of the General Accounting Office, Cameron, Virginia. (The volumes of the Journal which cover the Confederation period are not in order. The volume called "D" in Cameron, Virginia, is mislabeled, because there is a considerable jump in time between it and volume C.) It is already apparent how the usefulness of these volumes is limited. For example, wastebook "B" and part of "C," which are in the Records Section at Cameron, Virginia, tie in with Journal "A," which is located in the Library of Congress. In 1785, Morris published *A Statement of the Accounts of the United States of America During the Administration of the Superintendent of Finance,* but it is not as helpful as it should be because he fails to strike a comprehensive yearly balance. The original clean copy of this volume is located in the Fiscal Section, National Archives, but it is incomplete. Anyone interested in any department of the government previous to 1789 would do well to consult the very valuable typescript copy called "Preface to Prefederal Records" which is available in the main reading room at the National Archives at Washington.

For the later private business career of Morris, the sources cited earlier continue to be indispensable. In addition, it should be mentioned that a considerable number of Willing, Morris, and Swanwick letters to Tench Tilghman and Company in the Pennsylvania Archives — beginning with 1783 — become valuable for these years. They fit in with the full record of Morris' letters to Tench Tilghman in the New York Public Library. The Constable Letterbook also becomes important beginning in 1784 (see the explanatory note in Section B).

B. Other Manuscript Material

American Antiquarian Society:

Andrew Craigie Papers. These papers contain material which fits in with the Duer Papers and Holker Papers to help round out the story of Daniel Parker and Company. Joseph S. Davis in his *Essays* used some of this material with profit. The great bulk of the papers go beyond the immediate period covered in the present study. Many business and speculative trends from 1789 on are spectacularly illuminated. This part of the papers still needs to be exploited fully. They fit in perfectly with the Constable Papers in the New York Public Library and to a more limited extent with the Duer Papers in the New-York Historical Society.

Boston Public Library:

Chamberlain Collection. Used card catalogue index for the most part.

Clements Library:

Sir Henry Clinton Papers. Used to find specific data rather than thoroughly canvassed. Mass of material but little pertinent to this study.
Lord George Germain Papers. Used to locate specific data rather than thoroughly canvassed. Concerned largely with military and naval matters.
Nathanael Greene Papers. A rich collection of letters received and sent which needs to be worked much more thoroughly for the military aspects of the Revolution, particularly the Southern campaign after 1780. Illuminating background comments in addition to specific Morris letters.
John Holker Papers. This one volume of papers supplements the forty volumes in the Library of Congress.
Shelburne Papers. Again a rich but little exploited collection. For the present study, only specific data were looked for rather than intensive inspection of the entire collection. Excellent material. (A considerable amount of pre-Revolutionary material.)

Essex Institute:

Derby Papers. Inconsequential for my study.

   Other miscellaneous collections were inspected, but in most cases the data was either too fragmentary or too scattered to be of assistance.

Harvard University, Baker Library:

Amory Papers. Used Volumes LII and LIII ("Letters sent 1768-90" and

"Letters Received 1781-90") and Volume XLVI. These letters were moderately useful for my purposes. They are enlightening on the actions of a single firm, especially in their London connections.

Autograph Letters of Boston Merchants, 1780-90. The volume which covers this period is concentrated on Lopez Letters. It is useful material but, unfortunately, very incomplete.

Codman-Smith Letterbook 1780-83; Codman Letterbook 1783-85. These letterbooks are comparatively complete within their years although the second does not follow the first precisely. A great deal of information on trade and its problems — changes, connections, ingredients, etc.

Hancock Papers. So scattered in content for the period of the Confederation that they are of little value.

Daniel Parker Letterbook. Some revealing letters are contained in this Letterbook, but by no means does it describe completely the activities of Parker in this period.

Tudor Papers. Not very useful.

John Welsh Letterbook. The business of Welsh was not as extensive as that of many of his contemporaries, but he reflects the problems of the trading community.

Harvard University, Widener Library:

Sparks Manuscripts. Useful for Gouverneur Morris materials. Calendared and indexed.

Lee Papers. Useful for some factual material, but particularly good as an insight into Arthur Lee. Calendared and indexed.

Library of Congress:

Robert Beverly Letterbook, 1761-93. Not as valuable for trade as one would like to have it. More useful as insight into Beverly.

Ephraim Blaine Papers. These papers are almost exclusively letters to Blaine. Volumes III and IV are most useful for this period.

Levinus Clarkson Papers. Not too valuable for the Confederation. It is enlightening in the early part of the Revolution for Charleston trade to London and occasionally New York.

Stephen Collins Collection. Almost exclusively letters to Collins. The course of trade almost correlates with the bulkiness of the material. The correspondence is meager in 1782; it broadens out significantly in 1783, and then becomes scanty once again in 1784.

Papers of the Continental Congress.

12 "Book of Estimates" of Receipts and Expenditures, 1781-86.
20 Report of Committees on Letters from Governors of States. Some of these are published in the *Journals of Continental Congress.*
26 Reports of Committees on Treasury and Finance. Some of these are published in the *Journals.*
27 Reports on War Office and Department of War. Some of these are published in the *Journals.*
38 Papers relating to mutiny of a detachment of troops, 1783.
50 Letters and Papers of Oliver Pollock.
54 Papers and Accounts of Silas Deane, Beaumarchais, and Arthur Lee.
55 Letters and Papers of Tom Paine.
62 Letters and Reports of John Pierce, Paymaster General.
90 Letters of William Bingham (and others).

   91 Letters of Thomas Barclay (and others).
119 Transcripts of Letters of R. R. Livingston, Domestic letters.
133 Letterbook of Committee to transact Continental business in Philadelphia, 1776.
137 Reports of Board of Treasury.
141 Receipts and Expenditures of the United States.
142 Record of Accounts of the Registers Office, 1781-83.
143 Papers respecting state of accounts.
144 Letters relating to the Treasury, 1782-88.
148 Letters to the Board of War, 1780-81.
149 Letters and Reports of General Benjamin Lincoln, 1781-83.
155 Letters of Major General Greene.
188 Record of the Reports of Committees of Congress on Executive Departments, 1782-85. Some are printed in the *Journals*.

Samuel and John Galloway Papers. Maryland merchants of importance. Not too useful for my immediate period.

Hamilton Papers. Much of the papers for the early period are printed in H. C. Lodge, *The Works of Alexander Hamilton*, but not always with the care or accuracy they deserve. For the most part the early material is disappointing.

John Holker Papers. This invaluable collection of forty volumes is only second in importance to the Wadsworth Collection as a single body of material on business aspects of the period. With the Duer Papers in the New-York Historical Society, the Ridley Papers in the Massachusetts Historical Society, the Andrew Carnegie and the Holker Papers in Clements Library, it tells a relatively full story.

Hugh Hughes Letterbook, 1782 (beginning April 13). These letters are a much more formal record than the Pickering-Hughes correspondence and consequently less valuable. Less opinion is offered and less comment on current developments submitted. Supplements Hugh Hughes Letterbooks in the New-York Historical Society.

Letterbook of Samuel Miles (Deputy Quarter Master General for Pennsylvania), 28 March 1781 to 1 February 1782. Consists almost exclusively of letters between Miles and Hugh Hughes, DQMG for the Eastern Army.

Miscellaneous Letters (Force Transcripts). There are some letters of Joseph Reed, but their content is military rather than political. There are also some letters of Edmund Randolph to Madison which fit into those of Madison to Randolph published in E. C. Burnett's *Letters of the Members of the Continental Congress*.

Pickering Letterbook, Quartermaster General, 11 July 1781 to 28 April 1782. Letters almost exclusively between Hughes and Pickering. Relatively complete for the period specified. Supplements Letterbooks in the National Archives.

William Reynolds Letterbook, 1772-85 (for all intents and purposes it ends with 1783). Reynolds did not carry on an extensive business, but the volume does present a picture of a Virginia merchant who was subject to the injuries of the British invasion in 1781.

Letterbook of Charles Stewart, Commissary General, 1777-82 (Force Transcripts). This volume used very little.

Walter Stewart Letters, Inspector of the Northern Army, 1776-83 (Force Transcripts). Most of the letters are to Stewart. Rich in color, sketchy in information.

Charles Thomson Papers. Volumes I and II cover this period. It consists largely of letters to Thomson, some informative, others supplying color.

Jeremiah Wadsworth Papers. Comparatively little value for this period.

William Whipple Letters (Force Transcripts). Most of the letters deal with the early part of the Revolution.

Woolsey and Salmon Letterbook, 1774-84. This is a relatively complete record of a Baltimore firm, whose guiding hand demonstrates shrewd awareness of the changing economic scene. Because of the care and attention which was devoted to the business, and the lack of speculation on the part of the firm, it experienced less distress than did most of the others who faced the mercantile crisis after the Revolution. Highly useful for tracing the course of trade. Salmon writes almost all the letters after 1780.

Maryland Historical Society:

Mordecai Gist Papers. Used for information on Southern Army.

Tench Tilghman Papers. See Section A.

Massachusetts Historical Society:

Caleb Davis Letterbook, 1782-86, in Caleb Davis Papers. This is good for a study of Massachusetts but for my study its value was limited.

Heath Papers. A very valuable and complete collection which needs to be exploited much more than it has been. The letters printed in the Massachusetts Historical Society *Collections* are not only a fragment of the material available but often the least important.

Knox Papers. Useful, but not nearly as complete as the Heath Papers, and except for isolated letters, not as important.

Ridley Papers. An important collection which includes Letterbooks as well as much of the incoming correspondence. These papers fit in well with the Holker Papers in the Library of Congress to give a good picture of certain economic and mercantile aspects of the period. It also presents a full record of a firm during the early years of the Confederation. Some biographical material on Ridley is contained in the Papers.

Sedgwick Papers. Difficult to work with but they do give a good insight into the mind of the extreme conservatives in Massachusetts politics.

Higginson Papers, Bowdoin-Temple Papers, and the Miscellaneous Collections were used by means of a card index.

National Archives:

Pickering Letterbook. These twelve volumes of Quartermaster Records are found in the War Department Records Division. Together with the Hugh Hughes Letterbooks in the New-York Historical Society, this Collection makes up the most important existing record of this aspect of the Revolution.

Naval Academy at Annapolis:

Agent of Marine Letterbook. Described in Section A.

New-York Historical Society:

William Alexander (Lord Stirling) Papers. Provides useful background material.

James Duane Papers. These papers were used to answer specific questions. Not thoroughly canvassed.

William Duer Papers. For the greatest utility, these papers must be studied along with the Holker Papers in the Library of Congress, the Craigie Papers in the American Antiquarian Society, and the Parker Letterbook in the Baker Library. Two volumes are bound but some of the most valuable material is scattered through the miscellaneous boxes.

Gates Papers. These papers give a good insight into Gates and throw some important light on the virtues of Morris as well.

Greene Papers. Used to answer specific questions.

Hugh Hughes Letterbooks and Papers. This collection together with the Pickering Letterbooks in the National Archives make up the most important single sources of Quartermaster Records for the Revolution. It covers only up to 1782, so the value of the collection is unfortunately limited for this study.

Jonathan Lawrence Papers. Important in determining the working out of the contract system.

McDougall Papers. These papers were used extensively for this study. They throw some valuable light on the army, contracting, and trends of thinking in the period.

Osgood Papers. Useful for a point of view which is based on skepticism of the spirit rather than the actions of the Financier.

Reed Papers. Valuable papers for criticism of Morris. Some of the important letters, but by no means all, are printed in William B. Reed's *Joseph Reed*.

New York Public Library:

Samuel Adams Papers. This is a useful collection to trace criticisms of administrative action. A substantial part of the letters are not published. Those which are published in Burnett's *Letters* often omit some material which is valuable for local trends.

William Constable Letterbook, 1782-90, in the Constable-Pierrepont Papers. This is a very good letterbook from an indispensable collection. There is a gap in the Letterbook from 29 June 1784 to 16 August 1787. It is particularly good in conjunction with the Craigie Papers in the American Antiquarian Society for pressures on the new government from speculators in public securities.

Emmett Collection. Calendared.

R. R. Livingston Collection. Contains some useful material. Most of it is transcribed.

Schuyler Papers. This splendid collection was used only to answer specific questions. No attempt was made to inspect the collection thoroughly.

Wallace, Johnson, and Muir Letterbook, 1781-83. This volume is useful in determining the course of trade, particularly in tobacco.

Pennsylvania Archives:

Revolutionary Papers. This material was utilized by means of card catalogue. Much of it is printed in the Pennsylvania Archives. (See Part II.)

Historical Society of Pennsylvania:

Bank of North America Papers. Very important and complete, though formal, record of the first operational national bank in the United States.
Chaloner and White Papers. These papers are very full for the 70's but thin out in the 80's. Not too helpful for this study.
Coates and Reynell Papers. This correspondence helpful in the early part of the Confederation to determine the course of trade.
Dreer Collection. Only such material as pertained to my study was used from this valuable collection.
Franklin Papers. Contains Morris letters in addition to background material.
Benjamin Fuller Letterbooks. Helpful in analyzing course of trade.
Gratz Collection. Only such material as pertained to my study was used from this vast collection.
Robert Henderson. This business correspondence is extensive. Part of it threw some light on economic developments in the period.
Hollingsworth Papers. Only the correspondence between 1780-84 was used for trends of trade and business.
General William Irvine Papers. Particularly useful in working out of contracting and to some extent the attitude of the army to civilian measures.
Diary of George Nelson. Used in the analysis of the state of the country in 1780-81.
George Read Manuscripts. Only used to answer specific questions.
Society Collection. Contains Morris letters.
General Wayne Papers. Indispensable for military story, and very good for relationship between the army and the government.
Peletiah Webster Account and Letterbook. Sketchy, but with occasional comments on the broad politico-economic picture.
Wilson Papers. These papers are disappointing, but they do contain some important sidelights in the period.

II. PRINTED SOURCE MATERIAL

Adams, Charles F. (editor). *Familiar Letters of John Adams and His Wife Abigail Adams during the Revolution.* New York, 1918.
[Adams, John]. *The Works of John Adams.* (Edited by Charles Francis Adams.) 10 volumes. Boston, 1851-66.
Balch, Thomas W. (editor). *Willing Letters and Papers.* Philadelphia, 1922.
Ballagh, James C. (editor). *The Letters of Richard Henry Lee.* 2 volumes. New York, 1911-14.
[Blanchard, Claude]. *The Journal of Claude Blanchard.* (Translated by William Duane and edited by Thomas Balch.) Albany, 1876.
[Boston]. *A Report of the Record Commissioners of the City of Boston: containing the Boston Town Records, 1778 to 1783.* Boston, 1895.
Burnett, Edmund C. (editor). *Letters of the Members of the Continental Congress.* 7 volumes. Washington, D. C., 1921-36.
Carman, Harry J. (editor). *American Husbandry.* New York, 1939.
Chastellux, Marquis de. *Travels in North America in the years 1780, 1781, and 1782.* (Translated from the French by an English Gentleman who resided in America at that period.) 2 volumes. Dublin, 1787.
Cooper, Samuel. *A Sermon Preached before His Excellency John Hancock, Governor and the Honorable Senate and House of Representatives . . . 25 October 1780.* (Printed by T. and J. Fleet, and J. Gill.) Commonwealth of Massachusetts, 1780.

[Deane, Silas]. Deane Papers, 1774-90, in *New-York Historical Society Collections*, XIX-XXIII. New York, 1887-90.

[Deane, Silas]. Deane Papers: Correspondence between Silas Deane, His Brothers and their Business and Political Associates, 1771-95 in *Connecticut Historical Society Collections*, XXIII. Hartford, 1930.

Dearborn, Henry. *Revolutionary War Journals of Henry Dearborn, 1775-83.* (Edited by Lloyd A. Brown and Howard H. Peckham.) Chicago, 1939.

[England]. *The Parliamentary History of England: From the Earliest Period to the Year 1803.* London, 1814.

Force, Peter (comp.). *American Archives.* Series IV, 6 volumes. Series V, 3 volumes. Washington, 1837-53.

[Franklin, Benjamin]. *The Complete Works of Benjamin Franklin.* (Edited by John Bigelow.) 10 volumes. New York and London, 1887-88.

Guttridge, George H. (editor). *The American Correspondence of a Bristol Merchant, 1766-76: Letters of Richard Champion.* Berkeley, California, 1934.

[Hamilton, Alexander]. *The Works of Alexander Hamilton.* (Edited by Henry Cabot Lodge.) 9 volumes. New York, 1885-86.

Heath, William. *Memoirs of Major General Heath.* (Edited by William Abbatt.) New York, 1901.

[Hunt, John]. "John Hunt's Diary," in *New Jersey Historical Society Proceedings*, LIII, 26-43.

[Jay, John]. *Correspondence and Public Papers of John Jay.* (Edited by Henry P. Johnston.) 4 volumes. New York, 1890-93.

Johnson, Amandus (trans.). *Journal and Biography of Nicholas Collin, 1746-1831.* Philadelphia, 1936.

Landis, Charles I. (editor). "Letters of Mathias Slough to Robert Morris" in *Lancaster County Historical Society Papers*, XXIV, 59-65.

Mereness, Newton D. (editor). *Travels in the American Colonies.* New York, 1916.

Morris, Anne Cary. *The Diary and Letters of Gouverneur Morris.* 2 volumes. New York, 1888.

[Morris, Robert]. "Letters of Robert Morris," in *New-York Historical Society Collections*, XI. New York, 1878.

[Massachusetts]. Acts and Laws of the Commonwealth of Massachusetts. Boston, 1890.

[New York]. *New York Colonial Documents.* (Edited by Edmund B. O'Callaghan.) 15 volumes. Albany, 1853-87.

[North Carolina]. *The State Records of North Carolina,* XIV-XVI. Goldsboro, North Carolina, 1886-99.

Paine, Thomas. "The Crisis Extraordinary," dated 4 October 1780 in *The Complete Writings of Thomas Paine*, I. (Edited by Philip S. Foner.) New York, 1945.

[Pennsylvania]. *Pennsylvania Archives,* IV-X. (Edited by Samuel Hazard.) Harrisburg, 1853-54.

[Pennsylvania]. *Journals of the Pennsylvania Assembly,* I. Philadelphia, 1782.

Pettengill, Ray W. (trans.). *Letters from America, 1776-79.* . . . Boston and New York, 1924.

[Rhode Island]. The Commerce of Rhode Island in *Massachusetts Historical Society Collections.* Series 7, X. Boston, 1915.

Sparks, Jared (editor). *Correspondence of the American Revolution: being Letters of Eminent Men to George Washington.* 4 volumes. Boston, 1853.

Sparks, Jared (editor). *The Diplomatic Correspondence of the American Revolution.* 12 volumes. Boston, 1829-30.

Stevens, Benjamin F. *Facsimiles of Manuscripts in European Archives Relating to America, 1773-83.* London, 1889-95.

Thacher, James. *A Military Journal during the American Revolutionary War, 1775-83.* Boston, 1823.

[United States Congress.] *American State Papers.* 38 volumes. Washington, D. C., 1832-61.

[United States Congress.] *Journals of the Continental Congress, 1774-89.* (Edited by Worthington C. Ford, Gaillard Hunt, and John C. Fitzpatrick.) 34 volumes. Washington, D. C., 1904-37.

[Washington, George.] *The Writings of George Washington from the Original Manuscript Sources, 1745-99.* (Edited by John C. Fitzpatrick.) 39 volumes. Washington, D. C., 1931-44.

Webster, Peletiah. *Political Essays.* Philadelphia, 1791.

Wharton, Francis (editor). *The Revolutionary Diplomatic Correspondence of the United States.* 6 volumes. Washington, D. C., 1889.

III. SECONDARY WORKS

Abernethy, Thomas P. "Commercial Activities of Silas Deane," *American Historical Review,* XXXIX, 477-85.

Adams, James T. *New England in the Republic, 1776-1850.* Boston, 1926.

Allen, Gardner Weld. *Massachusetts Privateers of the Revolution.* Massachusetts Historical Society *Collections,* LXXVII. Boston, 1927.

Bates, Frank G. "Rhode Island and the Imports of 1781," *Annual Report* of the American Historical Association, 1894, pp. 351-59.

Beard, Charles A. *An Economic Interpretation of the Constitution.* New York, 1913.

Bemis, Samuel F. "British Secret Service and the French-American Alliance," *American Historical Review,* XIX, 474-95.

Bemis, Samuel F. *The Diplomacy of the American Revolution.* New York and London, 1935.

Bezanson, Anne (and Associates). *Prices and Inflation during the American Revolution: Pennsylvania, 1770-90.* Philadelphia, 1951.

Bidwell, Percy W. "Rural Economy in New England at the Beginning of the 19th Century," Connecticut Academy of Arts and Sciences, *Transactions,* XX, 241-399.

Bidwell, Percy W., and John I. Falconer. *History of Agriculture in the Northern United States, 1620-1860.* (Peter Smith reprint.) New York, 1941.

Bolles, Albert S. *The Financial History of the United States from 1774 to 1789.* New York, 1884.

Boyd, Thomas. *Mad Anthony Wayne.* New York, 1929.

Brant, Irving. *James Madison.* In progress. Indianapolis and New York, 1941-

Brown, Margaret L. "William Bingham in Martinque," *Pennsylvania Magazine of History and Biography,* LXIX, 54-87.

Brunhouse, Robert L. *The Counter Revolution in Pennsylvania, 1776-1790.* Harrisburg, 1942.

Bullock, Charles J. *The Finances of the United States from 1775 to 1789, with Especial Reference to the Budget.* Madison, Wisconsin, 1895.

Burnett, Edmund C. *The Continental Congress.* New York, 1942.

Channing, Edward. "Commerce during the Revolutionary Epoch," *Massachusetts Historical Society Proceedings,* XLIV, 364-77.

Clark, William B. *Gallant John Barry*. New York, 1938.
Clayton, W. Woodford. *History of Union and Middlesex Counties, New Jersey*. Philadelphia, 1882.
Clayton, W. Woodford and William Nelson. *History of Bergen and Passaic Counties, New Jersey*. Philadelphia, 1882.
Collier, Thomas S. "Revolutionary Privateers in Connecticut," in *New London County Historical Society Records*, Volume I, Part IV, 9-26.
Connor, Robert D. W. *History of North Carolina*. 6 volumes. Chicago and New York, 1919.
East, Robert A. *Business Enterprise in the American Revolutionary Era*. New York, 1938.
Eckenrode, H. J. *The Revolution in Virginia*. Boston and New York, 1916.
Ellis, Captain F. *History of Northampton County, Pennsylvania*. Philadelphia and Reading, 1877.
Felt, Joseph B. *Annals of Salem*. 2 volumes. Salem, 1845.
Ferguson, E. James. "State Assumption of the Federal Debt During the Confederation," *Mississippi Valley Historical Review*, XXXVIII, 403-24, (December, 1951).
Futhey, J. Smith, and Gilbert Scope. *History of Chester County, Pennsylvania*. Philadelphia, 1881.
Greene, Evarts B. and Virginia D. Harrington. *American Population Before the Federal Census of 1790*. New York, 1932.
Greene, George Washington. *The Life of Nathanael Greene*. 3 volumes. Boston, 1878-90.
Gray, Lewis C. *A History of Agriculture in the Southern United States to 1860*. 2 volumes. New York (reprint), 1941.
Griffin, Clarence W. *History of Old Tryon and Rutherford Counties*. Asheville, North Carolina, 1937.
Hall, Charles. *Life and Letters of Samuel Holden Parsons*. Binghamton, New York, 1905.
Harlow, Ralph V. "Economic Conditions in Massachusetts during the American Revolution, 1775-83," *Publications of the Colonial Society of Massachusetts*, XX, 163-90.
Harrington, Virginia. *The New York Merchant on the Eve of the Revolution*. New York, 1935.
Hart, Charles H. "Mary White — Mrs. Robert Morris," *Pennsylvania Magazine of History and Biography*, II, 157-84.
Hart, Freeman. *The Valley of Virginia in the American Revolution*. Chapel Hill, 1942.
Hatch, Louis C. *The Administration of the American Revolutionary Army*. New York, 1904.
Hedges, James B. *The Browns of Providence Plantations; Colonial Years*. Cambridge, Massachusetts, 1952.
Honeyman, A. Van Doren (editor). *Northwestern New Jersey.* . . . 4 volumes. New York and Chicago, 1927.
Howe, Octavius T. "Beverly Privateers in the American Revolution," *Publications of the Colonial Society of Massachusetts*, XXIV, 318-435.
Howell, George R. and T. J. Tenney. *History of the County of Albany, New York, 1609-1886*. New York, 1886.
Hufeland, Otto. *Westchester County During the Revolution, 1775-83*. Privately printed, 1926.
Hunt, Freeman. *Lives of American Merchants*. 2 volumes. New York, 1856.
James, James A. *Oliver Pollock*. New York and London, 1937.
Jameson, James F. "St. Eustatius in the American Revolution," *American*

Historical Review, VIII, 683-708.

Jensen, Merrill. *The Articles of Confederation; an Interpretation of the Social-Constitutional History of the American Revolution, 1774-81.* Madison, Wisconsin, 1940.

Jensen, Merrill. *The New Nation: A History of the United States During the Confederation, 1781-89.* New York, 1950.

Johnson, Emory R. (et al.). *History of Domestic and Foreign Commerce of the United States.* 2 volumes. Washington, D. C., 1915.

Johnson, Victor L. *The Administration of the American Commissariat During the Revolutionary War.* Philadelphia, 1941.

Johnson, William. *Sketches of the Life and Correspondence of Nathanael Greene.* 2 volumes. Charleston, 1822.

Konkle, Burton A. *Thomas Willing and the First American Financial System.* Philadelphia, 1937.

Kremer, J. Bruce. *John Hanson of Mulberry Grove.* New York, 1938.

Lawson, Murray G. *Fur: A Study in English Mercantilism, 1700-1775.* (University of Toronto Studies. History and Economic Series. Volume IX.) Toronto, Canada, 1943.

Lee, Richard Henry. *The Life of Arthur Lee.* 2 volumes. Boston, 1829.

Lewis, Lawrence. *A History of the Bank of North America.* Philadelphia, 1882.

Loughrey, Mary Ellen. *France and Rhode Island, 1686-1800.* New York, 1944.

Lundin, Leonard. *Cockpit of the Revolution.* Princeton, 1940.

Maclay, Edgar S. *A History of American Privateers.* New York and London, 1924.

McCormick, Richard P. *Experiment in Independence: New Jersey in the Critical Period, 1781-89.* New Brunswick, New Jersey, 1950.

Martin, Gaston. "Commercial Relations between Nantes and the American Colonies during the War of Independence," *Journal of Economic and Business History,* IV, 812-29.

McCrady, Edward. *The History of South Carolina in the Revolution, 1775-80.* New York, 1901.

McFarland, Raymond. *A History of the New England Fisheries.* New York, 1911.

Meredith, Gertrude E. *The Descendents of Hugh Amory, 1605-1805.* London, 1901.

Middlebrook, Louis F. *History of Maritime Connecticut During the American Revolution, 1775-83.* 2 volumes. Salem, Massachusetts, 1925.

Miller, John C. *Triumph of Freedom, 1775-83.* Boston, 1948.

Mills, Robert. *Statistics of South Carolina.* Charleston, 1826.

Monaghan, Frank. *John Jay.* New York and Indianapolis, 1935.

Morison, Samuel E. *The Maritime History of Massachusetts, 1783-1860.* Boston and New York, 1921.

Morris, Richard B. *Government and Labor in Early America.* New York, 1946.

Nelson, William (editor). *The New Jersey Coast in Three Centuries.* New York and Chicago, 1902.

Nevins, Allan. *The American States During and After the Revolution, 1775-89.* New York, 1924.

Newcomer, Lee. *Central and Western Massachusetts during the Revolution.* Doctoral Dissertation (to be published) for the Department of History, Columbia University, 1948.

[New England.] "The Privateer General Sullivan," *New England Historical and Genealogical Register*, XXIII, 289-92.

[New York.] *The American Revolution in New York*. Albany, 1926.

Nourse, Michael. "The Accounts of Robert Morris, Superintendent of Finance," *The Bankers' Magazine and Statistical Register*, New York, 1860, pp. 580-85.

Paine, Ralph D. *Joshua Barney*. New York and London, 1924.

Paullin, Charles C. *The Navy of the American Revolution*. Cleveland, 1906.

Peabody, Robert E. "The Derbys of Salem, Massachusetts," *Essex Institute Collections*, XLIV (1908), 193-219.

Peabody, Robert E. *Merchant Venturers of Old Salem*. Boston and New York, 1912.

Phillips, James Duncan. *Salem in the Eighteenth Century*. Boston and New York, 1937.

Porter, Kenneth. *The Jacksons and the Lees: Two Generations of Massachusetts Merchants, 1765-1844*. 2 volumes. Cambridge, Massachusetts, 1937.

Prime, Temple. *Descent of Comfort Sands and of his Children*. New York, 1897.

Ramsay, David. *History of South Carolina*. 2 volumes. Charleston, 1809.

Reed, William B. *Joseph Reed*. 2 volumes. Philadelphia, 1847.

Rumple, Jethro. *History of Rowan County*. Salisbury, North Carolina, 1881.

Rupp, Israel D. (comp.). *History and Topography of Northumberland, Huntingdon, Mifflin, Centre, Union, . . . Counties, Pennsylvania*. Lancaster, Pennsylvania, 1847.

Sabine, Lorenzo. *Report on the Principal Fisheries of the American Seas*. Executive Document 23. 32nd Congress, 2nd Session.

Sanders, Jennings B. *Evolution of the Executive Departments of the Continental Congress, 1774-89*. Chapel Hill, 1935.

Scharf, J. Thomas and Thompson Westcott. *History of Philadelphia*. 3 volumes. Philadelphia, 1884.

Schlesinger, Arthur M. *The Colonial Merchants and the American Revolution*. New York, 1917.

Scott, William W. *History of Passaic and Its Environs*. 3 volumes. New York and Chicago, 1922.

Sedgwick, Theodore. *Memoir of William Livingston*. New York, 1833.

Sheffield, William P. *Privateersmen of Newport: An Address delivered before the Rhode Island Historical Society*. Newport, Rhode Island, 1883.

Singer, Charles G. *South Carolina in the Confederation*. Philadelphia, 1941.

Smith, Philip H. *General History of Dutchess County, 1609-1876*. Rawling, New York, 1877.

Sparks, Jared. *The Life of Gouverneur Morris*. 3 volumes. Boston, 1832.

Steiner, Bernard C. "Maryland Privateers in the American Revolution." *Maryland Historical Magazine*, III, 99-103.

Sullivan, Kathryn. *Maryland and France, 1774-89*. Philadelphia, 1936.

Sumner, William Graham. *The Financier and the Finances of the American Revolution*. New York, 1891.

Taylor, Charles J. *History of Great Barrington, Massachusetts*. Great Barrington, 1882.

Thatcher, Harold W. *The Social Philosophy of William Livingston*. Unpublished Doctoral Dissertation for the Department of History, University of Chicago, 1935.

Tompkins, Daniel A. *History of Mecklenburg County*. 2 volumes. Charlotte, North Carolina, 1903.

Tryon, Rolla M. *Household Manufactures in the United States, 1640-1860.* Chicago, 1917.

Turner, Joseph K., and John L. Bridgers. *History of Edgecomb County, North Carolina.* Raleigh, 1920.

Upton, Richard F. *Revolutionary New Hampshire: An Account of the Social and Political Forces Underlying the Transition from Royal Province to American Commonwealth.* Hanover, New Hampshire, 1936.

Wallace, David D. *History of South Carolina.* 4 volumes. New York, 1934.

Wallace, David D. *The Life of Henry Laurens.* New York and London, 1915.

Waln, Robert. *Biography of the Signers to the Declaration of Independence,* V. (Edited by John Sanderson.) Philadelphia, 1824.

Weeden, William B. *Early Rhode Island: A Social History of Its People.* New York, 1910.

Weeden, William B. *Economic and Social History of New England, 1620-1789.* 2 volumes. Boston and New York, 1894.

Wells, William V. *The Life and Public Services of Samuel Adams.* 3 volumes. Boston, 1865.

Winfield, Charles H. *History of the County of Hudson, New Jersey: from its earliest settlement to the present time.* New York, 1874.

Winsor, Justin (editor). *The Memorial History of Boston, Including Suffolk County, Massachusetts, 1639-1880.* 4 volumes. Boston, 1880-81.

Young, John R. (editor). *Memorial History of the City of Philadelphia.* 2 volumes. New York, 1895-98.

INDEX

This index is prepared for the text alone, not the footnotes.